The Word of God Made Plain

Pastor Jim Kirkland

OlivePress
צהר זית
Messianic & Christian Publisher

Published by
Olive Press צהר זית
Messianic and Christian Publisher
P.O. Box 163
Copenhagen, NY 13626

Our prayer at Olive Press is that we may help make the Word of Adonai fully known, that it spread rapidly and be glorified everywhere. We hope our books help open people's eyes so they will turn from darkness to Light and from the power of the adversary to God and to trust in ישוע Yeshua (Jesus). (From II Thess. 3:1; Col. 1:25; Acts 26:18,15 NRSV and CJB, the *Complete Jewish Bible*)

In honor to God, pronouns referring to the Trinity are capitalized, satan's names are not. But not all Bible versions do this and legally must be printed as they are.

www.olivepresspublisher.com

Cover and interior design by Olive Press.
Cover photos are copyrighted property of 123RF Limited, their Contributors or Licensed Partners and are being used with permission under license.

The Word of God Made Plain

ISBN 978-0-9855241-6-6
Printed in the USA.
1. Christian Inspirational 2. Christian Spiritual Growth 3. Christian Devotional

All Scriptures are taken from the King James Version of the Bible.

Also by the author (with his wife Lyn):

Healing For Your Broken Heart

Also by Lyn Kirkland

The Lighted Path: 101 Practical Lessons Using God's Word As Guidance For Parents, Grandparents, And Anyone Who Loves Children

FOREWORD

This daily devotional is numbered rather than dated, so that anyone who purchases the book can start immediately at the beginning and work through it day by day. It is my hope that this format is more convenient for the reader.

On each page, it is suggested that you begin by reading the Scripture from your Bible that is listed first. The book is written from the perspective that the Word is the final authority, so spending a few brief moments reading it sets the stage for the Lord to bless, and will establish a framework which will make more sense of the comments that follow.

The main text is intended to expand your understanding of the Scripture you have just read, and can lead to spiritual growth.

A "faith profession" is listed on each page. This is intended to be read out loud. Since "faith cometh by hearing, and hearing by the Word of God" (Romans 10:17), your faith will be increased as you speak the profession, and it will be put out into the spiritual world around you.....having an effect there as well.

Lastly, some verses related to the original Scripture and the explanatory text are provided. Taking the time to look these up will be an additional benefit to your daily time with Jesus; will expand your understanding of that day's subject; and just might serve to trigger further study for you, which would deepen your appreciation of His Word even more.

It has been my pleasure to respond to the Lord's prompting to write this devotional. It is intended to lift up and glorify the most important person I know: Jesus Christ. HE IS LORD!

TABLE OF CONTENTS

Foreword   5
1. The Free Gift   13
2. Saying It   14
3. When You Pray   15
4. Pleasing God   16
5. Fear Exposed   17
6. It Won't Work Without You   18
7. The Toothless Lion   19
8. Heavenly Duct Tape   20
9. Defeating Worry   21
10. Unanswered Prayer   22
11. What is a "Buckler?"   23
12. Spiritual Circumcision   24
13. Totally Forgiven   25
14. Blotted Out   26
15. Blown to Bits!!   27
16. Jesus is Lord   28
17. Flip the Switch   29
18. Lessons From an Airplane Wing   30
19. Chastening   31
20. Your Confession   32
21. Removing Obstacles   33
22. Faith Prayer 1   34
23. Faith Prayer 2   35
24. Armor of God 1   36
25. Armor of God 2   37
26. Armor of God 3   38
27. Armor of God 4   39
28. Armor of God 5   40
29. Armor of God 6   41
30. Armor of God 7   42
31. Armor of God 8   43
32. Armor of God 9   44
33. Armor of God 10   45
34. Armor of God 11   46
35. Spiritual First   47
36. Who is "the Rock?"   48
37. True Worship   49
38. When Are You Strong?   50
39. Too Busy to Pray   51
40. Parable of the Sower 1   52
41. Parable of the Sower 2   53
42. Parable of the Sower 3   54
43. Parable of the Sower 4   55
44. Parable of the Sower 5   56
45. Parable of the Sower 6   57
46. Legion   58
47. Jairus   59
48. Touching His Garment   60
49. Jairus, Part 2   61
50. Limiting God   62
51. One Got Out   63
52. Why Prayers Take Time   64
53. Brothers and Sisters   65
54. The Death of John the Baptist   66
55. Jesus Fighting Back   67
56. A Little Boy's Lunch   68
57. Forgetting the Lesson   69
58. Walking on Water   70
59. Making the Word Ineffective   71
60. We Forgot the Bread   72
61. Spitting on a Blind Man   73
62. Creation 1   74
63. Creation 2   75
64. Creation 3   76
65. Creation 4   77
66. A Rewarder   78
67. Casting Out Devils   79
68. Hell   80
69. He Went Away   81
70. All Things Are Possible   82
71. Blind Bartimaeus   83
72. Removing the Mountain   84
73. When to Believe   85

TABLE OF CONTENTS, cont.

74. She Hath Done What She Could   86
75. A Religious Spirit   87
76. These Signs   88
77. Certainty   89
78. David's Seed   90
79. Four Gospels   91
80. The Size of Blessing   92
81. Jesus Prayed   93
82. Being Expectant   94
83. As He Is, So Are We   95
84. You Have Prosperity   96
85. A Bright Future   97
86. A Prayer and Promises   98
87. Benefits of Tithing   99
88. Jesus is Tempted   100
89. Jesus is Tempted 2   101
90. Jesus is Tempted 3   102
91. You Have Power!   103
92. Sympathy vs. Compassion   104
93. One Thing   105
94. The Father's Heart   106
95. A Note to Parents   107
96. Nathaniel   108
97. The Wine Issue   109
98. Born Again   110
99. Jesus as a Serpent   111
100. Two Kinds of People   112
101. Friend of the Bridegroom   113
102. The Woman at the Well   114
103. In Spirit   115
104. The Judge   116
105. Who's Going To Heaven?   117
106. Eyes of Faith   118
107. Knowing God's Will   119
108. Nice Family!   120
109. A Thirst to Know Him   121
110. The Spirit Flows   122
111. The Bigger the Belfry, the More Room for Bats   123
112. The Truth Shall Make You Free   124
113. Nasty Accusations   125
114. They Couldn't Kill Him   126
115. The Price of Truth   127
116. The Door   128
117. Good vs. Evil   129
118. Security   130
119. Raising the Dead 1   131
120. Raising the Dead 2   132
121. Raising the Dead 3   133
122. One Last Thing   134
123. Giving   135
124. Are You NUTS!?   136
125. The Perfect Lesson   137
126. Loving One Another   138
127. Good Intentions   139
128. The Way   140
129. What Does God the Father Look Like?   141
130. A Verse That Is Hard to Believe   142
131. The Comforter   143
132. You'll Have Peace   144
133. Outside the Camp   145
134. His Commandment   146
135. Friends   147
136. Killing in God's Name   148
137. Better Than Christ on Earth   149
138. The Holy Spirit's Ministry   150
139. A Train in a Tunnel   151
140. Be of Good Cheer   152
141. The Truth   153
142. How We Are Sent   154
143. Deeply Loved   155
144. The "I AM"   156
145. Peter's Problem   157

TABLE OF CONTENTS, cont.

146. Irrationality	158	
147. Cancelling Out the Word	159	
148. Innocent	160	
149. Beaten Unmercifully	161	
150. Where Are You From?	162	
151. King of the Jews	163	
152. Five Pieces	164	
153. Caring for Mom	165	
154. Two Brave Men	166	
155. A Sepulcher in a Garden	167	
156. Stunning Compassion	168	
157. Blind Faith	169	
158. Standing at a Fire	170	
159. Lovest Thou Me?	171	
160. Infallible Proofs	172	
161. The Promise	173	
162. Still a Little Confused	174	
163. My Father Loves Me	175	
164. A Sword and a Song	176	
165. Wishing vs. Hoping	177	
166. The Apostle Matthias	178	
167. The Death of Judas	179	
168. Scary Stuff!!	180	
169. Known Languages	181	
170. Wholeness	182	
171. Boldness	183	
172. Many Believed	184	
173. Our Response to Threats	185	
174. The Foundational Issue	186	
175. Paul's Eyesight	187	
176. A Miracle at Cornelius's House	188	
177. Antioch	189	
178. Rhoda	190	
179. You Reap What You Sow	191	
180. People of the Word	192	
181. To the Unknown God	193	
182. Apollos	194	

183. Complete Knowledge	195	
184. When the Church Began	196	
185. A Prayer for the Lost	197	
186. I'm Not Ashamed	198	
187. Constant Prayer, Part 1	199	
188. Constant Prayer, Part 2	200	
189. Dangerous Ground	201	
190. God Gave Them Over	202	
191. He Can Use You	203	
192. More About Salvation	204	
193. Blue Flashing Lights	205	
194. The Folly of Realism	206	
195. He Was Dead	207	
196. Belief And...	208	
197. The Key To Miracles	209	
198. Adoption	210	
199. Joint Heirs	211	
200. A Marriage Proposal	212	
201. No Miracles	213	
202. Romans 8:28 Clarified	214	
203. Saved to the Uttermost	215	
204. Your Body's Redemption	216	
205. Your Prayer Language	217	
206. Three Powerful Things	218	
207. Whose Side is God On?	219	
208. Nothing Can Separate Us	220	
209. Transformers	221	
210. The Measure of Faith	222	
211. The Powers That Be	223	
212. What's Required	224	
213. Your Body	225	
214. Divorce	226	
215. Escape From Trials	227	
216. Jesus is Lord	228	
217. Gifts	229	
218. One Body	230	
219. A Word to the Wise	231	

TABLE OF CONTENTS, cont.

220.	Love in One Chapter	232
221.	Are Tongues Forbidden?	233
222.	The Gospel	234
223.	No Last Name	235
224.	Eyewitnesses	236
225.	The First Resurrection	237
226.	Shaped by Companionship	238
227.	Rapture	239
228.	The Letter Kills	240
229.	Believe and Speak	241
230.	Light Affliction	242
231.	Walking By Faith	243
232.	Absent From the Body	244
233.	Christian Insanity	245
234.	Christian Judgment	246
235.	A New Creature	247
236.	Ambassadors	248
237.	Now is the Time	249
238.	Seeming Contradictions	250
239.	True Repentance	251
240.	A Little Common Sense	252
241.	Our Warfare	253
242.	False Apostles	254
243.	Serious Persecution	255
244.	Paul vs. Peter	256
245.	Crucified With Christ	257
246.	Redeemed	258
247.	Heirs of the Promises	259
248.	Cassie's Gifts	260
249.	Our "Daddy"	261
250.	The Works of the Flesh	262
251.	Good Fruit	263
252.	Living Like Him	264
253.	Sowing and Reaping	265
254.	God's Way	266
255.	Don't Lose Heart	267
256.	Whose Bad Eyesight?	268
257.	Amani Ku	269
258.	All Spiritual Blessings	270
259.	I'm Adopted	271
260.	The Deal is Sealed	272
261.	Your Guarantee	273
262.	You Are Quickened	274
263.	Seated in Heaven	275
264.	It's a Gift	276
265.	His Workmanship	277
266.	Not Strangers Any More	278
267.	We Are Him	279
268.	One	280
269.	He Descended	281
270.	Some of His Gifts to You	282
271.	Cunning Craftiness	283
272.	Volunteer Bondage	284
273.	The Devil Needs a Place	285
274.	It Hits Like a Hammer	286
275.	Don't Be Sad, Holy Spirit	287
276.	Redeeming the Time	288
277.	A Leaky Temple	289
278.	Balance in the Home	290
279.	Honor to Parents	291
280.	Nurture	292
281.	Rhema	293
282.	Saints	294
283.	Ruth…Four Seasons…#1	295
284.	Ruth…Four Seasons…#2	296
285.	Ruth…Four Seasons…#3	297
286.	Ruth…Four Seasons…#4	298
287.	A Pastor's Heart	299
288.	Seeing the Bright Side	300
289.	No Terror	301
290.	How to Get Along	302
291.	Not a Worm	303
292.	It's No More Than Dung	304
293.	Yokefellows	305

TABLE OF CONTENTS, cont.

294. Don't Worry, Be Happy	306	
295. Positive Thoughts	307	
296. I CAN	308	
297. The Reason For the Thanks	309	
298. All Your Need	310	
299. You're Not in the Dark	311	
300. Delivered	312	
301. Held Together By God's Hand	313	
302. It is Revealed	314	
303. Beware!	315	
304. Water Baptism	316	
305. Nourished in the Word	317	
306. The Right Perspective	318	
307. Satan Can Only Hinder	319	
308. Jesus is Coming Back	320	
309. Let It Go	321	
310. Pray for Leaders	322	
311. What is Jesus Doing Now?	323	
312. Who Can Be Saved?	324	
313. Clothing and Common Sense	325	
314. Mute Women	326	
315. Qualifications	327	
316. The Mystery of Godliness	328	
317. Refusing Nothing	329	
318. Meditation	330	
319. What You Value	331	
320. Fight the Good Fight	332	
321. Getting God's Approval	333	
322. In the Last Days	334	
323. Inspiration	335	
324. End-Times Advice	336	
325. Demas	337	
326. The Opposite of Demas	338	
327. Come Before Winter	339	
328. The Glory of Jesus	340	
329. Angels	341	
330. A Paralyzed Devil	342	

331. Delivered From Bondage	343	
332. Too Late	344	
333. Saying the Same Thing	345	
334. The Word is Alive	346	
335. He Understands	347	
336. He's Glad to See You	348	
337. Rightly Dividing	349	
338. Following the Results	350	
339. Your Witness That Jesus Lives	351	
340. To the Uttermost	352	
341. He Became Us	353	
342. A New Covenant	354	
343. Once	355	
344. Iron Sharpens Iron	356	
345. What Promise?	357	
346. Faith is NOW	358	
347. Goodbye, Charley	359	
348. A City Built by God	360	
349. Chastening	361	
350. Entertaining Angels	362	
351. The Everlasting Covenant	363	
352. Double-Minded	364	
353. God Doesn't Do It	365	
354. Be Careful With That Tongue	366	
355. Answered Prayer	367	
356. Power Given to Us	368	
357. Effective Prayer	369	
358. Do You Have a Reservation?	370	
359. A Random Blessing	371	
360. Guaranteed Success	372	
361. You WERE Healed	373	
362. Good Days	374	
363. Proper Suffering	375	
364. A Word to Ministers	376	
365. Hot Air	377	
366. You Sure Are Peculiar	378	

DEDICATION

This book is lovingly dedicated to my wife Lyn Kirkland, the absolutely lovely creature that the Lord sent to me in response to my prayers for a life partner who would, literally, be Jesus in the flesh.

She is the best half of me…..the love of my life…..the icing on the cake.

I know that He answers prayer…..I can see an answer every day in living, breathing form, and I am ever grateful for that.

DEVOTIONAL #1

THE FREE GIFT

Scripture: Romans 10:9-10

Jesus, the Bible says, died to "save His people from their sins." In fact, He is called "Savior," and, since that is so, there must be something to be saved FROM. What is that? It is the penalty for sin, which is eternal death (separation from God).

The Bible says, in several places, that everyone is a sinner, and is subject to the penalty for sin. Jesus died so that you and I and any other individual might escape that penalty. To do so, all we need to do is believe—to accept Jesus' work at Calvary as our own. Since His death and resurrection paid for sin, and He offers it to every human as a free gift, we need only believe this to receive the free gift of salvation (just as you receive any other gift); and it becomes yours to keep.

I received that gift when I believed…..and I told Him so. But that doesn't help YOU. Salvation is available for you, but you must receive it for yourself. Each person is asked to receive this great gift for himself/herself. When that happens, it is yours (Romans 10:13).

Remember: belief is the basis; confession (telling Jesus that you believe) is connected to that. Once that is done, salvation is YOURS—forever. It is that simple, and that profound. The greatest gift ever offered to mankind is free for the taking......IF one will believe.

Profession: "I believe that Jesus died for my sins. I receive His gift of salvation right now. Thank you Jesus for saving me and placing me into the family of God."

Study Scriptures: I John 5: 12-13; Romans 10:10-13

DEVOTIONAL #2
SAYING IT

Scripture: Mark 11:23

What you SAY…..it is the key to your entire spiritual life. As you look at Mark 11:23, notice how many times the words "say" or "saith" occur. Is that just a coincidence? No….. those words were chosen by the Holy Spirit on purpose…..to impress on the reader the importance of SAYING a thing in faith.

The "mountain" referred to in the verse is not a physical dirt and trees-type mountain, but anything in YOUR life that looms over you LIKE a mountain. It could be an illness; an addiction; a financial problem; a relationship issue. Whatever it is, it is HUGE in your life, and you have little hope of removing it.

Jesus says that your mountain can be removed from your life by FAITH in God's promises, and by SPEAKING them out of your mouth. They must be spoken in faith (*"and shall not doubt in his heart"*). They must be spoken from a believing heart (*"but shall believe..."*). But, with those two things present, you are promised that you will have "whatsoever" you say.

Implied is the fact that you are speaking a promise found in Scripture. That is the basis for any answered prayer. But, if you speak that promise in faith…..and KEEP ON doing so…..you WILL see it come to pass. It is an unconditional promise from the Lord, written down for you in Mark 11:23.

Faith Profession: "I believe God's Word to be THE TRUTH. I have a promise from Him, and I will SAY that verse, and believe it is true, until I SEE it happen with my own two eyes."

Study Scriptures: Matthew 17:20; Hebrews 11:1-6

Devotional #3

When You Pray

Scripture: Mark 11:24

Have you ever paid close attention to what people say as they pray? Have you noticed that many prayers are offered to God in DOUBT?

I have heard prayers that end with the phrase, "if it be thy will." Although this sounds very respectful, it is, actually, an admission that the one praying doesn't know if the granting of his/her request is God's will or not. This is surprising, since God's will is apparent all over the Bible.

Yes, it is. A few verses actually tell us that they are God's will. Based on John 6:38, everything Jesus did on earth was, and is, God's will. And, every promise given to us in Scripture is God's will.....each promise is a written guarantee from God Himself—it HAS to be His will!!

Armed with the knowledge of His will, the person praying is told, in Mark 11:24, that he/she is to *believe that ye receive.* When? When you see the result? NO..... "WHEN YOU PRAY." If you have a promise from God to begin with, then you CAN believe "when you pray." If you do that, and hold that belief while the answer is being sent through the spiritual world around us, YOU WILL RECEIVE YOUR ANSWER!

You believe WHEN YOU PRAY.....NOT when you see the results. THAT'S how real, effective, answered praying is done.....and YOU can do that!

Faith Profession: "I will pray a promise of God into my problem. I will believe for the answer I desire WHEN I PRAY. And God has promised me my answer."

Study Scriptures: I John 5:14-15; Romans 4:13-22

DEVOTIONAL #4

PLEASING GOD

Scripture: Hebrews 11:6

"Without faith, it is IMPOSSIBLE to please God." Wow! What a statement! Yet, it is placed in the Bible for everyone to see, because it is absolutely true.

Nothing…..NOTHING…..is done in the spiritual realm that is positive without the application of faith. The formula is: God supplies the Scripture, and the power. We…..humans…..His people…..supply the faith. When these things are combined, they produce an UNSTOPPABLE force that will mow down ANY satanic opposition.

We need to be reminded that we, as God's children, are part of the process. We have been told over the years that we are minor players on the spiritual stage; that we are little more than worms in God's sight (and in the devil's sight, too). But that just is NOT TRUE. You are given, among many other things at salvation, AUTHORITY…..the same authority Jesus earned when he overpowered the devil and his cohorts at Calvary. YOU have that, and you exercise it by speaking in FAITH…..in line with God's Word.

When you do that, NOTHING will be impossible; and you will have pleased your Heavenly Father…..who will unleash HIS POWER into the situation. That is how YOU PLEASE HIM…..and defeat your spiritual enemies at the same time!

Faith Profession: "I am a faith person. I speak the promises of God in faith. I believe God's Word, and because I do, He is pleased with me, and He unleashes His power on my behalf."

Study Scriptures: Mark 11:23-24; I John 5:4

DEVOTIONAL #5

FEAR EXPOSED

Scripture: II Timothy 1:7

Fear. It is common to all people…..all of us have experienced it…..all of us are familiar with it. Some of us even seek it out: in thrilling amusement park rides; at the movies; in daredevil stunts. It "gets our juices flowing"…..it is a thrill. Sometimes, fear is hideous; life-threatening; paralyzing. Sometimes it is so prominent in our lives that it literally controls us.

We've been taught that it is only an emotion…..that it is inevitable. And that is why today's Scripture is so important. Read it carefully, and you will discover a startling fact…..fear is a SPIRIT.

That means that, although it may produce an emotion, fear itself is NOT the emotion. It is a spirit that seeks to dominate us…..control us…..and it is hiding behind the false belief that it is purely a physical reaction to circumstance. No…..fear is a spirit. And, because that is true, it CAN BE CONTROLLED. And, it can be controlled by YOU. Only you can control the spirit of fear that seeks to dominate YOU…..by exercising the authority given to you by Jesus Christ (see the study Scriptures).

Notice, too, that God does not send fear. God is the one who deals in FAITH. It is the devil who uses fear, and it is always used for your harm. Refuse it! Chase it away! Don't be deceived into thinking that fear is natural or inevitable.

Faith Profession: "I understand that fear is a spirit, and that I have authority over it. I refuse to give in to fear. I will not let it have a place in my life. I am free of fear in Jesus Name."

Study Scriptures: Ephesians 4:27; I Peter 5:8-9; James 4:7

Devotional #6

It Won't Work Without You

Scripture: I John 5:4

If you pay close attention, you will hear this verse MISQUOTED almost every time it is referred to. (I'm not just throwing rocks here.....I misquoted it regularly for a long time.) And what you'll hear people say is, "*Faith is the victory that overcomes the world.*"

It's interesting, because that misquote is a reflection of a generally accepted doctrine that, unfortunately, is contrary to the Word.

Look at the verse again.....closely. See what it really says? "*...this is the victory that overcomes the world, EVEN OUR FAITH.*" (Emphasis added). So, it is not just faith in general..... or even God's faith.....that overcomes the world. It is OUR faith that does it! Yes! The world is overcome when we apply OUR faith to God's revealed Word.....which releases the power of God into the situation we are dealing with.

I know.....you've been taught that God does everything, and you play no part. SURPRISE!! You are in partnership with Him, and are vital to the faith process. In effect, you are the one who "pulls the trigger," or "flips the light switch." When you do that, something happens; but ONLY when.....or if.....you do your part.

That explains why so many Christians have so little power evident in their lives. Hey......try it. You just might like the results!

Faith Profession: "I am part of the Lord's faith process. I purpose to speak the Word into my situation, which will release God's power to change it for the better."

Study Scriptures: Genesis 1; Hebrews 11:6

THE TOOTHLESS LION

Scripture: I Peter 5:8

First Peter 5:8 is a familiar Scripture to many, but, all too often, we neglect to look at it as closely as we ought to do. From this Scripture, many have pictured the devil as a large, ferocious, man-eating lion. Such an animal would be powerful.....too powerful for us to handle: fast; nasty; and dangerous. It's no wonder Christians cower in fear of him!

But.....look at the verse. It doesn't say he IS a lion, but that he appears AS a lion. In other words, he'd LIKE you to believe he's nasty and overpowering, but he IS NOT!! You see, Jesus defeated him during the three days between the crucifixion and the resurrection..... and defeated him SOUNDLY and TOTALLY. So, he is a defeated foe.....it's good to remember that. And.....Jesus has given to you and me that very same victory that He won over the devil. That makes us more powerful than the devil.

That's why it says he walks about AS a roaring lion. Oh, he'll roar.....maybe even rush at you. But, you are commanded to STAND.....don't flinch; don't run; just stare him down. And you will see him RETREAT.......EVERY TIME!

Faith Profession: "I have the authority of Jesus Christ to use to resist the devil. I purpose to stand in the face of any attacks, and not to run. The devil is a defeated enemy, and he has no power over me."

Study Scriptures: I Peter 5:9; Ephesians 6:10-18; James 4:7

DEVOTIONAL #8
HEAVENLY DUCT TAPE

Scripture: Luke 1:5-22

Why did this angel strike Zacharias dumb? What had he done to deserve such treatment?

In Luke 1, we're dealing with the early part of the incarnation of Jesus Christ.....one of the most important events ever to happen on earth. When the angel discloses a miracle to Zacharias......that his barren wife was going to bear a child (who would be John the Baptist), Zacharias expresses doubt (see verse 18). We know from previous studies about faith that doubt cancels faith, and therefore short-circuits the action of God.....in this case a miracle birth.

Faith is activated by God's people speaking words of faith, which unleashes God's power. But here, Zacharias is speaking doubt, which would interfere with the process. So, he is rendered speechless so that he can't speak against this work.

The lesson? Watch what you say. If you can't speak in faith, then stick some duct tape over your mouth to prevent you from negating God's work. Okay, maybe not actual duct tape...but Heavenly duct tape. Be careful not to speak against God's work!

Faith Profession: "I will speak in line with God's Word, or I will not speak at all."

Study Scripture: Mark 11:23-24

DEVOTIONAL #9

DEFEATING WORRY

Scripture: I Peter 5:7

This Scripture tells us to cast all of our care upon Jesus, because He cares for us. It's an easy thing to read, but a little harder to actually do.

You see, we're conditioned to be like the rest of the world, and worry; fret; fuss; lose sleep; and expect the worst. We rationalize that we wouldn't be "caring people" if we didn't do such things. But, when we do worry, we are going directly against God's Will, as revealed in I Peter 5:7.

What is worry, after all? It is just considering something.....imagining the worst about it..... inventing disaster scenarios.....being caught up in the "what if's." Most people carry on this way, and it accomplishes nothing.

This kind of activity is, in reality, the opposite of faith. It is, in truth, the application of fear to your circumstances. Fear is of the devil.....faith is of God.....and God cannot operate for good unless faith is present. So, worry negates God's power in your life, and gives the devil a place from which to operate. It is, perhaps, the worst thing you can do.

Why not apply faith instead? Give your cares to Him. Expect Him to handle them effectively. Think about Scripture instead.....about positive things, and victory things. Believe God's promises, including I Peter 5:7.

Faith Profession: "I believe the Lord has my best interests at heart, and that He seeks to work things out for good in my life. I refuse to carry a burden that He is already carrying. I refuse to worry, because it is just a manifestation of fear, and I am a faith person, not a fear person."

Study Scriptures: Philippians 4:8; Ephesians 4:27

DEVOTIONAL # 10
UNANSWERED PRAYER

Scripture: Mark 6:1-6

What!? Jesus was hindered from doing any mighty works? How could that be?? Wasn't He God in the flesh; wasn't He "in control"? Isn't it amazing how, after all these years, Christians still lack a basic understanding of how Jesus works….. how faith works. And that we, as God's people, play a vital part in it all? It couldn't be more apparent than right here in Mark 6.

Jesus comes home to Nazareth, and, on Saturday, begins to teach in the synagogue. The response? "Hey…..isn't this the kid who used to live down the street? Isn't he the carpenter who used to build tables for us? Isn't he just another person from Nazareth?"

Because of this attitude of unbelief, Jesus "could there do no mighty work" (verse 5). Even Jesus Himself was astonished at their level of unbelief. But…..wait a minute. Wasn't He still Jesus? Didn't He still have power? How, then, could His ability to do mighty works have been hindered by mere people!? Why do the people make any difference at all? What do they have to do with it? Jesus can do anything He wants to do.

Really? Maybe you just don't comprehend the system He set up. He DOES have all power. He CAN heal, etc. He IS all-powerful, and sovereign. BUT…..He has set up a system, and He will not operate outside that system, because His integrity depends upon following His own plan. And that system includes, as a vital part of it working, the faith of those who believe in Him. When we show faith (or belief), then His power is released. If faith is not present, then His power lays dormant…..as it does here in Mark 6.

Do you see? Faith is the key that WE turn to start the engine. Faith is the switch the WE flip to complete the circuit and release the flow of electricity to our home.
TURN THE KEY, and you'll see the power flow in YOUR life!!

Faith Profession: "I WILL add MY faith to God's promises, and that will release His power into my situation."

Study Scriptures: I John 5:4; Mark 11:23; Mark 5:36

Devotional #11
What is a "Buckler?"

Scripture: Psalm 91:4

It says, at the end of Psalm 91:4, "His truth shall be my shield and buckler."

I've noticed that many descriptions of armor in the Bible are those describing first or second century garb.....the kind of thing worn by a Roman foot soldier. Of course, we don't see this kind of thing much anymore, so some of the terms can be a little vague.

I was riding along in my car with my wife one day recently, listening to some preaching. The speaker was commenting on Psalm 91 (one of the best chapters of Scripture in the Bible) when he mentioned verse 4. He was commenting on another aspect of the verse, but the Holy Spirit suddenly said to my spirit, "Did you notice the mention of a 'buckler' there? Do you realize what that is? It has the word 'buckle' in it, and you know what a buckle is for, don't you?"

Suddenly, it was clear. That Old English term "buckler" wasn't a mystery any more. It is simply a word that describes itself.....it is simple, really. When armor is put on, there needs to be something to hold it tight around you, to keep it from sliding around. That is what a "buckler" is.....and it works just like a belt buckle. It IS a buckle—probably in the back of the armor—which can be closed tightly.

And, do you see what YOUR "buckler" is.....what holds YOU tight as you fight the good fight of faith? It is TRUTH.....found only in God's Word. Your Christian life is only as good as the amount of the Word that you put into it…..it will hold you secure in life's storms.

Faith Profession: "God's truth is my shield and buckler. I am held secure in spiritual battle by the amount of the Word that I have placed into myself. And, I will add to that amount every day."

Study Scripture: Ephesians 6:10-18

SPIRITUAL CIRCUMCISION

Scripture: Colossians 2:11

This verse contains one of the few references to "spiritual circumcision" that I can find in the Bible. We know that circumcision was something commanded by God in the Old Testament to be the sign of His covenant with His chosen people, the children of Israel. Back then, it was a physical act performed on a male child shortly after his birth, and it involved the cutting away of some flesh.

Here in Colossians 2, it is mentioned again, but now in a spiritual context. It is addressed to all Christians, and it says that we are all circumcised with "the circumcision made without hands".....that is, it is a spiritual, unseen thing. So, it is different in that way, but it is the same as physical circumcision in a more important way. It involves a "cutting away" of something that formerly was a part of you. What is that thing? It is, as we see later in the verse, "the body of the sins of the flesh."

This is a vital truth, and one we tend to forget. At salvation, we were SEPARATED from the sins of our flesh in a supernatural way. Technically, the sins of our flesh are no longer a part of us. We, of course, can ACT like these sins are still connected to us (and we all too often do that), but, spiritually.....and as far as God is concerned.....they have been "cut away." We are free from bondage to sin because of this truth. It is our own choice to yield to the devil's temptations and act like we did before we became God's child, but WE DON'T HAVE TO!

THAT is one of the best things about our salvation.....we are free!

Faith Profession: "I have been supernaturally cut loose from the sins of my flesh. I choose to live in the freedom FROM sin that Jesus has given to me. Thank you, Lord, for this wonderful gift!"

Study Scriptures: John 8:32,36; Romans 8:1-2

TOTALLY FORGIVEN

Scripture: Colossians 2:13

I was sitting in a class one time at a Bible school when a student asked a pretty interesting question. The instructor happened to be the dean of the school, and the question was: "Are all of my sins forgiven at salvation, including those I commit AFTER salvation?"

The dean said nothing for too long a time. After a while, he said: "The sins you commit after you are saved are forgiven, provided that you repent and confess them." Hmmmmm, I thought. How could that be right? And yet, this man was the DEAN!

Later, after this question had found its way to other staff members of the school, a courageous speaker addressed it one day in Chapel. He pointed out Colossians 2:13—that it plainly says that you are forgiven ALL trespasses. "And," he added, "ALL means ALL!"

I know what was troubling the dean. Christian leaders are reluctant to teach that all sins are forgiven because they don't trust people with that information, and think people will see it as a license to sin. BUT.....that doesn't justify distorting the Word of God. Apparently, God trusts His children with this information. Anyway, weren't ALL of your sins future when Jesus died for them? Yes.....so He obviously paid for ALL of them.....past, present, and future.

Maybe Jesus trusts His children a little more than that dean. Maybe He wants us to turn away from sin, and lead a life pleasing to Him, because we appreciate what He has done for us. It works for many Christians who turn from sin because of love for our Savior. I think He'd rather have it that way.

Faith Profession: "I love Jesus Christ, and I want to live for Him, and bring honor to Him, in every way I can. Thank you, Jesus, for trusting me to love you and serve you with appreciation."

Study Scripture: John 19:23-30

BLOTTED OUT

Scripture: Colossians 2:14

This verse connects with the previous verse—Colossians 2:13—in verifying that ALL of your sins have been forgiven. It indicates that there was "handwriting of ordinances that was against us".....and guess who did the handwriting? The devil, who is called "the accuser of the brethren" (Revelation 12:10), spends his time trying to get God to be angry with us, and to mete out punishment. Of course, God is not inclined to do that kind of thing; and Jesus, who is our "advocate" (I John 2:1), counters every accusation with a reminder that our sins are covered by His blood.

I like the use of the term "blotted out." If our sins were written down on paper, they have been BLOTTED OUT.....completely removed! There is no evidence left that they even existed! And, for the believer, that is exactly the case. (Remember...ALL of your sins were in the future when Jesus died for them.)

In other Scriptures, we are told that He has removed our sins as far away from us as the east is from the west (Psalm 103:12); and that "their sins and iniquities I will remember no more" (Hebrews 10:17).

Jesus never does a thing incompletely. All that He does is done to perfection. And so it is with the payment for your sin: "blotted out;" "took it out of the way;" "remembered no more;" "removed as far as the east is from the west."

Take comfort in these truths. They are not a license to sin, but a treasured, precious truth of God's Word.

Faith Profession: "My sins have been forgiven. They have been blotted out completely. I am free to serve my Lord wholly and without guilt or shame, and I thank God for that fact."

Study Scriptures: Hebrews 10:16-17; Revelation 12:10

DEVOTIONAL #15

BLOWN TO BITS!!

Scripture: Colossians 2:15

Here is one of the most important Scriptures in all the Bible, because it gives us a revelation of our true place with God, and in relation to the devil. Notice first that Jesus spoiled "principalities and powers." Do you remember where you have seen that term before? Yes, in Ephesians 6 where it describes the whole armor of God. Principalities and powers are the devil's helpers.....his accomplices in his devious dealings with mankind.

Notice, too, the word "spoiled." In the original language in which your Bible was written, the root word translated "spoiled" here is the word from which we get our English word "dynamite." So, "spoiled" is correct, but may not be a strong enough term. More to the point would be "blown up," or "blown to bits"! When Jesus finished his work on the Cross, and during the three days afterward, the devil and his helpers had been defeated so completely that they are said to be "blown to bits"!

It also says He made a "show of them openly," meaning that He rose from the dead. He rose victorious from the depths of Hell itself, having defeated satan, the grave, death, Hell, and sin......so totally that they are said to be DESTROYED.

Now, when you think that the devil is too strong for you or too smart for you.....just think of this verse. He is not only defeated, but destroyed—blown to bits, and that victory is given to YOU by the precious, loving Savior who earned it for you. Praise God! We have the victory, and the authority!!

Faith Profession: "I have victory over the devil and his forces of darkness because Jesus blew them up, and gave His victory to me. They no longer have any power over me."

Study Scriptures: Ephesians 4:7-10; Ephesians 1:15-23

DEVOTIONAL #16
JESUS IS LORD

Scripture: Philippians 2:11

There will come a time, the Bible says, when every knee will bow to the Lord Jesus—"of things in Heaven, and things in earth, and things under the earth (Philippians 2:10), and that EVERY TONGUE SHALL CONFESS that Jesus is Lord.

That wonderful Scripture gives me a word picture in my mind. It is commonly believed that Philippians 2:11 is describing some future event, possibly taking place in Heaven itself. However, I see no indication of that in the verse. So, I see each demon and devil being forced, by the authority of Scripture, to bow down EVERY TIME THAT PHRASE IS UTTERED! Isn't that a marvelous thought?!

When I sense the presence of darkness around me, which sometimes happens as I travel through a particular area in a car, for example, I like to begin repeating this phrase out loud: "Jesus is Lord, Jesus is Lord." In my mind's eye, I can see these creatures of darkness scowling and complaining, but nevertheless obeying the authority of Scripture, bowing their knee.....EVERY TIME this phrase is spoken. It gives me great delight to do this! I love to think of them having to bow, though it pains them to do so.

Good. I don't think it will hurt to remind them of who really is in command. Someday, we may get to see this happen with our own eyes, and one pair of knees that will bow will belong to the devil himself. What a sight that will be! Until then, join me in speaking this phrase often, while thinking of them bowing—reluctantly, but SURELY.

Faith Profession: "Jesus is Lord.....over all things…...over my life.....over all the power of the enemy. JESUS IS LORD."

Study Scripture: Colossians 2:10-15

Flip the Switch

Scripture: I John 5:4

What would you say if someone came up to you with this complaint: "My house is dark every night! I called the electric company to put the lights on, but they didn't respond. Do you suppose I'm just not destined to have lights? Perhaps there is some lesson for me to learn from being in the dark. I know the electric company COULD give me light; but I still don't have any. I guess they know best."

Pretty silly, huh? Why sit in the dark, and blame the electric company, when YOU can simply flip the light switch?

Did you know that most Christians operate in exactly this same way with prayer? Maybe YOU operate this way. People pray, then get no result.....and they blame God, or rationalize that He has some unknown reason for withholding their answer. They know the power is there.....that He COULD answer. They know that He hears. But they can't figure out why He remains silent.

Well, it's the exact same reason that the guy didn't have lights. Because answered prayer is a cooperative effort. You play a part, and God plays a part. God supplies the power and the answer.....you supply the faith. You see, supplying the faith is like flipping the switch in your house to get lights. It's a simple little thing, but there are no lights unless you do it.

God gives you promises in His Word. They are the unconditional truth. If you'll take one, and apply it to your problem, and have faith in Him making it so, then you've flipped the switch......and you'll see your prayer answered. The switch is there in your Bible......all you have to do is use it. If you do YOUR part, God will certainly do His.

Faith Profession: "I will not blame God for my own failure to follow His simple system for answered prayer. I will exercise faith in His promises, which will release His power into my situation, and cause it to change."

Study Scriptures: Mark 11:23-24; Philippians 4:19

LESSONS FROM AN AIRPLANE WING

Scripture: Mark 4:26-27

I don't know about you, but, for many years, I rode on airplanes to various places without having the slightest idea how or why a large metal structure could get off the ground and fly through the air. It just did, and I accepted that by faith. It sure seems unlikely, though. How can something so big and heavy fly into the air?!

Well, the answer to that is found in the shape of the wing. If you could look at an airplane wing from the side, you'd see that the bottom is flat, but the top is curved—rounded over the top. When the plane moves forward, the air moving over the top travels slower than the air moving underneath. This causes a difference in pressure, which is enough to lift the plane upward. In fact, this force is called LIFT.

Now, whether you understand that science or not, you can get on a plane and fly. You don't need to understand it to have it work for you. And that is exactly how it is with faith. Many people complain that they don't understand why faith would work…..how can just believing in something that you can't see make any difference? Yet, it does work. It works so well that some of us have come to rely on it.

Do we need to understand it in detail? NO…..it works whether you understand it or not……just like an airplane wing. The Bible says as much in Mark 4—it likens the process to seed growing. We may not understand all of the science behind that, either, but we know it works.

Take a lesson from an airplane wing…..believe, and you will see!

Faith Profession: "I don't have to know why faith works. I am only asked to believe my Lord, who will make it work FOR me…..and I can do that!"

Study Scripture: Mark 11:26-29

CHASTENING

Scripture: Hebrews 12:6

I grew up as a Christian in a traditional, denominational church, so I have firsthand experience in the common interpretation of the verses in Hebrews which deal with chastening. The teaching? When you do something wrong, or when God just feels like making changes in you, unpleasant things happen. Things like: sickness; financial problems; family problems; trouble of any kind, really. The idea is that God is "chastening" you (hammering you; inflicting punishment on you) for your own good. "It might hurt now, but you'll be better off in the long run," they say.

This kind of interpretation of Hebrews 12:6 is consistent with the traditional belief about God Himself.....that He is somewhat strict; not easy to please; hard on you when you need correction.

What a sad testimony, especially since it goes against the teaching of Hebrews 12:6..... and even goes against the definition of the word "chasten." In the Greek from which Hebrews was translated, "chasten" means TO TRAIN, or TO EDUCATE. This is how you are to deal with your own children: you TRAIN them—you don't inflict them with cancer, or give them heartache to develop them.

Our God is consistent, and He is kind. As is usually the case, He "trains" through use of His Word. Therefore, He "chastens" the same way.....through his Word. Didn't you ever have the Word bring you to repentance? Haven't you ever felt convicted by some Scripture? Okay, then you have known God's chastening. It works for those who truly love Him, and who treasure their relationship with Him.

The Lord Jesus would never put sickness on you.....that would put Him in partnership with the devil! No, He uses His Word to "train and educate" (chasten). It is not pleasant, but it does work..... in a loving way.

Faith Profession: "I understand that my Lord chastens me with His Word, not with physical circumstances. He is trying to develop me spiritually, so He uses a spiritual book to accomplish that purpose."

Study Scriptures: Ephesians 5:26; Hebrews 12:5-11

YOUR CONFESSION

Scripture: Hebrews 4:14

The word translated "profession" here in Hebrews 4 is translated elsewhere in your Bible as "confession." Both words have the same meaning. A literal translation of the Greek word that is translated "profession" would be "saying the same thing." So, your profession, or confession, is "saying the same thing."

Okay…..saying the same thing as who? Well, there are two answers to that. First of all, you SHOULD be saying the same thing as the Lord says. That is, your conversation to the world—the things you SAY—should be in agreement with Scripture. Specifically, that should apply to your prayer life. In prayer, you SHOULD be speaking in line with God's will…..so you SHOULD be praying one or more promises from the Word.

If you pray a written promise, then you are obviously in agreement with the one who authored the promise. Your profession, or confession, would be "saying the same thing as God says"…..which will lead to answered prayer.

Secondly, your profession ought to agree with YOU. If you speak in line with Scripture today, but tomorrow you complain that you feel bad, that your prayer hasn't been answered, that you don't SEE anything yet…..then you have NOT spoken in agreement with yourself. Your first confession was okay, but your second confession nullified it.

It isn't hard to see why so many prayers remain unanswered. You might think that what you say, or how you say it, doesn't matter. But, in the spiritual realm, it is ALL that matters. Every time you speak, spiritual beings—good and bad—are listening. Your words give them freedom to move in your life. Which ones are you activating??

Faith Profession: "I purpose to focus on what I say, and how I say it. I will work to speak in line with God's Word, and the principles in it. I will work to change my speech patterns so that I'm saying the same thing as the Lord."

Study Scriptures: Hebrews 3:1; Philippians 4:8

REMOVING OBSTACLES

Scripture: Mark 5:24-27

The woman with the issue of blood had suffered with this disease for twelve years. According to the account in God's Word, she had spent all of her money on doctors, but was no closer to healing than when she started.

This woman was desperate. Certain traditions stood between her and Jesus: women with this ailment were not permitted to mingle with crowds; woman in ancient Israel were often not permitted to be in crowds of men at all. So, a number of things stood between this woman and her healing. She was going to have to overcome some obstacles, including tradition and fear, to achieve her goal. She was going to have to step out into an area that not many people dared to enter.

But.....notice that she didn't pray to God to have Him overcome these things FOR her. Apparently she realized that certain obstacles are only overcome if we do something about them ourselves. She realized that, to receive her healing, SHE would have some things to do, and God would supply the miracle. So, she went into the crowd, determined to touch the hem of Jesus' garment. When she did, she was instantly healed!

You, too, are expected to overcome some obstacles in the way of your miracle. The Lord will not do everything for you. It is a partnership, and YOU have a part to play if you want to see that miracle.....or that blessing.....or that answered prayer.

Receiving from God is a two-way street. Once you do your part—the faith part—He will supply the power to make the miracle a reality.

Faith Profession: "I will exercise faith in God's promises; and I will wait in certainty that the answer will come. For His part, my God will supply the power that will cause my faith to turn to sight."

Study Scripture: Mark 5:22-42

Faith Prayer 1

Scripture: Ephesians 1:17-23

As we learn more and more about faith, we begin to realize that our words are vitally important. This makes our prayer life equally important, since we are expected to pray, and speak, in line with God's Word. Obviously, we can do this when we speak some of the promises the Lord has placed for us all over the Bible. But there are certain places in the Bible where faith prayers are written down for us, and we can pray them exactly as they are written in Scripture. One such place is Ephesians 1:17-23, which will be our faith profession for today.

Faith Profession: "That the God of our Lord Jesus Christ, the Father of glory, may give unto you the spirit of wisdom and revelation in the knowledge of Him: The eyes of your understanding being enlightened; that ye may know what is the hope of His calling, and what the riches of the glory of His inheritance in the saints, and what is the exceeding greatness of His power to usward who believe, according to the working of His mighty power, which He wrought in Christ, when He raised Him from the dead, and set Him at His own right hand in the heavenly places, far above all principality, and power, and might, and dominion, and every name that is named, not only in this world, but also in that which is to come: And hath put all things under His feet, and gave Him to be the head over all things to the church, which is His body, the fullness of Him that filleth all in all."

Study Scripture: Matthew 12:34,37

DEVOTIONAL #23

FAITH PRAYER 2

Scripture: Ephesians 3:16-21

Once again I remind you of the importance of being in agreement with the Lord when you pray. Your faith, in combination with your mouth speaking one or more of the promises found in God's Word, WILL activate the power of Almighty God into your situation. That power WILL change the physical facts so that they line up with the truth of God's Word. There is in Ephesians 3 another prayer that you can pray verbatim from your Bible, and it is a faith profession. Let's make our faith profession today.

Faith Profession: "That He would grant you, according to the riches of His glory, to be strengthened with might by His Spirit in the inner man; that Christ may dwell in your hearts by faith; that ye, being rooted and grounded in love, may be able to comprehend with all saints what is the breadth, and length, and depth, and height; and to know the love of Christ, which passeth knowledge, that ye might be filled with all the fullness of God. Now to Him that is able to do exceedingly abundantly above all that we ask or think, according to the power that worketh in us, unto Him be glory in the church by Christ Jesus throughout all ages, world without end. Amen."

Study Scriptures: I John 4:8; Acts 1:4,8

ARMOR OF GOD 1

Scripture: Ephesians 6:10-11

In Ephesians 6:10, we find the beginning of the great discourse on the Christian's spiritual armor. It is compared to the typical armor worn by a first century foot-soldier, so some of the details will be unfamiliar to many readers. As we look at it in detail, please notice that every detail is significant.

Verse 10 begins by telling us to "be strong in the Lord," and then tells us how that is done.....by standing in the power of HIS might. Therefore, we immediately are focused on the fact that this is not armor designed to do battle in the physical realm. Further, it has nothing to do with our own power.....not our education; our intelligence; our bank account; how good looking we are; how famous we think we are; or our physical strength.

We are to STAND, and we'll see this word used throughout the description of the armor. So, on our part, we are expected merely to hold our ground, and not to run away. We are to do this based upon the LORD'S power, not our own.....remembering that He has given us access to His power at the moment of our salvation.

Verse 11 tells us what it is that we are to stand against—"the wiles of the devil." This identifies the enemy. Notice that he is said to use something called "wiles." In Genesis 3:1, the word is "subtle." Both words refer to the devil's tendency to use trickery; subversion; lying; and deceit. He will not come at you from the front. As a coward, he attacks when you aren't looking; when you are distracted; when you are hurt. His attacks are often disguised, and appear at first glance to be harmless—sometimes even helpful.

Be warned! The devil is not opposed to using ANY weapon against you, including your spouse; your best friend; or even yourself. We stand in the power of Jesus Christ.....who has already defeated the devil, and who gives that victory, and that authority, to us.

Faith Profession: "I will stand my ground based upon the power and victory supplied to me by Jesus Himself. I will wear the armor of God, which is invincible."

Study Scriptures: Ephesians 6:10-18; II Corinthians 10:3-5

Armor of God 2

Scripture: Ephesians 6:12

As we look at verse 12, we notice first that our battle is compared to the sport of wrestling. If you know anything about this sport, you know that it involves close contact of the combatants.....hand-to-hand fighting, you might say. It will involve being face-to-face with your enemy; and it will be a struggle.....though you have the assurance of victory if you wrestle in the power of HIS might (verse10).

Note that it is a purely spiritual struggle, with an invisible enemy. The only information you have on this enemy is what you find in your Bible. To struggle against flesh and blood—people, in other words—is to be focused on the wrong enemy. Our fight is with the SOURCE of the problem.....and that is found in the spiritual realm.

Our enemies are then named by category. You might want to turn to Colossians 2:15 and notice the use of the same terms there, where their defeat by Jesus Christ is described. THEY ARE DEFEATED! You need to keep that in mind. And Jesus has given His victory over them to YOU, because, at salvation, you have become part of His body.

From this verse, we can know that the devil's followers are organized into a sort of "level of command" structure. We see in verse 12 that each level is given a slightly different name. (See Daniel 10:1-14 for an example of this organizational structure).

Our spiritual enemies are organized, experienced, devious, nasty.....and defeated. They KNOW they have been defeated, but are counting on YOU not knowing that. So, operate in the TRUTH that they ARE defeated.

Faith Profession: "My battle with principalities and powers will be a struggle, but I WILL PREVAIL through Jesus Christ, who strengthens me."

Study Scriptures: Daniel 10:1-14; Colossians 2:10-15

ARMOR OF GOD 3

Scripture: Ephesians 6:13

Although it is described in detail in subsequent verses, verse 13 plainly exhorts you to take unto you the WHOLE armor of God—not just bits and pieces. The devil will notice a missing piece, and is sure to attack there.

It is also important to note that you are instructed to PUT ON this armor. God does not put it on FOR you. Nor will it help YOU if HE has it on. It doesn't jump onto your body of its own accord.....YOU have to put it on. As is always the case with Bible things, YOU are given some responsibility in the matter, and YOU are accountable for your failure to comply. Christians are fond of failing to put on their armor, then blaming God for their defeat. That is the easy way out of the responsibility issue, but it will not work with the Lord.....He is the author of the Book. He knows what He has written.

So, you are admonished to TAKE ACTION.....put on the armor! Why? So that you may be able to STAND in the evil day. What is this "evil day"? It is any day that the devil puts you under attack (which, by the way, is every day). Having put on the armor, you are simply commanded to STAND. If you look at the whole passage on God's Armor, you'll notice that this word "stand" is used four times: (in verses 11; twice in 13; and 14). Obviously, the Lord is trying to tell us something.

The devil, who is described in I Peter 5:8 to be "AS a roaring lion" (emphasis on AS is mine), will rush at you making lots of noise. The idea is to get you in fear, and to get you to give in to the natural urge to take off running. (This is deadly in spiritual warfare, as we'll see further on in our discussion of the Armor).

You KNOW the devil has been defeated, and that YOU have this victory, and its attendant authority, because Jesus gave it to you at salvation. So, just STAND when the devil rushes at you. Refuse to move. Withstand his bluster (which is all it is) with the quiet confidence that comes from KNOWING you are victorious.

He will be defeated.....every time!

Faith Profession: "I will stand against the devil's roaring attacks, knowing that they are nothing but noise and hot air. I am victorious in Christ, and in Him I stand firm."

Study Scriptures: I Peter 5:8,9; James 4:7; Ephesians 4:27

ARMOR OF GOD 4

Scripture: Ephesians 6:14

Verse 14 begins with the important admonition to STAND, rather than to take any physical action. As previously discussed, we are to simply stand our ground…..fight the tendency to run…..and refuse to fear.

Now begins the discussion of the specific pieces of the armor. The first thing mentioned is protection for your "loins." In a human body, your "loins" would be called your "core"—the strongest part of your body, consisting of your mid-section; lower back; and thighs. This is the source of your power. In the armor, this piece is called "truth." So, the TRUTH is the foundation upon which the remainder of the armor depends.

John 17:17 defines truth for us, and tells us that God's Word is truth. The Bible, and all that is in it, is basic, universal TRUTH. If you have experience in the Bible—if you have devoted your time to the study of it—if you know the Word—then you will have a solid foundation for the rest of your armor. The truth of God's Word is your greatest strength, so there is nothing more important to success in the spiritual realm. If you don't already do so, please make time in your schedule to study the Word each day.

The second piece mentioned is the breastplate. This, for a foot soldier, was the piece of metal that fit over the chest area, protecting the heart, primarily. In ancient warfare, as in warfare today, they know the value of HEART. If your heart is damaged, it is not likely that you will be able to fight. More than that, your WILL to fight is another definition of "heart." So, too, you will be ineffective without the WILL to do battle. Your shield is defined as righteousness, or "right thinking and actions." Thankfully, we are given the righteousness of Christ at salvation, so we don't have to rely on our own righteousness, which could never be effective. He died because our own righteousness could never save us. So, we do spiritual battle using Jesus' righteousness, which is perfect, and gives us this needed protection.

Faith Profession: "I stand in my spiritual battle, strengthened by the truth of God's Word that I have studied for myself, and protected by His righteousness, which gives me the will to stay in the fight."

Study Scriptures: II Corinthians 5:21; John 17:17

Armor of God 5

Scripture: Ephesians 6:15

God provides special protection for your feet because He knows how vital your feet are in combat. The armor being described is that of a first century foot soldier. One can only imagine how important this protection was for that kind of warrior. Should the enemy strike a blow to the feet, the soldier's mobility would be severely hampered. Loss of mobility made death a near certainty. So, one's feet needed the best protection possible.

For us, in these last days, it is our own mobility—our ability to move from place to place—that puts us in a better location to give out the Gospel. We need to be able to "go to where the people are." So, our feet represent our ability to be mobile, and therefore become just as vital to our efforts in ministry as a soldier's feet were to him in hand-to-hand combat . In these modern times, we can reasonably get to any place on the globe. Protection during these times of trouble is not only vital, but is promised for you.

Isaiah 52:7 says, "How beautiful upon the mountains are the feet of him that bringeth good tidings, that publisheth peace; that bringeth good tidings of good, that publisheth salvation; that saith unto Zion, Thy God reigneth!." So, you have beautiful feet (not stinky ones like some others), which give you the needed mobility to fight this fight effectively.

Faith Profession: "I am promised protection from God Almighty as I move from place to place to spread the Gospel. My feet are beautiful in God's sight, because they move me into necessary places to do battle with the enemy."

Study Scripture: Isaiah 52:7-10

Armor of God 6

Scripture: Ephesians 6:16

"ABOVE ALL," this verse says, "taking the shield of faith...." Although every piece of armor was important for the foot soldier, his shield was his first layer of protection. If he could deflect oncoming arrows; sword strikes; spears; etc. with his shield, he could prevent damage to the other pieces of his armor. Without the shield, enemy projectiles would strike his breastplate or helmet directly.

Eventually, these things would receive damage, and possibly even let damaging enemy projectiles through. So, deflecting them with a shield was the best idea.

The ancient shield was usually almost as tall as a man—he could hide behind it totally. Notice, though, that it specifically says that it must be TAKEN ("taking the shield..."). That is, the shield did not automatically jump into one's hand. You had to reach down and pick it up, then USE it, for it to be effective.

So it is with faith. It is not some automatic thing that just appears when you need it. It must be TAKEN, and APPLIED. That is, YOU activate faith for yourself.....by speaking the Word of God; reading it; studying it (see Romans 10:17). IF you will do that, you will have the protection that the shield of faith provides.

Note: God is not going to apply it FOR you. If you expect the shield of faith to work, you'll have to DO something with it. Pick it up! Use it! Apply it to your own life! Start by reading—and speaking—some faith verses.....until they become imbedded in your spirit. THEN your shield of faith will be most effective.

Faith Profession: "I have a solid shield, which is called faith. It will do the job, but I must take it and use it. The Lord makes it totally effective, but I must be the one to apply it."

Study Scriptures: Hebrews 11:1,6; I John 5:4

Armor of God 7

Scripture: Ephesians 6:16

Last time, we discussed the first part of this verse. Today, let's focus on this part: "...wherewith ye shall be able to quench all the fiery darts of the wicked." It is important to notice that the Word of God is not shy about saying that the shield of faith will quench ALL the enemy throws our way. ALL. This is possible because, when Jesus defeated the devil in the three days after His death on the Cross, that defeat was TOTAL. When you TAKE UP the shield of faith, you are putting up protection that has already won the victory over everything and anything the devil can throw at you. Amen!!

The verse calls the enemy's attack weapons "darts." In other places, it says "swords." Both darts and swords are WORDS (see verses 16 and 17). You defeat the devil's words with GOD'S WORDS. That is why it is so vital to know some Scripture promises, and to say them—out loud—daily.

Remember.....WE are His body. Jesus is no longer present physically on the Earth, but WE ARE. There's a reason for that. We are His voice.....if WE don't speak faith promises into a situation, who else will do it? When we do that, EVERY weapon of satan is nullified, because this shield quenches ALL the fiery darts of the wicked.

Notice, too.....it QUENCHES them. To "quench" means "to put out completely" .....as the application of water does to a fire. It negates the attack COMPLETELY.

So, IF we will TAKE this shield, it will afford us perfect protection against ALL the enemy throws our way!

Faith Profession: "I have a shield that negates ANY weapon used against me by my spiritual enemy. If I will take it up, it will give me total protection."

Study Scriptures: Colossians 2:15; Luke 10:19

Armor of God 8

Scripture: Ephesians 6:17

As we move on in this description of our armor, the next important piece is the helmet. It's a no-brainer that one's helmet is a vital item of protection. Obviously, our ability to function is dependent to a great degree upon our brain, and our senses in general, being fully intact. We need to think effectively as we battle our enemy. Although it is a spiritual battle, we are expected to use our mind. In fact, our mind is one of the battlefields in this conflict. Ours needs to be fully functional; clear; and full of the Word of God.

Our helmet is compared to our salvation. Once a person has truly received Jesus as his/her personal savior from sin, they will give you a "yes" answer if you ask them if they are saved. Above all other things in the Christian life, certainty about salvation seems to be prevalent. This is a good thing, because the devil will try to inject doubt into your life….. especially about your salvation….if he can. Our spiritual battle is complicated enough without having to wrestle with doubts about our status as a child of God.

So, with salvation firmly settled in our mind, we can move on to other areas of the conflict with confidence. If you are having any doubts about your own salvation, take a minute to get it settled. Just say something like this to Jesus: "Lord, I believe in You. I believe You died on the Cross to pay for my sin. I believe You rose from the dead, and I now accept You as my savior from sin's penalty. Thank You for saving me, and making me part of the family of God. In Jesus' Name. Amen."

Now…..go ahead and move forward into the battle…..with confidence!

Faith Profession: "I know that I am saved. I have that matter settled in my mind and heart. I am saved because of what Jesus did for me on the Cross. And I wear this like a protective helmet."

Study Scriptures: I Thessalonians 5:8; Romans 1:16

Armor of God 9

Scripture: Ephesians 6:17

Our next piece of armor is the only one mentioned that is an offensive weapon (offensive in the sense of offense vs. defense, not repulsive). So, our part in this battle is not only to ward off the devil's attacks, but to strike back at him.

The sword that was prevalent in the first century—and which made the Roman army effective—was a smaller sword which was sharp on both edges (called a two-edged sword in Hebrews 4:12). Previously, combat swords had been large, and had become larger over the years. The idea was that you could do lots of damage if you hit your enemy; but the thing was heavy, and you were in trouble if you missed. Old swords had only one edge on them. This new sword was easy to handle, and could cut in either direction. In use against larger, heavier swords, it was incredibly effective.

It is to this two-edged sword that the Word of God is compared. It is lightning fast, and wildly effective. (Just ask the devil.....if he wasn't such a liar, he'd tell you that it's REALLY effective against him.) You use this sword by SPEAKING the Word of God. Every time you speak a Scripture, angels are activated on your behalf in the spiritual realm (see Psalm 103:20).

Even satan himself is subject to the commands and demands of the Word of God. That is why he works so hard to get you to believe anything else except that YOU need to speak the Word. Do that, and watch the devil run. The Word of God is his worst nightmare..... and a Christian willing to speak it is his second worst nightmare. Anyway, it's about time we struck back at these forces of darkness.

Faith Profession: "My sword in the spiritual battle is the Word of God. It is a highly effective weapon, and I intend to use it by speaking Scripture. When I do, the devil will be forced to flee!"

Study Scriptures: James 4:7; I Peter 5:9; Ephesians 4:27; Mark 11:23

Armor of God 10

Scripture: Ephesians 6:18

The Bible's discussion of the whole armor of God ends with an admonition for prayer. This is not surprising, since we are encouraged to pray throughout the Word, and since Jesus Himself spent much time during His earthly ministry in prayer.

Prayer is our method of spending time with the One who built and perfected the armor. If the armor is our protection, then prayer is the glue that binds it in place. Prayer invites the power of God into the battle, which is what guarantees the victory.

We are told to pray "always," or, as stated in I Thessalonians 5:17, "without ceasing." Obviously we can't spend our whole day bent over, hands folded, and eyes closed. The idea is to be in an *attitude* of prayer at all times…..in constant contact with the Lord…..living in the realization that He is with you, and in you, every second.

Notice, too, that you are asked to pray "in the Spirit." That is, you are to pray in your secret prayer language (in tongues), so that your prayers might be that much more effective. If you haven't yet come to an understanding of this great New Testament gift, do yourself the favor of prayerfully studying it. NO prayer is more effective than that done in the Spirit.

Faith Profession: "My spiritual battle is fought in my prayer place, where I can fellowship with my Lord and Savior, Jesus Christ. The effectiveness of my armor is dependent upon His power, so I request that power as I battle our common enemy, the devil."

Study Scriptures: Romans 8:26; John 17:1-23

ARMOR OF GOD 11

Scripture: Ephesians 6:10-18

Although we have completed our look at the armor of God, I want to take the time to point out to you that there are two pieces of armor missing from the description in Ephesians 6.

A typical first century foot-soldier wore a sort of fitted plate on his back; he also wore a pair of shin guards, called "greaves." These two pieces of armor are obviously necessary for physical hand-to-hand combat.

However, in our spiritual warfare, we are given no protection for our back. Why? Because we are commanded to "stand" in the face of the enemy's attack (Ephesians 6:11,13,14). If you turn and run in the spiritual conflict, you are on your own.

The missing shin protection should be obvious: you don't need protection for your shins when you are fighting a battle on your knees. According to Ephesians 6:18, that is where this battle is fought.

Once again, we see that the Lord has made every provision for our needs.....and has made no provision for those things we don't need. Some would like to believe that our battles are fought FOR us by the Lord. But, what would be the purpose of armor.....given to US.....if that were the case?

No.....WE are the part of His body that remains on the Earth. WE face the daily conflict against the forces of darkness. He has not left us alone; nor powerless; nor without protection. It is up to US to TAKE this armor.....put it on.....and USE it. There will be certain victory if we do that.

Faith Profession: "I will take my stand WITH Jesus, and AGAINST the devil. I will take up my armor daily, and go into battle as a prayer warrior for the Lord. And, I WILL be victorious, in Jesus' Name!"

Study Scriptures: Philippians 4:19; Isaiah 54:17; I Samuel 17:26, 45-51

SPIRITUAL FIRST

Scripture: Matthew 6:33

At the end of Matthew chapter 6, Jesus is speaking about worldly things, and how to react to them. He sums up His narrative with verse 33, telling His listeners (and readers) to focus on spiritual things FIRST.

This information, like most everything else He spoke, was stunning to the crowd because it was the exact opposite of the thinking of the world. Perhaps that's why our Bibles collect so much dust in America. A preacher from Florida I once knew said, "If everyone in Florida picked up their Bibles at the same time, the state would disappear under a cloud of dust." Yes, Jesus' methods are quite unlike the world's practices…..which is why they work so well.

You might want to think about that for a second. When you or someone in your family becomes sick, what do you think to do first? Call a doctor? Run for the medicine cabinet? If you're like most people in this country, that's exactly what you do.

I wonder what the world would be like if we took Jesus' advice? We would read and study the Word every day. If we got sick, we'd pray about it FIRST. If we developed a money problem, we'd take it to the Lord first. If we had a conflict with another person, we'd follow His process in Matthew 18…..but we'd attempt to avoid harsh words at all costs. Our first reaction to any person would be LOVE.

"Seek ye FIRST the kingdom of God, and His righteousness, and all these things shall be added unto you." It's the best of advice from the One who knows.

Faith Profession: "I will try to change my approach to life's situations, beginning today. I will put spiritual things first in my life, and react to circumstances by looking to the spiritual FIRST."

Study Scripture: I Kings 3:11-14

WHO IS "THE ROCK?"

Scripture: Matthew 16:18

THE ROCK. Whatever or whoever it is, the church is built upon it; so it has to be vitally important to us as Christians. As you might know, there is some confusion and misunderstanding of this passage of Scripture in our world. Let's look at verse 18, and see what it is really talking about, using simple English grammar and common sense.

In verse 16, Jesus asks His disciples who they think He is. Peter gives the correct answer, and, in verse 17, Jesus reveals that the answer was given to Peter supernaturally….from God the Father. Of course, Peter had to be "tuned in" to the Lord for this information to be received.

Verse 16 is the key. The fact that Jesus is "the Christ" (the "Messiah," or, literally, "the Anointed One") is the foundational truth here. So, in verse 18, Jesus says He will build His church upon "this rock." Prior to that, He calls Simon by the name "Peter" (rather than Simon as in verse 17). So, some have concluded that the church was to be built upon Peter—a mere man, and a flawed one at that!

No, verses 17 and 18 both refer to "it," not "him." The "it" being referred to is the statement of verse 16. It is referenced again in verse 20. Besides that, the name "Peter" has a meaning, which is "rock…..as in small pebble." The word "rock" used to describe the foundation of the church in verse 18 has the translation of "huge rock"—like the Rock of Gibraltar.

In the original language, the difference is quite obvious. Nobody back then had any doubt what Jesus was saying: the church was going to be built upon the *truth* that Jesus was "THE CHRIST, THE SON OF THE LIVING GOD"…..as stated by Peter in verse 16. Obviously, no mere man could possibly measure up to that.

Faith Profession: "The church of Jesus Christ is built upon Jesus Himself…..The Christ, and Son of the Living God. He Himself is the chief cornerstone, and the Rock of my salvation."

Study Scripture: Ephesians 2:20

DEVOTIONAL # 37

TRUE WORSHIP

Scripture: Matthew 26:39

This verse is one of the most powerful in the Bible because in it, Jesus is yielding His will to that of the Father. Had this not been done, none of us could be saved.

But, today, I want to focus on another aspect of this verse: the phrase "…and fell on his face…"

We talk about worship. We sing in church. We say we like the music. Some of us actually get "in the Spirit" during worship. But, here in this verse, we find TRUE WORSHIP. By definition, it is bowing down flat on the ground. The idea is giving yourself totally to the Lord.....complete submission.....complete trust.

Now, it probably isn't the norm in your church to see people lying face down in worship. But the IDEA is valid, because true worship is to be LIKE that. It is to be from the HEART.....the bowing down of your SPIRIT.....an attitude of complete worship; adoration; trust; immersion.

We are to "give ourselves to Him" in a very real way. Some visible signs of it are: raised hands; tears; closed eyes; kneeling; praying in the Spirit; clapping of hands. That is, we are to become "lost" in the worship of Him.....paying no attention to our surroundings, who is nearby, or what they think. Our total attention is on the Lord.....He has our entire focus, and nothing else is being allowed to enter our consciousness at that time.

As always, Jesus is our example. He gave Himself to His Father. Why would we expect Him to do less?

Faith Profession: "I will worship the Lord with abandon, allowing myself to be immersed in the flow of the Spirit of God."

Study Scriptures: Psalm 141:2; Psalm 134:2

DEVOTIONAL # 38

WHEN ARE YOU STRONG?

Scripture: Matthew 28:17

To get the true sense of this verse, we will have to look at the context. Verse 16 tells us that the disciples had traveled to Galilee, as instructed in verse 7. When Jesus appears, they worship Him, but…..SOME DOUBTED.

Doubted what? That it was really Jesus? No…..they doubted THEMSELVES. How do we know that? Well, they had just experienced the greatest failure of their lives. Peter wasn't the only one who had forsaken Him at the Cross. When the chips were down….. when it was a matter of life or death…..they ran and hid.

Imagine the shame and guilt they must have been feeling when they saw Him alive again. Our Bible puts it rather gently….. "some doubted." Yeah…..you bet your life they did!

What is Jesus' reaction to this? Well, the disciples are just off their greatest failure as His followers; and it is THEN that Jesus speaks verses 19 and 20. In effect, He says "Okay fellas,…..let's go take the WORLD!" What's the point? It's this: the Lord is never counting on just people. He knows them all too well. No, He is counting on His power working THROUGH people. All the people need to be is WILLING.

So, YIELDEDNESS is the key to service. The Bible says that He uses the weak, not the strong. Why? Because that's when His power works best. It's flowing through vessels who are less likely to get in the way…..who are less likely to "do it their own way."

Yieldedness is the key. When I am weak, then I am strong!

Faith Profession: "I yield to the power of the Lord working through me. I do not seek control of it, but simply let it do its own work. Nothing could be more effective."

Study Scriptures: I Corinthians 1:26-31; II Corinthians 12:10

Too Busy to Pray

Scripture: Mark 1:35

Our Scripture reading for today tells us that Jesus rose up early in the morning; found a place where He could be alone; and prayed. No surprise there.....we know Jesus often prayed. It's one way we know that WE should pray. If He prayed, then surely we will have to do the same.

But, I'd like to look at this verse a little more closely. If we look back at the earlier part of Mark 1, beginning at verse 23, we'll see that Jesus had quite a busy day prior to His early-morning prayer session in verse 35. According to verses 23 to 32, He was busy healing people ALL DAY. At even (6 o'clock PM), there were even MORE crowds. Jesus continues to heal them until late—well after sunset, and well into the evening.

It must have been an exhausting day for Him! Yet, instead of sleeping in, we find Him rising early—well before sunrise.....to get alone to pray. And, in that we can find some valuable lessons for ourselves. Jesus knew where His strength came from.....and it wasn't necessarily from sleep. He knew that real power came from the spiritual, not the physical. He also knew this: the busier we get, the MORE we need to pray.

We tend to do just the opposite. In fact, in our society, many of us can rarely find time to pray. We're blessed just to get to church once a week. But, my friend, that won't do it. It isn't enough to sustain you through the tough battles we face. No, we need to resolve to pray MORE—in proportion to how busy we are. That's what He did. It's an important lesson for us.

Faith Profession: "I resolve to pray more as my schedule gets busier. I will do whatever I have to do to get some prayer time in every day."

Study Scriptures: Luke 18:1; I Thessalonians 5:17

Parable of the Sower 1

Scripture: Mark 4:1-20

The Parable of the Sower is one of Jesus' more famous discourses, and most Christians are somewhat familiar with it. Notice that, in verse 10, the disciples ask Him to explain what they heard. Apparently even they didn't always understand all that He said!

A parable is sometimes defined as "an earthly story with a heavenly meaning." Jesus often used similar methods to get His point across. He compared spiritual things to things familiar to His listeners.....things they could relate to from their everyday life. This made it easier for them to comprehend His ideas and concepts. Parables were also intended to increase the difficulty of understanding to skeptics, such as the Pharisees. Jesus knew that they were not trying to understand, but to find some way to accuse Him of wrongdoing, so He cloaked some of His ideas in parables.....later explaining them in detail to those who really wanted the truth (as in Mark 4).

This practice reveals something about our Lord. He sees into our hearts. As it says in Hebrews 4:12, He knows the "thoughts and intents of our heart." When He sees that you actually desire to know His Word, He will have it find you. If your motive is to find fault with the Word, its truth will be elusive to you. Or, put another way..... "believing is seeing." You can't hide your true motives from God Almighty, to whom all things are revealed. But when you hunger for His Truth, you will become bathed in it.....and it is a wonderful thing!!

Faith Profession: "I will seek the truth of God's Word with pure motives. I want to know my Savior better, and to come to understand who He is, and who I am in Him."

Study Scriptures: Hebrews 4:12; Mark 4:11-12

DEVOTIONAL #41

PARABLE OF THE SOWER 2

Scripture: Mark 4:13-20

Having given the parable in verses 3 to 9, Jesus is asked by His disciples to explain what has been taught. Because they truly wanted to know, Jesus accommodates the request. First, though, He mentions that some, whose motives are not to know, but to trap Jesus, will not comprehend the teaching until they are "converted."

He also mentions something else in verse 13 that is well worth noticing. He indicates that, if they don't understand ("know") this parable, they will not understand any of the other parables. Therefore, there is something special about this particular parable, and we need to be aware of its importance. In fact, certain principles in this parable are foundational to our understanding of many other portions of the Bible, and a working knowledge of THIS parable is extremely helpful if you are ministering the Word yourself. It helps to know why the Word tends to just bounce off many listeners. (By the way, if you haven't found out yet, YOU are not responsible for your listeners UNDERSTANDING and APPLYING the Word. You are only responsible for DELIVERING it faithfully (see I Corinthians 4:2).

As to the parable itself, His explanation starts off with a bang in verse 14. The sower in the parable represents someone who is giving out the Word of God..... "the sower soweth the word." This reveals that the Word is like SEED. Therefore, if you want to know how the Word of God works, you'll need to study how seeds work. They both work the same way.

So, when you speak the Word, you're casting seed into your listener's lives. As He tells us, not all of that seed will produce fruit. But, if it does, it will BE LIKE SEED: it will need time to grow; be watered; be "weeded;" be given careful attention with patience. And, we must NEVER stomp on our seed by speaking words of doubt or negativity..... that will surely destroy the growth process. Today, remember this.....the Word of God works like seed!!

Faith Profession: "I will treat the Word of God as seed, giving it time to grow, and being careful not to hinder its growth by speaking in opposition to it."

Study Scripture: Romans 4:12-22

DEVOTIONAL # 42

PARABLE OF THE SOWER 3

Scripture: Mark 4:15

Four groups of hearers are listed in this parable, and the first of these is discussed in verse 15.

First, the Word of God is clearly "sown" (or preached) in this case. This group of listeners is immediately victimized by our enemy, as he takes action to steal away the Word that they have heard.

I have preached the Word for well over 30 years. As you stand behind a pulpit, you can clearly observe this type of thing taking place. I have seen the following: people nodding off to sleep; people applying makeup; people texting messages on their cell phone; people checking messages on their cell phone; people writing notes and letters unrelated to the preaching; people staring off into space, daydreaming about something unrelated to the Word of God; people who just HAVE to go to the bathroom during the service; people distracted by unruly children; and, one time, I saw that a shaft of light had peeked in through an unclosed window, making a small circle of light just above the preacher's head on the wall. A teenager noticed it, too, and was making shadow shapes of rabbits, etc. that were showing up on the wall behind the preacher.....while he was delivering his sermon! So, not only was the teenager having the Word stolen, but he was facilitating the same thing for the whole congregation!

It is imperative that you stay focused on the Word as it is being preached. There is a concentrated effort being made.....every time the Word is spoken.....by the devil and his minions.....to steal that Word away from you. Sadly, his efforts are all too successful, and the Word never has a chance to make the difference that it CAN make. Be aware of this! Guard yourself and your family by making them aware of it. At least give the Word a fighting chance in your life!

Faith Profession: "I will focus on the preaching of the Word as I listen to it. Where possible, I will take notes. I will be aware of the devil's attempts to steal the Word from me, and I'll not let him do it!"

Study Scriptures: James 1:22; Romans 10:17

PARABLE OF THE SOWER 4

Scripture: Mark 4:16-17

Verses 16 and 17 describe the second group of hearers of the Word of God. The "ground" upon which this seed lands is said to be "stony," so it is hard rather than soft and pliable, making growth difficult if not impossible.

Notice that this group of hearers hears the Word, and initially receive it with gladness. They are excited at what they have heard, and usually show it. As a preacher of the Word, I originally got excited myself at this type of response. However, as I gained experience, I began to realize that the initial excitement often withers as quickly as it occurred.

Verse 17 indicated that the Word is unable to "take root" in stony-ground Christians. It simply is not received into their heart and life solidly. Therefore, when hardships occur.... as they always do in the Christian life, because we are opposed in this life by the devil and his helpers.....this type of hearers get offended, and turn away from the Word they heard.

Many Christians are "thin-skinned," and are fine as long as things are going well. But when the fighting starts, they want no part of it. That is, they lack toughness—essential for the soldier in the Lord's army. As God's people, we live in enemy territory. OF COURSE we're going to be persecuted and afflicted! But we have the ability, and the authority, to strike back! When we do, the enemy is taken back. Ultimately, our enemy cannot win, because we are given authority that has already proven victorious over him.

So, this second group looks good initially, but fades fast when real life, and true spiritual warfare, begins.

Faith Profession: "I know that the enemy is going to oppose me as I take a stand for Jesus Christ. But, because Jesus is Lord, I have the authority to prevail over the enemy..... in Jesus' Name."

Study Scriptures: James 4:7; I Peter 5:8-9; Ephesians 6:10-18

Parable of the Sower 5

Scripture: Mark 4:18-19

Jesus goes on to explain that there is a third category of people who hear the Word, and this group is described as those who have the seed cast among thorns. Now, if you have ever planted a garden, you know the difficulty presented by trying to garden through thorns.....it is VERY difficult, and the crops have a tough time competing with the aggressive weeds.

In this third group, the Word is heard, but the effectiveness of the Word is choked out by the things of the world. Because some of us live in the United States, this is an especially prevalent problem for us.

We live fast-paced lives, packed with obligations and responsibilities. We have families; children; jobs; church volunteer work. We add in baseball; dance class; gymnastics; soccer; football; tennis; various summer camps; church youth group; etc., and, as parents, we have multiplied our "busy-ness." For ourselves, we go to the gym; go to women's club; do hobbies.....and don't forget the summer vacation (where we rush to the beach, or to a campground, to do as much as we can squeeze into a week's time).

It's exhausting just writing about it! And what is the effect? We simply don't have time to read the Bible, pray, study; and don't even THINK about meditating on the Word quietly!

As a result, we hear it, but it rapidly fades from memory, engulfed by the cares of the world, and our lust for "other things" (many of which are "good" things.....but they still keep us from the Word).

The result? The Word becomes unfruitful.....it bears no fruit, because we have had no time to think about it; process it; plant it in our heart.

Faith Profession: "I resolve to MAKE time to pray and think about Scripture. I will even turn off the TV to do so."

Study Scripture: Matthew 19:16-22

Parable of the Sower 6

Scripture: Mark 4:20

The fourth group described by Jesus is the one that bears fruit, and therefore is a blessing to Him.

In this case, the seed (the Word of God) falls on good ground.....ground that has been tilled.....it is soft, receptive, ready, fertile.

With regard to the hearers, I notice that, in this case, they not only HEAR the Word, but they RECEIVE it. That is key to fruitfulness. Many people HEAR the Word, but not everyone RECEIVES it. It's interesting that, when you preach the Word to an audience that you can see, you can discern the receivers. They are the ones locked onto your words..... they are the ones actively taking notes.....they are the ones responding verbally when their heart is touched by a statement.

People like this hear the Word, and then receive it by faith. They think about it later..... mulling it over in their mind (called "meditating on the Word".....it is a Bible concept, not an eastern religion one, at least not originally). As a result, the Word settles into their spirit, where the indwelling Holy Spirit can speak through it.

THESE are the ones who bear fruit. Fruit-bearing is done in varying degrees, described in Mark 4 as thirty, sixty, and a hundred-fold. So, not everyone bears fruit equally, because not everyone applies Scripture in faith, and not everyone plants Scripture in their heart in equal measure.

The bottom line is this: the "seed" is good.....it is perfect, in fact. It WILL work, and bear fruit.....as long as you do your part, which is to receive it in faith, and apply it faithfully.

Jesus said that, if you understand this parable, it is the basis for understanding the rest of the parables, and the Bible itself. RECEIVE the Word! Then rejoice over the fruit!

Faith Profession: "I not only hear the Word, but I receive it. It WILL bear fruit as I apply it in my life, adding my faith to God's Word, which releases His power!"

Study Scriptures: Romans 8:16; II Timothy 2:15; John 15:16

Legion

Scripture: Mark 5:1-20

This remarkable story relates a true life event involving a man so possessed by devils that he was physically abusing himself. Actually, this incident reveals some common features of devil possession. Notice that this man dwelt in the cemetery; had supernatural strength; roamed around at all hours of the day and night; was wild and undisciplined; was naked; and actually cut himself with stones. He was crying out, but no one knew how to help him.....until Jesus showed up.

Did you notice that this wild man immediately recognizes Jesus? (See verse 6). Why? Because even devils know about spiritual things.....that are true. You have to be an educated American to believe otherwise.

Notice, too, that Jesus speaks directly to the devils, and that they obey Him. When Jesus asks the devils their name, they answer "Legion, for we are many." A Roman legion was a military grouping of 6,000 soldiers, so there were apparently 6,000 evil spirit-beings in this man! They were driving him to do harm to himself; revere death and dead things; to be active at night; to tend toward nakedness; to have unnatural strength.

What defeated these 6,000 spirits of darkness? Simply a word from Jesus Christ.....which is found in Matthew 8:32. It is the Word of God that defeats our spiritual enemies.

What was the result? See verse 15. The man had been set free: he was calm, clothed, and rational.....and those who came to him were AFRAID! (They were okay with him when he was nuts.....NOW they are afraid!!) Jesus sent him out to tell his story to others, and he obeyed.....as we should.

Devils tend toward destruction and harm. Jesus sets us free.....and He does it with HIS WORD (which WE can speak in His Name!)

Faith Profession: "I am so glad I have been set free by Jesus! I have the authority to use His Name in just the way He did.....and devils WILL OBEY!"

Study Scriptures: John 8:32,36; Luke 10:19

DEVOTIONAL #47

JAIRUS

Scripture: Mark 5:21-24

As Jesus leaves the man from Gadara to witness to others, He travels, as He often does, by ship to another location. Verse 21 tells us that, as soon as He came to land, He was met by another large crowd of needy people. (This man rarely had time to rest!)

A rather surprising person came out of the crowd to ask Jesus for a miracle. Jairus was a "ruler of the synagogue," and it was rare that such a religious leader would publicly appeal to Jesus for anything. Usually the religious leaders in Israel were trying to kill Him. So, it was a humbling thing that Jairus was doing.

He pays Jesus homage by falling at His feet. Then he makes his request known: his daughter was dying, and he wanted Jesus to come with him, lay hands on her, and heal her. I am struck by how definite he is. In verse 23, he says, "Lay thy hands on her, that she may be healed; and SHE SHALL LIVE." There is no doubt in his mind; therefore his request is one of faith, and Jesus can work with that.

I like the fact that Jesus doesn't point out that Jairus's actions are contrary to those of his colleagues.....He simply goes with him, and He does so immediately. I like that. Jesus responds immediately when we have a need, regardless of our past. He holds no grudge; He is love, and responds just as love should. Jairus is very pleased, and eagerly leads Jesus through the crowd.

Faith Profession: "The Word of God is true, so I can speak it with certainty. God always keeps His promises, and I can count on that."

Study Scriptures: Proverbs 30:5; John 17:17

DEVOTIONAL #48

TOUCHING HIS GARMENT

Scripture: Mark 5:25-34

Mark chapter 5 is packed with great information, and this account is one of the best. Jesus has just agreed to accompany Jairus to his home to heal his daughter. As He pushes through the large crowd, He passes an unnoticed woman.

This woman had been sick for twelve years. She had spent all her money on doctors, and was not one bit better. Now she was desperate. Though she was forbidden to mingle with crowds according to Jewish law, she had her faith focused on one thing.....touching the hem of Jesus' garment. She believed that, if she touched this, she would be healed. Her faith was strong, and it was focused. She was going to allow NOTHING to get in the way of her healing.

So, she slips unnoticed through the crowd and touches Jesus' garment as He passes. Immediately (verse 29), her disease was healed. At the same time, Jesus strongly sensed the movement of healing power from Himself, and He stopped, saying, "Who touched me?" His disciples reacted just as you and I would.....hey, you're moving through a huge crowd of people, and you ask, "Who touched Me?"

Of course, Jesus meant that someone had touched Him with purpose, and faith.

At this, the woman comes forth, and Jesus speaks kindly and gently to her (verse 34). Jesus said that her faith had made her whole. That is, her faith released His power, and a miracle occurred. That's how it happens, folks. Your faith releases His power, and the facts get changed by the Truth.

In this case, the fact was that she was diseased. The Truth (spiritually) was that she was healed. It was her faith that moved the Truth to replace the fact.....changing the physical circumstances so that they came into line with the spiritual truth. And so it will always be.

Faith Profession: "I will believe the promises given to me in God's word. I will add my faith to them, which will release God's power into my circumstances, changing them to get in line with the promise."

Study Scriptures: I John 5:4; Hebrews 11:6

Jairus, Part 2

Scripture: Mark 5:35-42

We had left Jairus standing—probably impatiently—waiting for Jesus to finish with the woman with the issue of blood. All the while, Jairus' daughter was getting closer to death.....the delay was maddening to him!

And.....it turned out to be too late. As Jesus finished speaking to the woman, messengers arrived from Jairus' house to give him the bad news that his daughter had died. What a moment! I can see Jairus looking at Jesus, thinking, "If you hadn't delayed, my daughter might have lived."

However, Jesus reacts immediately to the words spoken by the messengers. Before Jairus can say anything, Jesus looks at him and says, "Be not afraid, only believe." That is, before Jairus can utter anything negative (against faith), Jesus cautions him to STAY IN BELIEF. Not stated, but there anyway, is Mark 9:23. (Read it for yourself.)

Jesus is saying, "Don't speak against the miracle.....even now. It isn't over yet. I promised to heal your daughter, and I intend to keep that promise." (By the way, that's exactly what He says to YOU with each promise given in the Bible.)

They continue to Jairus' house, where they find people weeping over the daughter's death. Jesus calmly goes in to the little girl, and commands her to arise.....and she responds. She is ALIVE!! Once again, faith has been rewarded! A miracle has occurred because someone stayed in faith, which allowed Jesus' power to flow into the situation, and change the physical facts.

Faith, my friend, works. YOUR faith in God's promise WILL change the physical circumstance! Even death itself, as in this case! There is NOTHING that can't be done if we mix our faith with God's promises!!

Faith Profession: "I believe! I believe that God's Word is true, and when I place my faith in it, then it becomes real for me! I expect a miracle!"

Study Scriptures: Mark 10:27; Romans 4:16-22

DEVOTIONAL # 50

LIMITING GOD

Scripture: Psalm 78:41

You probably can't believe the title of today's devotional. You ask, "How can humans limit God!?"

Yes, we're conditioned to believe that God can do anything.....and that He does EVERY-THING. That's why you pray the way you do.....because you have been taught that "God is in control," and that whatever happens is God's will.....even if it is a nasty illness, or even a death.

So, what do you do with today's Scripture? It plainly says that the Israelites— HUMANS— have limited God. Matthew 13:58 tells us that Jesus "did not many mighty works there..." Do you see the rest of the verse? "...because of THEIR UNBELIEF." That is, Jesus was "limited" by humans.

We need to get rid of this teaching that everything that happens to us is either FROM God, or ALLOWED by Him. Don't you see? That is EXACTLY what the devil wants you to believe, because it gives him free access to you.....to do whatever nasty thing he wants to do to you, and then to sit back and laugh while you blame it on God!

God DOES have all power and authority. He IS all-powerful, and sovereign. BUT.....He has set up a system. (See lesson #10.) We can limit God because His Word plainly decrees that WE—with our faith—are important partners in the unleashing of His power on earth. WE hold the key.....OUR faith is the trigger. And God WILL NOT TAKE AC-TION unless we exercise faith. If we don't, we "limit" what He is able to do. YES.....we CAN limit Him. Let's not do that!

Faith Profession: "I will speak God's promises (Scripture) into the spiritual world around me. This will activate His power, and release it into my life."

Study Scriptures: I John 5:4; Matthew 13:53-58

One Got Out

Scripture: Revelation 22:20

I would like to relate to you a story I have just read. I cannot take credit for it, but the message is undeniably from the Holy Spirit.

The author relates that, as he and his 5-year-old son were passing by a cemetery one day, the boy noticed a pile of dirt beside a newly excavated tomb. He pointed and said excitedly, "Look, Dad, one got out!"

It was a funny event, and the Dad laughed. Yet, he relates, the more he thinks about it, the more he hangs onto those three words. Every time he passes a graveyard, every time he sees a cross at the front of a church, he is reminded of those three words: ONE GOT OUT. That event is why we can move forward in life.

It's hard to find something to say when someone tells you that they've been diagnosed with cancer. What do you say to a couple who has just lost a small child? But those three words seem to stick in your mind.....ONE GOT OUT.

Death couldn't keep our Savior in the ground. Jesus broke the chains of death, rose from the dead, and promised us eternity with Him. It is the central fact in human history, and our focal point as Christians. He spread His arms wide on a rugged cross one awful day some 2,000 years ago. There was nothing good about that day. It left eleven followers in agony, and the rest of His followers devastated. Perhaps they locked themselves away, asking questions that nobody could answer.

Until that glorious Sunday when ONE GOT OUT! "When the heart broken by our sin began to beat once again."

One day soon, those same arms will spread wide again, welcoming us home. It is a wonderful, glorious thought! Let that mental picture fill your heart to overflowing. Let it guide the way you live, the way you handle adversity, the way you deal with people.....both charming and not so charming. "Even so, come, Lord Jesus."

Faith Profession: "I live in the reality of my risen Savior. I keep in the front of my mind the fact that "one got out."

Study Scripture: Revelation 22

WHY PRAYERS TAKE TIME

Scripture: Daniel 10:10-14

In our text, the prophet Daniel had received a vision of things that were going to happen in the end times. He didn't understand all of what was revealed to him, so he began to pray about it.....just as you or I would.

Three weeks after he began to pray, he was visited by the angel Gabriel, who explains to Daniel what has been happening since he began to pray. Notice in verses 12 and 13 that Daniel's prayer was heard as soon as he spoke, and the answer was sent immediately. However, there is opposition to good things in the spiritual world; and the angel messenger in this case was delayed by an angel of darkness called, in verse 13, the "prince of the kingdom of Persia." Michael, the Bible's only Archangel, was dispatched to fight with this dark opponent, and, when he defeated him, Gabriel was able to continue on his way with the answer to Daniel's prayer.

So, sometimes, when we pray and don't get an immediate answer, we begin to rationalize: "Maybe God is saying 'no;'" "maybe God is saying 'maybe;'" "maybe God is mad at me for something I've done." Or.....maybe there are spirits of opposition in operation who seek to hinder the progress of the answered prayer. Maybe, instead of thinking that God is holding back for some reason, we ought to give Him credit for being the God of Love that He truly is, and be patient while spiritual opposition is thrown back.

While this spiritual battle is going on, and your answer is temporarily delayed, it is the devil who is trying to get you to give up.....not God! God is the one who is working to get the answer to you.....as you might expect. Let's stand firm WITH our God, trusting Him and holding fast in our belief in Him.

Faith Profession: "Prayer is not always answered immediately because there is opposition to it in the spiritual realm. I will hold fast to God's promise, patiently expecting the answer to my prayer."

Study Scriptures: Psalm 84:8-11; Ephesians 6:12

BROTHERS AND SISTERS

Scripture: Mark 6:1-3

I want to take a short look today at Jesus' family, because, through tradition, some confusion has arisen over the years about this topic.

Notice in our text verses that Jesus had traveled back to "his own country," meaning that He was back in His hometown of Nazareth. On Saturday, the Sabbath day, He began to teach in the synagogue. As He taught, the listeners became offended, uttering the words in verses 2 and 3.

Look closely at verse 3, please. In it, you find a list of the names of Jesus' brothers. There are four mentioned. It also mentions His sisters (plural), so we know that there were at least two of them.

This means that Jesus grew up with brothers and sisters. There were at least seven children in the family—Jesus being the oldest. If you search around, you can find teachings that indicate that Jesus' mother, Mary, was sinless; and that she bore no other children (they say she was a "perpetual virgin").

This would come as quite a surprise to her husband, Joseph, who knew otherwise.....the six other children being testimony to the error of that teaching.

No, Mary was neither sinless nor perpetually a virgin. She was a Mom who raised lots of kids. She was a good woman, and loved the Lord. And I, for one, will be looking to talk to her in Heaven. But sinless? Perpetual virginity? I'm afraid that is contrary to the plain teaching of the Bible.

Faith Profession: "I believe the Bible to be God's Holy Word, and the Final Authority in all matters.....period. I take my beliefs directly from Scripture, and from no other source."

Study Scripture: Matthew 13:53-58

DEVOTIONAL # 54

THE DEATH OF JOHN THE BAPTIST

Scripture: Mark 6:17-28

In many ways, this is a very sad story.....not just because of the death of a great warrior for God, but because of the way it happened.

Herod, the Roman ruler in Galilee at the time, had married his brother's wife. John the Baptist, never at a loss for words, told Herod that what he had done was not lawful. This infuriated the new wife, Herodias (as the truth often does), and she demanded John's imprisonment.

While John was in prison, Herod threw a drunken party. During the party, Herodias' daughter danced for Herod and the crowd. Her dance was rated "R," and induced the drunken Herod to promise to give her anything she asked. (People in a drunken state tend to do this kind of thing). However, this situation had been anticipated by Herodias, who schemed with her daughter to ask for the head of John the Baptist. Since Herod had loudly promised her anything—in front of the whole crowd—he felt he could not go back on his word.....and had John beheaded.

Isn't that ironic? Though it meant killing an innocent man, Herod does it to protect his "honor." To "keep his word," he commits murder. (Don't you find the people in the world to be irrational? Isn't that outrageous to you??)

John the Baptist, one of the Bible's finest men of God, is killed because of a promise made to a lewd dancer in the middle of a drunken stupor. What a waste. What a shame.

Notice verse 26. Herod was "sorry." (Oh, great.....that should make John feel much better about things). Yes.....he was "sorry".....but he murdered an innocent man anyway. Perhaps Herod was "sorry" in another sense of that word.

Faith Profession: "I am a stranger and a pilgrim in this world system. This world is not my home any longer. I am a citizen of Heaven since I received Jesus as my personal savior, and I miss my home."

Study Scriptures: Proverbs 14:12; Proverbs 26:12

DEVOTIONAL # 55

JESUS FIGHTING BACK

Scripture: Matthew 14:10-14

There is so much about Jesus that we simply don't comprehend.....at least at first glance. He is a complex being, and one needs to contemplate Him to begin to understand Him.

Such is the case here in Matthew 14. Verses 1 through 12 tell the story of the death of John the Baptist. In verse 12, the disciples give this bad news to Jesus.

Although it doesn't say so in the Bible, I can imagine how hard this news was for our Savior. John was not only Jesus' friend, but they were cousins.....family. Furthermore, John was an unyielding voice for God, and Jesus had precious few helpers quite like John. The loss of this man was enormous.

When I first noticed Jesus' reaction to this news, I was puzzled. In verse 13, He gets away by Himself. The ever-present crowd, upon hearing that Jesus had gone apart to be alone, promptly follows Him. As Jesus emerges from praying, He sees the multitude. Instead of being irritated with them, He is "moved with compassion," and spends the day healing the sick among them.

What? No mourning period? No funeral arrangements for His cousin? No, Jesus, as always, does just the right thing. John's death has been a blatant attack by the devil. So, Jesus hits back in this spiritual battle.....He gets into serious prayer. Then He spends a whole day un-doing what the devil had done to the multitude.

It's Jesus' subtle way of saying "in your face, devil." Jesus reacts by striking back at the true enemy where it hurts him most. He heals.....He shows compassion (not anger).....He prays. In sum, He enters the battlefield with the devil, and inflicts maximum damage on him. And that's EXACTLY what should have been done.

Faith Profession: "I recognize that my daily battle is a spiritual one. I recognize that my true enemy is not flesh and blood, but spiritual entities who try to motivate humans to do their dirty work. I react as Jesus did.....with prayer; compassion; and spiritual warfare."

Study Scriptures: Ephesians 6:10-18; I Samuel 17:47

A Little Boy's Lunch

Scripture: John 6:5-14

This account of the feeding of the 5,000 (it is 5,000 men, plus women and children.....more like 10,000 people) is found also in Mark 6 and Luke 9. It is a rather famous story, so I'll trust that you know the details.

Notice, first of all, that Jesus knew from the start what would happen, but was looking to teach something to His disciples (verse 6). Philip states the impossibility of the task, but Andrew, who suspects that a miracle is possible here, points out that a lad is present, and this young fellow has brought his lunch along to the preaching service. It is a modest amount.....two small fish, and five loaves (we'd call them dinner rolls), but sufficient for a small boy to eat.

Jesus instructs His disciples to have the crowd sit down in an orderly fashion (because ours is a God of order). Notice that Jesus gives thanks FIRST.....from which we derive our habit of praying before we eat. Then He distributes the food to the crowd, and.....miraculously.....it multiplies as He distributes it. He not only feeds the crowd of 5,000, but they gather 12 baskets of leftovers (one for each disciple). That is, the amount left over is more than they started with!

This is a principle that we need to lock into our hearts. If Jesus is in a thing, there is no limit to how big it can grow, or how effective it can be. Jesus is not concerned about the size of the original. So, we are much better off leaving things in His hands, and simply being obedient to him, because that's how miracles occur. It's when we get ourselves involved.....when we think too much; when we do it ourselves; when we insist on looking at the facts.....that His work is hindered.

This miracle simply teaches us that nothing is impossible with our Lord. Believe me, a little boy was convinced that day. His willingness to give all he had for the benefit of others was key to this miracle.

Faith Profession: "I believe my God can do the impossible. If I will give to Him without reservation, He can and will multiply my gift so that others will be blessed as well as me."

Study Scriptures: Luke 6:38; Mark 9:23

FORGETTING THE LESSON

Scripture: Matthew 14:22-33

Immediately after the feeding of the 5,000 (see verse 22), Jesus asks His disciples to get into a ship and "go before Him unto the other side" of the Sea of Galilee. Jesus Himself takes time out to get alone and pray…..to refresh Himself after the labor of the day.

While He is alone praying, the disciples find themselves out on the Sea of Galilee in the midst of a pretty violent storm. They apparently battle this storm for many hours, because it is the "fourth watch of the night" before Jesus appears to them, walking on the water. (More on that later).

Let's look at that…..a Jewish day was set up in two twelve-hour periods; but, unlike our setup, they started their day at 6 o'clock in the evening (our time). They counted twelve hours of "night" (6 PM to 6 AM); then twelve hours of "day" (6 AM to 6 PM). Each twelve-hour period was divided up into four parts of three hours each. Each three-hour period was called a "watch"…..a descriptive term because that's what was done during these hours…..someone "watched" (and was called a "watchman").

The twelve-hour "night" period has four parts…..6 PM to 9 PM; 9 PM to midnight; midnight to 3 AM; and 3 AM to 6 AM. This last three-hour period is called the "fourth watch" for obvious reasons, and it is during this time that Jesus appears. That means that the disciples have been rowing against the storm for something over six hours or so

Suddenly, they look up…..in the midst of their fatigue…..and see Jesus walking toward them on the water!! They "freak out," as you can imagine. I like Jesus response: "It's okay, guys…..it's just me. Be of good cheer." The scene makes me smile. Here is Jesus being completely nonchalant about standing on top of the water in the middle of the deep sea. He seems to take His own miracles in stride…..and to expect that His followers would do the same by now.

Do you? Do YOU?? Do you expect miracles from Him? Or are you startled by His presence, and by His miracle-working power? You shouldn't be. Hasn't He worked miracles for you over and over? "Be of good cheer…be not afraid" (verse 27)

Faith Profession: "I expect miracles from my Lord. I know He is THE power in the universe, and He routinely does the supernatural in my life."

Study Scriptures: Zechariah 4:6; Mark 10:27

DEVOTIONAL # 58

WALKING ON WATER

Scripture: Matthew 14:22-33

In our last installment, we left the disciples out on the Sea of Galilee, fighting a storm; rowing and bailing for all they were worth for anywhere from five to eight hours. During the "fourth watch" of the night (3 AM to 6 AM), Jesus appears to them, walking up to the boat ON THE WATER!

After Jesus calms them down, they are still skeptical that it is Him. They are talking to Him, but He remains standing on the surface of the water. Peter, as usual, speaks up first, saying "Lord, if it be thou, bid me come to thee on the water."

I like this! Peter is not absolutely sure it is Jesus, but knows that, if it is, Jesus can do any miracle. So he asks the impossible.....that HE (Peter) be permitted to walk on the water, too. Jesus replies, simply….. "Come." Then, in verse 29, we find PETER walking on the water!!

You know, much is said about the fact that Peter looks at the waves and the storm, and begins to sink, and has to be rescued. But I've noticed that none of the other eleven disciples had the guts to get out of the boat in the middle of the sea. None of them had enough faith to even TRY it. So, let's not be too hard on Peter. Yes, he begins to look at the physical circumstances, and his faith wavers. BUT..... while he remained in faith, NOTHING WAS IMPOSSIBLE. And, he DID walk on the water.

The lesson? You and I can "walk on water," too. Our faith releases Jesus' power into our situation. As Jesus said, "O thou of little faith, wherefore didst thou doubt?" Doubt is the thing that negates a miracle. Faith is the thing that makes them happen. DO NOT DOUBT.....ONLY BELIEVE!

Faith Profession: "I believe in Your miracle-working power, Lord. If need be, I believe I can walk on water, because there is no limit to Your power."

Study Scriptures: I John 5:4; Mark 4:35-42

Devotional # 59
Making the Word Ineffective

Scripture: Mark 7:1-13

As Jesus ministered on earth, He endured many hostile encounters with the "religious authorities" of His day. In fact, Jesus shows hostility to only these people. We need to see why that is, and we need to avoid it in our own lives.

In our text verses, the whole encounter centers on the fact that the Pharisees are criticizing Jesus because His disciples are not following "tradition." That is, the Pharisees had a complex system of "things" that they did, and things that they did not do. To them, this was the essence of their lives. The more you followed these traditions, the more spiritual you were (in their eyes).

But, Jesus attacks this type of thinking in no uncertain terms. He states that the following of a set of "rules" (ritual; ceremony; repetitious practices) is exactly the opposite of what God desires.

Jesus calls the followers of tradition "hypocrites" (verse 6), and says that their tradition has made the Word of God "of no effect." Jesus knew that real faith in God is based on one's heart, not on his outward practices. Jesus knew that these outward practices, these traditions, could be faked.....that a person could go through the motions without any real conviction about the truth behind the practices.

That was the case with the Pharisees. I've seen this same thing in my own life. I lived with a person who faked it in the "religious "realm, and who got away with it for quite a number of years.

Traditions, repetitious practices, ritualistic ceremonies.....are religion, not faith. They are empty and meaningless as far as Jesus is concerned. More than that, they appeal to humans so much that they are substituted for real faith in Him. In that way, they nullify the Word of God in that person's life.....and Jesus is none too happy about it!

Faith Profession: "I have a relationship with Jesus, not a religion. I worship Him in spirit, and in truth."

Study Scripture: Romans 1:21-32

Devotional # 60
We Forgot the Bread

Scripture: Mark 8:14-21

The disciples, my friend, were as human as you and I. Some days, they were as dumb as a rock. Some days, they were full of faith and love. In today's lesson, we'll see one of those "dumb as a rock" days.

Notice, in the verses, that Jesus begins to teach them as they were traveling in a boat. He is using "leaven" (yeast) as an example of evil in His teaching. The disciples are having a "thick" day, and, when they hear Him mention leaven, their minds go to physical things..... in this case food.....and they begin to feel guilty because they forgot to bring bread for the journey. They reason that His teaching is His way of chastising them for their forgetfulness.

Hey.....don't be too hard on them. You and I can both recall times when WE didn't get it, either. Jesus, in verses 17 and 18, addresses this misunderstanding. He references the feeding of the 5,000; and the feeding of the 4,000. His point? To jog their memory..... to get them focused on spiritual things rather than on physical things. To get them to REMEMBER (verse 18).

Remember what Jesus has done. Hasn't He done wonderful things in your life? OK..... He wants you to keep those things fresh in your mind. Keep those things close to your heart, because what he has done, HE CAN AND WILL DO AGAIN.

Faith builds upon itself. An answered prayer today gives me confidence to pray about this new situation. A miracle over here makes me more inclined to believe in a miracle in my own circumstance. That's why it's important for each of us to share our answers to prayer.....and to keep them fresh in our own minds.

Faith is believing not only that Jesus CAN.....and that He WILL.....but that He already DID.

Faith Profession: "Jesus has worked many miracles in my life. I keep them in mind, and in heart, because they are reminders of what He WILL do again."

Study Scriptures: I Thessalonians 5:24; Lamentations 3:23

SPITTING ON A BLIND MAN

Scripture: Mark 8:22-26

Sometimes I read about the things that Jesus did while He was on the earth, and I think, "If He were to do that today, somebody would have Him in court for abuse." Unfortunately, that's the sad state of our world these days.

But, you have to admit that some of the things He chose to do when He was healing were pretty odd. Sometimes He just spoke to them; sometimes He placed His hand on them. One time, He used some spit to mix a clay from the dirt, which He placed on a blind man's eyes. Here in Mark 8, He just spits right on this guy's eyes!!

Now folks, it seems to me that if you're going to do something like this, you'd better be mighty sure that it will work! Otherwise, you'll be looking awfully foolish! Of course, Jesus WAS sure.....just the same as you and I can be (though I don't recommend this particular method in your healing ministry).

Now, have you noticed that the Holy Spirit uses almost an infinite variety of ways to do miracles? Did you notice that there is no pattern for it.....that it is essentially different in each case? Our traditional brethren have trouble with this. They think God's ways should be consistent so that they'll be easier to recognize.

However, this variety is the beauty, and essence, of the ministry of the Holy Spirit. He is compared to water.....a well.....a fountain.....a river. He is LIQUID, and as such can conform to whatever the situation calls for. It's one of the best things about the Holy Spirit! He is not held to traditions.....is not confined to a "box." He is free.....to work with your personality.....that circumstance.....this situation—no matter what it is. Sometimes it looks odd to us, but it's just the Lord adapting to the needs that He finds in us..... no matter what they are!!

Faith Profession: "I recognize the freedom of the Holy Spirit to flow as He sees fit, and to adapt to any circumstance. I will not try to force Him to conform to my ideas of what He should be doing."

Study Scriptures: John 9:1-7; Mark 7:31-37

DEVOTIONAL # 62

CREATION 1

Scripture: Genesis 1

"In the beginning God created...," the Bible says. So, God Himself is a Creationist rather than an Evolutionist. Please notice that, in verse 3, God begins to establish a pattern that He will use to create the heavens and the earth.....and which will be in play right up to today as you read this writing.

That pattern is this: For something to be created out of nothing, God needs to speak..... in faith. He does this in every day of creation.....He speaks, and things pop into existence. When He does this, something appears in the physical creation that was not there before.

It is immediate in Genesis chapter 1, but the pattern does not change. When God wants something done, or changed, He arranges for it to be SPOKEN.....and spoken in FAITH.....first. Then, it comes to pass.

This is the principle behind all prophecy. Every prophecy deals with a future event. The prophet speaks it, in faith, and it eventually appears in the physical realm.

In the New Testament, which is where you and I live, that principle has not changed. In our own case, it works this way: God has given us numerous promises in the Bible. Each one is a truth, backed up by God's own integrity. For the promise to become a physical reality, the pattern of Genesis 1 must be followed. That is, someone needs to SPEAK that promise.....in FAITH.....and it will appear in the physical realm where we can see it.

That's OUR job these days. WE are His voice, and, if WE won't speak His promises in faith, WHO WILL? This is our primary assignment in this earthly life because it is the only way to get miracles to occur in these last days. It is a pattern set up on the Bible's first page.....and it is still going strong!

Faith Profession: "I will do my part to be God's audible voice on this earth, speaking His promises.....in deep faith.....so that miracles can be accomplished in our world."

Study Scriptures: Mark 11:23-24 ; I John 5:14-15

CREATION 2

Scripture: Genesis 1

As God continues to speak physical things into existence, let's notice a few particulars:

In verses 3 and 4, God creates "light." But look at verses 14 through 19.....the sun and the moon aren't created until the fourth day! Whatever this "light" is in verse 3, it is not sunlight. No, it is supernatural light emanating from God Himself, and it is spiritual in nature (see the study Scriptures below).

On the second day, God creates a "firmament." He calls this firmament Heaven in verse 8. If you look up that word in a dictionary, you'll find that a "firmament" is a large, open expanse.....and that fits the description of Heaven that we know. However, notice verses 6 and 7. This firmament is said to divide "waters." In fact, there are waters above this firmament, and waters under it. Plainly, the firmament is Heaven, because it is called that in verse 8. So, now we know something new (to us).....there is water ABOVE the area we know as Heaven.

Now, look at II Corinthians 12:2. Paul speaks of a "third" heaven, telling us that there are three! The first is our earth's atmosphere. The second is what we know as "outer space." The third is the home of God. The water mentioned in verses 6 and 7 appears to sit right above the second heaven, which means we would have to travel through it to get to the place of God's throne. If you meditate on that, you might find new meaning to water baptism, especially in view of the Rapture of the saints in the last days.

Isn't the Bible a wonderful book!? What marvelous treasures it holds for us! And we're only on page 1!!

Faith Profession: "I believe that God's Word is God's Truth, exactly as it is written. I marvel at what I see, but I believe every word!"

Study Scriptures: John 1:1-5; John 9:5; Revelation 21:23

CREATION 3

Scripture: Genesis 1:9-19

On day three, dry land is created. In verse 11, we are introduced to the concept of "seed," which is going to be one of the central themes in the Bible. Notice that seed yields fruit "after his kind" in every single case. We will see this same thing in verses 21, 24, and 25. God establishes this principle right away, because of its importance in His overall plan. Simply put, oak trees produce oak trees; corn seeds produce corn; cows produce cows. Now, we know that this principle can be altered somewhat by man, but, left to itself, seed reproduces "after his kind."

Later on, in the New Testament, humans are going to be able to produce spiritual seed. This seed.....like any seed.....will produce after his kind. That is, good spiritual seed will produce good spiritual results. Bad spiritual seed will produce bad results. Good spiritual seed is nourished by FAITH, and that is essential to producing sound, valuable results in a life. (See Matthew 7:17-18.)

On the fourth day, the sun and moon are created, and their stated purpose is to divide the day from the night; to determine the seasons of the year; and to permit time to be counted. I like the statement in verse 16: "...and He made the stars also." It's almost as if He did that as an afterthought. Billions of stars, filling unknown numbers of galaxies..... mentioned in an offhand manner, as if it was nothing!

Lastly, we're told that light is to be divided from darkness. As it is intended in the physical, so it is in the spiritual. Light is to remain separate from darkness, and there is to be no merging or blending of the two—under any circumstances. Light stands alone. Light always dominates darkness, as you can see when you turn on a lamp in a dark room. Light needs no assistance, because it is perfect in itself.

Jesus is the Light.

Faith Profession: "I am a child of Light, and I am given pure spiritual seed from God's Word. I will not mix it with any form of darkness, so that it might reproduce after his kind."

Study Scriptures: Genesis 8:22; I Peter 1:23

CREATION 4

Scripture: Genesis 1:26-29

We have moved ahead to Day 6 and the creation of man. Notice with me, in verse 26, that God refers to Himself in the plural. Why? Because He is a trinity.....three unique persons, yet one entity. It is important to note that man is the only creation who is made in God's image (likeness). You know what an image is.....you look at one every time you gaze into a mirror. It is an exact replica, and that is how mankind is created.

In verse 28, we read the first thing God spoke to man: He blessed them (God refers to Adam in the plural because he really is two persons. Eve will be created from Adam's body). This blessing is also very important, because it is this that satan steals from man. In his hands, of course, it becomes a curse. But God's original purpose is to bless man. The Plan of Redemption is all about God restoring this blessing to man.

Lastly, man is given two vitally important things here: dominion (verse 26), and seed (verse 29). In Genesis 3, dominion is stolen, and the seed is corrupted through sin. What you ought to know (but few Christians do), is that, when you get saved, you become a new creature (creation) in Christ, which means, among other things, that this dominion and pure seed are RESTORED to you. Essentially, you are restored, spiritually, to exactly the same place that Adam enjoyed in Eden.

Romans 8 says that this is your inheritance.....but you don't live in the reality of it unless you receive it through faith.....EXACTLY as you received salvation. You are made in God's very image. You are important to Him. You are His partner in the spiritual work here on Earth. But He will not force this on you.....you must receive it for yourself.

Faith Profession: "I am made in the image of the Living God. When I was born again, this image....along with dominion and pure seed.....were restored to me. I am valuable and important to God Almighty!!"

Study Scriptures: II Corinthians 5:17; Romans 8:16-17

DEVOTIONAL # 66

A REWARDER

Scripture: Hebrews 11:6

This verse is one of those that I immediately think of when faith is mentioned. It begins with a basic premise in the Christian life: that God works with faith, and faith only. For God's presence and power to be mobilized, there MUST be faith. And, guess who provides that faith? Yes.....YOU provide it for you, and I provide it for me.

This verse gives all Christians two qualifiers that are also necessary for God to work in a life. First, one must believe that God is. That is, a person must believe that God is real, and present, and interested.

Secondly, a person must believe that God is a *rewarder*. Do you see that? Are you beginning to see why so many Christians live with few answered prayers, and little fruit in their lives? Listen, dear reader, most Christians pray in a way that reveals that they do NOT believe God is a rewarder. They pray the same prayer over and over, hoping to convince God to act. If you ask them about their prayer, they'll tell you that they have no idea whether or not it will be answered. They believe that sometimes God tells them NO. They believe that God sometimes sends disease; heartache; debt; pain; trouble; and discouragement to them.....to "teach them a spiritual lesson" of some sort (which they don't know, either).

Can you see that they are praying in DOUBT? Do you know that doubt is the opposite of faith?

No.....to receive answers from God, one must believe that He is a rewarder.....that He is seeking to bless, not curse.....that He would never send pain, nor would He be in partnership with the devil to allow him to send it. Ours is a God who IS LOVE. He cares for you, and seeks to bless you. He is a REWARDER!

Faith Profession: "I believe that God is, and that He is a rewarder. I reject the false notion that God sends or allows evil. I believe that satan does all evil, and God is the one who can take that evil and make some good come of it."

Study Scriptures: John 10:10; Jeremiah 29:11

CASTING OUT DEVILS

Scripture: Mark 9:17-29

Jesus, in this passage, is seen casting out a particularly difficult evil spirit which had been tormenting a young man for a long time. The disciples had tried to cast it out, but had failed. Jesus casts the spirit out, and then explains that some spirits are a little more difficult to deal with, and require some fasting and prayer to be done before they can be successfully cast out. It's a good lesson for us.....we should keep ourselves in a high state of spiritual readiness, and regular fasting and prayer would be a good start.

What I want you to notice about this section of Scripture, though, is that Jesus casts out devils on a regular basis, but He never makes a big deal out of it. I have people approaching me at times wanting to talk about something they call "deliverance ministries." They are referring to the casting out of foul spirits from folks, done through a fairly long process that includes delving into their past to dredge up the "root cause" of the presence of this devil, then going through a rather violent process of cleansing that involves loud yelling, throwing up, etc.

I've never been much of a fan of "delving into the past." If I read correctly, we're told to think about things that are "lovely; pure; honest; true; just; and of good report." Plus, I've noticed that whenever Jesus casts out a devil, He simply speaks to it, and it obeys. No long process; no delving into the past; no digging for the root; no puking.....just a simple command. Since you and I have been given this same authority over spirits of darkness (James 4:7; I Peter 5:9; Ephesians 4:27), it follows that, for us, the process would be the same. Just command them, in Jesus' Name, and they will depart.

Like all things truly Biblical, it is simple, but effective. Let's not complicate what the Lord took the time to make easy for us.

Faith Profession: "I have authority over spirits of darkness, given to me by Jesus in His Word. I speak to these spirits in His Name, and they obey."

Study Scriptures: Philippians 4:8-9; I John 4:17

HELL

Scripture: Mark 9:43-48

Hell. It's an offensive word to many, including some Christians. I preached for a time in a church that preferred the word "hades" to the word "hell," and they substituted "hades" when they repeated the Apostle's Creed. Did you know that "hades" is not even an English word? It is the Greek form of "hell" left untranslated.

I believe we need to ask ourselves why the word "hell," and preaching on "hell," is so offensive to us. Are we afraid of the word? Do we just hate to consider the implications of it? Are we so pampered that we can't even say the word? Did you know that Jesus used this word "hell"? Did you know that He didn't substitute another word for it? Did you know that He preached on hell more than any other subject while He was on earth?

It wasn't that He liked the subject. On the contrary, He knew all about it, and spoke of it so often because He desperately wants the humans that He loves to avoid it. It was not designed for humans, but for fallen angels and the devil. But, if a human fails to choose to receive His divine gift of redemption (salvation), that human is still in sin, and sin cannot be let into Heaven.

It is not that Jesus wants any person to be in hell, or that He sends people there. He has made the way to Heaven free and simple. When a human stubbornly refuses to accept the free gift of eternal life, he or she condemns THEMSELVES to hell. It is never His will that anyone be in hell…..yet people go there every day, and it is sadly unnecessary. If only they would choose to receive God's greatest free gift.

Today, take the time to look up the study Scripture below. In it, you'll find a complete description of hell, and it is factual, not a parable.

Faith Profession: "I intend to do whatever I can to get God's message of salvation out to lost souls so that they can escape hell. Thank you, Lord, for paying the price of redemption for me, and giving me eternal life with You."

Study Scripture: Luke 16:19-31

DEVOTIONAL # 69

HE WENT AWAY

Scripture: Mark 10:17-22

When we think of Jesus and His ministry on earth, we are tempted to believe that everything He accomplished was due to the fact that He was God. He was, of course, but He obviously was not operating in His divine powers while on earth. If He had been, then He could not have paid fully for our sins, nor completely related to us as indicated in Hebrews 4:15. No, He put aside His divine attributes, and functioned as a man, but using the power of the Holy Spirit within Him.....just as we are able to do. (That's why He could state John 14:12, and why I John 4:17 is true.)

Among other things, He witnessed to those with whom He came into contact.

Now, you would think that, with Jesus Himself delivering the message, everyone that He talked to would get saved.

However, in this passage of Scripture, we see Jesus failing at His attempt to witness to this unnamed man. Take a second to consider this: Jesus.....in the flesh.....is witnessing to this man. And the man rejects the message and walks away unsaved.

Why do I mention this? For the same reason that the Lord placed it in the Bible..... you need a little encouragement once in a while. As you witness, you will find that some people (too many) refuse to believe what you're saying. Some are rude about it, laughing and scoffing at what you say. It can be discouraging.

Just remember that even Jesus did not succeed every time He witnessed. Not everyone is ready to receive right now. Remember that, even if they haven't received.....you have planted a seed, and that seed will grow in their heart. You might be surprised in Heaven to see how many people did respond positively, later, based on something you said to them. Take heart.....don't be discouraged.....let Jesus be your example, and keep on trying.

Faith Profession: "I am a faithful witness for Jesus, but not everyone is ready to receive right now. Some pray for salvation.....some walk away carrying spiritual seed inside them. Both are victories, and I praise the Lord for that."

Study Scriptures: I Peter 1:23; Acts 1:8

DEVOTIONAL # 70
ALL THINGS ARE POSSIBLE

Scripture: Mark 10:27

I'd like you to read the text Scripture again — out loud if you can. Perhaps you might be willing to repeat it every day from now on. Reading it is good.....saying it is better, because Romans 10:17 says that "faith cometh by hearing, and hearing by the Word of God." So, when you say a Scripture out loud, you increase your faith (because you hear it), and you activate angels on your own behalf (see Psalm 103:20).

Consider this wonderful truth: with God, ALL THINGS ARE POSSIBLE.

Do you have unpaid bills? Have you lost your job, or have you been forced to accept a cut in pay? Is a loved one sick or injured? Are you sick or injured? Is it cancer, or heart disease, or diabetes, or some other seemingly insurmountable illness?

Has a friend betrayed you? Has your trusted spouse betrayed you? Are you alone and without hope? Has your heart been so badly broken that you think the shattered pieces can never be put back into place? Is some besetting sin getting the best of you all too often? Are you addicted to something in this world?

Okay.....these are legitimate problems, and they're big ones. You alone might not be able to find the solution. But, I have good news for you. Jesus has the answer, and He's more than willing to share it with you. Not only does He answer prayer, but He can (and has) solved EVERY problem that has come up, or ever will.

Your part? Just believe, and you will see. Believe FIRST, and you will see..... that is the catch (if you want to call it that). If you can do that.....and YOU CAN.....then you will see your problem solved by the God to whom ALL THINGS ARE POSSIBLE.

Faith Profession: "I believe in Jesus Christ. I believe the Word. I believe that all things are possible with God, and that He will answer my prayer of faith."

Study Scriptures: Mark 9:23; John 11:40, 43-44

Devotional # 71
Blind Bartimaeus

Scripture: Mark 10:46-52

Okay.....I guess this installment would more accurately be called "formerly" blind Bartimaeus, because, after meeting Jesus, he was never blind again.

The fame of Jesus had spread so widely that even beggars had heard of Him. Here is a blind man.....unable to work, and so reduced to a life of begging.....sitting along the road from Jericho to Jerusalem. Once he realized that Jesus was near, he began to cry out..... we'd say that he was yelling at the top of his voice! He was so loud that some in the group tried to get him to quiet down. His response? He yelled even louder!

Why? What is motivating him? It is the possibility of HEALING.....being free of this curse of blindness. He believed.....deep within his heart.....that Jesus could do this. And, he was willing to do ANYTHING to get Jesus' attention.

In verse 49, Jesus stops, and commands that this man be brought nearer. When he comes to Jesus, he is asked what Jesus can do for him. (What? Doesn't Jesus know he's blind? Didn't He see him stagger over to him? Yes. But Jesus knows the importance of WORDS. He asks because He wants Bartimaeus to SAY it, because speaking the word is part of the faith process.)

In verse 51, Bartimaeus speaks his request, and immediately can see!! Look at what Jesus says in verse 52: "...thy faith hath made thee whole." More specifically, Bartimaeus's faith released Jesus' power, and the combination caused healing. It has worked that same way ever since then, and will work that same way for you.

Jesus provides the supernatural power, but it is not released until WE act (speak out) in faith.

Faith Profession: "I understand how this works now. The power is always there, but it is not released into my situation until I provide the faith. This is how the faith process works, and it works every time."

Study Scriptures: I John 5:4; Romans 4:17; I Corinthians 1:28

REMOVING THE MOUNTAIN

Scripture: Mark 11:12-14, 20-23

The incident with the fig tree brings out one of the clearest and most important teachings of faith in the New Testament. In verse 14, Jesus speaks a curse onto a fig tree. The next day, as the disciples pass by this same tree with Jesus, they notice that it has already dried up, and they are amazed. Jesus says: "Have faith in God.," then gives a short but potent explanation in verse 23.

The "mountain" in verse 23 is not necessarily made up of dirt, rocks, and trees. It represents any large, seemingly insurmountable problem in your life.....disease; divorce; discouragement; poverty; fear; etc.

Notice in verse 23 that there are 3 references to "saying." Therefore, we conclude that the saying of a thing is a crucial part of the faith process. If we will speak to our problem in faith.....without doubt (which will blow up the whole process)..... and will STAY in faith regardless of what we see or hear.....we will receive our answer. That is, the "mountain" will be dissolved.

Is that all there is to it? Just saying "go away?" No.....our faith must be IN something. Our words alone will accomplish nothing. BUT.....if what we speak is SCRIPTURE..... specifically a promise that has been given to us in God's Word (which means it is already established, and we are just adding our faith to that promise), THEN we will have what we say.

Your words matter. They are critical to the faith process. If you won't speak a promise from the Word, then God cannot act on your behalf. Some of us have tried this process, and seen that it works.....every time. It requires patience, and the laying of a foundation of belief in the Word of God.....but it does work.

Faith Profession: "I purpose to begin to speak promises that I find in God's Word into my life. I will say them out loud, and expect this to release God's power into my problem (mountain), changing it for the better."

Study Scriptures: Hebrews 11:1,6

DEVOTIONAL # 73

WHEN TO BELIEVE

Scripture: Mark 11:24

Mark 11:24 is one of those verses that, too often, is read incorrectly. Most Christians read it as if there were no comma after the word "desire." That is, they just read through the verse, and take their preconceived notions through with them. If you remove the comma after "desire," you are left with the impression that you desire certain things, and they'll come to pass.....somewhere out there.....maybe.

However, there IS a comma after the word "desire." The verse says: "Whatsoever ye desire, when ye pray, believe that ye receive them..." More specifically, it tells you to believe that you have the answer to your prayer WHEN YOU PRAY.....NOT when you see the result.

Now THAT'S something most Christians have trouble with! It's too bad, too, because this is how faith is to be applied.....if it's applied properly. Faith is believing not only that God CAN.....or that He WILL.....but that He ALREADY HAS. When you connect a promise from God to your prayer, you start with the answer (oh, yes you do!). God's promises are already done.....already established.

So, when you put your faith in one of God's promises, you are just coming into agreement with what God has revealed to you in His Word. If He has promised something, then it's already completed.

So, now Mark 11:24 should make more sense to you. You pray, and believe that you have what you pray for WHEN YOU PRAY (based on God's promise). What's left is just to wait patiently as the answer works through from the spiritual realm to the physical..... which it will most definitely do!

Faith Profession: "I believe that I have the answer to my prayer when I pray, not when I see the result. This is true Bible faith in the promises of God."

Study Scriptures: Matthew 18:19; Romans 4:17

DEVOTIONAL # 74
SHE HATH DONE WHAT SHE COULD

Scripture: Mark 14:8

The incident in question in today's Scripture involves a woman (Mary—see John 12) pouring out a box of very costly ointment onto Jesus. She is doing this in thanks and tribute to Jesus for raising her brother back to life (see John 11, then the first part of John 12). Judas Iscariot raises a fuss about the ointment being wasted, since it could have been put to better use (his judgment, not that of Jesus), but Jesus commends her actions, saying, "She hath done what she could..."

We are a results-oriented culture.....we tend to focus on numbers; scores; size. I've noticed that Jesus was not particularly concerned about those kinds of things. He didn't have a large church; He didn't have a huge income; a jet; or fancy clothing.

And, I find no place in Scripture where He had that expectation of those who followed Him. Instead, His approach to our efforts is summed up in this phrase: "She hath done what she could"—which is said without condemnation.

Here is the lesson: Do what you can.....where you are.....with what you have. Then, be satisfied with that, because your Savior is satisfied with it. Just do your best, regardless of how much it is, or how big. If you'll do that, you might see God increase what you can do.....increase your vision, and your capacity.

But, whether He does that or not, you need to take the spiritual viewpoint of your efforts. Our concern should be for what Jesus thinks, not for what the world thinks or says. Jesus is not asking for an amount, but for faithfulness.....just faithfulness, and that is all.

Faith Profession: "I will do the best that I can do with what I have been given. I will be faithful, and that is all it takes to please my Lord."

Study Scriptures: I Corinthians 4:2; I Chronicles 4:10

DEVOTIONAL # 75

A RELIGIOUS SPIRIT

Scripture: Mark 14:3-6

If you read the companion passage to this one in John 12:1-8, you'll see that the person who complained about what he called "the waste" of this ointment was none other than Judas Iscariot, the eventual betrayer of Jesus. It also reveals in John 12 that his concern was not so much for the poor, but that the money be placed into the "bag" (because Judas was the keeper of the bag—the "treasurer" among the disciples—and he was stealing from it).

Notice verses 4 and 5. There is "indignation" shown "within themselves," so it is unspoken indignation. That is, some who witnessed this woman's act of worship, and selfless sacrifice, saw it as a bad thing. They piously thought that the ointment could have been sold for money, which could then have fed some poor folk.

It sounds so good, doesn't it? It sounds like they are concerned for the poor, which is a good thing in itself. People would be impressed by this kind of thinking, perhaps thinking that this was a very spiritual idea.

But.....do you know what this really is? It is a religious spirit. It is a critical spirit, generating negative thoughts about the use of the ointment. It second-guesses the action (after the fact, of course). It SOUNDS so holy and pious!!

Of course, we know from John 12 that the REAL reason behind this thinking is THEFT. A religious spirit always LOOKS good, but it is a deception for the real thought process hidden behind the piousness.

Jesus was not fooled. His words seem harsh until you realize that He recognized this religious spirit, and contradicted it. That's what always should be done.

Religious spirits..... they're present in every church. They look good at first glance, but their actual motives are ROTTEN. We get our cues from the Holy Spirit within us, not from the religious Pharisees who plague our churches.

Faith Profession: "I will look to the inner voice of God's Holy Spirit for my promptings. I will be wary of high-sounding pronouncements that tear down others in the name of spirituality."

Study Scriptures: John 12:1-8; Matthew 23

THESE SIGNS

Scripture: Mark 16:17-18

When I attended a traditional Bible school, they addressed this passage of Scripture by pointing out that the audience in this case was the eleven remaining disciples (verse 14); therefore, this information applied to them only. In the book of Acts, the disciples use these sign gifts; but, the school taught that they were only temporary and died out with the disciples. Interestingly, they give no Scripture to back up this idea that the sign gifts died out with the disciples. Do you know why? Because there isn't any.

In fact, these sign gifts did NOT die out. In fact, it plainly says in verse 17 that "These signs shall follow THEM THAT BELIEVE." Do you believe? Are you a believer? Okay.....then these sign gifts SHALL FOLLOW YOU. They don't, you say? I wonder why not? I wonder who it is who would want you to believe that these sign gifts are not for you? Who would benefit from that?

Did you know that these five sign gifts are the backbone of the Holy Spirit's ministry for New Testament Christians? They were used in the book of Acts because that is the pattern for YOU. They didn't die out. They were spoken against by the devil and his crowd until Christians began to believe the deceptive LIE that they are not for us today. I believe that the failure to recognize and use these five gifts is the biggest failure of the end times church.....and that the Holy Spirit is sorely grieved by that fact.

Look at the verse. It's God's Word. And it says that these signs shall follow them that believe. That's true, dear reader, and it's your job to conform to what the Scripture says, regardless of what you were taught in the past.

Faith Profession: "I believe the Word of God as the final authority in all matters. I therefore believe what is written in Mark 16:17-18, and I seek to apply these signs in my life."

Study Scriptures: I Corinthians 14:18, 22, 39-40

CERTAINTY

Scripture: Luke 1:1-4

In his introduction to his first book of the Bible (Luke also wrote Acts), Luke explains why things are recorded for us in the Scriptures. That explanation appears in verse 4, where we're told that they are written down so that we can know the CERTAINTY of those things.

Aren't you glad that Bible things are certain? We live in a world where so much is uncertain.....where the hallmark idea is "it depends," and nothing is ironclad. In such a world, everything is questioned, and the bottom line turns out to be whatever YOU think is truth.

So, every person decides for themselves, and what's true for you isn't necessarily true for me. This kind of thinking (or lack thereof) is done by folks who are supposedly educated, but appear to have lost touch with basic common sense (which is not so common these days).

It's nothing new.....people thought that way as far back as the days of Samson (see Judges 17:6). It led to disaster then, as it will in our day as well, because it removes God's blessing from the equation.

I'm thrilled that, in this life, there is something that I can count on.....absolutely. I'm so glad that the Lord loved us enough to give us certainty, and to have it written down where we can get to it every day. All of us have an inherent need for certainty. I know.....we're told that certainty limits our "freedom to choose." Hogwash. Certainty gives us stability, and a foundation that we can trust. That's important to our sanity in general. In the Bible we have CERTAINTY. Thank God.

Faith Profession: "I can count on the Bible to be absolute truth.....not just because I believe it, but because it IS truth on an infinite scale."

Study Scriptures: John 17:17; John 8:32,36

Devotional # 78

David's Seed

Scripture: Luke 3:23-38

Hold on, there.....don't skip over these verses because they're boring (you might have done the same thing in I Chronicles). "Yeah," you say, "but they're just lists of "begats." Who cares?"

Well, let's look more closely, shall we? This list begins with Jesus, then traces His ancestry back to God. You might know that there are unconditional promises given to David that guarantee that one of his descendants will reign as King in Israel forever. Therefore, to be the true Messiah, Jesus will have to have ancestry that goes back through David.

So, this list starts with Jesus, and traces back through Mary's family line. Since customs in Bible days emphasized the male part of a family, this genealogy is given through Mary's father, whose name is Heli (verse 23). Notice verse 31..... it says she's related to David through David's son, Nathan.

If you look in Matthew 1, you'll see another genealogy, this time of Joseph's family. In this case, it starts with Abraham (verse 2) and works up to Joseph through his father, Jacob. Notice, in Matthew 1:6, that Joseph is related to David through David's son, Solomon.

We know that Joseph was not the father of Jesus in the scientific sense, but I think it's comforting to know that both Mary (who bore Jesus) and her husband are direct descendants of David. This confirms prophecy and preserves the great covenant that God made with David (see study Scriptures).

I know it's tedious to read these "begats," but sometimes there are important nuggets in there. Aren't you glad that we serve a God who is this precise?

Faith Profession: "Every Word of God is true, and I can rely on the Bible totally, because our God is exact in what He does."

Study Scripture: II Samuel 7:12-16

FOUR GOSPELS

Scripture: Matthew 4:1

Have you ever wondered why there are four books that we call the "Gospels"? Why couldn't all the information have been written down in just one book.....it would have been simpler, right? Don't they all tell of the same events anyway?

Actually, no, they don't. While some events are recorded in two or more of the Gospel books, there is much unique information in each book.

One of the main purposes for four separate books is found right here in Matthew 4:1. Notice the wording: "Then was Jesus led up of the Spirit into the wilderness..." (This is the beginning of the account of Jesus' temptations at the hand of the devil.)

Now, look at the wording of the same event in Mark 1:12: "And immediately the Spirit driveth him into the wilderness." Do you see the difference? Why is the wording so different?

The answer comes from discovering the intent behind having four Gospel books. Each book is written by a different person, with a different personality. Each author writes from a slightly different perspective. For example, Matthew writes in a way that presents Christ as a King. His whole book is written with that in mind. Therefore, he writes that Jesus was LED into the wilderness (as you would do with a King). Mark, on the other hand, writes from the perspective of Jesus as a suffering servant, so his record of the same event says that Jesus was DRIVEN into the wilderness.

Luke presents Jesus as the Son of Man, and places emphasis on His humanity. John's writing presents Jesus as The Son of God, and therefore emphasizes His divine attributes. Each Gospel presents a different aspect of our Savior, who is too complex to be described in one book by one author.

Four Gospels give a more complete picture of Him. Read them all, and appreciate the Bible's attention to detail.

Faith Profession: "Lord, You have given an amazing Book to your children. Thank You for its detail, and its completeness. It is truly a book set apart from all others."

Study Scriptures: All four Gospels, as you have time. Read with today's lesson in mind.....you'll get a blessing.

THE SIZE OF BLESSING

Scripture: Luke 5:4-9

It happened a few times.....the disciples, most of whom were seasoned fishermen, were given instructions about fishing by a carpenter. As you might guess, they were skeptical about His advice, forgetting, it seems, that He was the Messiah.

So, here in Luke 5, Jesus tells Peter to let down his nets for a catch of fish. Peter, who has fished all night with no results (verse 5), is reluctant, but obeys.....well, sort of. Notice that Jesus said to let down nets (plural), and Peter lets down only one net (verse 5).

Peter's partial obedience gives away his true thoughts about the advice. But, he is shocked to discover that the carpenter was right, and the seasoned fisherman was wrong (himself) when they attempt to bring in the huge catch of fish. The net begins to break because of the enormity of the catch. In the end, they fill two ships with fish, almost to the point of sinking (verse 7).

Peter learns an important lesson that day, and it never left him afterwards. He is so overwhelmed by what has happened that he utters verse 8. It's a lesson we all need to learn, and it is this: Jesus thinks big. Peter, not sure, obeys, but not fully. As a result, he is shocked at the size of the blessing.

Listen, reader.....never sell Jesus short. Expect a miracle, and expect it to be big!! Jesus is in the miracle business, and He deals in QUANTITY! Got a big debt? Got a serious disease? Expect even bigger victories and blessings!! Ours is a generous God, and He loves to give to His children!

Faith Profession: "I expect big things from my Father. He is able, and He is more than willing to bless in abundance. I believe for big things from Jesus!"

Study Scriptures: Mark 9:23; Philippians 4:19

DEVOTIONAL # 81

JESUS PRAYED

Scripture: Luke 5:16; 6:12

It should be a humbling thought to those of us who know Jesus as our Lord and Savior that, while He was on the earth, He stopped to pray.....often.....sometimes all night.

What about that? Or, as the kids say, "What's up with that?" Why did Jesus pray if He was God, and was operating as God while on earth? Well, it's just another indication that He was not operating as God while on earth. He was operating as a human being, but acted in the power of the Holy Spirit that was given to Him at His water baptism (the same Holy Spirit that YOU have since the moment you were saved).

So, because He was operating in His humanity, He spent time in prayer. Notice that, in Luke 6:12, He prays all night because the next day, He would be choosing His disciples.....a very important event (see verses 13-15).

The lesson is obvious. It should move us to follow His example. Yet, most Christians can't really say that they pray a lot. Oh, they pray when they need to.....when some problem comes up.....when they have a sudden need. You don't find many Christians who pray every day, let alone all night.

I don't think I need to belabor the point. If He needed to pray often, then it's for sure that you and I need to. My guess is that both of us need to do more praying than we've been doing lately. I wonder. How much better would life be if we would just do that one, simple, free thing?

Faith Profession: "I need to pray more, and I purpose to do it. I will set aside some time EVERY DAY to spend in prayer with my precious Heavenly Father."

Study Scriptures: Luke 18:1; I Thessalonians 5:17

BEING EXPECTANT

Scripture: Luke 6:47-49

You've heard this story.....one guy builds his house on a foundation of rock; one guy builds on the ground, without a foundation; and when the storm comes (as it always does), one house stood, and one was ruined.

Okay.....obviously we know that we should build on a solid foundation. But there is a little more to this story, and it has to do with faith. Did you know that it is IMPOSSIBLE to please God without being in faith? Are you aware of the critical LACK of faith in the Body of Christ?

Read these verses again. Notice that the guy in verse 49 is passive.....he expects nothing. He hears, but pays no attention.....as if the Word of God was of no importance. He doesn't expect anything from the Word, and gets exactly what he expected.

The guy in verse 49, on the other hand, is EXPECTANT.....faithful.....he hears the Word, and believes that it can make a difference.....that it makes THE difference. This man believes that the Word of God has effect in our physical world.....that it causes miracles..... that it makes miracles LIKELY, if not CERTAIN.

When the storm comes, one man is safe, secure, confident, expectant.....knowing that he serves a God who rewards faith. The other guy experiences ruin, and will probably blame God for it.....or say that God "allowed" this tragedy for some unknown reason. He'll try to convince himself that he has faith, but, in reality, he's just living like the world: believing that everything that happens is unavoidable.....that he's subject to random chance..... then trying to rationalize the bad result.

No.....real faith is EXPECTANT of a miracle!

Faith Profession: "I believe what God's Word says. I believe that God is a rewarder of them that diligently seek Him. I am expectant!"

Study Scriptures: Hebrews 11:6; James 2:18-26

DEVOTIONAL # 83

AS HE IS, SO ARE WE

Scripture: I John 4:17

Today's verse will test your belief in God's Word. Many of God's children call themselves Bible Believers…..and they really think they are. In truth, they believe some of the Bible…..maybe even most of it. But, they jump off the train when confronted with verses like today's, among others.

I'm referring specifically to the last phrase of the verse. "As he is" is a reference to Jesus Christ. The phrase is in the present tense, so it means right now. As Jesus is right now…..."so are we." Many of the Christians I have known would begin to wobble at this point, but could stay on track by rationalizing that we will be just like Jesus in Heaven….. that this verse applies to later…..after death or the Rapture. I've noticed that lots of God's kids tend to apply things in the Word to their time in Heaven. That's because they don't expect much from this present life, where, they're convinced, they are assigned the task of bearing up under suffering and persecution until they are set free from this world.

That sounds nice, and is almost believable…..if you don't read the remainder of today's verse. It closes by saying, "in this world." We are just as He is…..in this world. That would be here and now. That would be IN THIS LIFE.

Yes…..that is exactly what it says, and exactly what it means. It also means that some of you have missed parts of the New Testament, because your life is nowhere like that of Jesus so far. He healed people…..He did miracles…..He cast out devils…..He spoke with authority. Reader…..YOU are to be like that. You CAN be like that, but you'll have to change your thinking and get on board with the ministry of the Holy Spirit…..including tongues (oh, no). It's the ministries of the Holy Spirit that make today's verse possible….. that make miracles possible, likely, and more common than you ever thought.

Think about it. You became one with Jesus at your new birth. You and He are one.

Faith Profession: "What a privilege I have in Jesus! As He is, so am I…..in this present world!"

Study Scriptures: John 14:12; John 17:1-11

DEVOTIONAL # 84

YOU HAVE PROSPERITY

Scripture: Psalm 1:1-3

The Book of Psalms…..most of which was written by David…..opens with a very positive message about how any person can be blessed. In a nutshell, it revolves around your heart attitude toward the Lord, called "delighting" in Him in today's reading. You "delight" in Him if you spend time in His Word…..spend time with Him in prayer…..think about Him…..and live your life with Him close to your consciousness.

I would like to focus, though, on verse 3, which tells about some of the advantages for you if you do "delight" in the Lord. Verse 3 is one of those Bible promises that are found here and there in the Word. Notice that it is stated as fact. It is already done as far as the Lord is concerned. If you are a child of God—and if you "delight" in Him in your life—then you can expect the promises made in verse 3 in your life.

These promises are all about prosperity. It promises that you will be like a tree planted near water. Such trees are blessed, because they have a plentiful supply of life-giving refreshment at all times. Because of this, that kind of tree….. you…..will bring forth fruit. That kind of tree…..you…..will have moist, green, fresh leaves, full of life. Best of all, you are promised that "whatsoever he/she doeth shall prosper."

Do you see that? Whatever you do SHALL PROSPER. It is a promise from God Almighty. It is written down in plain English for you. The only condition is that you "delight" in Him.

Well, do you? Is the Lord your best friend…..your daily companion? Do you hear from Him in your spirit? Does He guide you in life? Are you happy and content in His presence? Are you aware of the fact that He loves you more than anyone else could? Do you know that He's FOR you, not against you? Okay…..then you "delight" in Him…..and that means today's promise is YOURS.

Faith Profession: "I do delight myself in the Lord. Therefore, whatever I do will prosper…..WHATEVER I do!!"

Study Scripture: Philippians 4:13,19

A Bright Future

Scripture: Jeremiah 29:11

It was the lowest point of my life up to that point. My whole world, and especially my future, had been destroyed in one conversation. My (former) wife…..who was supposed to be my trusted friend, and the other half of me…..had confessed adultery, and was not entertaining any thought of preserving the marriage she had wrecked. It was a wreck….. very much as if I had been hit by a speeding freight train. I was dazed, confused, hurt, shocked, afraid, and disbelieving. The efforts of nearly 27 years had been blown to bits.

In the long nights and days that followed, I found some comfort in listening to praise and worship music. I knew the Lord had not done this to me, and I needed to keep His Word pouring into my broken heart.

One particular song never failed to bring a tear to my eye. It was based upon a Scripture I wasn't familiar with…..and it happens to be our reading for today. In it, the singer softly proclaimed the promise of "a future and a hope" for those who dared to believe.

I wanted to believe it. The thought of a restored future seemed too good to be true, especially for a man in his early 50's. But…..I looked up the verse in the Bible and found it to be a promise. In the King James version, it said, "to give you an expected end." That wasn't the wording in the song, so I looked at other versions, and found several different variations…..one of which plainly said that He would give me "a future and a hope." My life seemed hopeless, but this promise said otherwise.

I clung to it with every ounce of faith I had, and I have lived to see it come to pass.

Today's promise is for YOU, too. If you're reading this through tears…..please take hold of this promise from God. He can't lie. He loves you, and grieves for your situation. And He wants you to have a glorious future, filled with joy. Believe it.

Faith Profession: "Though it seems so unlikely just now, I choose to put my faith on this wonderful promise from my Lord. I believe there is a wonderful future in store for me, full of life and hope. It is promised to me by a loving God."

Study Scriptures: Psalm 3:3; Hebrews 6:18

DEVOTIONAL # 86
A PRAYER AND PROMISES

Scripture: Psalm 91

Yes, I know I gave you an entire chapter to read today. But, it is one of the most powerful chapters in the Word of God, and is well worth reading at least once a week.

This chapter is both a prayer and a promise. Well, actually, it is a bunch of promises. All are unconditional…..all are yours just because you're His child, and He loves you. You may claim one or more of the promises in Psalm 91 as your own any time you want.

As for the chapter, it is unique in that it contains words that are given from four different speakers. Verse 1 is spoken by the Holy Spirit. Verse 2 is spoken by the man or woman of faith…..it is a declaration of faith. Verses 3-13 are spoken by Jesus…..He is confirming your own faith statement from verse 2, and He does this as the High Priest of your profession (see first study Scripture). Lastly, verses 14-16 are spoken by God the Father. Knowing this, you can plainly see the divisions in the chapter…..the wording indicates a change of speaker.

This chapter provides promises for safety; prosperity; health; protection from both physical and spiritual harm; long life; delivery; honor; and authority over the forces of darkness. It is a wonderful profession to make over those in our armed forces; policemen; firemen; emergency responders; and anyone else directly in harm's way. We know of reports of this Psalm having delivered soldiers in combat in Iraq.

The last three verses are especially precious to me, because they are the Father confirming all that has been said previously. He is giving it His stamp of approval. That being the case, you can rely on it absolutely.

Faith Profession: Simply repeat the entire Psalm 91. If you do this out loud, you will benefit; angels will be activated; and it will make a difference in the spiritual world around you.

Study Scriptures: Hebrews 3:1; Romans 10:17; Psalm 103:20

Benefits of Tithing

Scripture: Malachi 3:10-11

"Oh…..here we go," you say. "We knew he'd get around to money sooner or later." I marvel at the attitude of many Christians about the principle of tithing. Most are very touchy about it, and get angry instantly at the mere mention of the subject.

So….read this carefully: WE DON'T CARE WHETHER YOU GIVE OR NOT. The Lord certainly doesn't need your piddly few dollars. Churches have their needs supplied through supernatural means…..if they're doing it right (that is, Christians who DO understand tithing WILL give). You keep your money if it's that important to you. Your attitude about it gives you away anyhow.

Tithing isn't some scheme invented by church people to take your cash. It's an OPPORTUNITY…..given to you by the Lord…..to sow financial seed.

The problem is that Americans are like a farmer who wants the harvest first. Give me the money FIRST, they'll say, and I'll give some back. Of course, it doesn't work that way on a farm, or in your garden…..and it won't work that way spiritually, either.

Your tithe is your financial seed. Seeds tend to produce in multiples of themselves. But how is the Lord going to multiply your seed if you don't give Him any? Or how can He produce the harvest you desire with that lonely dollar bill you pry out of your clenched hand each week? No, He promises that, if you willingly and cheerfully give a tithe, He will "open you the windows of Heaven, and pour out a blessing, that there shall not be room enough to receive it." Furthermore, He promises in verse 11 to "rebuke the devourer for your sakes."

He does both if you yield your tithe to Him. He does neither if you don't.

He promises prosperity; blessing; and protection…..given supernaturally…..to the person who will trust Him with their finances. It can be difficult to do, as money is a big issue for many folks. Dare to do it, and you'll be amazed at the results!

Faith Profession: "Since nothing that I have is really mine, it is no big deal for me to give 10% back to Jesus. I get to keep 90%, and get blessed, too!!"

Study Scriptures: Psalm 1:3; II Corinthians 9:6-8

DEVOTIONAL # 88

JESUS IS TEMPTED

Scripture: Luke 4:2-13

Early in His earthly ministry—perhaps right at the beginningJesus is tempted (tested) in a face-to-face confrontation with the devil. You probably are familiar with the basics of this event: Jesus is tempted three times; answers each test by quoting Scripture; and emerges victorious.

Nevertheless, let's look at this situation in some detail. Jesus is in the desert for the purpose of fasting.....which He does for forty days and nights. This would be the kind of preparation we would expect from Jesus for His earthly ministry. The denial of food is not really the point of fasting; but rather it is a time of complete focus on the task of prayer, not taking time out to eat. It is a spiritual exercise, and the needs of the body are given second place because the spiritual task is of that much more importance.

As soon as it ends, the devil is there to try to negate the positive effects of the focus on prayer. Since the Lord has been without food, the tempter begins with that; he reasons that this will be an area of weakness, which he will be able to exploit. So, he begins in verse 3. Notice that two of the temptations begin with the word "if": "IF thou be the Son of God..." This is the devil trying to anger the Lord by questioning His status.

I've noticed that Jesus ignores this childish tactic, giving it the attention it deserves. This first temptation—to change stones into bread—is answered by Jesus quoting Scripture..... in this case, Deuteronomy 8:3. Jesus is very hungry, as you might imagine, but refuses to give in to the desires of the flesh. With Jesus, it is always the spiritual first and foremost. Actually, it is somewhat infantile for the devil to believe that he would have any chance at success with this attempt. He fails, and immediately moves to something else.

Faith Profession: "My focus is on the spiritual FIRST. Unlike the world, my body does not take precedence in my life."

Study Scriptures: I Thessalonians 5:23; I Corinthians 6:19-20

Jesus is Tempted 2

Scripture: Luke 4:2-13

Having failed miserably in the first temptation, the devil moves on to the second try. You'll find the details in verses 5 to 8.

Here, the devil is being kind of "in your face" with Jesus. He shows Him all the kingdoms of the world; then offers to GIVE THEM TO JESUS if Jesus will fall down and worship him (the devil). What unmitigated gall! We know from the Word that these kingdoms are the Lord's.....that He will redeem them legally. But, in Luke 4, the devil is RIGHT..... they are his at that point.

The devil has desired worship from the beginning of his sin (see study Scriptures), and is trying to get Jesus to give him what he could not get back then, and will never have. (He wants to be God Almighty.) Jesus responds by quoting Scripture.....this time Deuteronomy 6:13.....and the devil is again stopped in his tracks.

The third temptation occurs in verses 9-12. Again, it is a complete failure, and is blown away by the quoting of Scripture. The idea of this temptation is to get Jesus to exalt Himself—His own powers and talents in the flesh. (It was a popular belief at this time that the Messiah would appear suddenly in the midst of a crowd.) To counter Jesus' annoying (to the devil) habit of quoting Scripture, the devil quotes some in verse 11. He quotes Psalm 91: 11-12. But, if you look up those Scriptures, you'll see that he misquotes.....he leaves part out. Typical of the devil.....he tries to use Scripture, but can't get that right, either.

Jesus defeats him by quoting Scripture properly. This time, Jesus quotes Deuteronomy 6:16.....and again, the temptation is stopped dead.

Faith Profession: "I defeat the devil by quoting Scripture, just as Jesus did. Since the Word of God is the final authority, the devil must obey it, and has no answer for it."

Study Scriptures: II Corinthians 4:4; Isaiah 14:12-15

JESUS IS TEMPTED 3

Scripture: Luke 4:2-13

I'd like to mention two more things about this wonderful passage of Scripture. Did you notice that these three temptations match satan's three methods found in I John 2:16? Temptation # 1 is the lust of the flesh. Temptation # 2 is the lust of the eyes. Temptation # 3 is the pride of life. Sadly, the devil has only these three methods, and uses them over and over. You'd think humans would catch on and be more effective in deflecting these attempts.

Lastly, I want to mention the depth of deceit in these temptations, because they go much deeper than the obvious. Each has a connection to the Second Coming of Christ. In Revelation 12:6-14, the Lord WILL make bread in the wilderness! In Revelation 11:15, Jesus WILL rule the kingdoms of the earth! In Revelation 19:11, Jesus WILL come down from the sky!

So, these temptations are not simply to get Jesus to make a mistake, or supply His flesh..... but they go to the heart of God's plan, and are an attempt to break Scripture! That is, Jesus is being tempted to do some things that ARE Scriptural.....but to do them in the WRONG TIME FRAME.....which would violate Scriptural principle, and give satan a way to accuse the Bible of being wrong.

The devil is sneaky, subtle, tricky. There are usually many levels to what he is doing. You can ALWAYS defeat him with your knowledge of Scripture, and your willingness to speak it at him, as Jesus did. You can "count it all joy" when you are tempted (as it says in James 1:2) because each temptation is another opportunity to defeat the devil, and solidify his true calling.....which is to be a FAILURE.

Faith Profession: "The devil is subtle and deceitful, but the Word of God defeats him EVERY TIME. Jesus is LORD!"

Study Scriptures: James 1:2; I John 2:16; Revelation 20:10

YOU HAVE POWER!

Scripture: Luke: 10:17-19

In Luke 10, Jesus has a following of disciples that numbers far more than the twelve who remained with Him to the Last Supper. In fact, large crowds followed Him for much of His earthly ministry. In this case, there are 70 who are sent out to minister to the people of Israel. (They had spent time with Him; heard His words; and were now applying them in a practical way.)

These 70 disciples return in verse 17, and they do so with JOY! They have had success, and are pleased! In fact, they comment that "...even the devils are subject unto us through thy name." Jesus is not surprised by this statement. In fact, He elaborates on it in verse 19, saying that He had given to them.....mere humans like you and me.....power over ALL THE POWER OF THE ENEMY, and that nothing would (or could) hurt them.

Notice: they exercised this power "through His name" (verse 17). Obviously, flesh and blood people like us have no power of our own over spiritual beings. But, of course, we are not on our own.....not after we have received Jesus Christ as our Lord and Savior!

I think I know what you've been taught.....that you're nothing but a lowly worm, not worthy.....only a sinner saved by grace. But, that's just the point! You are no longer "only a sinner." You are now a child of God.....a born again believer.....a disciple of Jesus Christ! And, He has given YOU the same authority over devils (and THE devil) that these seventy folks had!

Read the study Scriptures, and you'll see that it is true. Satan has no power over you, because Jesus has given you.....freely at your salvation.....HIS power, and HIS authority..... to use against the devil. And it WORKS!

Faith Profession: "I am God's child, bought with the sinless blood of Christ. I have the authority of Jesus Christ, given to me freely. I may use it any time I choose to get victory over the devil."

Study Scriptures: Ephesians 4:27; I Peter 5:9; James 4:7; Philippians 2:10

SYMPATHY VS. COMPASSION

Scripture: Luke 10:33

The context of this verse is the familiar story of the Good Samaritan.....a story told by Jesus to the religious leaders of Israel.....and which simply enraged those religious leaders. You see, the Pharisees and Sadducees (who bitterly opposed Jesus) were the religious leaders of Israel in Jesus' day. They believed Samaritans to be inferior people, and they wouldn't even socialize with them. So, Jesus used a man from Samaria (a Samaritan) as the hero in the story. (You could have lit a match on His listener's faces, they were so red with anger!)

However, today let's concentrate on just one part of this very potent story.....the word "compassion." It says in verse 33 that the Samaritan saw the wounded man, "and he had compassion on him." How do we know that it was compassion? Why is the Bible so certain? Because of the definition of the word.

Sympathy is evident when you FEEL for the situation.....it moves you to an emotional response, like sorrow. In the story, it appears that the priest and the Levite had sympathy for the wounded man. Compassion, on the other hand, is more than just sympathy.....it moves one to become INVOLVED.....to DO something. The Samaritan man showed compassion, because he took action.....which you can see for yourself in verses 34 and 35.

Friends.....as Christians in the last days, I believe it would be safe to say that we spend too much time in sympathy, and not enough time in compassion. Ask yourself.....when was the last time you called someone who was ill, or sent a card? When was the last time you took a meal to someone recently out of the hospital? When was the last time you took some action to get the truth of the Gospel to the lost people of the world? Do you pray for missionaries, or better yet, support any of them financially?

Action is the difference. If we are to be like Jesus, we will be people of compassion, not just people feeling sympathy.

Faith Profession: "I am a person of compassion. I am moved to become involved in helping others, especially those in ministry."

Study Scriptures: Matthew 9:36; Matthew 14:14; Matthew 20:34

ONE THING

Scripture: Luke 10:38-42

Here in Luke 10, we find Jesus taking a short break from the daily grind (just kidding), visiting with His good friends Mary and Martha—sisters to Lazarus, whom Jesus raised from the dead.

Martha, who is the worker of the family, is all about preparing the meal and setting the table. Mary uses the opportunity to sit at Jesus' feet and listen to Him speak the Word (verse 39).

Martha complains, prodding Jesus to make Mary help her. Instead, Jesus gives a valuable lesson in His response. In verses 41 and 42, He indicates that fussing over the things of this world is not of high importance. He says that "one thing is needful, and Mary hath chosen that good part."

What is He talking about? The "one thing" He recommends is a vital, productive spiritual life in close contact with Him. Mary was spending time with Him. Not only did He commend her, but He plainly says that this shall not be taken from her.

Mary CHOSE this.....Martha did not. So, it is a CHOICE. And, it is a choice that each of us is responsible to make.

These days, it is common to hear a Christian say, "Well, I'd have time to pray and read the Bible, too, if I didn't have a job, kids, a spouse, and responsibilities." Not to mention soccer practice, swimming meets, wrestling, basketball, football, baseball, dance class, Brownies, Boy Scouts; etc.

Hey, folks.....if you're too busy to pray, you're TOO BUSY! If you'd give it some thought, you'd conclude that you're too busy NOT to pray. In Scripture, Jesus prayed MORE as He got busier.....and so should we.

Lastly, He says that this would not be taken from Mary. NOBODY.....including the devil (especially the devil) can take that away! Only you can take it away from yourself. DON'T DO IT!.....FOR YOUR OWN GOOD!

Faith Profession: "I will MAKE time for prayer and Bible reading daily. It is something that Jesus values, and that will benefit me and my family."

Study Scriptures: Mark 1:35; Luke 5:16; Luke 18:1

THE FATHER'S HEART

Scripture: Luke 15

What!? You want me to read the whole chapter?? Yes.....it will do you good. Take it in small chunks if you have to.

Luke 15 opens with some information about Jesus hanging around with "publicans and sinners".....the common folk of the day....."regular" people; not rich.....not famous..... people with common, unglamorous jobs. In verse 2, the "bigwigs" murmur (meaning to find fault, but to do so in whispers because they lacked the guts to confront Him) about this.

Jesus does not comment directly to these religious bigots, but immediately gives three stories highlighting the value of lost people. Verse 4 begins the story of the lost sheep. Verse 8 begins the story of the lost coin. Verse 11 gives the account of the lost son. (You can read these for yourself).

What is He doing? He is sharing His Father's Heart.....which is about PEOPLE. People.....like you and me.....like the homeless guy downtown.....like the cashier at the grocery store.....like the fireman who drives by in the big truck. Just people.....ordinary, everyday, regular, unspectacular folks. THAT is what the Father's heart is all about. He loves people. He loves to spend time with us. He loves to give to us. He especially loves it when we show faith—in Him and His Word. He loves it when we come into His throne room to pray with Him. He notices when we open His Word.

He's been nuts about us since He spent every evening visiting with Adam and Eve in the garden. If God has a wallet, there's a picture of YOU in it. And, if He has a refrigerator, YOUR picture is hung on it with a magnet. Face it, folks.....He's WILD about YOU! Do you want to know what makes God's heart warm? It's you.

Faith Profession: "I love the thought that God's heart is focused on people. He cares about ME. And I'm going to spend time with Him every day!"

Study Scriptures: I John 4:8; John 3:16; (See also the song "Jesus Loves Me")

A NOTE TO PARENTS

Scripture: Luke 15:11-32

Let's look a little closer at one of the stories from yesterday. Try to focus on verses 25 to 30. These verses have to do with the Prodigal Son's brother.....the one who stayed at home and did not foolishly spend all of his inheritance.

As you read, you'll probably become disgusted with him. He whines; throws a hissy fit; refuses to celebrate with the family; and displays massive selfishness. You begin to wonder just what kind of parent these sons had. It looks like they had too permissive an upbringing. One is a fool; the other is a resentful brat.

The prodigal's brother shows no forgiveness. He can't let go of what has been done. He is spiritually immature. Like many folks, he can't rejoice when others are blessed.

But, today I want to make a point to parents. We tend to make judgment on the dad in this story because of what his kids are doing. However, did you know that children make their own choices? And that they are responsible for those choices? Did you know that they can make really bad choices despite proper parenting? Parents aren't the only influence in a child's life. In the end, it is the child who has to choose his or her own course of action. And, parents are not responsible for those choices.....they are only responsible to do the very best they can to raise the child properly.

Do you have a rebellious child? One who is on drugs? One who has been in jail? It's not your fault, and don't let the devil tell you that it is. If poor choices on the part of children were the only measure, then God Himself would be a bad parent, because of what His first kids pulled off in Genesis 3.

Faith Profession: "I will not let the enemy convince me that the choices made by my children are my fault. I will raise them right, and set a good example for them.....it is all that I can do."

Study Scriptures: Genesis 3; II Timothy 3:2

DEVOTIONAL # 96

NATHANIEL

Scripture: John 1:43-47

Here in the early parts of the Book of John, the twelve disciples are being gathered. Today's Scripture focuses on one of these, a man named Nathaniel.

Philip was the man who went to Nathaniel. Apparently they were friends, and, when Philip knew that he had found the Messiah, he seeks out his friend to tell him this wonderful news. Nathaniel's first reaction is interesting: he finds it hard to believe that anything good can come out of a dump like Nazareth (which was a city held in low regard in it's day). Deuteronomy 18:18 says that something good indeed came out of there!

In verse 47, Jesus looks up and sees Nathaniel for the first time, and says: "Behold an Israelite indeed, in whom is no guile!" Now, you won't appreciate the depth of the compliment paid to Nathaniel until you know the meaning of the word "guile." It means deceit, deception, sneakiness, trickery. A person without guile could be defined as "innocent, naïve, open."

That is, with Nathaniel, what you see is what you get. He hides nothing. He has no trouble believing, because his first tendency is to believe that everyone is telling the truth. Lying doesn't even occur to him. If he tells you something, it will be honest, open, and simple. In short, people like Nathaniel are some of the best people to know, because they're trustworthy. Now, the world will make fun of folks like this, chiding them for being so naive. Jesus, however, saw it as an advantage, and a thing of value.

I'm blessed to be married to a person like this, though her name is not Nathaniel. I can pull loving tricks on her, because she believes whatever she's told.....we laugh a lot over that. But, as the bottom line, she is absolutely trustworthy; consistently honest; and one of the kindest, most loving people I've ever met. My prayer is that YOU might find a Nathaniel as a spouse or friend.

Faith Profession: "I will strive to be a person who is without guile. Jesus marvels over such people, and considers them to be of great value."

Study Scriptures: Deuteronomy 18:18; Romans 12:17; Philippians 4:8

DEVOTIONAL # 97

THE WINE ISSUE

Scripture: John 2:1-11

Well, I guess every Christian, and non-Christian, knows that Jesus made water into wine at the wedding feast at Cana.....which is our subject today.

I recently heard a preacher use this passage of Scripture to give Christians an opening to drink alcoholic beverages. His explanation of this passage was that, since it just says "wine," and doesn't specify whether or not it was fermented, then we can't say that Jesus didn't make alcoholic wine in this incident. In the end, he gave tacit approval to the drinking of alcoholic beverages to his congregation!

He was right about one thing: it just says "wine," and doesn't elaborate on whether or not it was fermented. The word "wine" in your Bible can signify grape juice, or it can signify fermented, alcoholic wine. Why is that? Because you are expected to be able to compare Scripture with Scripture to figure this thing out.

Can we tell if the wine Jesus made was alcoholic? I think we can. Look with me at Habakkuk 2:15. Look also at Proverbs 23:29-35. These verses clearly speak against the giving of "strong drink" (alcoholic beverage) to ANYONE.

Jesus came to this earth to fulfill the Law. That is, to live under the Law of the Old Testament without sin, so that the Old Testament Law could be done away with. He did that.....which is why you and I can be saved and declared righteous.....we are given HIS righteousness when we receive Him as our Savior.

My friend, based upon those facts, Jesus COULD NOT have made fermented wine in John 2. If He did, then He violated the Law, and we are not saved. No, He made wine—as in grape juice—and He made it from pure water. It was His first miracle on earth, and is not to be used as an excuse to drink.

Faith Profession: "I have been declared righteous by the one Man who EARNED pure righteousness. Jesus was sinless, and never violated Old Testament Law. I will not twist Scripture in order to justify my fleshly desires."

Study Scriptures: Proverbs 20:1; Ephesians 5:18

Born Again

Scripture: John 3:1-13

Did you know that all Pharisees were not bad guys? Some of them actually listened to Jesus, and were drawn to Him by the Truth. One such Pharisee is Nicodemus.

I like this story. It is an actual event. Nicodemus comes to Jesus at night (verse 2) because he does not want to be seen (and kicked out of the "Pharisee Club"). He does, though, have some honest questions. He doesn't understand "born again;" he does not understand spiritual things. But he does recognize that what Jesus is teaching is powerful and changes lives.....and that his religious practices produce no such results.

Did you notice that Jesus doesn't even say "hello"? He just gets right to the heart of the matter.....you MUST be born again. Nicodemus does what most people do.....he tries to interpret spiritual things in his physical understanding. It will never work. Jesus shows that there is a difference between the physical and the spiritual (verses 5-8).

Jesus emphasizes BELIEF—not facts (verse 12). It is a spiritual, unseen, faith transaction, based entirely upon belief in what God says. Nicodemus was used to dealing with facts, information, scholarly things, where one's knowledge gave him superiority.

But salvation is not a "mind" thing.....it is a "belief" thing. And Jesus takes the time to try to explain it to Nicodemus because the man is asking genuine questions.....he REALLY wants to know!

In the end, Nicodemus takes a stand for Jesus, so we conclude that he DID believe, and was born again. (See study Scriptures). Are YOU born again? You can be, because Jesus died for everyone. Believe, and you will see.

Faith Profession: "I believe that Jesus is the Son of God; that He died for MY sins; that His resurrection proves that He is THE ONE; and I place my faith in His finished work on the Cross as the payment for my sins."

Study Scripture: John 19:38-42

DEVOTIONAL # 99

JESUS AS A SERPENT

Scripture: John 3:14

"As Moses lifted up a serpent…even so must the Son of man be lifted up." What!? Jesus is being compared to a serpent? I thought a serpent was symbolic of the devil in the Bible! What's going on here!?

Well, the reference is to an incident that is found in Numbers 21. There, fiery serpents were sent among the people because they were griping about everything God was doing. When they were bitten, they died! The solution was for Moses to make a serpent of brass, put it on a tall pole, and hold it up where the people could see it. When they looked on it, they were safe from the deadly snakebites.

So, how does that apply to Jesus? Well, we've been taught that Jesus "took all of our sins on Himself at Calvary." We sing a few songs to that effect. Did Jesus take all sin on Himself? Yes, of course.....but it isn't quite that simple. If you look with me at II Corinthians 5:21, you'll see that Jesus actually did something more profound than just taking your sins onto Himself.

It says there that "He (God the Father) hath made Him (Jesus) TO BE sin for us…" Do you see that? Jesus did more than simply take your sins on Himself. He actually BECAME SIN. That is why the Father had to turn His back on His Son at Calvary (see Matthew 27:46).

Did Jesus love you? Well, He BECAME SIN for you, so that the righteousness He gives back to you is complete, and it is not able to be questioned by the devil. No, John 3:14 has it right: Jesus is represented by a serpent because He would BECOME SIN on the Cross. (And, God knew about this as early as the Book of Numbers.) It is almost too horrible a thought to bear. But, then again, Jesus doesn't do anything half way. Nobody will ever love you that much again.

Faith Profession: "Jesus became sin for me, so that the righteousness He gives to me would be perfect, and above the questioning of the devil. Jesus loves me, and I intend to love Him back."

Study Scriptures: II Corinthians 5:17-21; Matthew 27

T<small>WO</small> K<small>INDS OF</small> P<small>EOPLE</small>

Scripture: John 3:18

Verse 18 is connected in context to verses 16 and 17. Most of us are familiar with verse 16.....we used to see it at every NFL game. In verse 17, the Lord explains that Jesus was not sent to condemn anyone, but to set them free through salvation. Then in verse 18, He explains who is not condemned, and who IS condemned.

It is actually very simple, as most things are with God. It was not, nor ever has been, God's intention that anyone be condemned. Notice that, in verse 16, salvation is open to WHOSOEVER believeth.....which includes everybody. He also mentions in verse 17 that Jesus was sent to SAVE people, not to condemn them.

What, then, places folks in condemnation? Well, they do it themselves. (Sorry, but that's the truth). They have the option to choose the salvation offered by Jesus to all ("whoso-ever"). If they choose NOT to believe, then condemnation is the only alternative. Is that God's fault? Did God make them choose poorly? Did God hinder them from making a good choice? "No" to all of these.

People find themselves in condemnation because they refuse to believe God when He tells them that Jesus saves them from an eternity in Hell. And, God, who is always a gentleman, will not force them to make the right choice. God does all the work.....then He offers that finished work for free to anyone who will believe. There is no cost for this; it is free.....and it is so simple that a child can understand it. But the one thing He WON'T do is make the choice FOR you.

So, when God looks down onto our world, He sees only two kinds of people: believers, and non-believers. Believers are not condemned, and are part of the family of God. Non-believers have brought condemnation onto themselves by their refusal to believe God. It is that simple, and that profound.

Faith Profession: "I believe that the Bible is God's Holy Word. I believe in Jesus Christ and His finished work on Calvary's Cross. As a believer, I am not condemned, and will spend eternity in Paradise."

Study Scriptures: I John 5:11-13

DEVOTIONAL # 101
FRIEND OF THE BRIDEGROOM

Scripture: John 3:25-36

Ahhh.....John the Baptist. You couldn't ask for a better friend than this man. He was, in fact, Jesus' cousin, and was sent by God to be the "herald"—or the announcer—of the arrival of the Messiah. John understood his calling. He was the one who was to announce Jesus. John never called attention to himself; he never glorified in his own accomplishments.

You know, it's hard to "play second fiddle," as they say. Most people want to be the star..... have their name mentioned.....enjoy the spotlight. John, though, knew that Jesus was the One, and never failed to deflect the glory toward Him. Here in John 3 is another example of it. He says, "I am not the Christ, but that I am sent before him" (verse 28). John then calls Jesus the Bridegroom.....apparently knowing that He would have a bride, which we know is the church (all believers in Jesus throughout the ages).

John says, in verse 29, that he is the friend of the bridegroom.....and he indicates that his own joy is fulfilled in this role. Unlike Lucifer, John does not seek the limelight, and resists any temptation to be rebellious. He does not seek Jesus' rightful place in God's plan. He is faithful; loyal; and "has Jesus' back" at all times.

Friends like this are hard to find, and Jesus values John's trustworthiness very highly. Our goal.....to BE a friend like John. Such a thing greatly pleases God.

Faith Profession: "I purpose to be content with my God-given role in His plan. I reject rebellion; I do not seek the spotlight; my goal is to deflect all glory toward Jesus."

Study Scriptures: Matthew 3:1-17; Luke 7:26-28

DEVOTIONAL # 102
THE WOMAN AT THE WELL

Scripture: John 4:1-30

The people of Samaria were shunned by most Jews. Samaritans were so despised that, when a Jew traveled north.....even though the most direct route was through Samaria..... he would travel extra miles to avoid going through Samaria.

Jesus, of course, defies that tradition, and goes straight through. On the way, He stops at a well and has a conversation with a woman whose name is not given. It starts as a request for water, but moves into a discussion of spiritual things. In other words, Jesus is witnessing to this woman, and she is intrigued by Him, starting with the fact that He was there at all (being a Jew).

This discussion has been recorded by the Holy Spirit, and has touched many lives besides this unknown Samaritan woman's. In the end, she becomes a believer (verse 29), and a witness to others, bringing them to Christ (verse 30).

Has it occurred to you that Jesus uses Samaritans as the subject of good, positive stories on several occasions? Did you know that it infuriated the Pharisees, and the other religious leaders in Israel? Jesus was revealing their lack of love.....their lack of true, heartfelt compassion.....and some of them never got the hint.

I'd like to find this woman in Heaven. She's one of many important people in the Gospels whose name is unknown. That's okay, too, because it is Jesus and His redemption that should be the focal point.....not people. Still, I'd like to hear her version of this event, and see the light in her eyes and the smile on her face as she tells it.

In effect, she is us.....just an ordinary person who chose to believe, and whose life was changed forever because of it.

Faith Profession: "The Holy Spirit always glorifies Jesus, so that is my calling as well. He is the focal point.....He is the Giver of Life, and I have the privilege of being a small part of His process."

Study Scripture: I Peter 5:5-6

Devotional # 103

In Spirit

Scripture: John 4:24

I've noticed that, in the New Testament, our Lord seldom insists on anything. So, when He does, I'm thinking we should take careful notice. One such case is found here in John 4:24. It says that our worship of Him MUST be in spirit, and in truth. Both elements are essential.....and it is surprising how often neither are present when Christians worship and study.

We live in this world, where almost everything relates to our senses. We experience this world through sight, sound, taste, touch, and smell. Unfortunately, we tend to interpret the Bible that same way, and it is a serious mistake.

In my thirty-seven years of study and experience, I've noticed that most Bible teaching, and most church activity, is based on the physical senses, or interpretations related to the physical. We think "spirituality" consists of coming to church regularly; serving in the church; getting our name mentioned in the Sunday Bulletin.....that is, it's about what we DO.

But here in John 4:24, the Lord points us in a completely different direction. He says that it is SPIRITUAL, not physical. You don't learn the Word, or about Him, by accumulating facts, but by receiving the Word into your spirit as the truth that it is. God wants you to remember that He is a Spirit.....you'll never relate to Him through your senses. It is a spiritual connection.....internal.....invisible.....based entirely on faith.

So, real contact with God MUST be done first of all in the spiritual realm, and secondly MUST be based on Truth.....which is, we know, the Word of God. There is no real contact with Him unless it is spiritual, and connected to His Word. He sees it as a MUST!

Faith Profession: "I will strive to change my approach to my Lord. I will receive the truth of His Word into my spirit, and it will place me into intimate contact with Him. It is the only way that it can be done."

Study Scriptures: Hebrews 11:6; I Corinthians 2:12-16

THE JUDGE

Scripture: John 5:22

What a peculiar picture we have in our heads about the final judgment day. Most Christians expect to see a huge throne with God seated upon it, and a zillion little people gathered in front of it.

Most expect God's judgment to be strict.....maybe even harsh. Many live in fear of it. Of course, that's because most people have an Old Testament idea of who God is.....and they don't seem to be able to come to the realization that they live in the NEW Testament. We are under the NEW COVENANT.....which is characterized by grace and mercy, not harshness.

The sad case of the incredible misunderstanding of God's character aside, the picture of the final judgment is incorrect, too. Do you see what it says in John 5:22? God the Father will not be the Judge.....Jesus will be. You remember Jesus, right? He is compassionate; a healer; tender; patient; merciful; loving. HE will be our judge when life is over, and I'm relieved to hear it!

Now, don't misunderstand.....Jesus will not be giving out free passes.....He will administer justice, and will do it fairly. Still, I know what He's been doing since the resurrection. I John 2:1 says He's been my Advocate. I Timothy 2:5 says He's been the Mediator on my behalf when the devil has accused me. And, I know that He loves me enough to have died on the Cross for me.

We will face judgment, and I, for one, am sorry to say that I have let the Lord down all too many times. But I find comfort in the thought that the Man judging me is the One who loves me more than anyone else. He died for me.

Faith Profession: "I will not live in fear of final judgment. I strive to live for my Lord, and I am not always successful. I trust Jesus to judge me fairly, and in ultimate love."

Study Scripture: Revelation 20:11-15

Who's Going To Heaven?

Scripture: John 5:24

Here is the Gospel message in a nutshell.....all tidied up in one verse. That can be done because Jesus is into simplicity. He doesn't design His truths for college graduates, but for simple, childlike people who will accept His Word as The Truth.

There are only two elements to it. First, one must hear the Word. Second, one must believe it.

You can hear the Word in any number of ways. Most churches have a time for a sermon. You can listen to recordings of the Word. You might hear it in a song. Or, it might be part of a conversation you're in. God designed His Truth to be passed from person to person.....we have some advantage today because of the technology we enjoy. Once you hear the Word, it is up to you to choose to believe it. If you DO believe the message of Jesus' death on the Cross, you have eternal life.....right there.....on the spot.....instantaneously. (Notice that, in verse 24, the verb is present tense).

Based upon your choice to believe God's Word about your eternity, it emphatically says that.....from that point on.....you "shall not come into condemnation..." This is your assurance of eternal life. You'll need that, because the devil will try to convince you that your salvation isn't a reality. And, he has a good many well-meaning, but confused, Christians helping him create this doubt for you.

Lastly, it repeats your assurance..... "but is passed from death unto life." That combination of words "is passed" is a special verb tense in the original language. It simply means that your choice to believe has effect now, and forever more, and can never be changed. It is simple, yet profound, and has eternal consequences.

Faith Profession: "I believe that Jesus is the Son of God; that He died for me; that He paid the penalty for my sins; and that He rose from the dead. I have eternal life based on God's Word and my choice to believe that Word....and it is forever."

Study Scriptures: Romans 10:9-10,13; John 3:36

DEVOTIONAL # 106

EYES OF FAITH

Scripture: John 6:1-14

Have you noticed how often Jesus is looking at the same scene as His disciples, but seeing something completely different? Perhaps that's what is meant by looking at things with "spiritual" eyes.

A large crowd was gathered around Jesus and the disciples, and it was apparently time for lunch. The disciples are thinking, "Let's get away from here so we can eat in peace." Jesus looks at the crowd and asks where they could buy enough bread to feed everybody. The disciples scoff, seeing it as impossible (verses 7-9). But Jesus calmly has the crowd sit down in an orderly fashion, and proceeds to feed everybody with five small loaves and two small fish. It turns out to be one of His most famous acts.

The disciples see impossibility. Jesus knows that all things are possible with God. The disciples are thinking of themselves. Jesus is focused on each person in the crowd. The disciples, looking at the physical, are sure five loaves and two fish are nowhere near enough. Jesus feeds 5,000 men, plus whatever women and children were in this crowd, and there are twelve baskets of leftovers gathered afterward (one for each disciple).

Jesus just sees something different when He looks at people and situations. He sees each thing spiritually.....with the supernatural in mind.....not limited by scientific laws or human reasoning. When we get to know Him, WE begin to see situations the way He does. Not in the physical realm, where there are limitations.....but through faith in the supernatural power of a Holy God. It makes the impossible a daily reality.

Faith Profession: "I plan to spend time with my Lord and His Word.....enough that I will get to know Him intimately. Then I will see the world through the eyes of faith, and with limitless possibility."

Study Scriptures: Mark 9:23; Mark 11:23; I John 5:4

KNOWING GOD'S WILL

Scripture: John 6:38

Here in John 6, as Jesus is giving a dissertation about Himself being the Bread of Life, He mentions, in passing, something that I have found to be immensely important.

The average Christian lives in the dark with regard to knowing God's will. Most Christians think that God's will is a mysterious secret, and that only a select few get to know that will…..even then, only occasionally. I used to think that way, too…..because most of the people I knew thought that way.

However, there's nothing like some study in the Word to open one's eyes. It turns out that God's will is not a secret…..it is openly revealed all over the Bible. Here's what I mean….. check these Scriptures, and you'll see that they tell you God's will: Romans 12:1-2; I Timothy 2:4; II Peter 3:9; I Thessalonians 5:18; I Thessalonians 4:3.

Here in John 6:38, you're told that all Jesus did on earth was the Father's will. So, what is the Father's will? All that Jesus did on earth! Lastly, the Father's will is revealed in every promise given in the Bible. If the Lord promises something, then it is a done deal…..He has already decided that it is so. Therefore, every promise is God's will revealed to you.

It is no secret. Why would God hide His will from His children? Answer: He didn't. It's evident all over the place. Once you realize that it's there, you wonder how you missed it in the first place.

We can know His will. A loving Father would see to it that His kids would know….. and He did.

Faith Profession: "My Lord has revealed His will to me in everything that Jesus did on earth; in several Scriptures; and in every promise that He gave. I can know God's will….. it is not hidden."

Study Scriptures: II Corinthians 4:3-4; I John 5:13

NICE FAMILY!

Scripture: John 7:1-5

Have you ever considered the pain and difficulty Jesus endured while on earth? I'm not talking about the Cross right now.....I mean in everyday life, as He tried to minister the Truth to people, including His own family.

Here in John 7, Jesus has retreated into Galilee (north of Judea—Jerusalem was in Judea) where His earthly family lived. He left Judea because the Jews there sought to kill Him (verse 1). Did His family know that? You have to believe that they did.

Yet, in verses 2 through 4, they are trying to get Him to return to Judea! His own family! Attempting to get Him to go back into the area where people were seeking to kill Him!

Verse 5 tells you why.....His family did not yet believe on Him. Not yet. Don't you think that, at this point, they were a little put out with him? He was stirring up trouble everywhere He went.....and there was, no doubt, some backlash onto His family from the community. They weren't believers at this time, so they were doing what unbelievers do..... trying to rid themselves of their problem, even if it meant putting Him in harm's way. Nice family!

Have you ever had a similar experience? I've been preaching the Gospel for almost 37 years. I have brothers and sisters who have become strangers to me because they're offended at what I believe. My own mother effectively disowned me for the same reason. Listen, folks, putting yourself on the line for your Savior is going to cost you something.....the devil will see to it.

I wouldn't change one day of my service to Jesus Christ. Maybe my family will end up believing the Truth.....Jesus' family did. And they did so after He returned to Judea..... where they did put Him to death.

Faith Profession: "Jesus paid the ultimate price for me. My service to Him, done out of gratitude to Him, will not be understood by everyone. But I will remain faithful to Him to the end."

Study Scriptures: Matthew 10:34-39

DEVOTIONAL # 109
A THIRST TO KNOW HIM

Scripture: John 7:14-37

Controversy swirled around Jesus every day of His earthly life. By John 7, Jesus had become well known. His miracles had become common knowledge.....the depth of His teaching undeniable.

Many people—the common folk, mostly—believed on Him. The religious leaders..... who were jealous of Him, who feared Him, who could not match His wisdom, who were afraid of losing their elevated position in the community..... hated Him and plotted to put Him to death.

That controversy is apparent in today's reading. To some extent, it rages in our society today. The point is.....then or now.....anyone COULD know Jesus if they wanted to. In-formation about Him is all over the New Testament. Believers will tell you of Him if you give them a chance. Changed lives pretty well speak for themselves.

Yet many still do not know Him. Many are angered by Him, just as they were when He was on earth. Tragically, many believers don't know Him. What's lacking? He reveals it in verse 37.....to really know Him, there must be a thirst to do so. A THIRST.....like when you are hot, dry, parched, and desperate for a drink of water. A thirst that COMPELS you to study. A thirst that isn't satisfied until it KNOWS for sure.

If you have a thirst to know Him, He WILL see that it is satisfied. But, it has to be more than curiosity.....more than an angry demand that He reveal Himself.....more than an oc-casional look at the Bible. A THIRST. A compulsion. A passionate search. .....which WILL BE SATISFIED. Pray for this!

Faith Profession: "Lord, I want to know You. I NEED to know You in an intimate way.....as a true friend.....deeply.....and completely. I thirst to know You."

Study Scriptures: II Timothy 2:15; Ephesians 3:16-19

Devotional # 110
The Spirit Flows

Scripture: John 7:38-39

In these two verses, Jesus speaks of the receipt of the Holy Spirit that would occur after He was glorified. As such, it is a prophecy, and shows us that Jesus was aware of future events before they happened.

He mentions that the Spirit would flow out of one's "belly." We tend to think of a belly as that hunk of flesh positioned right above our belt; but the meaning of the word translated "belly" here can also be "heart" or "inner being." He's saying that the Holy Spirit will be sent to believers, and He will flow forth out of the depths of their innermost contact with God.

Notice that the Holy Spirit is compared to a river. Although the Holy Spirit is a person.....a member of the Godhead, and is given human-like characteristics all over the Scriptures..... He is always compared to something liquid. Here it is a river. Elsewhere in the Bible, it is a stream, a well, a fountain. Why? Because that best describes how the Holy Spirit works. He is unique because He is adaptable. He can adjust to any situation, any personality. He is not held to "lines and boxes".....meaning rules and fixed methods of operation.

Many Christians are thrown off by this. They speak and teach against the ministry of the Holy Spirit in today's world because they can't find any consistency to what He does. GOOD! AMEN! Why should He be held to consistent methods?

No, He has the freedom to adapt to you and me. He operates with me in the best way for me.....and for you in the way best suited for you. He is "liquid," and is infinitely adaptable.

Think about it.....it is, by far, the best way for Him to be!

Faith Profession: "I will not try to hold the Holy Spirit down to a set of rules that I think is best. I glory in His adaptability, because it maximizes His effectiveness!"

Study Scriptures: Rev. 7:17; John 4:14

THE BIGGER THE BELFRY, THE MORE ROOM FOR BATS

Scripture: John 7:45-52

"Belfry" is the old word used to designate a tower—specifically, the bell tower, or steeple, of a church. The meaning of the title today is that higher scholarship.....more education.....does not necessarily translate into more wisdom.

Here in John 7, the religious leaders have sent soldiers to arrest Jesus. They come back empty-handed, and an argument begins about His status as a prophet. The leaders reason that, since none of THEM believe on Jesus, why should anyone? (No arrogance there, of course.) When Nicodemus speaks up and asks them to be reasonable, they answer with verse 52.

So, here are the religious leaders, in what may have been the most religious nation on earth, rejecting Jesus as a prophet because He was from Galilee. Nazareth is in the area of Israel then known as Galilee, and no prophet in the Bible is from that area.

That's interesting to me because, if you look carefully, you'll see that the religious leaders were wrong about that. Look at II Kings 14:25. Notice that Jonah was from a place called Gath-hepher. If you look on a good Old Testament map of Israel, you'll see that Gath-hepher is in Galilee. So, it looks like the Scribes and Pharisees were in such a hurry to condemn Jesus that they missed an important fact or two.....and they were supposed to be the experts!

What do we learn from this? Be careful about taking everything that's preached or taught about the Bible as fact without checking on it yourself. Just because the preacher or teacher has a degree in theology doesn't make him or her infallible. Here were doctors of the Old Testament Law being incorrect about an important fact because they were blinded by their own prejudice against Jesus. Listen.....you have the Holy Spirit, and He has promised to guide you into all truth. Trust HIM, not some human being. Check things for yourself.....use the Bible as your final authority. Mere men can be wrong.....and often are.

Faith Profession: "I will check out what I am taught by verifying it in God's Word. The Word is my final authority because men can be led into error."

Study Scriptures: John 16:13; II Timothy 2:15

Devotional # 112
The Truth Shall Make You Free

Scripture: John 8:32

The truth. Some people don't believe that there IS any such thing. They believe that everything's relative.....that it all "depends on you and your circumstances."

Jesus speaks of truth as an absolute thing.....something that you can know and use in your daily life.

Here in John 8, He tells you that this truth SHALL MAKE YOU FREE. Free from what? Well, free from doubt.....from fear.....from relativity.....from chaos.....from disillusionment. There's something comforting about knowing that you have the truth, and that you can count on it. Those who believe otherwise must live tormented lives.....because they can't be sure of anything.

Verse 32 says that you shall know the truth.....so it must be possible to know it. And, it follows that truth must be available somewhere. Notice also that Jesus speaks of THE truth.....so He apparently believes that there is only one truth, and that all other opinions are just that.....opinions.

The truth that Jesus speaks of, that is basic to life, and that can be found, is the Bible. The Bible is otherwise known as God's Word. Why? Because all of it was given by God to men, so that they could record it, and make it available to others. You have it available to you today, and so do I.

Study of the Bible—with a believing heart—is one of life's most important opportunities. It gives you a solid anchor in life. It proves itself to be true, time and again. And, it permits you to live life free of burdens, doubt, confusion, and lack of understanding. In short, it gives you peace of mind.....and heart. You can relax about life, and enjoy it without all that shadow of doubt in the background.

The truth shall make you free.....supernaturally, but definitely. Nothing else can accomplish that.

Faith Profession: "I want to live in spiritual freedom, having truth in my life that I can count on absolutely. I find that in one place.....God's Word."

Study Scriptures: John 8:36; John 1:14-17

Devotional # 113
Nasty Accusations

Scripture: John 8:33-41

To really get the full effect of today's Scripture reading, you would benefit by reading the chapter from verse 1. Notice that the nastiness begins as early as verse 13. Who is angry? The religious leaders in Israel—the Scribes and Pharisees (supposedly the most pious and holy people in the land). Why are they mad? Because Jesus is exposing their sin, and their hypocrisy. (They looked good on the outside to the average person, but were rotten on the inside.)

By verse 33, the discussion has heated up. They state that they are related to Abraham (verse 33), and that this makes them free. Jesus counters with verse 34, telling them that they are servants to sin.....and proves it by exposing their desire to kill Him (verse 37). When they assert that Abraham is their father, Jesus points out that Abraham would never have wanted to kill someone who was telling him the truth.

They counter with what is known in boxing as a "low blow" (see verse 41). You see, Jesus was born to a virgin.....a woman who was engaged to Joseph, but not yet married to him. Believers knew that the birth was supernatural, but unbelievers, like these Pharisees, drew the worldly conclusion.....that Mary had conceived through a relationship with another man.

It is a nasty thing to say.....both to Jesus, and ABOUT His earthly Mom. And, this ugliness is coming from men who professed holiness!! (See Matthew 12:34.) Actually, they should have been embarrassed to even THINK such a thing! The statement betrays their deep hatred for Jesus (who is God manifest in the flesh)! It is no surprise that they finally succeeded in putting Him to death.

All was not niceness and love for Jesus on earth. He endured criticism, hatred, banishment, and death threats, even as He healed the sick and gave only love.

Faith Profession: "I will watch what comes out of my mouth, and be careful to speak well of others.....just as Jesus would.....and does."

Study Scripture: Matthew 23

Devotional # 114
They Couldn't Kill Him

Scripture: John 8:59

The heated argument between Jesus and the Pharisees continues all the way through John 8. As we near the end of the chapter, Jesus reveals Himself as the great "I AM" of Scripture, which takes the Pharisees "over the edge," so to speak. They take up stones in verse 59, intending to stone Him to death for what they believe is blasphemy.

In fact, Jesus IS the great "I AM" of Scripture. He is the promised Messiah.....the One the Jewish leaders had been waiting for. The problem was that He didn't show up in the form, and with the grandeur, that they had expected. Neither did they expect that He would be in opposition to them. That in itself was gross pride and arrogance, but when He opposed them publically, it moved them to consider murder.

Have you noticed that, in the several instances where the religious crowd makes a move to kill Jesus, He simply walks away unharmed? Here in verse 59, He walks right through the midst of them.....men who had already picked up stones to throw at Him.....yet they never throw even one rock. Why is that?

Two reasons stand out to me. First, Jesus is fulfilling prophecy, which states that he will die on a cross. Bible prophecy always comes to pass 100%, so that accounts for part of it. The second reason why He escapes is that they simply cannot hurt Him. Jesus is operating under the Covenant, as described in Deuteronomy 28, and is totally obedient to it. That Covenant promises that He would be safe from any harm.....and He is! I'm guessing that, if they had thrown stones, all of them would have missed. Jesus was under the divine protection of a Blood Covenant with God.....and NOTHING can supersede that.

So, you say, they DID eventually crucify Him. Yes.....but they didn't kill Him. He voluntarily gave up His life at Calvary. Even when He DID die, it had nothing to do with mere men doing it. Jesus GAVE His life.....for YOU and for me. They COULD NOT kill Him.

Faith Profession: "Jesus volunteered to give His life in exchange for mine. He died a cruel death so that I would be spared that pain. Nobody loves me like He did.....and does."

Study Scriptures: Deuteronomy 28; Exodus 3:13-14

Devotional # 115
The Price of Truth

Scripture: John 9:1-38

Oh, go ahead and read all the verses.....it will do you good. Every Scripture reading can't be only one verse! Today's account is one of my favorites. Jesus heals a man who was blind from birth. When the Pharisees realize that this healing was done on the Sabbath Day, they conclude (incorrectly) that Jesus could not be of God.

Nevertheless, the healing speaks for itself, and, in the discussions that follow, it's obvious that the man who was healed is angered by the Pharisees' focus on the fact that this was done on the Sabbath. They're missing the point (again), and the healed man quickly grows tired of their pettiness. The Pharisees even call for his parents because they are questioning that the man was even blind in the first place.

In the end, they belittle the healed man (rather than rejoicing over the miracle) for attributing the event to Jesus, and finally cast him out of the synagogue. All he had done was tell the truth about his healing and who had done it.

The point is that the miracle itself pointed to the fact that Jesus was of God, and was undoubtedly the Messiah. But, rather than believe, the Pharisees cling to their petty little traditions, and refuse to give credit where it is due.

After he is cast out of the synagogue (a big deal back then), Jesus comes to him with words of comfort, and the healed man becomes a believer. He has received his physical sight and his spiritual sight all in the same day!! (See verses 35-38.)

The Pharisees have never died out.....they are with us as I write. They look different today, but their pettiness, refusal to believe, refusal to see anything but their own ideas, and hostility remain the same. I've experienced it firsthand on several occasions. The answer? Just stick to the truth. Jesus notices, and blesses that.

Faith Profession: "I know whom I have believed. I know what Jesus has done for me. No Pharisee will make me back away from my love and faith in Him."

Study Scriptures: John 9:39-41; II Timothy 1:12

DEVOTIONAL # 116

THE DOOR

Scripture: John 10:1-2

These verses begin the great dissertation of the sheepfold and the true shepherd. Jesus is, of course, the true shepherd.....with satan being the imposter. The distinction is made right away.....in the first two verses of the chapter.

Notice that the true shepherd enters the sheepfold (the place where the sheep were kept at night—a place of safety) by the door. The one who does not enter by the door is revealed to be a thief and a robber.

The door in this story is symbolic of physical birth. The idea is that you enter the door of this life through physical birth. That's what gives you the right to be part of humanity, and part of the world's human population. Jesus went out of His way to do this, because it is critical to the Plan of Redemption that all be done properly and legally. Jesus WAS born into this world physically.....it's just that He didn't have a human father as part of the process. He was conceived supernaturally (so that the sin of the human mother involved [Mary] could not pass on to Him). He WAS human, and lived a life on earth as a human. That's what makes it possible for Him to legally pay for the sins of humans.

Satan, on the other hand, was not born physically.....he had no physical birth. Therefore, he has no legal right to interact with humans. He does so as an outlaw.....illegally interacting. He did not enter humanity by the door, and is revealed as a thief and a robber..... taking that which doesn't belong to him.

Many people these days can't seem to tell whether to worship Jesus or satan. If these two verses were all we had, it would be enough. Satan is a liar, a thief, and a destroyer, and deceives humans into believing that he's harmless.....just a cartoon character, or a Halloween personality.

No.....he is deadly, but he smiles at you while he destroys. Beware.....and be faithful to Him who came to you through the door.

Faith Profession: "Jesus is the way, the truth, and the life. He accomplished my redemption legally, and in a way with which even satan cannot find fault."

Study Scriptures: John 14:6; Luke 1:26-38

DEVOTIONAL # 117

GOOD VS. EVIL

Scripture: John 10:10

There is perhaps no better verse in the Bible to see the sharp contrast between the Lord and the devil. Here in John 10:10, it is capsulated in all of its stark reality. The "thief" in the verse is our enemy, the devil. His three major motives are then listed.....he comes to steal, kill, and destroy. There is no good motive to him.

Humans who believe that following the devil somehow gains his favor are simply playing into his hands, and are naive beyond reason. The devil has no other motive than to do harm. He may spare you some grief while he is able to use you to accomplish some purpose, but he'll reward you with violence and evil eventually.

He steals.....your reputation; your finances; your possessions; your peace of mind; your confidence. He kills.....he'll take your life if possible, but he'll settle for killing your initiative; your good name; your desire; your boldness. He destroys.....lives; marriages; friendships; ministries; churches; leaders; families; futures. Nothing about him is good, or kind, or the least bit compassionate.

By contrast, the Lord is the "I" in this verse. His goal? To give you life (not death).....but not just any life. Life is good, but Jesus intends for you to have ABUNDANT life. Not just a regular, every-day, OKAY life.....but one marked by blessing; joy; purpose; fulfillment; accomplishment; confidence; fellowship; safety; and health. This life is founded on love.....but, again, not just regular love. This love is the love of Jesus—characterized by giving so much that you can hardly receive it all. And, this life is not waiting for you in Heaven, but is intended for you right now.....on this earth! (See study Scriptures.)

It makes you wonder why anyone would choose to neglect Jesus Christ, and believe that they are neutral, and not controlled by either Jesus or the devil.

Faith Profession: "I make the obvious choice.....I choose Jesus, and the abundant life that He offers—and promises. My joy is overflowing.....I am loved by the Creator of the Universe!!"

Study Scriptures: I John 4:17; I John 5:20

DEVOTIONAL # 118

SECURITY

Scripture: John 10:27-29

Yes, I know that there are many reading this who have been taught that you can lose your salvation. Yes, I know there are some New Testament verses which appear to teach that. And, yes, I know that some will find this teaching offensive. Sorry about that.....I'm charged to teach the truth of the Word as it has been made apparent by the Holy Spirit. There are just too many Scriptures.....and too many supporting Scriptural principles..... teaching that salvation is a secure thing.

Today's verses are one example. If saved, you are gripped by the Hand of God. No man.....or "no one".....can pluck us out of His hand. (Who is able to overpower God?)

Ephesians 5 (see study Scriptures) tells us that, when we are born again, we become part of Christ's body.....and the words imply that it is PHYSICAL as well as spiritual. How could part of Christ's body end up in Hell?

Romans 8 (see study Scriptures) tells us that we are legally adopted into God's family.....we become His children. I have children of my own. They are not always people who I'm proud of. They have disowned me at various times in our lives. Even if they deny being part of my family and change their name, would any of that change the fact that they are my children? No, because they are my children forever.

It is exactly the same with Jesus. When you are born again, you become one with Him, and He becomes one with you. You, in effect, melt into each other. You couldn't separate the two of you after that if you wanted to.

I know our conduct isn't always the best. He knew that when He saved you. The thing is….. He loves you with a deeper love than we can imagine. He doesn't go back on His Word.....He doesn't take back what has been unconditionally given. To think otherwise is to discredit the Lord of Glory.

Faith Profession: "I have eternal life and oneness with God as a permanent possession, because my salvation is not because of me, nor is it dependent on me. It is of Him, and depends on Him.....and He never changes."

Study Scriptures: Ephesians 5:30-32; Romans 8:15

RAISING THE DEAD 1

Scripture: John 11:1-16

John 11 gives the account of one of the most famous miracles Jesus did while on earth. Almost everybody has heard of it, and it is a true account, not a legend or fairy tale.

If you had read the last couple of chapters before John 11, you'd know that the religious leaders in Judea (southern Israel, including Jerusalem) had tried to kill Jesus after a particularly nasty verbal exchange. Jesus went north to Galilee, near his home town. But when He hears that His good friend Lazarus has died, He decides to go to him and his sisters (Mary and Martha). That's interesting, because Lazarus and Mary and Martha lived in a town called Bethany.....which is very close to Jerusalem.

As you have read, Jesus did not go right away.....in fact, it would be 4 days until He arrived in Bethany (more about that later). But He did decide to go.....without hesitation.

Notice, too, that the disciples misunderstand the situation. They think Lazarus is just sleeping. Jesus sets them straight in verse 14. And, notice that Thomas—though later a doubter—is also a man of courage (verse 16).

Some think that Jesus had gone to Galilee to run away from the death threats.....to get someplace safer. But, He doesn't hesitate to return when He needs to. I doubt that Jesus ran away.....it's just not like Him. He was not a coward.....or a weenie, either. Jesus was one of the bravest, strongest (physically, mentally, and spiritually) and purposeful men who ever lived. He had no fear of mere Pharisees.....He had successfully defeated the devil himself in Matthew 4. No, Jesus knows it's time to go back into Judea, and that's where He goes.

Faith Profession: "My Lord Jesus Christ is the toughest, most courageous man I've ever known. He backed down from nobody, and even faced, then defeated, death itself."

Study Scriptures: Luke 22:41-42; John 19:1,5

Devotional # 120

Raising the Dead 2

Scripture: John 11:17-35

They didn't understand. They were some of His best friends on earth, but they didn't know Him like they should have. They were like many people today.....like many Christians today.....they just underestimate His power and ability.

Jesus waits.....on purpose.....before leaving for Bethany. He arrives four days after Lazarus has died, and Mary and Martha are a little put out with Him.

Martha is the person of action, so she goes out to meet Him (verse 20). She starts the conversation with an accusation (verse 21), then quickly backpedals in verse 22.

Jesus' reply is short and sweet: "Thy brother shall rise again." Martha responds with a statement (verse 24) that betrays her ignorance of Scripture. She is much like people today.....both saved and lost. She believes in one general resurrection of the dead at the end of time ("at the last day" verse 24). That is, she knew some Bible, but not enough.

Jesus immediately corrects her theology in verses 25 and 26. He states that those who believe in Him shall resurrect BEFORE the general resurrection in the "last day." Lazarus was shortly going to be one example of that. There are TWO resurrections, my friends, and you don't want to be a participant in the second one.....the big, general one at the end (see Revelation 20).

Jesus was not late. As always, He was right on time, as we'll see shortly. He did, however, weep.....not because Lazarus had died, but because the belief among the crowds was still so weak. So, He prepares to do another miracle, and this one is going to be one of the best!

Faith Profession: "I am a believer in Jesus Christ. I will be bodily resurrected in the first resurrection, not the second, because I am part of the body of Christ."

Study Scriptures: Revelation 20:1-6; 11-15

RAISING THE DEAD 3

Scripture: John 11:34-45

Tears trickle down the precious face of our Savior. He has worked so hard to teach these people.....to love them.....to show them His miracle-working power. And still they doubt. It is disheartening, but He is not done trying.....even though some of them (the cruder, more insensitive among them) continue to speak out accusations (verse 37).

It is time. Jesus walks to the grave.....straightens Himself to full height.....and boldly says, "Take ye away the stone." Even Martha is stunned! What? We can't do that! He's been dead four days, and he stinks by now! Jesus looks at her and reminds her of what He had said a few moments before.....that her brother would rise again (verse 23). He meant NOW!

So, they obediently roll the stone away from the front of the tomb. Jesus takes a moment to pray.....thanking His Father for hearing Him.....and shouts, "Lazarus, come forth!" It is a command, not a guess. He KNOWS what is going to happen, because He knows that the power of the Holy Spirit within Him is more powerful than death.

Sure enough.....to the utter amazement of the crowd.....Lazarus hops out of the tomb, still bound with the grave clothes and the napkin on his head. (Notice: two pieces of clothing, not one). Jesus commands the stunned onlookers to unwind Lazarus from the wrappings, because he was alive!! They did, and HE WAS!!

NOW they believe on Him. NOW they are converted. It is a miracle that no one can deny. NOW they see why Jesus waited so long to arrive.....had He come earlier, some would have doubted that Lazarus was really dead. Nobody doubted it now. NOW they have a glimpse into what Jesus meant when He said verses 25 and 26.

Jesus is the resurrection and the life, and He has proven it!

Faith Profession: "I believe. I have not seen Lazarus, or Jesus (yet), but I believe God's Holy Word. That belief connects me with Him, and gives me life everlasting!"

Study Scriptures: Hebrews 11:1,6; Romans 10: 9-10

DEVOTIONAL # 122

One Last Thing

Scripture: John 11:41-44

One last thing before we move on from the miracle of the raising of Lazarus from the dead. Did you notice anything about the prayer Jesus prayed at this event? In verse 41, as they were moving the stone away from the grave, Jesus begins to pray. It is a prayer of thanks to the Father for this miracle, and thanks that the Father HAD HEARD HIM (verse 41). That is, Jesus is praying IN FAITH.....thanking God for the answer BEFORE it occurs in the physical.

Once again, He is setting a pattern for US. If you have a promise from Scripture when you begin to pray, that promise IS your answer. It is already so, or it wouldn't have been written down as a promise. So, the faith process in prayer is: you have the promise.....you pray the promise.....then you thank Him for the answer.....BEFORE YOU ACTUALLY SEE IT. Why is this valid? Because you are praying an already established promise from God, and that means that it must come to pass.....IF you stay in faith about it.

Jesus isn't having a hallucination here in John 11. He is thanking God for an answer before it is seen. That can be done because God always honors His Word.

Jesus is teaching us something here. This is how we SHOULD be praying. Instead, we often pray in a way that indicates that we don't know the answer, and aren't sure what it might be. Why would you do that when you have established promises given to you by God Himself? Why would you do that when Jesus shows you the proper way to pray..... expectantly, and in faith? As always, it is a choice.....YOUR choice. It just seems odd to me that folks would insist on praying differently than Jesus did.

Faith Profession: "I will pray in faith, based on a promise I find in the Word. I will thank God for the answer that's indicated in the promise BEFORE I see the results."

Study Scriptures: I John 5:14-15; Mark 11:23-24

DEVOTIONAL # 123

GIVING

Scripture: John 12:1-9

After the raising of Lazarus, the chief priests and Pharisees got together to plan Jesus' death (see John 11:53). A while later, just before the Passover feast, Jesus re-appears in Bethany to see his good friends, Lazarus and his sisters Mary and Martha. As He is seated at supper, Mary gets a container of very costly ointment, and anoints His feet with it. (This ointment was expensive.....what Mary did was very sacrificial.)

Judas immediately begins to complain that this act was a waste of the ointment.....that it could have been sold for 300 pence, and the money given to the poor. Oh, yes.....so pious.....so religious. It sounds so "spiritual".....until you find out that his real motive was to steal some of it, and anointing Jesus' feet made that impossible. (See verse 6.....Judas was the treasurer of the group.....they trusted him!!)

Jesus does not condemn Mary for her act of worship. In fact, He commends her. What was she doing? She was saying thank you in the best way she knew how.....because Jesus had given her brother back to her. She was giving to the Lord the most precious thing she had. She was showing love in the way Jesus showed it. She was giving totally.....with abandon.....because she knew He deserved it

.

It's not a bad example to follow, either. We tend to be careful with our "things," but you don't get to take them with you when you die. You could do a lot worse things with what you have than giving them to the Lord. He does deserve it.

Faith Profession: "Nothing that I have is mine anyway. Giving back to the Lord is actually giving Him that which He gave to me in the first place. I will be more generous to the Lord, showing my appreciation to Him."

Study Scriptures: Luke 6:38; II Corinthians 9:7

Are You NUTS!?

Scripture: John 12:10-11

I'll tell you what, dear reader.....I had to read today's Scripture a couple of times, because I couldn't believe my eyes! In chapter 11, Jesus had raised Lazarus from the dead. And, there was NO DOUBT ABOUT IT, because Lazarus had been dead four days before Jesus performed the miracle.

Many people became believers that day (see 11:45). Well, I guess so! What other conclusion could you come to? Okay.....you COULD be a Pharisee, and conclude that you needed to put Jesus to death (see 11:47-53). And, if that wasn't goofy enough, now they decide to kill Lazarus, too!!

Do you see how twisted people become when they begin to oppose God Himself? Do you see the rampant irrationality in all of this? Here's a guy who claims to be your Messiah, and raises people from the dead (among many other things). He is fulfilling prophecy every day. You could choose to believe on Him, as many did.

Or.....you could decide that the best thing to do is KILL HIM. And, let's kill the guy He raised from the dead while we're at it.

Man, are these guys out of it! You're going to try to kill a guy that Jesus already proved that He can raise from the dead? This is your plan?! Listen, folks.....when people get in opposition to Jesus, their thinking goes haywire something awful. They become irrational, and stop making any real sense. When you see that kind of thing.....beware. They're capable of ANYTHING.

Faith Profession: "Jesus is Lord. I love Him.....He is THE TRUTH and THE LIFE. Where would I go to find someone better?"

Study Scriptures: John 6:66-68

THE PERFECT LESSON

Scripture: John 13:1-17

It is only chapter 13 out of 21 chapters in the book of John, but we're well into the last week of Jesus' life on earth already. Here in John 13, they are at the last supper. It is the last opportunity Jesus had before Calvary to speak to His disciples.

But He gives no speech. Instead, as the meal ended, He quietly took a towel and some water, and began to kneel at the feet of each disciple, washing their dirty, smelly feet. It is not the best of jobs.....one which you would normally avoid, and which was done by the lowest servant. Yet, here is the Creator of the Universe, on the floor in front of mere men, washing their feet. (Remember, they wore sandals.....their feet were DIRTY). What is He doing? He's giving the most powerful example of love that can be given.....of His love for them.....and of how THEY were to love others. Sacrificially. Without pride. Doing the lowest, dirtiest job, as long as others benefitted. With no paycheck, and no expectation of even a thank you.

Did they get it? Did they learn anything? No, not right away, because I notice that no disciple moves for the towel and water after Jesus finishes. No disciple thinks to wash HIS feet. They did get it later.....after He had gone back to Heaven. I guess you just have to let some things sink in a little.

Jesus.....the Messiah.....King of Kings, and Lord of Lords.....kneeling on the filthy floor, washing the grime off the feet of the men He had created. I can't think of any act that would convey the love of God for His creation better than that. Serving the Lord is not easy work, if it's done right. The work is often not glamorous.....it is done alone much of the time, without help. It can be frustrating, lonely, and difficult. You won't get rich in worldly ways.....many, many people abandon you along the way. So why would anybody do it? Because they deeply appreciate a Savior who loves them enough to be willing to wash their feet.

Faith Profession: "I love Jesus. I love Him enough to serve others, even if it is not rewarding on earth. He asked me to serve others in the least glamorous ways, and I'll do it because He did it first."

Study Scriptures: II Corinthians 11:22-28; Revelation 5:9-14

Devotional # 126

Loving One Another

Scripture: John 13:34-35

They are still at the last supper, and will be until the beginning of chapter 18. John's Gospel spends lots of time giving the details of what Jesus said to His disciples at that last meal. And here, in our verses for today, He summarizes their duty as He sees it. He tells them to love one another as He has loved them. And, He lets them know that other people.....who are not yet disciples themselves.....will know that they are His disciples because of the love that they will show for one another.

Now, that seems pretty simple. You'd think adult believers in the USA could get the message of these two verses, especially since they seem to be so central to all that Jesus expects from those who follow Him. Yeah.....you'd think that.....but it wouldn't be true of Christianity in these last days.

Look at churches. What do you see? People loving each other so obviously that others want to be part of it? No.....you see ritual that is so cold and dead that you feel moved to fall asleep. Or, you see entertainment (which you could see on TV or at a concert). Or, you see little cliques of people who stay to themselves. Or, you find people who are so judgmental that they'd make a Pharisee blush. Or, you hear pleas for money.....over and over and over, because that's what's most important to that group.

Jesus' own words.....out of His own mouth.....were that people were SUPPOSED to know His followers by the love they had.....and SHOWED.....to one another. You know what? People would be attracted to that. People WANT that. Jesus knew that. And, if you want to please Him, it's simple.....just love people, and don't be afraid to show it. If only we could get that simple concept right.

Faith Profession: "Jesus lives inside me because I am a born-again Christian. His love should therefore show through in my life. I resolve to love others in every way I can."

Study Scripture: I Corinthians 13:4-8, 13

Good Intentions

Scripture: John 13:36-38

Of all the disciples, the one I can most relate to is Peter. Here is a man with an outgoing personality (which I wish I had) who doesn't hesitate to drop everything to follow the Messiah. He loves Jesus.....really LOVES Him, and will do anything for Him. He says that, and he really means it.

His problem is that he fails to deal with some of his more obvious fleshly tendencies. Let's just say that sitting down and thinking things over before he speaks is not one of Peter's characteristics. Plus, he is constantly putting his own feelings and opinions above the Word of God, and he pays dearly for this flaw.

So, here at the last supper, Jesus begins to talk about going away from His disciples (verse 33), and Peter doesn't want to hear that. In verse 36, he asks the Lord where He is planning to go.....he has picked up on the words of verse 33.

Jesus, who is making reference to Calvary, and His descent into Hell itself in the three days and nights after the Cross, tells Peter that he can't go with Him now, but that he will follow Him afterwards. Peter, of course, is not getting the hint.....he has no idea that Jesus is speaking of His death on the Cross (though Jesus has told them about it plainly on several occasions). So, he begins to push the issue. "Why can't I follow you now?" he whines. And then, letting his pride get the best of him, he says, "I will lay down my life for thy sake."

You have to like this guy. He meant what he said.....he loved Jesus that much, and Jesus knew that. But Jesus also knew that talk is cheap, and that some pretty potent forces would be moving in Peter's life in a few short hours.....and that Peter would openly deny Him. Notice: Jesus tells that to Peter; then moves on to other things (see 14:1). Peter is left there with his intentions hanging out. He has spoken his bold, prideful words in front of the other disciples, and that would be used against him by that most despicable of all enemies, the devil. (More on that in later pages).

Faith Profession: "I will weigh my words before I speak, so that I won't have to publicly eat them later."

Study Scriptures: Matthew 16:21; Luke 9:22; Matthew 17:22-23

DEVOTIONAL # 128

THE WAY

Scripture: John 14:1-6

Beginning here in chapter 14, and continuing through chapters 15 and 16, Jesus begins to prepare His disciples for His departure. He explains it for three chapters before praying for them in John 17. But here, as He begins the explanation, He utters one of the most well-known statements of His earthly ministry.....John 14:6. You hear this quoted at funerals a lot, but I thought we'd take a look at it today.

Verse 6 is about as definite a statement as you will find about Jesus being the one and only person to turn to for salvation. He says, without apology, that HE is THE way, THE truth, and THE life. We can safely conclude then that there are NOT many ways to Heaven.....as too many people believe.

I know it's not popular to put that into print. Most folks think it is "narrow-minded" to believe that there's only one way to get to Heaven. But, if you think it through, you'll see that it's not too unusual. The sky is blue. You can believe otherwise, but it doesn't change that truth. You can get all fussy about that being narrow-minded, but the sky is still blue. Some things are so just because that's the way it is.

Jesus is THE WAY, because He's the only man ever to have resurrected from the dead of His own power over sin. That's the truth.

Now, you can believe something else if you want.....it's a free country, after all. But if your alternate belief doesn't get you to Heaven, please don't blame anyone other than yourself. Jesus has told you that HE is the way, the truth, and the life. Believe, and you will see. Choose otherwise, and you're on your own.

Faith Profession: "I believe that Jesus Christ died for my sins, and that His resurrection proves that He is THE WAY to Heaven. Thank you, Lord, for being honest with me."

Study Scriptures: Acts 4:12; II Peter 3:9

WHAT DOES GOD THE FATHER LOOK LIKE?

Scripture: John 14:7-11

As Jesus begins to explain His coming departure, He mentions God the Father and His similarity with Him. Philip, in verse 8, asks Jesus to show them the Father.

Jesus' reply is given kindly, and is quite revealing. Jesus tells Philip that if he has seen Him (Jesus), he has seen the Father.

Wow! That's so simple it almost makes your head hurt! We tend to believe, as Christians, that God the Father is some remote, mysterious figure dwelling above the clouds, and sitting on some massive throne. We aren't sure what He looks like; what He does all day; or even how He feels about us.

Yet, here is Jesus telling us that it really is simple.....the Father is just like Jesus. Do you want to know how the Father feels about you? Okay.....how does Jesus feel about you? Right.....He loves you in a way that is so big, and so intense, that it is hard to comprehend.

What is God doing? Like Jesus, He is caring for us.....trying to teach us.....trying to keep us safe and well.....trying to provide for us. The Father, if He is like Jesus, is gentle; wise; loving; forgiving; understanding; compassionate; caring; tender; and has a sense of humor. He is NOT a nasty bully who is searching your every move, looking for something wrong so that He can punish you. That is the image of God that the devil would like you to have.

God the Father is exactly like Jesus. In fact, they worked together to devise the Plan of Redemption.....a plan that has completely befuddled the devil, and which has zero flaws. It was all done so that the Father.....and Jesus.....and the Holy Spirit.....could have friendship and fellowship with you and me. Amazing!!

Faith Profession: "I DO know what God the Father is like. He is just like Jesus, and that is really good news. He is MY Father. Better yet, He is my DAD."

Study Scriptures: John 12:45; Hebrews 1:1-3

DEVOTIONAL # 130

A Verse That Is Hard to Believe

Scripture: John 14:12

You know, I went through both Bible school and seminary without anyone pointing out this verse to me. It was never mentioned in all the classes I attended, and now that I have seen it and studied it, I have to wonder how it was missed.

Jesus is speaking these words. These words are Scripture.....God's Holy Word. They MUST be true. Jesus prefaces these words by two "verilies".....the Bible way of signaling that something extra special and very important is about to be said. It says that, if you believe in Jesus as your Savior, the works that He did, YOU can do also.....and even greater works than He did!! Wow! How can that be!?

Well, the verse IS true, and applies to all believers. It is possible because, when Jesus was on earth, He was operating as a human being, but He was utilizing.....to the maximum..... the power of the Holy Spirit that indwelt Him (see study Scriptures below). I know there is disagreement about that. Most people just figure (in their mind) that Jesus healed people and cast out demons because He was God. But, if He was operating as God on earth, then His death could not have applied to humans in all ways (Hebrews 4:15).

No.....it is just that we have been poorly taught with regard to the amazing power that is ours.....you and me as believers.....once we are indwelt by the Holy Spirit. With Him present inside us, we have the capability to do anything that Jesus did on earth. (Hey, don't get mad at me.....I'm only repeating what HE said here in John 14:12): ANYTHING that He did on earth. That's what the disciples did in the early part of the Book of Acts. Why? Because they believed and applied this verse and this principle.

Why doesn't it happen so much today? Because we've been taught that this verse couldn't be true (which is a denial of God's Word.....hello, satan, when did you come in?) That God does everything for us, and that we are capable of very little, if anything. That God does everything.....period. No. No. No! This verse is God's Holy Word. It has to be true. And, if so, then we'd better get tuned in to the Holy Spirit within us.....we're missing out on a lot of power!!

Faith Profession: "I am who Jesus said I am. I can do what Jesus said I can do. I have what Jesus said I have. Amen."

Study Scriptures: Mark 16:17-18; Acts 1:8

DEVOTIONAL # 131

THE COMFORTER

Scripture: John 14:16-17

This is it. This is THE promise.....the most important one given by Jesus as He prepared to leave this world. It is the promise He referred to just before He ascended (see Acts 1:4). He knows it is the most important thing for His followers because it is from the Holy Spirit that they will receive the power that He used on earth. It is what makes His statement in John 14:12 possible.

Jesus was about to leave the earth in physical form because He had to. He knew that humans place a great importance on comfort, and that they hate to be left alone. So, He arranges for a member of the Trinity to be with them at all times while He is away from them (physically). Notice that, in verse 17, Jesus says that the Holy Spirit, or Comforter, SHALL be in you (future tense). That's right, because the Holy Spirit didn't begin to permanently indwell believers until Acts 2. Since then, He has indwelt every believer from the moment they believe.

The Holy Spirit is said to be a Comforter. That's good, because we often need comfort. We get hurt.....we get sick.....we get frustrated.....we feel like crying..... we get mad as a hornet.....we get confused. In each case, comfort has already been provided.....it lives in your heart, and you can get to it any time you need to. The Holy Spirit can only be received..... and used.....by those who believe.

The world knows nothing of Him or His ministry.....that's why they look at you funny when you say something about "hearing" from the Lord. It is just the Holy Spirit communicating.....internally and spiritually.....with your spirit. You know that it happens, because you've experienced it. They cannot know unless and until they trust Jesus as their Savior.

The Comforter.....He lives in my heart, and yours, too..... if you are a believer. We can communicate with Him any time we want. It is among the greatest of gifts!

Faith Profession: "As a believer, I know I have the Holy Spirit living within me. He is my personal Comforter, and is available to me anytime."

Study Scriptures: Acts 1:4; Acts 2:1-4; John 16:7-14

Devotional # 132
You'll Have Peace

Scripture: John 14:27

Did you know that most people are seeking peace? Some of them don't even know that they desire this…..they just think they're "stressed out" or "too busy."

Here in this little-known passage, Jesus is plainly telling us that, when He is away from us in Heaven temporarily, He is leaving His peace with us. Notice that we don't have to strive for this…..we don't have to pray for it (in fact, it would be insulting to Him if we did that)...we don't have to sit around wringing our hands and hoping for it. He gave it to us. It's ours as a free gift, just because He loves us. It is ours…..IF we receive it as a gift.

Many Christians don't, you know. Despite clear passages of Scripture like this one, many are still seeking peace; or, worse yet, asking God to give it to them, and wondering why He doesn't. Hellooooo…..are you there? He DID give it to you. John 14:27 says so. All you have to do is receive it as you would any gift!

This peace of God, by the way, is always present when you're in the will of God. In fact, it's one of the indicators that you are in His will, and it's okay to trust that. The Holy Spirit won't mislead you. So, when you are struggling with a decision, and you make a choice that gives you a sense of peace in your heart…..that's a good indicator, and that peace is no doubt from God.

It is not the kind of peace the world knows…..fleeting; dependent upon the circumstances; hard to find. No, this is always there…..and comes into play as verification from Him that your decision is sound. (It was based on Scripture, right? Then it must be solid.) Trust this inner peace. Trust the Holy Spirit. It is given to you for your benefit, by a God who loves you desperately.

Faith Profession: "I will make decisions based upon Scripture, and consistent with God's revealed will. When I do, I have a sense of peace within me. It is given by a loving God, and it is a precious gift."

Study Scriptures: Philippians 4:7; Colossians 3:15; Romans 5:1

Devotional # 133
Outside the Camp

Scripture: Hebrews 13:12-14

Today I was sitting in an office in my local church, folding bulletins for the Sunday service, when a young man who is relatively new to our church popped his head in the door to say Hi. In the course of the conversation, he mentioned that he had been asked to preach the sermon this Sunday while the pastor is away. I felt like I had been punched in the stomach. Here I am…..an experienced pastor and teacher, folding bulletins while the new guy, with minimal experience, is asked to preach. He has preached before in our church. I have never been asked.

So, I was feeling sorry for myself, and more than a little hurt. Then I sat down at my computer to write a devotional for the Lord, and He brought today's Scripture to my mind. The Pharisees didn't even let Jesus fold bulletins. They followed Him around….. not to learn from Him…..but to catch Him in some error so that they could accuse Him, and discredit Him. (They tried this for over three years, but could find nothing.) They publicly argued with Him. They hated Him, and plotted on many occasions to kill Him….. eventually managing to get the Roman ruler of Judea to do that for them.

Jesus was innocent. He was guilty only of loving them. He was their Messiah, promised and prophesied throughout Scripture. He hurt no one. He did only good. He told them the truth, because He was the Truth personified. But, instead of them rejoicing over Him, and celebrating His presence…..they sought to destroy Him, finally doing so OUT-SIDE THE WALLS OF THE CITY.

Jesus was always outside…..of the social camp; the political camp; and the religious camp. They were afraid of Him, and didn't understand Him, so they banished Him.

As for me, my suffering was limited to being held at arm's length in a church where I was sent (by Him) to serve. I was being gently placed "outside the camp" of my own home church. It is a mild thing…..hardly worth mentioning….. compared to what He endured. Still, it is a little taste of what He experienced. I should thank these folks for giving me this chance to know a little of the type of thing He suffered. It lets me know Him more intimately, and that is a blessing.

Faith Profession: "I will try to see events in my life from Jesus' perspective rather than to just sit and suck my thumb. Nothing I experience can compare to the suffering He endured for me."

Study Scripture: Isaiah 53

Devotional # 134
His Commandment

Scripture: John 15:12

It's the New Testament…..why is Jesus giving commandments? Actually, this wording is not meant to convey the idea that you either do this or He will be angry at you. Rather, it is stated this way to give the thought emphasis…..so that you and I will pay close attention to it.

Jesus is with His disciples for the last time before Calvary, and is spending time giving them "last minute instructions." Here, He says simply that it is His earnest wish that His children love one another.

What do you suppose this would look like? I think it would mean that we pray for each other. I think it means that, if we are sick, someone who knows us will come and pray; offer to do some things around the house to help out; provide a meal or two. I think it means that we won't be out in the world looking for someone to replace our spouse. I think it means that we will encourage each other instead of criticizing. I think it means that we would encourage our brother or sister to minister in the anointing given by the Holy Spirit. I think it means that we would try to share…..in an inoffensive way…..some of the information given to us by the Lord.

Sadly, this is not a picture of end times Christianity…..but it should be. How does it change? One person at a time. It starts with you…..deciding to change your approach to those around you. (You can do it, too…..Jesus says so…..see the study Scriptures.) Your willingness to change, and love those around you as Jesus did, will be noticed by someone else. They will decide to change…..and it will begin to multiply. That's Jesus' way…..multiplication. But it starts with one person.

Faith Profession: "Jesus has asked me to love others as He did. It must be possible to do…..and I'll try it, starting today."

Study Scriptures: Philippians 4:13; John 15:5

Devotional # 135

Friends

Scripture: John 15:15

What have you been taught about your relationship with Jesus? If you're like most Christians, you've been taught that you are saved, but you're still a lowly worm.....a sinner barely saved by grace.....a person who fails repeatedly, and deals with large amounts of guilt and shame. An onlooker in the Kingdom of God, watching Jesus battle satan, and hoping that Jesus wins in your case.

I call that an "Old Testament" view. It's amazing to me how difficult it seems to be for children of God to leave the Old Testament practices behind, and live in the glorious blessings of the New.

In the Old Testament, one's relationship to God was based upon conduct. Do good, and get blessing. Do bad, and get punishment. In that time frame, your relationship with God was that of a servant.....and it says so in John 15:15.

But you are not in the Old Testament! Because Jesus took your sins away when He died on the Cross (something that wasn't true in the Old Testament), you are given an entirely new relationship with Him. As unbelievable as it may sound, His work on the Cross..... GIVEN to you at salvation.....has changed you from a servant into a FRIEND. Yes!! You are a child of God now.....His kid! That makes you a prince or princess in His Kingdom.

You have been made into a family member! You have become one with Jesus Himself! And your relationship with God has been improved because of all that. You are now considered to be God's friend.....by God. It is all too wonderful..... almost too hard to believe! Yet, what I have just written is the truth of the Word of God.....it cannot be false.

You are His friend. He wants to spend time with you. He wants to confide in you. He wants to bless you, and share what He has with you. You are His friend!

Faith Profession: "God considers me to be His personal friend. It is written in His Word. I receive it, and I will BE His friend!"

Study Scriptures: I Corinthians 12:27; John 1:12; Colossians 2:13

Killing in God's Name

Scripture: John 16:1-4

Jesus warned His disciples. In doing so, He warned us. One of the things I really love about the Lord is that He always tells the truth, even if it is not what we want to hear.

You'd think that, if you decide to serve God with your life.....which is a good thing.....that your path would be an easy one. You'd think that, if your desire is to help people; and serve them; and love them; and tell them truth.....they would be appreciative. You'd also be very naive, and someone who failed to heed the many warnings Jesus gave about this.

There are people.....and they are among us today.....who think they are doing God service by opposing and persecuting those who are trying to spread the Gospel. The Apostle Paul was such a person before the Lord set him straight on the road to Damascus. The Pharisees.....at least some of them.....thought they were ridding their country of a bad influence when they crucified Jesus. As we approach..... and live through.....the last days before Jesus' return, the world will get more and more irrational. The Word says that evil will be called good, and good will be called evil. I call it irrationality, and it is a sure sign of demonic activity.

So, as you devote your life to His service, don't be surprised if you lose some friends; get betrayed by some of your closest companions; are silently pushed to the side and not permitted to participate in the activities of your local church; and are held in suspicion. Even worse, you could be accused of things that your accusers should be ashamed to speak. Don't be surprised. It happened to Jesus, and He warned you about it as early as John 16.

Faith Profession: "I do not expect to serve the Lord without experiencing opposition. I have the authority of His Name to use against those who oppose Him, and opposition will not make me quit. And, if I won't quit, I cannot be defeated."

Study Scripture: Acts 9:1-20

DEVOTIONAL # 137
BETTER THAN CHRIST ON EARTH

Scripture: John 16:7

As Jesus speaks with His disciples just before His death, burial, and resurrection, He begins to introduce the concept of the indwelling Holy Spirit. The Holy Spirit had not permanently indwelt any human before. I guess the closest person to that in the Old Testament was David, but he prayed that the Holy Spirit be not taken from him (Psalm 51), so it was possible.

Jesus knew He would have to leave His disciples, who had grown used to seeing Him every day. Being without Him would be quite an adjustment for them, so He is trying to prepare them. Here in verse 7, He says that it is "expedient" for THEM that He go away. The word "expedient" means suitable, or better. Jesus, then, is telling them that it is BETTER for them that He go away! They must have been thinking….. "How can that possibly be better?!"

That's a pretty good question, and one which you may have asked yourself. The answer is this: When Jesus was on earth, He was in physical form, and so could be only one place at a time. When He sends the Holy Spirit to indwell each believer, He can be inside every child of God at the same time. Therefore, each believer has direct access to Jesus (in the form of the Holy Spirit) any time at all. It IS better!

I don't think they understood all of that right away. But they did get it later, and the Book of Acts gives testimony to that. You, dear reader, if you know Jesus as your Savior, have Him dwelling inside you right now, and every minute of your time on this earth. What could be better than that??

Faith Profession: "I am indwelt by the Holy Spirit of God from the moment I was born again. I have direct access to the Trinity at all times. It is a rare and blessed privilege."

Study Scriptures: Colossians 1:27; Acts 2:1-4

THE HOLY SPIRIT'S MINISTRY

Scripture: John 16:13-14

If you ask the average Christian believer if they have the Holy Spirit living inside them, they'll answer an enthusiastic "Yes!" If you probe further, though, you might be surprised to find that the presence of the Holy Spirit has little or no practical effect for them.

Here in John 16, as Jesus explains why He needs to leave, He tells them some basic truths about the Holy Spirit who will be His replacement for them. Notice, first of all, that the Holy Spirit will guide believers into all truth. All truth..... nothing but truth. Therefore, you can rely on the Holy Spirit's leading.

You know…..that still, small voice within your spirit that is guiding you gently. He WILL NOT lead you into error. He CAN not. So, when He begins to lead you into the Biblical areas of authority over devils; prosperity; healing and health; and safety…..you can follow with confidence.

Next, notice that He will show you things to come. So, to some extent, you can know the future.....at least from the standpoint of Bible prophecy (which is 100% accurate). You can know where you're going when your body dies; what Jesus' return will be like; some things about Heaven. He is here to show you these things.

And, lastly, the Holy Spirit will glorify Jesus (verse 14). He glorifies JESUS….. not Himself. When you hear someone glorifying the Holy Spirit, you are hearing something contrary to the Word. Jesus is the focal point, because it was Jesus who did the difficult work of Redemption, and it is Jesus who does the work now of mediation, intercession, and advocacy.

When things are in proper Biblical order, Jesus will be exalted, not the Holy Spirit. But, He can be relied upon to guide you faithfully into truth, and revelation of future events.

Faith Profession: "I can rely on the inner moving of the Spirit within my heart. He is faithful to His own ministry, and is my Comforter, and the revealer of TRUTH."

Study Scriptures: John 14:26; Philippians 2:9-11

Devotional # 139
A Train in a Tunnel

Scripture: John 16:20-22

Jesus understands what is about to happen. He knows that His death on the Cross will be traumatic for them, and that they will not grasp the significance and miraculous-ness of it right away. He knows.....and He loves them so much.....so He does His best to prepare them.

"You will weep and lament," He says. Who wants to hear that? Well, it's not good news, but it is the truth, and He always tells them the truth. As you weep, the world will rejoice! Amazing, isn't it? The thinking of the world is often exactly opposite of our thinking. BUT.....and you have to love this..... "Your sorrow will be turned into joy."

Okay. If I have to have sorrow, I can handle it if I know that it will be turned around. Have you ever been in this situation? I have. I have known sorrow so deep that I thought it would engulf me, and take me to my death. It is a place of deep darkness, and hope seems so far away. As I was in that place, my son said to me, "Pop, you're like a train going through a dark tunnel. There's a bend in the track, so you can't see the opening, and it seems like there is no end. But you will emerge from this tunnel, and the light you enter into will be so bright that you will be shocked at it. Not just light, but brilliant sunlight!"

As it turned out, his words were prophetic. As I write, it is 8 years later, and I have lived to see my son's words come true. The life that looked so hopeless and dark has become so bright a light that it is almost too good to be true. Almost..... but I live every day in that brilliant sunshine now.

I was in a place of weeping and lament, but my sorrow was turned into joy. And, if you find yourself in that place today, take heart. The disciples lived to see their sorrow turned to laughing. That same thing happened to me. And our Lord will see to it that the same happens to you. "...Your heart shall rejoice, and your joy no man taketh from you." Amen.

Faith Profession: "My Lord wants me to live in joy and laughter. He will turn my present situation into joy, no matter how unlikely that may seem."

Study Scriptures: Luke 22:54-62; Acts 2:14-36

Devotional # 140

Be of Good Cheer

Scripture: John 16:25-33

The disciples' darkest days were just about to be on them. The Master, whom they had followed for over three years, would shortly be crucified, and would die alone on a hill outside Jerusalem. They would know no greater tragedy.

As Jesus prepares them for these trying times, He is speaking to them in plainer terms than ever before, clearly indicating that He was destined to die.....but that it would just be temporary.

He sums it up in verse 33, which may be the epitome of understatement. He tells them..... and us.....that we shall have "tribulation" in the world. That is….. trouble, pain, frustration, unfairness, betrayal, sickness, attack, persecution, loneliness. If you've lived as long as I have, you know what an understatement that is!

Then Jesus says, "But be of good cheer; I have overcome the world." Hey, don't even give all that trouble a thought.....I've overcome all of that. First, He is speaking in faith, because, as He says these words, He has not yet died on the Cross, nor descended into Hell to battle and defeat the devil. Secondly, He is telling you and me that we have victory over whatever we face in this world through Him. When He rose from the grave, He did so as victor over death, Hell, the devil, sin, and the grave. Then He offered to give that hard-earned victory to every one of His children. We become His children through belief in Him and His finished work on and after the Cross.

We CAN live in the reality that the difficulties of this world are nothing more than temporary, pesky inconveniences. We have authority over them, and can (and should) oppose and cancel them (see study Scriptures). We can live in good cheer despite the temporary circumstances of our earthly life, because we have been given His victories.....and the resurrection power of the Holy Spirit.....to use against these troubles. So, be of good cheer! We have reason to be cheerful!

Faith Profession: "I have victory over all the trials and tribulations that I face in this earthly life. I live in a state of peace and joy, knowing this."

Study Scriptures: I Peter 5:8-9 ; Ephesians 4:27; James 4:7: Proverbs 4:20-22

DEVOTIONAL # 141
THE TRUTH

Scripture: John 17:17

If there is one Scripture that the devil has worked harder to destroy, I can't think of what it might be. You can't help but notice that, in our world today, the idea that everything is relative.....that whether or not an action is "right".....DEPENDS. It depends upon the person involved.....on the situation.....on the politics.....on the possible outcome. We live in a world where nothing is for certain anymore. This kind of thinking.....which is FALSE TEACHING, by the way.....has become the prevailing train of thought.

How sad, and how tragic. Satan has worked long and hard to develop and implement this deception. By my estimates, he has been at this for some 150 years, and is just now beginning to see fruit from his efforts. Of course, at the same time, he has been working to get the Bible put out of schools, government, and politics.....and, very sadly.....even out of our churches. The goal? To put the Word of God in a secondary place in society..... as if it were not relevant.

Satan could not find fault with it legally. He could find no mistakes in it. He could not break Bible prophecy. But he HAS been able to change mainstream thinking enough to get most people to forget the Bible. It is not read, studied, or spoken.....at all.....by most people. To their great shame, the same can be said of God's own blood-bought children. In effect, our world has adopted the thinking of Pontius Pilate, who, when Jesus spoke to him of the truth, he replied..... "What is truth?" (See study Scriptures.)

The answer.....from Jesus' own mouth and heart..... is in John 17:17. God's Word is absolute truth.....eternal truth. All facts, and all knowledge, find their basis in the Word of God. It is the Word that gives all other things validity. I know folks who are unsatisfied with the Bible because it won't prove itself to them. Because they approach it in a challenging way, the truth becomes elusive to them. But to those who approach it with a believing heart, and an open mind, it is a treasure of truth. It is a faith book, so it will not "prove" itself to the unbeliever. Why should it? The Bible has to prove itself to you? I don't think so. THE TRUTH stands alone. You can take it or leave it.....that doesn't change the fact that it is TRUTH.

Faith Profession: "I choose to take it rather than leave it. I choose to believe rather than to doubt. I am of the persuasion that believing is seeing."

Study Scriptures: John 18:28-38; John 14:6

Devotional # 142
How We Are Sent

Scripture: John 17:18

Anybody who has read Acts 1:8 or Matthew 28:19-20 knows that Jesus left us in the world after He saved us so that we could pass the salvation message on to others who do not know it.

Here in John 17, as Jesus prays to His Father, He mentions this fact. In doing so, He says that He is sending us (His disciples) into the world just as the Father sent Jesus into the world. So, what does that mean, exactly?

Well, we will be sent out in the flesh, but with the added power of the indwelling Holy Spirit within us…..just as He was. We will be in the world, but we will not be OF the world. We were changed spiritually when we were saved, and that change forever made us different. Like Him, we will probably not be rich, famous, or well-liked (John 17:14). That's okay with me, because there's no record of Jesus ever missing a meal.

We will be living on the earth, but we will not be earthly beings any more. We will be faith people…..people who are not enslaved by sin…..people who are not compelled to follow the devil…..people who see the world as it really is (twisted, irrational, upside-down). Our lives will be marked by the habit of doing things against the prevailing religious practices of our day. We will be misunderstood; disliked; held at arm's length; and will minister from outside the normal and accepted places and ways.

Haven't you noticed that in your own life yet? We will be held on the outside of even the churches of our day…..more so as His return nears. Why? Because too many churches are in compromise with the world system, and refuse to take a stand with God and His Word. We are different, as He was different.

Take heart…..He can relate…..and He DOES relate. You'll see evidence of that when you see Him face to face.

Faith Profession: "I am sent into this world just as Jesus was sent. I am His child, and I am happy to be thought worthy to minister in the same way He did."

Study Scriptures: John 15:19; Matthew 23

Devotional # 143

Deeply Loved

Scripture: John 17:23

At this point, we are only three verses away from the end of Jesus' prayer prior to His crucifixion. We know that all of this lengthy prayer is meant for us today. He said so in verse 20. Now, as He finishes, he says something vitally important. He prays that the world may know that Jesus was sent by God Almighty. Furthermore, He prays that the world might know that God the Father loves US just as He loved.....and loves.....Jesus Himself.

Hey, folks.....I didn't write it. But that is definitely what it says. You know, we get to feeling sorry for ourselves sometimes. Life isn't always a day at the beach. It gets old being on the outside.....being different.....having convictions in a world which has less and less every day.....telling and living the truth.

In those times, I need to know that I am loved and appreciated. I need that, and I suspect that you do, too. Well, how about verse 23, then? The Father in Heaven loves you just as much as He loves His own Son, Jesus. Folks, I don't know that there is any love that is bigger than that. We tend to think of ourselves as small and insignificant. That's been drummed into us by well-meaning traditional teachers and preachers, but it is a doctrine directly from Hell itself.

You are NOT small and insignificant if God in Heaven loves you just as much as He loves His own Son. Somebody special thinks you're wonderful. If God has a refrigerator, your picture is on it. If He carries a wallet, it contains pictures of YOU. He's nuts about you, and me, too. We are loved by the God of the whole universe! I don't know about you, but that makes up for lots of this life's difficulties!

Faith Profession: "God the Father in Heaven loves me just as much as He loves Jesus Christ. I am blessed. I am loved completely. And it makes a difference."

Study Scriptures: John 3:16; John 15:15

Devotional # 144
The "I AM"

Scripture: John 18:1-6

Some of the things I read in Scripture are downright dumbfounding. It is stunning to see the irrationality of the actions of some Bible people. We have such a case in today's Scripture reading. As you may know, Judas left the Last Supper, and went to the Pharisees..... making a deal to receive money in return for betraying Jesus. He has already done that as John 18 begins. Judas knows that Jesus has a habit of going to Gethsemane to pray, and he leads a group of armed soldiers to that place.

If you have a King James Bible, notice with me that the word "he" in verses 5 and 6 are in italics. Words that do not appear in the original text were put in italics by the translators of the King James. They were trying to be honest about the addition, and thought the addition helped to make the verse more clear. Therefore, what Jesus actually says when asked if He is Jesus of Nazareth is, "I Am."

Now.....did you notice that, when Jesus said, "I AM," the soldiers and Judas were knocked backward onto the ground! Do you know why? It is because that phrase....."I AM".....is how God identifies Himself (see study Scriptures). It is, essentially, the Name of God. As such, it has the force behind it to knock men off their feet. (You wouldn't think that mere words could have that effect, but these are not mere words.....and words CAN have that effect.) Jesus calls Himself the great I AM of Scripture, because He is!!

That title knocks armed men to the ground. You'd think they would stop and consider that. Instead, they get up, dust themselves off, and proceed to tie Jesus' hands as they arrest Him!! Think about that! This guy can knock you down with just words.....and you proceed to tie Him up as if that could actually matter! Incredible! Irrational! But absolutely true!

Faith Profession: "My Lord is the power of the universe. He can defeat enemies simply with His spoken word. He is truly All-powerful!"

Study Scriptures: Exodus 3:13-14; Revelation 19:15

PETER'S PROBLEM

Scripture: John 18:7-13

We need to be well aware of the details of the setting for today's lesson. Jesus has been praying in Gethsemane with His disciples nearby. Suddenly, Judas appears, bringing with him a group of soldiers who intend to arrest Jesus. It does not say how many soldiers there were, but we can safely assume it is somewhere between six and twelve armed men. Jesus, in verse 8, makes an appeal that His disciples be allowed to leave the scene. But, before anything else can happen, Peter draws his sword and takes a swipe at the nearest soldier, who turns out to be a man named Malchus (verse 10).

What has happened? Despite more than three chapters of preparation, the disciples still don't understand what has to happen to Jesus. Peter has made a public vow to lay down his life for Jesus (John 13:37). Furthermore, there had been a mention of swords at the Last Supper (see study Scriptures).....although Jesus was speaking of swords spiritually, but Peter was hearing in the physical realm, and thinking that Jesus meant a real metal sword.

So, these soldiers attempt to arrest Jesus, but Peter is not going to let that happen! Quick as a flash, he draws his sword and cuts at the nearest soldier. Peter, who means business, is aiming for his neck. Malchus flinches, and Peter's sword takes off his ear. Immediately, Jesus commands Peter to stop! He knows the arrest is necessary for His death at Calvary.

Peter, though, is left in an emotional state. He loves Jesus, and can't bear the thought of His arrest. But, when he tried to prevent it, Jesus ordered him to stop. Now, Peter can do nothing.....and he is angry and frustrated. He can't fight for his Savior like he wants to do, and he can't bear the thought of Jesus' possible death. It is a turmoil that will lead to the fulfillment of Jesus' prediction in John 13:37, though Peter doesn't know that yet. It is anger and frustration that lead to the denials.

Faith Profession: "I see how imperative it is to follow Scripture. I see how raw emotion can lead to problems. I will make the effort to live by the Word, no matter how I feel."

Study Scripture: Luke 22:31-38

DEVOTIONAL # 146

IRRATIONALITY

Scripture: John 18:28

As I grow older in the Lord, the one thing that seems to become more and more prominent in the world around me is irrationality. No doubt it is symptomatic of the end times, but it is always obvious, and very odd. I keep thinking the people of the world will HAVE to see how absurd their actions have become.....but they don't seem to do that.

On occasion, one sees this same irrationality even as far back as Jesus' time on earth. I'm thinking that it is related to sin.....and that it seems to increase in direct proportion to the amount of sin that is active in a life or a situation at the time.

Here in John 18, we have a classic example of what I'm talking about. Jesus has been placed under arrest in Gethsemane, and is now being taken from place to place for examination by various leaders in the community.

According to verse 13, He is taken to Annas first; then to Caiaphas, who was the current High Priest in Israel. You should know that every one of the six "trials" that Jesus endured that night were illegal under Jewish law. Nevertheless, their zeal to condemn Him is so great that they put aside their attention to the detail of the law for this occasion.

Now, notice that, in verse 28, they take Jesus from Caiaphas to the hall of judgment, but they are careful to avoid actually going in to that building. Why? Because it was a Gentile (Roman) building; and they didn't want to defile themselves, which would disqualify them from partaking of the Passover. It is completely irrational! They are taking an innocent man to illegal trials.....but they take care not to "defile" themselves by going into a building!! They are in the process of killing the Son of God, but they're worried about ceremonial defilement. You wouldn't believe it unless you read it in the Word! Mark it down.....where sin is rampant, irrationality is always present.

Faith Profession: "I reject irrationality as a product of the devil's attempt to force sin into a situation. Where I see it, I know that sin is out of control."

Study Scripture: Acts 10:28; 11:3

Cancelling Out the Word

Scripture: Mark 7:13

What would it take to cancel out the Word of God? What could possibly be so powerful that it would nullify the precious Word? Nothing? That would probably be the answer most people would give. Some might guess that sin could cancel it out, or ignorance, or death.

To me, there is nothing more powerful than God's Word. He spoke the world into existence with it. And, He will defeat His enemies at Armageddon with only His spoken Word. What then could ever defeat it? The answer is found in our verse for today..... and it is tradition. Tradition makes the Word of God of no effect..... according to Jesus Himself.

So, what IS tradition? Well, you are no doubt familiar with it, and just don't know it. Back in Jesus' day, it was the belief that the Messiah would conquer the occupying Roman army. And the belief that one was holy because of his/her actions.....what they did, and what they did not do. Today, it takes other forms.

Tradition differs from religion in this way: tradition is unbelief practiced by believers. Oh, they believe in salvation.....even tithing (some of them) and the need to regularly attend church. They also believe that God sends, or permits, the problems that you experience in life. They believe the Book of Job confirms that. They believe that Paul's thorn in the flesh was an illness, like bad eyesight. (See more on this in #256.) They believe that God heals, but not in every case (that is, He CAN heal, but not necessarily that He WILL).

Tradition teaches people to pray in a hopeful way, and that certain prayer is ridiculous . It teaches that you have the Holy Spirit within you, but that He never communicates with you, or does miraculous works through you. Tradition, in fact, will not permit the idea that God communicates back to people, except through His Word.

And tradition is what is causing the end-times church to be so cold and worldly. Those in tradition call themselves "Bible Believers." In truth, they believe parts of the Bible.....but not all of it. When confronted with a Scripture different than they believe, they ignore it, or quote some book they read—written by a traditionalist.

Faith Profession: "I believe the Bible. ALL of it, not just parts."

Study Scriptures: II Timothy 2:15; Matthew 15:1-9

Devotional # 148

Innocent

Scripture: John 18:38

I'm sure you're familiar with how a courtroom works. Someone is on trial.....there are lawyers for the defense and for the one charging a crime. In modern courtrooms, there is a jury, but in Bible times, the judge WAS the jury.....he made the decision, and it was final.

So, the Jewish leaders have finally succeeded in getting Jesus to trial. They don't have the legal power to put Him to death themselves.....it must be done by the occupying Roman officials—in this case, Pontius Pilate. So, they bring Jesus to Pilate, accusing Him of being against Pilate's boss (Caesar). (The charge is false. It is also a different charge than they started with. And, Jesus has been given no defense lawyer—all illegal.)

Nevertheless, Pilate is hearing the case because it has raised such a turmoil. Notice in verse 38, however, that he declares Jesus innocent of all charges. Amazingly, he does it again in John 19:4.....and AGAIN in John 19:6! Pilate is the judge! He declares the prisoner (Jesus) innocent.....not once, but three times!!

And still Jesus is sentenced to death.

I know it had to happen. I know He was dying for my sin.....and for yours. Still, it is quite unusual for the judge to pass a sentence of "not guilty," but the prisoner be given the death sentence anyway. Another example of irrationality (which I discussed two days ago).

Jesus died for our sin, and I'm glad for that. But, just in case there was any doubt that He was dying for someone else's sin.....remember that the presiding judge in this case publicly declared Jesus INNOCENT. And, He most certainly WAS!

Faith Profession: "Jesus died for MY sin. He could not have died for His own sin, because He didn't have any.....and the judge in His trial said so!"

Study Scriptures: Hebrews 4:15; John 8:46

BEATEN UNMERCIFULLY

Scripture: John 19:1-3

I am saddened at pictures of my Lord Jesus hanging on the Cross which show Him as a wimpy, thin fellow covered by a loin cloth…..with a little trickle of blood running down from His brow. Someone is trying to be "politically correct," no doubt. I think, though, that you ought to know what He really endured.

The scourging was a vicious beating, administered on bare skin by a burly Roman foot-soldier who probably loved his work. He used a whip made up of multiple strands of leather, each strand having a piece of bone or metal at the end…..so that, when the strand landed on flesh, it would tear out big chunks as it was pulled back.

Thirty-nine lashes were given…..if the prisoner could survive that many. Often, the prisoner died from the scourging. Jesus did not because He was a strong man, not some skinny wimp. He was physically tough, and that impressed Pilate (see study Scriptures). In addition, His beard was plucked out…..He was punched in the face repeatedly…..and slapped. Then, a crown of thorns…..large, sharp, three to four inch thorns…..was jammed onto His head, then beaten down with sticks. It would have been very painful, and would have produced torrents of blood.

Isaiah 52:14 tells us that His "visage" (facial appearance) was marred more than any man. In other words, the beating, and the other indignities, had torn his flesh so grotesquely that He was hardly recognizable as a man. His back had been beaten to the bone. Blood was everywhere. The robe they put on Him would have stuck to the torn flesh, resulting in great pain when it was removed for the crucifixion. Had He lived, He would have been horribly disfigured for the rest of His life.

How much did Jesus love you? He was innocent…..but He endured this so that YOU WOULDN'T HAVE TO. Nobody else loves you that much. Nobody!

Faith Profession: "Lord, it makes me sick to think of what was done to you. I am in awe of the depth of your love for me. How can I ever say thank you enough?"

Study Scriptures: John 19:5; Isaiah 50:6; Isaiah 53

Devotional # 150
Where Are You From?

Scripture: John 19:1-9

We are in the middle of the final trial.....the one that counted the most.....the one before the Roman governor and judge, Pontius Pilate. This whole thing was like a nightmare to Pilate. He knew Jesus was innocent, and said so three times. At the same time, the crowd was vehement for His death, and Pilate didn't want to disappoint them, either. To add to it all, Pilate's wife warned him not to have anything to do with Jesus' death. Pilate tried to have the worst criminal in the jail put to death in place of Jesus, and the crowd released the criminal, as Jesus was calmly explaining that He was not of this earth.

Things escalate rapidly, and they're getting out of control by the second. Pilate is desperate to release Jesus, and fearful of killing Him, but he is just as fearful of the crowd. In the middle of this pandemonium, Pilate, hearing disturbing things from both Jesus and the crowd, goes back into the judgment hall and asks Jesus a mighty peculiar question.

In verse 9, He says to Jesus, "Whence art thou?" We would say, "Where are you from?" Now, folks, that's a very revealing question. Pilate knew where Jesus was from ON EARTH.....He had just sent Jesus to Herod (trying to push the problem off on someone else) because he had heard that Jesus was from Galilee (see Luke 23:5-7). Oh, yes.....Pilate knew that Jesus was from Galilee. Yet he storms into the judgment hall asking Jesus..... "Where are you from?!"

Do you know why? Because Pilate was beginning to suspect that Jesus was not just an ordinary "earthling," that's why. And, no, it's not so far "out there".....it's exactly what Pilate was thinking. Pilate is in a panic, and suspects that this man is supernatural in some way that he doesn't quite understand. It is a very revealing question. One wonders why Pilate gave permission for Jesus to be crucified under the circumstances. One wonders whatever became of Pilate, who wilted to pressure, and put the Son of God to death.

Faith Profession: "I know that Jesus was.....and is.....the Son of God. More than that, He is my Savior, and my Friend."

Study Scriptures: Matthew 27:19; Luke 23:13-25

Devotional # 151
King of the Jews

Scripture: John 19:19-22

Details.....the Scribes and Pharisees were all about details. They were careful to tithe even the spices in their house. They were careful to avoid entering a Gentile building (for fear of defilement) while they were gathering false witnesses to kill their Messiah. They were careful to avoid the "unclean" people.....the publicans and sinners. They fussed about details so much that the whole point of their spiritual experience had been lost.

So, when they finally get their satanic wish, and Pilate agrees to have Jesus crucified, they begin to argue about what Pilate had written on the sign that was to hang on the Cross above Jesus' head. Notice verse 19. Pilate writes, "JESUS OF NAZARETH THE KING OF THE JEWS." When the religious leaders see this, they protest. Their point is found in verse 21: don't write that He WAS king of the Jews, but that HE SAID He was king. Pilate, who by now is pretty tired of the whole mess, refuses to change it.

Details.....they wanted the public sign to say that Jesus CLAIMED to be king. Instead, in a point of irony, Pilate.....who had the power to set Jesus free.....writes the CORRECT TITLE on the sign. It is the hand of God entering into the scene. As the crucifixion took place, the truth hung on a sign over a dying Savior for all to see, and it had been written by His executioner. He WAS, in fact, King of the Jews. More than that, He WAS, and IS, King of the Entire Universe.....and will be forever.

And it was right there on the Cross.....for all to see. They were killing their King.

Faith Profession: "Jesus Christ is not only my Savior, but He is King of Kings, and Lord of Lords."

Study Scripture: Matthew 23:23-28

Five Pieces

Scripture: John 19:23-24

Jesus has been placed on the Cross (verse 18). His suffering continues. And even while He writhes in agony a few feet away, the soldiers turn their attention to more urgent matters (for them). Since the victim of crucifixion was rapidly on his way to death, those who were killing him took the time to divide up his possessions.

In Jesus' case, He had two garments. There were four soldiers, so they tear the first garment into four pieces, each man taking one piece. Then they look at the coat, and notice that it is a more valuable piece. It is seamless, which was rare in those days. So, instead of tearing it into pieces, they decide to "cast lots" for it (gamble, with the winner getting the coat). This action was predicted in the Bible 1,000 years earlier in Psalm 22:18, so it fulfills a prophecy.

It also verifies some things you may have noticed about numbers in the Bible. Did you know that there is some significance to numbers in the Word? It is not 100%, but it is true too often to be co-incidental. The number five is often connected with death. In fact, the word "death" has five letters in it. When men are killed in the Old Testament, their wound is often specified to be under the fifth rib (II Samuel 2:23; 3:27; 4:6; 20:10).

Romans 5 talks about Christ's death. In II Samuel 21:8-9, David hangs five sons of Michah. In I Samuel 6:17-18, the Philistines are killed by five plagues. The first man who dies in the Bible of natural causes is mentioned in Genesis 5:5. In Acts 5:5, someone dies. The Brazen Altar in the Tabernacle was five by five cubits (Exodus 27:1).....sacrifices were killed there.

And, at Jesus' death, He had five wounds (I'll give you time to count them), and His garments ended up being five pieces.....one garment torn into four pieces.....the coat left whole. Have you noticed that the distress signal at sea is "May Day"? May is the fifth month.

You might want to notice numbers in the Bible. While not infallible, you can nevertheless learn some things from them. And the number five figures prominently in the crucifixion.

Faith Profession: "The Word of God has so many ways to teach us truth! Even the numbers are significant! How wonderful are your ways, O Lord!!"

Study Scriptures: Psalm 22; Isaiah 53

CARING FOR MOM

Scripture: John 19:25-27

It is so grotesque that it is difficult to look upon. Our beloved Savior is hanging on a rough cross, bleeding profusely and covered with blood and bruises. He is naked.....contrary to popular depictions of Him in a loin cloth (the Romans were not that considerate). This explains why the women stood far off. He is in agony.....He can only breathe if He pushes up on the nails in His feet, which is in itself agonizingly painful. And.....He is dying.

Several of the women closest to Him, including His earthly Mom, Mary, have moved close enough to hear Him speak. John is there, too.....his face twisted in disbelief and sorrow. They know that the end is near.

It is in this setting that Jesus does something so touching that it is simultaneously unsettling and unbelievably tender and loving. He looks down through swollen, bloody eyes and sees Mary. He says to her: "Woman, behold thy son." Then His gaze shifts to John, and He says to him: "Behold thy mother." Notice that John "gets it" immediately. He is to look after Mary as if she were his own mother. And he'll do it, too. He would do anything for Jesus, his Lord.

Notice, too, that Jesus is careful not to call her "Mom" or "Mother." He knows that this would cause some confusion later.....that some would begin to regard Mary so highly that they would begin to worship her. So, He calls her "Woman." It is not disrespectful..... it simply makes the point that she is not his mother in the scientific sense. He was conceived supernaturally.....and He doesn't want to confuse that important issue.

He is in extreme, almost unbearable pain. He is an innocent man being tortured. Yet He takes the time to see to it that His earthly mom will be cared for by someone He trusts. Isn't that just like Jesus? Isn't that exactly what love would do?

Faith Profession: "My love for Jesus deepens as I learn more about Him. His focus is always on others, just as mine should be. This is the love of Christ in action."

Study Scriptures: I John 4:8; Luke 1:30-35

DEVOTIONAL # 154

TWO BRAVE MEN

Scripture: John 19:38-40

It has ended. Jesus was not killed on the Cross. His blood was not "spilled," which gives the connotation of an accident. No, there was nothing accidental about it. He SHED His blood and GAVE His life.....voluntarily, and on purpose.

Suddenly, and unexpectedly, there is a visitor in Pilate's office.....a member of the Jewish leadership named Joseph of Arimathaea. He has come to request the body of Jesus so that he can bury it in his own tomb. He does this out of love and respect for the man in whom he has come to believe.

Notice in verse 38 that he had been a believer for some time, but secretly, because he feared the Jewish leadership would expel him from their group. But the death of Jesus has been so brutal, and so unfair, that he does not care to remain secret anymore. And, it surely won't be a secret after this! And he doesn't care.....he is going public with his faith in Jesus, no matter what the consequences.

He is not alone, either. He has a companion with him.....someone you may have heard of. It is Nicodemus, the Pharisee who had come to Jesus at night to ask Him some questions in John 3. Like Joseph, Nicodemus has been moved deeply by the crucifixion.....you might say it moved him from the night into the daylight, because all of the Jews would now know of his belief in Jesus, too.

Two men.....both Pharisees. Both too timid to go public with their faith.....until Jesus was cruelly put to death. That awful event spurred their courage and conviction, and they have been rewarded by having their faith and boldness recorded in the Bible for everyone to see. You'll get a chance to hear their story in Heaven. I can't wait to hear their account!!

Faith Profession: "Lord, give me boldness to step out of my "comfort zone" and become known as a follower of Jesus, and a witness of His love and truth."

Study Scriptures: John 3:1-12; Acts 4:13

DEVOTIONAL # 155

A Sepulcher in a Garden

Scripture: John 19:41

There is a garden near the place where Jesus was crucified…..a place of quiet beauty close to a place of killing, cruelty, blood, and death. And in this particular garden, there is a "sepulcher," which is the old English term for a tomb, or grave. This information is seemingly placed in verse 41 almost as an afterthought. Yet, I wonder if anything in the Word is accidental. A sepulcher in a garden may not be as unusual a thing as you might think. It seems contradictory, and yet…..

As I write, a famous golfer…..a billionaire actually…..with more sports talent than you can measure; lots of money; two healthy children; a beautiful, devoted wife; and what seemed to be a spotless reputation…..has confessed to an extra-marital affair that has ruined his reputation. It is a garden, to be sure, but a sepulcher has been found in it, and the garden will never be the same.

I'd been visiting homes on behalf of my church, only to hear violent arguing coming from inside one of the homes through an open window. The home was beautiful…..it was nicely landscaped…..it was clean and well-kept. But the people inside were nasty to each other…..a sepulcher in a garden.

Jesus knew about this kind of thing. A Pharisee looked to others like a pristine religious leader you'd want to look up to. But inside, they were so corrupt that they would plot to murder an innocent man…..and they did! Jesus exposed this "sepulcher in a garden" in Matthew 23…..and their reaction simply proved His point.

Not everything is as it seems. There are true gardens in this life, and some don't have sepulchers in them. It's my prayer that yours is like that.

Faith Profession: "What I look like on the outside is not always the real me. My goal is to be purified by the Word so that my "garden" is free of deadness."

Study Scripture: Matthew 23:1-39

Devotional # 156
Stunning Compassion

Scripture: John 20:11-18

It is very early on Sunday morning, three days and nights after the crucifixion. There is some commotion at the tomb where Jesus had been buried. Mary Magdalene is devastated. First, her beloved Jesus had been taken from her, and now somebody has taken His body. It is too much, and she begins to weep uncontrollably. Through her heaving sobs and vision blurred by tears, she can see the form of a man standing nearby. Supposing him to be the caretaker (verse 13), she asks him, through her sobs, to tell her where he has taken the body so that she can care for it.

It is not the caretaker (gardener). It is the risen Lord Jesus Christ. He says to her..... gently..... "Mary." She is stunned! She recognizes the voice instantly! It is JESUS!! She whirls around, looking at Him closely, and cries out in surprise and delight..... "Master!!" With that, she does what anyone would do.....she rushes toward Him to hug Him. She is ssoooooo happy!!!

Instantly, He says, "Stop! Touch me not! For I am not yet ascended to my Father." He has just come up from His victory over the devil, sin, death, and Hell. In fact, He is in the middle of His vital trip to Heaven to complete the Reconciliation by the sprinkling of His sinless blood on the mercy seat there. Because of this, He cannot be defiled by human touch…..at least until that task is completed.

It is the most important thing history has ever seen. Yet, He stops off in the garden on His way up to Heaven to comfort someone He loves. Do you see that? Can you believe that? Yes…..if you think about it…..it is just like Him to do that! Amazing!

Faith Profession: "How do I know that Jesus loves me deeply? Because of incidents like this. If He loves me half as much as He loved Mary, I am loved more that I could ever hope for."

Study Scriptures: Hebrews 9:1-14; 10:1-14; I John 4:8

BLIND FAITH

Scripture: John 20:19-29

We, as Christian believers, are often criticized for believing something we can't see and touch. There are many in the world whose thinking goes like this: if I can't see it, or I haven't experienced it, then it just isn't so.

As you can see from today's Scripture reading, that kind of thinking is not new. Thomas was that kind of person, and he had been with Jesus, and had seen some spectacular miracles. Apparently that isn't always enough.

So, the risen Jesus Christ appears.....alive and functional.....to several of the disciples after His resurrection, but Thomas is not present at the time (verse 24). When they tell Thomas what has happened, he refuses to believe them. "Unless I see it for myself," he says, "I will not believe."

Eight days later he gets his wish, so to speak. Jesus shows up in a closed room (verse 26), which is mentioned because He did not open a door to enter.....He just came through the wall. Among those present are Thomas; and Jesus knows what Thomas has said. Jesus immediately turns to him and offers to let him thrust his hand into His side. Implied is this thought: "Maybe then you'll believe." There is no mention of Thomas putting his hand into Jesus' side, but he sure is convinced now!

Jesus then says something that we should note: "Blessed are they that have not seen, and yet have believed." Yes, there are still "Thomases" among us. But, for you and me, it might be good to dwell on what our Lord said. Those who have believed without seeing WILL BE BLESSED. I don't know about you, but it has surely been the case for me in this life.....and it can only get better! If you have believed by faith alone.....EXPECT BLESSING!!

Faith Profession: "I believe that Jesus is risen from the dead, and that He is my Savior and Lord forever. I have not seen Him.....YET.....but I will!"

Study Scripture: Luke 24:36-49

Devotional # 158

Standing at a Fire

Scripture: John 21:1-13

It is a few weeks after the resurrection. All the disciples are relieved that Jesus has risen from the dead. One of them.....Simon Peter.....is still troubled. He had publically declared his allegiance to Jesus.....even to the death. But, only a short time later, he had denied his Lord in public. It was his greatest failure in life, and affected him so deeply that he had quit the ministry and gone back to commercial fishing.

That's where he is in verse 3, having worked all night, catching nothing. As daylight breaks, a man calls to them from shore.....then instructs them to let down their nets for a catch. They are reluctant (hey.....THEY are the professionals), but they do it.....and catch so many fish that their net begins to break! As they work, John suddenly recognizes the man on shore as Jesus (verse 7).

Peter is conflicted. He had hesitated to let down the net, but, once again, was startled at a miracle from His Lord. He comes to shore and walks up the sand to find that Jesus has started a fire to cook the fish. He walks up.....slowly and reluctantly.....and stands there looking into the flames. Jesus is standing there, too, looking at the same scene. Both men are acutely aware of what had happened the last time Peter was standing at a fire (see study Scriptures).

Peter, for once, is speechless. He is so ashamed.....so very aware of his failure.

But.....the Lord is there. He has come to Peter. He is not condemning him. And they eat in silence. (See tomorrow's lesson for the conclusion).

Faith Profession: "As long as I am in this flesh, it will tend toward sin. If I fail my Lord, I'll find.....as Peter did.....that He will come to me. I can count on that."

Study Scriptures: Luke 22:54-62; Luke 5:1-10

DEVOTIONAL # 159

LOVEST THOU ME?

Scripture: John 21:15-17

Peter has failed the person he most loved in the world. He is crushed, and has lost his will to preach. But, here on a seashore in Galilee, he has found that Jesus has come to him.

Of the many interpretations of verses 15-17, the one that makes me smile is the one where we're told that there are different Greek words used for the word "love" in this passage. The idea is that the Lord is getting Peter to confess deeper love each of the three times he asks, "Do you love me?" That's nice.....and it may even be true.....but it isn't the point at all.

Jesus has come to this seashore specifically to minister to Peter. He is not intending to challenge him with variations of the word "love." He is here to restore his disciple to service with an object lesson.

So, He asks Peter if he loves Him.....once.....twice.....three times. Each time, Peter speaks his love publicly. He SPEAKS it.....so HE hears it; the rest of the disciples hear it; and the unseen spiritual world around them hears it. Peter denied the Lord three times with his mouth.....now he has professed his deep love for Jesus three times. Each time, Jesus gives Peter some gentle direction: "Okay, feed my sheep."

Do you see? Our words are vitally important in the Kingdom of God. What we say DOES make a difference. Here in John 21, the Lord restores Peter to service, and renews his confidence. Jesus has come to Peter.....has had him profess his love enough times to cancel the denials.....and has quietly forgiven him in the process.

That's what Jesus does. That's how He loves. His mercy endureth forever. He is the God of second chances.

Faith Profession: "I love the Lord Jesus. He is a forgiving, merciful, and good God. He knows me, and understands my failures. He does not give up on me. He is the "lifter up of my head."

Study Scriptures: Psalm 3:3; Psalm 136

Devotional # 160
Infallible Proofs

Scripture: Acts 1:3

The resurrection of Jesus Christ is the single most important event that has ever happened on earth. No other leader of any other religion can truthfully make the claim of resurrection…..which is why following Jesus has to be right.

This resurrection is not a matter of speculation. Looking out into time, Jesus apparently realized that there would be many skeptics, so He showed Himself alive by many "infallible" proofs. The word "infallible" means "incapable of error"…..and that is just what is needed for an event this important.

What are these proofs? Well, here in verse 3, it indicates that He showed Himself alive to people for a period of forty days after the resurrection. The body that He showed up in still had the marks from the nails, and the wound from the spear piercing His side. The people who most wanted to prove that He did not rise from the dead…..the Romans….. were unable to do so. Instead, the guards were bribed to tell a lie about it, and that lie was spread around the community (see study Scriptures).

We also know that Jesus was seen by over 500 people in that forty-day period. I can think of no other historical event that has that many eyewitnesses testifying to its accuracy (see study Scriptures). Jesus gave up His life on the Cross, and died. That He was actually dead was witnessed by several Roman foot-soldiers, who were used to seeing death….. you didn't fool them by merely fainting. He battled the forces of darkness in a literal Hell, emerging victorious, and proving it by returning from the dead…..alive and well, but with all the marks of the crucifixion still on His body.

There is no doubt about it…..Jesus rose from the dead. He is alive. He conquered death. And He is the only one who ever has. Jesus is the One.

Faith Profession: "I place my faith in the only person who ever rose from the dead….. Jesus Christ. I trust Him for my salvation from sin's penalty, and receive it as a free gift."

Study Scriptures: Matthew 28:11-15; I Corinthians 15:1-8

THE PROMISE

Scripture: Acts 1:4

It is late in Jesus' time on earth. In fact, He is just minutes from His ascension. He gathers His devoted followers, and tells them to go to Jerusalem and wait for what He calls "the promise of the Father." THE promise.....not just any promise. There are hundreds, if not thousands of promises given in the Bible. But, here in Acts 1, Jesus designates one as THE promise.....because it is that important.

This promise has already been discussed….. "which ye have heard of me." Jesus has already told them some detail about it (see John 14 and John 16). He's referring to the new miracle that will forever define the New Testament church.....that supernatural phenomenon that will allow the Holy Spirit of God to permanently indwell each and every believer from then on. Nothing like this has ever happened. It is a gift so immense, and so vitally important, that its value cannot be measured. It is so important that Jesus refers to it twice in the final moments of His time on earth.....because that is what He wants to impress on His followers.

This promise is what gives unlimited power to every believer. This promise guarantees victory over the enemy of the followers of Christ, the devil. This promise gives each believer supernatural ability to release the power of God into earthly circumstances, causing them to change for the better. This promise is what enables believers to communicate with God in a language that He understands, but the forces of darkness don't.....making them unable to counteract what's being said.

This promise gives each believer the ability to lay hands on sick people, and see them get well. This promise gives each believer assurance of protection, and prosperity..... and authority over the powers of the devil and his followers. It is the foundation of the New Testament church. It is what makes the New Testament believer a new species of being.....a new creation.....different from anything ever seen before. It is THE PROMISE, and it is magnificent!!

Faith Profession: "Since Jesus emphasized the promise, it would be foolish if I did not do the same . I receive this rare privilege of having the indwelling Holy Spirit living within me. It makes all the difference in my life."

Study Scriptures: II Corinthians 5:17; John 16:7-15

DEVOTIONAL # 162
STILL A LITTLE CONFUSED

Scripture: Acts 1:6-8

Okay. The disciples have seen so many incredible things that their heads must be spinning. Their leader was crucified. Then He was alive. He appeared to them in a glorified body, and spent forty days with them, proving that He was resurrected. He has explained.....over and over.....that He was now going to leave, but that He would send the Holy Spirit to be with them permanently. He had told them that He would be coming back some day.

For the Jewish people of Jesus' days on earth, the thing they wanted most was to be free from the oppression of having a foreign army occupying their land. In this case, it was the Roman army. They wanted freedom from that, and expected their Messiah to release them from that bondage. So, here in Acts 1.....very, very late in the game.....they have still not gotten that idea out of their heads. They are still asking Him if He will restore the kingdom to Israel at this time.

It must have been a little frustrating for Jesus, but He didn't show it. He just says that it's not for them to know such things.....those are in the hands of the Father. In other words, "Forget about that and concentrate on what's really important here."

Then, in verse 8, He brings them back to focus on the miracle of the Holy Spirit's indwelling of them that is soon to come. Much has been made of the witnessing aspect of verse 8.....and it does tell us that we're to witness. But the vital thing is the receipt of POWER. It will be unlike anything they have ever experienced. It will make the difference in the world, and in the lives they touch. This power is the same power that was used to raise Jesus from the dead.....and now it will be the possession of every individual believer! It is too incredible to imagine! Can there be a better gift?! Can we doubt the depth of God's love for us?

It's the last thing Jesus mentions before He rises up into Heaven. The last thing.....it's that important.

Faith Profession: "I will place my focus on this amazing gift given to me by Jesus Himself. I have the Holy Spirit of God living inside me, and I have access to His power. It WILL make a difference in my life. How could it not?"

Study Scriptures: Ephesians 1:17-23; Acts 3:1-7

MY FATHER LOVES ME

Scripture: Psalm 112

When you read through this psalm, you are no doubt struck by the fact that so many of the things listed here <u>don't</u> apply to the modern-day person…..or the modern-day Christian.

David, the author of Psalm 112, is glorifying the Lord by listing all the benefits that are part of a relationship with Him. Why, then, is this list of benefits and blessings so rarely found among God's children?

I believe the answer lies in the widespread belief—that has <u>not</u> always been generally accepted—that God controls all events in a person's life…..that everything that happens is His will.

Many Christians…..<u>most</u> Christians…..will tell you that their sickness was sent (or allowed) by God to: punish them; give them opportunity to witness to some people; teach them some spiritual lesson; or another reason that they simply don't know. They chalk it up to God's way of doing things that we simply are too small, or unimportant, or incidental to understand. In this way, <u>all</u> life events are attributed to God…..good and bad….. and the way faith is shown is by tolerating it all, and trusting His "unknown ways."

But…..maybe we should re-read Psalm 112, verse 1. All of the benefits listed in the psalm come to the person who "delights greatly in His commandments" (or, we would say, His Word, the Bible).

What follows verse 1 is <u>dependent upon you</u>. <u>If</u> you will make the effort to study the Word, you will discover that the traditional, common view that God is the author of every event in your life is <u>FALSE</u>. If you study the Word, you'll get to know <u>Him</u>. As that happens, you'll see that He would <u>never</u> put sickness, poverty, etc. on those He loves. The devil is responsible for that type of thing…..of course!

Study the Word. Get to know your Dad. Notice His love, and His promises. And begin to see the benefits listed in Psalm 112:2-10 show up in <u>your</u> life.

Faith Profession: "My Heavenly Father loves me, and wants what is best for me. My part is to study His Word…..and I will do that daily!"

Study Scriptures: Matthew 8:17; James 4:7; Psalm 91

Devotional # 164
A Sword and a Song

Scripture: Psalm 149

The Bible has much to say about praise and worship, but sometimes we fail to pay attention to <u>why</u>. The Lord loves us…..and is trying to give us tools for victory in this life….. <u>that's</u> why.

So, here in Psalm 149, we're instructed to praise the Lord, and sing songs to Him. This causes the Lord to take pleasure in us (verse 4), and beautify us with salvation (in the Hebrew, it is the word "<u>wholeness</u>" – verse 4).

When are we to do this? Just when everything is going well? No…..verse 5 says to "sing aloud upon their beds." Those "beds" are more literally translated "beds of affliction." So, we're to praise Him in sickness <u>and</u> health…..in good times <u>and</u> bad.

Why? Because praise and worship <u>inflict</u> our spiritual enemy, and drive him away. Satan, you see, is <u>not</u> omnipresent. So, how does he choose where he operates? He looks for strife…..because he can't operate in the presence of God, or in the presence of people giving <u>praise</u> to God!

Look at verse 8. When you praise the Lord (even when you might not <u>feel</u> like it), you <u>bind</u> the enemy. It's kind of like why the armor of God works so well…..the devil can't tell who's in there…..you or Jesus….but he backs away just in case.

The Study Scriptures will guide you to more examples, but they just make the point more firmly. Praise and worship unleash God's blessing and power into our situation and life. At the same time, they drive the devil and his slimy followers back into the darkness they came from…..so you benefit both ways!

That song you sing is, in fact, a sword. That praise you freely give is a weapon. And it has <u>always</u> worked. Remember…..praise is the only thing you can give to God that He does not already have!

Faith Profession: "I will make a conscious effort to include praise and worship into my daily schedule. I will also give praise during times of trouble…..even though I may not feel like it. It will please my God, and frustrate my enemy!"

Study Scriptures: Psalm 50:23; Psalm 47:1-7; II Samuel 22; Exodus 17:8-16

DEVOTIONAL # 165
WISHING VS. HOPING

Scripture: Hebrews 11:1

You live among a large population of God's people who worship and speak of a God about whom they know very little. As a result, they believe that their problems.....sickness, lack of funds, relationship issues.....are part of what they believe is "His will" for their lives. I'd like you to consider, dear reader, a point of view that may give you a different attitude about Him.

You see, there's wishing, and there's hoping. Wishing is saying, "I believe God can heal." That's fine, but it isn't a belief as much as it is an opinion. It's general, and therefore unspecific.

If you really believe a thing, you'll be specific. You'll have an accurate picture of what you're praying for. And your prayer about it will reflect those specifics. Go ahead—don't be afraid! Get locked in on a promise He gave you in Scripture, and pray it. If you do, that will give you hope. Hope is more definite, and hope releases faith. (Our text verse says that faith is the substance of things hoped for.)

Hope is specific, and definite.....which is exactly how faith is. And the Lord responds to faith (Mark 11:23).

When I prayed for my wife, I wrote down what I wanted in a woman. I began with spiritual qualities.....I wanted her to be saved; completely trustworthy; and to love the Lord with all her heart. But I wrote down other qualities, too.....that she have a nice smile; love animals; be creative. I even specified her height and the color of her hair. In all, I gave the Lord 29 specifics.....and He provided someone who matches all 29 of them. She lives in my home with me as my wife as I write.....and will be with me always.

So, look at your life. What you have.....whatever it is, or is not.....is a direct result of what you believe (not what you have wished for). That belief spawned faith, and our Lord can work with that!

So, you believe.....and if you can believe, and dare to do so.....then the doing of it is up to the Lord. And He will do it!

Faith Profession: "I'm done wishing my life away. I'm going to start building hope by being specific with my prayer requests, because that will generate faith, and faith is the thing the Lord is looking for in me. My life will be different as I replace wishing with hope!"

Study Scripture: Mark 11:23; Psalm 118:6; Matthew 7:7

THE APOSTLE MATTHIAS

Scripture: Acts 1:15-26

Judas is dead.....the rest of the apostles and friends (120 in all) are meeting secretly, praying as they wait for THE PROMISE (see verse 4). As they wait, Peter brings up the need to replace Judas as an apostle, quoting Psalm 109:8 as his precedent.
Verses 21 and 22 then give us the qualifications for a person to be considered an apostle. Notice that: he had to have been with Jesus and the apostles all the time that Jesus was among them; and he needed to be a witness of the resurrection.

In this group, two men qualified.....Joseph called Barsabas, and Matthias. They pray (verse 24), then they cast lots (the Bible version of a vote.....same principle as today, but more directly guided by the Holy Spirit). In verse 26, it says that Matthias was chosen, and he was numbered with the eleven apostles.

The problem, if there is one, is that Matthias is never mentioned again. Does that make his selection invalid? Well, it was done with Scriptural precedent, which is good. They did it after prayer, which is also good. Yet, he is never mentioned again, which may not be good.

We tend to think that there were only 12 apostles.....just like we tend to think there were only 12 disciples. In truth, there are about seventeen people mentioned in the New Testament as being apostles.....and there were many more than 12 disciples following Jesus, even when He walked the earth. Some say that Paul should be considered to be the twelfth apostle, not Matthias.

I wish I had a definitive answer, but the Bible just doesn't give one, so we'll have to wait until we get to Heaven to get the answer for sure. Matthias, though, was validly elected, and qualified to be an apostle. Though he wasn't the only one called an apostle after Acts 1, I believe it's safe to count him as one.

Faith Profession: "I am definite about anything that Bible is definite about. With other things, I am content to get my answer in Heaven rather than argue the point here in this life. The Lord knows, and He will let me know, too."

Study Scriptures: Acts 14:14; Romans 16:7

Devotional # 167
The Death of Judas

Scripture: Acts 1:16-18

Judas Iscariot was not right from the beginning, and Jesus knew it all along (see study Scriptures). So, it was no surprise to Him when Judas left the Last Supper to go out to the Pharisees and make the deal to betray Jesus for thirty pieces of silver (the Old Testament price for a female slave.....a further insult to Jesus).

Judas.....moved by the dark spirits that he allowed to control him.....leads the arresting soldiers into the Garden of Gethsemane, and identifies Jesus with a kiss (the "kiss of death".....not all kisses are sincere, as you may know).

When Jesus is actually taken to Pilate and condemned to death, Judas scrambles into reverse and "repents himself" (see Matthew 27:3—not true repentance). He tries to give back the paltry amount of silver he had received for the betrayal.....and, when he sees that he can't undo it, goes out and hangs himself (Matthew 27:5). The Pharisees, of course, have no more concern for Judas than they have for Jesus. However, in Acts 1:16-18, it says that Judas died by falling headlong, bursting asunder in the midst. So, what do we have here? A contradiction? Some would say so.

But, a simple comparison of Scripture with Scripture will give the answer (as always). Judas did hang himself as recorded in Matthew 27. Shortly afterward, there is a violent earthquake during the crucifixion (Matthew 27:50-51). The place where Judas hanged himself is very near a high ledge. The earthquake caused his already dead body to fall violently to the ground below, and the impact burst the body, spilling his bowels out (sorry for how graphic that is.....it's Bible).

Both accounts are true. There is no contradiction. The Bible always gives the absolute truth.....and you can stake your eternal life on that.

Faith Profession: "The Word of God is true. Apparent contradictions are just that..... apparent. Some simple Bible study always dispels so-called contradictions."

Study Scriptures: John 12:4-6; John 6:70-71

Devotional # 168
Scary Stuff!!

Scripture: Acts 2:1-4

Oh, no!! Not that!! Not tongues!!! You know, people can believe almost anything in the Bible except for this. I've been taught, in both Bible school and Seminary, that tongues were of the devil. That's a fairly common teaching in traditional circles.....maybe you've been taught that way. But, do me a favor, will you? Take a few deep breaths, and let's just look at what it says.....okay? There can't be any harm in that.

Look at verse 4. Can it get any plainer? They spoke with other tongues, "AS THE SPIRIT GAVE THEM UTTERANCE." Do you see that? Tongues were the result of the action of the Holy Spirit of God.....NOT the devil. Tongues are one of the gifts given to believers.....something new.....as a result of being filled with the Holy Spirit. It is not something to fear.....it is from a member of the Trinity.

Plus, you are told in John 16:13 that the Holy Spirit will guide you into ALL TRUTH. So, if the Holy Spirit is giving tongues, then it is TRUTH.....from Heaven. How did Christians come to fear and despise a holy ministry sent by the Lord to aid His people?? There can be only one answer.....our enemy the devil fears this gift, and has worked overtime to cast dirt on it, deceiving believers into thinking of it as something evil. That is the opposite of the truth, and is characteristic of the devil (John 8:44).

Hey.....haven't you gotten tuned in to satan's ways by now? Don't you recognize deception when you see or hear it? Can you read Acts 1:4? That settles the matter, and it's your job to change your thinking to get in line with the Word (instead of furthering the devil's deception on this matter). Hard? Yes, it's hard to admit that you've been wrong.....that you've been working against a ministry sent by God. He forgives you. He understands peer pressure. But you are His child, and can stand on your own. Make the Word your final authority. Tongues are holy.

Faith Profession: "I repent of my thinking contrary to the Word. I see that tongues is a ministry of the Holy Spirit, and was sent to help us as believers."

Study Scriptures: Mark 16:17-18; I Corinthians 14:39

KNOWN LANGUAGES

Scripture: Acts 2:4-11

Those who fight against the gift of tongues are fond of pointing out that, in Acts 2, the tongues turned out to be languages known by those hearing the tongues. They apparently think this makes some point against speaking in tongues, since many instances of tongues occur in unknown languages.

It's true that they spoke known languages here in Acts 2. It says so right in the passage— verses 7-11. The people SPEAKING did not know the languages (which made them unknown tongues to them), but the hearers recognized what they heard.....and it came out in many different languages. What is the Holy Spirit doing here? He's using tongues to capture the attention of the crowd. Once that happens, Peter preaches to them, and whole bunches of them get saved (verse 41).

So, they say.....if tongues aren't recognizable by somebody in the crowd, then they're not from the Lord. Oh, yeah? Where did you get that? Don't you know that the Holy Spirit is compared to liquids.....water, fountains, wells, streams, rivers? He is not held to one or two methods of operation.....He adapts to the situation. Here in Acts 2, it is known languages.....because that's what works here. In other places, it is languages known to nobody. The unusual nature of the occurrence is sufficient to draw a crowd, or capture somebody's interest. Tongues are a gift.....a tool that can be used to spread the Gospel. It is called a "wonder" because that's what it does.....it makes people wonder what is happening, and draws them in.

But the Holy Spirit is not held to patterns, or man-made boxes. He doesn't operate by rigid rules, even though traditional Christians prefer that. No.....He is free to operate in whatever way is best for the given situation. He is "liquid," you might say. Why? Because that is the best way to be.....if He's adaptable, he can fit any situation or any person's needs.

So, chill out, as they used to say. Relax. Don't get all frustrated trying to put the Holy Spirit in the box you made for Him. He'd leak out through the seams anyway.

Faith Profession: "The Holy Spirit adapts Himself to any situation. I'm glad that's true, because that method will reach many more people for Christ."

Study Scriptures: John 7:38; Revelation 21:6

Devotional # 170

Wholeness

Scripture: Acts 4:5-12

In Acts 3, Peter and John were part of the healing of a lame man who had sat begging at one of the gates to the temple. When a crowd had gathered to marvel at this event, Peter preached the Gospel to them (another example of the Holy Spirit's gifts being used to spread the Gospel). In response, the priests and Sadducees (verse 1) had them arrested.

The next day, Peter and John were put on trial in front of Annas and Caiaphas (the same characters who had put Jesus to death). The officials demand to know by what power this lame man was healed. Notice: they have no gladness at the miracle.....they are distressed, and want it stopped. Peter boldly declares that the man was healed by Jesus, and points out that they had crucified Him.

Notice with me, though, something interesting in this passage besides the boldness. In verse 9, Peter mentions that the man was made whole. In verse 12, the last word is "saved." The connection is that they are both the same word in the original language..... even though they are translated differently here.

What do we learn from that? We learn that salvation means "wholeness." Wholeness is not just a healing thing.....it is a salvation thing. That means that, when you receive Jesus Christ as your Savior, you not only receive eternal life, but WHOLENESS. This wholeness includes eternal life, but also includes healing and health; protection; prosperity; authority; peace; joy; and all the other fruit mentioned in Galatians 5.

At salvation, you are made WHOLE.....in every respect. You are not who you used to be. You are a new creature.....a totally unique creation on the earth. You have been made WHOLE.....COMPLETE.....and Jesus never does anything partway.

Faith Profession: "My salvation has made me whole. I own every promise the Lord has given in His Word. I am what He says I am.....I have what He says I have."

Study Scripture: Galatians 5:22-23

DEVOTIONAL # 171

BOLDNESS

Scripture: Acts 4:13

It is true that the outstanding characteristic of Jesus Christ is love. We are to show the love of Christ to the world around us. That is why we have been left on earth after salvation.

But the outstanding characteristic of the earthbound Christian is revealed in today's verse. It isn't love.....at least not in the sense that you usually recognize it. It isn't compassion, though that surely is needed in our world. It certainly isn't tolerance.....especially the kind that has become prominent today.

Look at the verse. The religious leaders could easily see that Peter and John were not college men, but uneducated fishermen. Yet the leaders had been stopped in their tracks in their attempts to intimidate or confuse Peter and John. What they noticed most about them was their BOLDNESS. They refused to back down.....they spoke with authority..... they made perfect sense.....they were not radical lunatics.....and they had the proof of what they said standing beside them (verse 14).

Notice that it says that, when they saw the boldness in these men, they took knowledge of the fact that they had been with Jesus. That is, they recognized the same traits in these fishermen that they had experienced with Jesus Himself. They were bold; they were right; they did miracles; people noticed what they did. And, it didn't look good for the religious leaders to be opposed to miracles that so obviously came from God.

So many Christians sit quietly on the sidelines, leaving the heavy work for pastors, teachers, and those who they think are "more spiritual." No.....if you are a saved, blood-bought child of God, people should notice your BOLDNESS. You are shy, you say? You don't know what to say? Okay.....are you saved? Do you have the Holy Spirit within you? Then boldness should seep out of you despite your unwillingness to use it. It's something that we just can't help.....it's in us from Him.

Faith Profession: "I am bold in my witness for my Savior. I believe His Word, and defend it as opportunity presents itself."

Study Scriptures: Philippians 1:20; II Corinthians 7:4

DEVOTIONAL # 172

MANY BELIEVED

Scripture: Acts 4:4

Have you noticed in your reading of the Bible that huge numbers of people came to know Jesus as their Savior early in the book of Acts? In today's Scripture, it is about 5,000 people. In Acts 2:41, it is about 3,000. That's pretty impressive, no matter who you are.

I don't know about you, but I've never seen that many people come to know Jesus at one time. It must be staggering to see. I've seen a person or two respond to an invitation for salvation. I have led about thirty to the Lord at a time in Africa. I hear of large numbers of people getting saved overseas, but rarely, if ever, in America.

I wonder why that is? We have the same God that they did in Acts. We have the same Holy Spirit, who has the same power now as then. I have noticed that these large numbers of salvations were connected to the gifts given through the Holy Spirit. Did you notice that? Tongues were spoken in Acts 2.....people gathered as a result.....the Word was preached.....3,000 got saved. In Acts 3, it was a miracle healing that drew the crowd. The Word was preached.....5,000 were saved. These days in America, we tend to downplay the gifts of the Spirit. Many Christians don't believe in them at all.....or believe that they are from the devil. (Guess where that came from?)

So, there is an absence of teaching, and therefore belief in, the gifts of the Spirit. Simultaneously, there are very few instances of crowds of people getting saved. Doesn't that make you wonder if there isn't a connection? We have been deceived into believing that these supernatural, wonderful, potent miracles from the Holy Spirit of God are not for today.....are devilish.....are to be avoided.....are for those "Pentecostal nuts." Yes, everything except what is taught in the Bible. They are from HEAVEN. They WORK. People get saved when they are used. What else do you need to know?

Faith Profession: "The Bible.....God's Word.....is my final authority. I look to IT as my source of wisdom. Sign gifts are from the Lord, and they result in salvation."

Study Scriptures: Acts 2:40-47; Acts 3:1-12

Devotional # 173
Our Response to Threats

Scripture: Acts 4:29-30

Well, there's been lots of action since Acts 2. The local church is flourishing; the sign gifts are working (and not being inhibited by unbelief); and souls are being saved by the thousands. Naturally, the devil is not pleased. Naturally, he retaliates. In Acts 4, Peter and John are placed on trial by the religious leaders (!) because of the healing of the lame man. In verse 18, Peter and John are threatened, even though the religious leaders decide that, due to public opinion, they can't do what they would like to do.

Upon their release, Peter and John gather with their fellow believers (verse 23) and tell them all that has happened. The response is immediate prayer by the whole group (verse 24). They don't make plans to go into hiding. They don't ask revenge on their accusers. Instead, they utter verses 29 and 30. In response to the threats, they ask the Lord for BOLDNESS TO SPEAK THE WORD.....and that more signs and wonders (which is what the indwelling Holy Spirit is about) be done in Jesus' name. (Notice.....the signs and wonders are in JESUS' name.....not from the devil.)

This is the proper response to threats, dear reader. No revenge.....no thought of getting even. Just more power.....more supernatural signs and wonders.....which will result in more salvation decisions.....and more glory to God. The Lord's response? See verse 31. The place is physically shaken.....they are filled with the Holy Ghost.....and their request for boldness is immediately granted. In verse 33, we see that they had great witnessing power, and great grace was upon them, plus they prospered in earthly needs (verse 34).

Don't worry about threats. I was told once, by the head of a Christian Bible school, that I would never preach the Gospel even one time.....because he disagreed with me for false reasons. I asked the Lord to intervene and, as I write, it is 29 years later and I have preached the Gospel.....in person or on the radio..... EVERY SUNDAY since he made that statement.....every Sunday for 29 years. Just ignore the threats.....ask for power, boldness, signs, and wonders.....and you'll see your own world shaken for Christ!

Faith Profession: "I will not be intimidated by threats. God hath not given me the spirit of fear, but of power, love, and a sound mind. I will preach the Word with boldness, to the glory of my Savior, Jesus Christ"

Study Scriptures: II Timothy 1:7; Acts 16:23-26

DEVOTIONAL # 174
THE FOUNDATIONAL ISSUE

Scripture: Acts 4:15-18

If there ever was any doubt about what the religious leaders fear.....or what causes the most violent reaction in the world, today's verses clear it up once and for all.

If you want to "get by" with today's Pharisees.....if you want acceptance by your local ministerium.....if you want the devil to treat you like a nuisance instead of a real warrior..... just avoid today's issue. It's easy to do.....many Christians do it unconsciously.

In Acts 4, as we've seen, two of the disciples have been brought to trial by the religious leaders over the healing of a lame man outside the temple. The leaders are outraged by this event. They aren't interested in looking into it. They aren't concerned that the healing was miraculous. They don't show any joy over the lame man's sudden recovery. They want to know who gives two uneducated fishermen authority to do things like this (verse 7).

They admit, when they confer among themselves, that it is a notable miracle. But they want this kind of thing stopped (and you wonder why), so they decree verses 17 and 18. Their decision? Peter and John were told to stop speaking or teaching in the name of Jesus (verse 18).

And there it is. We have found the problem (as far as the religious people are concerned). The issue.....the foundational issue.....is the name of Jesus. If you check the study Scriptures today, you'll see why His name is such a big deal. These religious leaders in Acts 4 didn't even have the book of Philippians for reference (it hadn't been written yet), but they were reacting to the truth of the authority and power of the name of Jesus anyway.

THAT'S what presses their button. THAT'S what gets them agitated. They know to react to this name because they are of their father the devil (see study Scriptures again). When you listen to church people, try to pick up on how they refer to their Savior. If they use general terms, like "God" or "the man upstairs," they are telling you something about themselves.....they don't know Jesus personally, or at least don't have a close relationship with Him. To us who know Him well, it is JESUS, the Name above all names. That's where we get our authority!

Faith Profession: "I serve my Lord Jesus Christ. He is God, but He is also my personal friend, and I call Him by His more personal Name.....Jesus."

Study Scriptures: Philippians 2:9-11; John 8:44

PAUL'S EYESIGHT

Scripture: Acts 9:1-18

Nobody else in the Scriptures got saved quite the same way the Apostle Paul did. His was a unique experience, so don't be expecting your salvation to be like his.

He is rounding up Christian believers for imprisonment, thinking he's serving God. He is stopped in his tracks by the Lord Himself, who gets his attention by blinding him totally. It's not lost on Paul.....he "gets it" quickly (see verse 6).

When Paul gets off the ground, his eyes are open, but he can see nothing. They have to lead him by the hand into the city. He sits in this unexpected darkness for three days. Then, the Lord instructs a man named Ananias to go and minister to Paul (who still goes by his old name of Saul at this point). Ananias is no fool, and has heard about this man persecuting true believers. Nevertheless, being assured by the Lord, he obediently goes to find Paul. This obedient servant of the Most High God follows His instructions.

In verse 17, Ananias enters the house.....finds Saul praying.....and lays his hands on him. (Please stop and notice that. Some today make fun of that practice, but it is Biblical. Here, it is done in obedience to the Lord. Perhaps you should be looking into it instead of laughing at it.) And, Paul miraculously has his sight restored. Two verses later, Paul is preaching the Gospel publically.

Some say, based upon their interpretation of Galatians 6:1, that Paul suffered with bad eyesight. This, they say, is what he was praying about in II Corinthians 12:7-9. They go on to interpret the book of Job in such a way as to justify their interpretations. But let me ask you something.....if Paul had any physical problems as he aged, what makes you think bad eyesight would be one of them? It doesn't say that in II Corinthians 12. If Paul wrote with big letters, don't you think it was because his READERS had problems seeing? Paul's eyesight was healed by the Lord Himself. I have not known Him to do shoddy work.

No.....Paul's eyesight was perfect until the day he died.....and the interpretations of Scripture built around that erroneous teaching are themselves erroneous. Know your Lord..... it will save you some error.

Faith Profession: "I choose not to read anything into Scripture, or to blindly accept standard teachings as truth without checking them out.....Scripture with Scripture. That way, I'll avoid misinterpreting the Word."

Study Scriptures: Joshua 23:13; Numbers 33:55

Devotional # 176
A Miracle at Cornelius's House

Scripture: Acts 10:34-46

The miracle repeats itself. The Holy Spirit once again IS moving in the lives of people through the miracle of speaking in tongues. Sometimes God repeats things to impress their vital importance on us. That's how we learn.....by repetition. If we see something enough times, we'll eventually get the point.

So, Peter has been called to the home of a Roman centurion named Cornelius by the Lord. Peter is very much aware that this man is a Gentile, and that, when he traveled with Jesus, they ministered only to Israelites. Nevertheless, a vision has been given to him (Acts 10), plainly telling him to go to Cornelius.

Once he arrives, Peter begins to preach the same Gospel he had preached in Acts 2 to a Jewish audience. This time, though, just as he is getting near his conclusion, the Holy Spirit interrupts the service (see verse 44). The last thing Peter has said was, "Whosoever believeth in Him shall receive remission of sins" (verse 43). Immediately, the Holy Spirit is poured out on the Gentile listeners, and they begin to speak in tongues as evidence of it. The Jews who had come with Peter were astonished at this event.....because the Holy Spirit had not been given to Gentiles up to now. But.....they are convinced when the Gentiles begin to manifest the supernatural gift given only by the Holy Spirit. Peter was learning as he went along. He always followed the leading of the Lord, and was blessed as a result.

Notice, too, that, as the people speak in tongues, they MAGNIFY GOD (verse 46). So, it is NOT something from the devil. A pattern has been set here. In Acts 2, they got into repentance for crucifying the Lord before they received the Holy Spirit. Here.....with Gentiles.....the Holy Spirit appears as soon as they believe. And this is the pattern ever since. A person is saved by believing in his/her heart, and confessing with the mouth (see study Scriptures). Immediately afterward, the Holy Spirit indwells them.

Faith Profession: "I see that the Lord is instructing the apostles through the early part of the Book of Acts, and that the pattern set here in Acts 10 is the prevailing pattern for New Testament believers and witnesses."

Study Scripture: Romans 10:9-10,13

ANTIOCH

Scripture: Acts 11:25-26

The persecution that broke out against the church had begun to spread believers out from Jerusalem. Early on in the Book of Acts, all the activity was in Jerusalem. But, the Lord had decreed Acts 1:8, and it wasn't going to happen if they didn't move. The persecution.....led by Saul for a time.....was from the devil, but it did get the believers mobile.

And one important place they went was a town called Antioch in Syria. A church had formed there, and it was a good one. As you read the book of Acts, you'll see that Paul's missionary journeys began from Antioch. It became the most important center for believers for a long time.

So great was the power of the church there that it has a unique distinction: the disciples (all followers of Jesus Christ, not just the original eleven) were called Christians for the first time here.....in Antioch.....NOT Jerusalem.

Christian: a follower of Christ.....people known for their relationship with Jesus Christ. That's a good name to have! Did you know that "Christ" is a title, not a name? It means "anointed one".....anointed by the Holy Spirit. Jesus Christ is THE anointed one. But, if you are a Christian, you have become one with Him.....part of His body. What, then, does that make you? It makes YOU an "anointed one," too!

To be called a Christian is a privilege! It is a meaningful, special title. It means that we are not only followers of THE Christ, but we are anointed as well! Amen! Wear this title well. Be blessed to be called a Christian.....it is the people of the world giving you a title of distinction.....even if they don't realize it!

Faith Profession: "To be called a Christian is a compliment. It identifies me as a follower of Jesus Christ, and an "anointed one." I am one with THE anointed one."

Study Scriptures: Acts 1:8; Acts 13:1-3

DEVOTIONAL # 178

RHODA

Scripture: Acts 12:1-16

The persecution has begun. Although Saul (Paul) is no longer leading it, others have taken up the activity.....including the wretched Roman ruler, Herod. After killing James (Zebedee, brother of John), he puts Peter in prison.

Immediately the believers gather for prayer (verse 12), and they continue hour after hour. Meanwhile, their prayer is being answered. An angel shows up in Peter's cell. He causes the chains to fall off Peter's hands.....all the while not waking the two soldiers sleeping right beside Peter (verse 6). (Did you notice that Peter was fast asleep just hours before he was supposed to be executed? That's confidence in the Lord, brother. Peter wasn't afraid to die.....he knew where he was going. Do you?)

Anyway, the angel leads Peter out of the prison.....doors opening as they approached (verse 10). For a while, Peter isn't sure whether he's dreaming or not, but finally realizes that this thing is real (verse 11). He heads for the prayer meeting. Now, when he gets there, he politely knocks on the door. A believer named Rhoda comes in response. When she hears Peter's voice, she leaves him standing outside.....and in her excitement just runs back to the meeting with the wonderful news.

Their response is interesting.....they don't believe her. Here is a group of believers praying that a miracle will happen, and, when it does, they don't believe it!! (Don't be too hard on them.....you and I have been guilty of selling the Lord short a time or two.) Finally, they go to the door themselves.....and there Peter is! It says that they were astonished.....but they shouldn't have been. We serve a Lord who answers prayer. If we get into agreement with a Scriptural promise when we pray, we will see lots more answered prayer. Every answered prayer is a miracle.....no less than this one in Acts 12. We serve a GOOD LORD!

Faith Profession: "I will pray more expectantly, knowing that my Lord desires to answer my prayers. And I can increase the occurrence of answers if I pray in agreement with a promise I find in the Scriptures."

Study Scriptures: James 5:16; Matthew 18:19

DEVOTIONAL # 179
YOU REAP WHAT YOU SOW

Scripture: Acts 12:18-24

Herod the Great was the Roman ruler of the part of Israel that contained Jerusalem.....
that's why you find him mentioned so often in the Bible accounts about Jesus. You might
recall that he was the one who deceived the Magi in Matthew 2, telling them that he wanted to know the location of the Christ child so he could worship Him, when all the while
he intended to kill Him (see study Scriptures). His son was the one who, in response to a
drunken promise made to an exotic dancer, had John the Baptist beheaded.

Here in Acts 12.....after Calvary.....after the resurrection.....after several miracles done by
the disciples.....his grandson is still at it.....persecuting Christians instead of joining them.
His attempt to have Peter put to death is foiled by an angel, who frees Peter in answer
to the fervent prayer of believers. Herod had already killed James, the brother of John,
with a sword. Then he relished the fact that this murderous act pleased the religious Jews
(verse 3).

Now, Herod (Agrippa) dresses in royal apparel (he had ego, too), and delivers a speech to
the people. They are so taken by this pomp and ceremony that they publically declare that
Herod is not a man, but a god (verse 22). (People tend to get hysterical like this over mere
men, and flowery speeches.....but not over God Himself appearing to them. Go figure.)

It is insult added to much injury. The speech is barely over before Herod is smitten
with a terrible disease, and dies after being eaten by worms (ugh!). You think God is too
harsh.....too brutal? How about the innocent lives.....including the Lord Himself.....that
this man and his relatives snuffed out? How about the unmitigated gall of permitting
people to declare you a god, when you know very well that you are just a man.....and not
a very good one at that?

No, dear reader, the Lord is not harsh. If He was, Herod would have been blown away
long before this. But it is true that you reap what you sow (see study Scriptures). Want to
kill people for no reason other than political gain? Expect the same for yourself. It is a
law of life.....no less than the law of gravity.....and maybe more, because it is a spiritual law.

Faith Profession: "The Word of God is true, and that includes all spiritual laws found
in it. You reap what you sow.....and I intend to reap righteousness and glory to my Lord."

Study Scriptures: Galatians 6:7; Matthew 2:1-16

DEVOTIONAL # 180
PEOPLE OF THE WORD

Scripture: Acts 17:10-12

I was listening to some well-meaning people recently. They were discussing Heaven..... and their conclusion was that your choice of church wasn't important, but what was important was that you exercised faith. Actually, that's right.....as far as it goes. But it doesn't go very far. Faith is right, but you need to know what you're putting your faith in. If the object of your faith isn't the finished work of Jesus Christ on the Cross, that faith will not get you to Heaven.

The reason why there is such confusion about heavenly issues is a lack of practicing something mentioned in today's Scripture reading. When Paul and Silas preached at Berea, the people there received the Word.....but they took one more step, which is critical.....and it is found in verse 11. They searched the Scriptures to determine whether or not the things that were preached were so.

Think about that a minute. The preacher was the apostle Paul! They gladly received what he said, but they did not see Paul as the final authority.....they checked out what he said against the Word. And that is what is missing in modern Christianity. We have faith, all right.....that's not the problem. What we fail to do is check what we're being told against the Scriptures.

There are lots of teachings floating around that have nothing to do with the Bible. If you're naive enough.....and foolish enough.....to accept things without checking them against the Book, then you're likely to be led astray. For example, you need to check on me. I'm just a man.....I'm trying to teach truth here, but I'm not the final authority. And if what I write is not consistent with the Scriptures, then just dismiss it as my opinion. The point is.....you need to check. The Bible is God's Word, and therefore the final authority.....not some man or woman.

Take a hint from the believers at Berea, who didn't blindly accept the teachings of even the apostle Paul.....because Paul wasn't the final authority, either. And he'd be the first to tell you that. Search the Scriptures to see whether these things are so.

Faith Profession: "I am a person of the Word. I eagerly listen to the Word being preached and taught, but I always check what I hear against the Word."

Study Scriptures: II Timothy 2:15 and 3:16

DEVOTIONAL # 181

TO THE UNKNOWN GOD

Scripture: Acts 17:22-23

Almost 2,000 years ago, Paul and Silas spent some time in Athens, Greece. While there, Paul visited a place called Mars Hill.....where local scholars often met to debate issues. Paul skillfully uses an inscription he saw on an altar as a steppingstone to preach the Gospel. That inscription is found in capital letters in verse 23 of today's reading. The Athenians spent time debating about gods that they didn't know. They certainly didn't know the true God, or His Son, Jesus Christ.

That was 2,000 years ago.....yet, today.....as you read this page.....that inscription could accurately be placed on most church doors in America. Did you know that one reason the religious leaders in Israel failed to recognize their Messiah when He was standing in front of them was that they had developed a picture of God as a hard man.....a being of justice.....a being to be feared.....a harsh dispenser of punishment. But when Jesus came, He talked of God as His Father. He told of the Father's love and care for His people. He revealed the Father as a Daddy..... one who delights in His children.....one who desires His children's friendship and fellowship.

So, Jesus came to earth and showed us what the Father is really like.....He is just like Jesus. Yet, despite the New Testament.....despite the indwelling Holy Spirit.....despite the completed Word of God.....Christians continue to fear God, and shrink from His Almighty justice. Like the Scribes and Pharisees of Jesus' day, they've never seen the love side of the Father that Jesus came to reveal.

Do you know Him? Do you understand that He is GOOD.....all the time.....and that He could never send evil upon you, or conspire with the devil to allow him to do it? If you think that God sends or allows sickness to accomplish some good in a person's life, then you've misunderstood Him. To you, He remains the UNKNOWN GOD. Sadly, you've progressed no further than the unsaved scholars of Mars Hill in Athens. The Father revealed Himself through Jesus. Look at Him.....study Him.....spend time with Him. Get to know Him.

Faith Profession: "My Father in Heaven is a generous, good, giving, merciful, forgiving friend, who cares for me like nobody else ever could. He loves me."

Study Scripture: John 14:6-9

Devotional # 182

APOLLOS

Scripture: Acts 18:24-28

Today's Scripture reading introduces us to one of my favorite Bible characters—Apollos. He isn't mentioned much, but he has a quality that is both rare and vital for the child of God.....he is teachable.

Notice that, when Aquila and Priscilla first encounter him, he is already preaching boldly, and is said to be an eloquent man, and mighty in the Scriptures. Amen! A man of the Word! A man of conviction, who draws his authority from the Book.

The problem was, he was preaching incomplete truth. Notice verse 25: Apollos knew only of the baptism of John. He was unaware of Jesus, Calvary, the resurrection. So, he was a mighty man of God.....the Scriptures are his authority.....he is a wonderful speaker.....but his knowledge is incomplete.

Aquila and Priscilla do something both important and difficult. They take Apollos aside and tell him the rest of the story.....all about Jesus. This places Apollos at a crossroads. It is a vitally important place in his life. He is the mighty orator. He is the man of the Word. To believe what he hears from Aquila and Priscilla, he must publically admit that he has been wrong in his preaching.....or at least that he didn't have the whole story.

A man's pride will often not let him make that admission. But this is the test for Apollos. Is he a Bible believer, or does he just say that? Because, if the Bible IS his final authority, and what he is being told by these two strangers is true, then he'll have to make some big changes.

As it turns out, he IS a man of integrity and IS a true Bible believer. He checks out what he is told, and finds it to be consistent with Scripture. Immediately, he changes his preaching to reflect this further revelation of truth, and goes on preaching mightily (verse 28). He is a rare individual. He is not full of himself. For him, the Word is the authority, and he changes to conform to IT. Amen!

Faith Profession: "I pray that I might be found to be as solid a Bible believer as Apollos. If what I think is different than what the Word teaches, then I MUST CHANGE."

Study Scriptures: Acts 9:1-6; John 17:17

Devotional # 183
Complete Knowledge

Scripture: Colossians 1:9

Before Jesus had completed the most important work in history.....during the three days between Calvary and the resurrection.....He attempted to prepare His followers for the fact that He would be going back to Heaven. In John 14, He tells them.....and us.....of the plan to have the Holy Spirit indwell each and every believer. In John 14:26, He mentions that the Holy Spirit will teach them ALL things, and bring ALL things to their remembrance.

Today, we are in Colossians 1. In verse 9, we find a companion verse to John 14:26. Notice that the prayer is that they might "be filled with the knowledge of His will..." Let's stop for a second and dwell on that word "knowledge." When we look at it in the original Greek in which your New Testament was written, we find that it is translated "complete knowledge." COMPLETE knowledge of His will. That is what you have because of the presence of the Holy Spirit within you.

Yet, most Christians act like, and pray like they have no idea what God's will is, or how to find it. Why? Because they have been taught poorly.....or, more precisely.....what they have been taught is incomplete. Most Christians..... blood-bought, born-again children of God.....think that God keeps them in the dark about His will. Well, they ARE in the dark, but that isn't what the Lord intended. In fact, today's verse plainly tells us that the Holy Spirit is trying to give us complete knowledge of God's will.

Is it possible that it is US.....Christians.....who aren't listening.....aren't hearing enough of the truth of the Word.....aren't studying the Word enough on our own?? Well, it isn't that God is hiding His will from us. Obviously, He sent the Holy Spirit to see to it that we have all we need. You SHOULDN'T be in the dark. If you are, maybe you need to spend some time listening to the Spirit, and studying the Word, because both are trying to reach you.

Faith Profession: "Complete knowledge of God's will is well within the realm of possibility for me. The Word says He wants me to have it. I will study the Word as much as necessary to receive that."

Study Scripture: John 14:16-27

DEVOTIONAL # 184
WHEN THE CHURCH BEGAN

Scripture: Revelation 1:5

Yes.....I know.....you've been taught that the church began in Acts 2 with the arrival of the indwelling Holy Spirit. I was taught the same thing, and I always accepted it as fact. The problem is, I never seriously looked into it.....until today. If you'd think about it, you might be surprised at how many Bible things you have just accepted as being so without personally checking them.

Revelation 1:5 tells us that Jesus was the first person ever born again. That's what "first begotten of the dead" means. He died spiritually (meaning that He was spiritually separated from the Father); descended into Hell; got victory over death, Hell, satan, sin, and the grave through faith in God's Word; and rose victorious.....forever free from all five of the things just mentioned. Those who appeared at His tomb after the three days were convinced that He was alive.....they believed. They believed on Him, and trusted Him with their eternity, so they were saved. If the church consists of all people who were ever born again, then it includes those who believed prior to Acts 2.....and that number includes more than just the apostles.

The indwelling Holy Spirit appeared for the first time in Acts 2, but He appeared to the existing church. When He did, they received the promise Jesus had given them.....the gift of the Holy Spirit.....and they immediately began to speak with other tongues. It is one of the gifts given by the Holy Spirit to the church. It was a valuable tool for the early church, and it is a sad fact that today's church is so leery of something given to it by God Himself.

It's not something that I'd want to argue with you about.....in the Kingdom of God, you are free to believe whatever you choose to believe.....even if it's not given to you by Him. But the church's first member was Jesus Himself, and the resurrection marks the beginning of it.

Faith Profession: "I am a Bible believer. If the Word says something different than I have been taught, I change my thinking to conform to the Word."

Study Scriptures: John 20:19-22, 26-29

A PRAYER FOR THE LOST

Scripture: Acts 26:18

All of us know people who are lost. They don't know Jesus as their Savior, but are not interested in your attempts to witness to them, either. So, we pray for them. But, let me ask you.....what exactly do you pray?

Some ask Jesus to save these precious souls. Okay, but that request is an insinuation that He does not want to save them, or that He has to be begged to do so. Plus, it is against Scripture, since the Word plainly tells us that He DOES want them saved (see study Scriptures). Some pray that the lost person would be made to choose salvation. This, too, is against Scripture. The Lord has obviously given every human free will. (It is vital for the love principle to be valid, and He never goes against that. If He did, the devil would jump on it, and salvation would be made invalid).

So, what should we do?? Well, maybe we should consider praying things that God can and will do.....that are consistent with His Word, and don't violate the exercise of free will. We COULD pray the words in today's Scripture. That would be valid.....it would be God's revealed will.....and it just might work!

Will God open their eyes? He can do that.....make them more aware of what is being said to them. Will He send people and circumstances into their lives that will maximize the possibility that they'll choose Jesus as their Savior? Yes. Will He force them to choose salvation? NO. The choice is theirs to make. You and I, though, can make a correct choice more likely by praying Acts 26:18 for them. Let's do that, and not let up for even one day.

Faith Profession: "I know that Jesus wants all people to be saved. I also know that it is every individual's free will choice to accept salvation, or not. I will ask my Lord to send every influence to my loved ones to give them the best possibility for a good choice."

Study Scriptures: I Timothy 2:4; II Peter 3:9

DEVOTIONAL # 186

I'M NOT ASHAMED

Scripture: Romans 1:16

Here in today's verse, Paul makes a statement that, I think, every Christian would agree with. More than that, I believe that almost every Christian would believe that he or she is following this verse. I wonder, though, if that's true.

If you really were unashamed of the Gospel, wouldn't you be bold enough to bow your head and pray before you ate your meal.....even in the middle of a public restaurant? If this verse applied to your life, wouldn't you be able to recall some recent attempts that you have personally made to witness to the lost? If it were true, wouldn't the people you work with be well aware that you are a Christian? If you really are unashamed of Jesus, wouldn't you be spending time in His Word every day? Isn't that the logical place to go for information about Him? Wouldn't you want to know Him intimately, as you would any best friend? Do you know what the word "Gospel" means? Can you turn to a place in your Bible that gives the Gospel plainly?

If Jesus Himself were to suddenly appear in the room, would He agree that your life is a testimony to the fact that you are not ashamed of the Gospel? Hey.....I can't answer those questions for you, dear reader. I can only answer for myself.

If you can't answer them to your own satisfaction, you need to know that it's not too late. You can do something about it. Your Bible is available. You can look for opportunities to speak out in His Name. You can change your present situation, and He will help you.

Remember.....the truth of the Gospel is the power of God unto salvation to EVERY-ONE who believes!

Faith Profession: "I am NOT ashamed of the Gospel of Jesus Christ; and I am determined to live a life that shows that."

Study Scriptures: I Corinthians 15:3-4; Acts 1:8

Constant Prayer, Part 1

Scripture: Acts 12:1-5

As we read in Acts 12, some time has passed since Jesus ascended into Heaven. Notice that Herod.....one of the people opposed to God's work on earth.....had "taken" James the brother of John (that would be the sons of Zebedee) and had killed him. Seeing that this had worked, Herod then arrested Peter and placed him into prison, intending to deal to him the same fate.

The question we should be asking is this.....why is this happening? Or, more to the point.....how is it able to happen to people operating under the protection of the armor of God and in the power of the Holy Spirit?

The answer is not even all that profound, and certainly not surprising. If you read verse 5, you will see that the church reacted to Peter's imprisonment by praying "without ceasing, or, we might say "constantly." That is, they got serious about their prayer life. And, if you know the rest of the story in Acts 12 (if not, you can read the chapter), you know that a remarkable miracle occurred to allow Peter to be set free from the prison. Why? Because of the constant prayer of the people of the church.

We have all heard sermons on prayer. We all know that, as God's children, we have access directly to His throne room, and are welcomed there (see study Scriptures). Yet, we live busy lives, and often find that we have gone days without spending any time there. Though we tend to excuse ourselves, it is not that simple. Yes, Jesus forgives us, but what have we sacrificed by our neglect of this fantastic opportunity to walk right into God's presence? Well, we have reduced our reservoir of "God power." We have made ourselves easier targets for the enemy. When faced with a problem, we have no reserve to fall back on.....we start from scratch, scrambling to gather the power we need to defeat the attack.

That's why James was able to be killed. The flow of defeat was not stopped until God's people began to pray constantly, building up a reservoir that they could tap into.

Faith Profession: "I have a great privilege in being permitted into God's throne room at any time. I will not waste this privilege."

Study Scriptures: Hebrews 4:16; I Thessalonians 5:17

DEVOTIONAL # 188
CONSTANT PRAYER, PART 2

Scripture: Mark 9:14-29

I have read this Scripture many times without coming to an understanding of what it meant. Sometimes it takes years.....in this case, for me, 37 years.....to be enlightened on a passage. But it sure is sweet when it happens!

This Scripture is related to yesterday's lesson from Acts 12. Notice that, here in Mark 9, the disciples cannot cast out this evil spirit. Jesus does it, and then explains that it takes fasting and prayer to handle some evil spirits. What is He saying?

Many well-meaning Christians believe that Jesus accomplished this task.....and many others.....due to the fact that He was God in the flesh. We know, however, that He had purposely set aside His divine attributes to operate on earth as a man. How, then, you may ask, did He do all those miracles? Through the power of the Holy Spirit within Him..... the same power from the same Holy Spirit that you and I have.

More than that, Jesus prayed.....and He did so constantly. The Gospels are full of examples of Him going apart from the crowds to pray.....sometimes all night. Why? Why would Jesus have to pray so much? The answer is this: He was preparing Himself for battle. He was building up a reservoir of power from being in God's presence. When He was confronted with the particularly difficult situation that occurs in Mark 9, He could tap into that reservoir and defeat this devil spirit. The disciples couldn't do that because they were sleeping when He was praying all night.

The lesson? Constant prayer is vital for your success in this life. You need to build up your own "reservoir" of "God time," so that you have that power available when you need it.....like when your child suffers a sudden accident. That's what Jesus did. He was showing us something. We need to pray.....constantly.....to build up our power base. It keeps us "ready" for whatever the devil throws at us.

Faith Profession: "I will spend more time in prayer. I see that it is the key to success in my spiritual battle."

Study Scriptures: Matthew 14:23; Mark 1:35; Philippians 2:7-8

DANGEROUS GROUND

Scripture: Romans 1:25

When I attended Bible school, this verse, along with verses 20 through 28, were commonly attributed to the unsaved people around us. Although they do apply to them, that is not their only application.

Verse 25 identifies two serious problems as far as the Lord is concerned. Changing the truth of the Word is so serious that the Bible contains three warnings about it (see study Scriptures). But did you know that God's own children do this very thing every time we deny a truth revealed in His Word? I know lots of people who deny Mark 16:17-18; John 14:12; I Peter 2:24; and James 4:7, to name a few. These are valid Bible verses, but are denied in classrooms and in church sanctuaries every week.

Don't you know that you change the truth of God's Word into a lie when you blame God for the things satan does? Some people violate this verse every time they pray.

And, lastly, God's children tread this dangerous ground of opposing the Word by interpreting the Bible in physical terms instead of spiritual. We believe something we hear from a preacher because we like him, or because he/she is famous, and on television. When we do that, we're exalting the creature more than the Creator, who is also the Author of the Book.

Hey, thank you for reading this book of daily devotions, but don't go thinking that what you see is right just because it's in a book. You need to check on what I've written..... look in the Bible to see if it is so. The Bible is the final authority, not me.....or any other person, either.

God's Word is TRUTH. God is GOOD, all the time.....it's the devil who's putting all that junk on you. And the Bible is interpreted SPIRITUALLY if it's interpreted correctly. Get those things right, and you'll be in line with verse 25.

Faith Profession: "I believe the Bible to be the Words of God. It is a spiritual book, because God is a spirit, and the eternal part of a human is spirit. And, I refuse to blame God for what the devil does."

Study Scriptures: Deuteronomy 4:2; Proverbs 30:5-6; Revelation 22:18-19

Devotional # 190
God Gave Them Over

Scripture: Romans 1:28

The last few days' lessons have not been as uplifting as I'd like, but my calling is to preach the whole council of God, so I cannot shy away from the less popular truths. Today's verse is one of those, and I can't help but think of my own beloved country of the USA as I read the verse.

As a population, we have permitted our "leaders" to slowly and systematically remove the Bible from our seminaries, our colleges, our high schools, our elementary schools, our holidays, our courtrooms, our churches, and therefore from our consciousness. As a country, our testimony, sadly, is that we tend not to retain God in our knowledge, and it's getting worse instead of better.

It might be good to pay special attention to today's verse. God does not lie. When people are dead set on removing Him from their lives, He will patiently try to appeal to them. After a while, though, when He realizes that their heart is set in stone against Him, He "gives them over to a reprobate mind." That is, He stops trying to change their mind about Him, and releases them to drift away to wherever they are going (a destination that even they don't know).

I don't think it's accidental that the verses immediately before verse 28 are speaking about homosexual behavior. We'd do well to remember Sodom and Gomorrah. This kind of activity seems to signal the end of God's patience with mankind, and His reluctant withdrawal from those who willfully depart from His designs in this fashion. I know that is an unpopular viewpoint these days (I guess I'm "intolerant" and "bigoted"), but I didn't arrange these verses. Why don't you take it up with the One who DID arrange the verses? By the way, He's not trying to be punitive, but rather to guide you away from harm.....the way He always does.

At any rate, you do NOT want to get to the point described in verse 28. There is no way back from this point, and that's sad when you realize that He died for YOU.

Faith Profession: "I love the Lord, and make an honest attempt to live His Word in my life. I may be imperfect at it in this fleshly body, but He knows my heart, and I am trying. My goal is to retain the knowledge of God in my heart."

Study Scriptures: Genesis 18 and 19

DEVOTIONAL # 191

HE CAN USE YOU

Scripture: I Corinthians 1:27-28

Traditional Christianity has been pounding away at its own members for years, emphasizing their weaknesses and shortcomings. The result is a fragile, timid body of Christ that expects Him to do all the work. But.....He can use YOU. He prefers to use you. And here's how I know that.

The Lord used the smelliest, foulest, least popular people He could find to minister with Him. The idea was to make it unlikely that we would begin to deify them (which, unfortunately, has not worked). Look at who He chose. Peter was an impetuous, loud-mouthed, opinionated, smelly fisherman. Mary Magdalene was a hooker. James and John were called "sons of thunder" because you could hear them long before you could see them. Matthew was a traitor to his own homeland.....you can only imagine how popular he was with the rest of the group. Simon the Zealot killed Romans on the side.

This is perhaps the most unimpressive group that Jesus could possibly have assembled. They had absolutely no standing in the community. Yet, we speak of Peter reverently, and like to think that this group of people contained some sort of "super-saints." No.....they were just the opposite.

What's the point? If Jesus could use that bunch, then there's hope for US. He's not looking for the smartest person.....or the best looking.....or the wealthiest.....or the most charming. No.....most of the Bible's evangelists and leaders were ex-convicts, murderers, or folks who held the lowest jobs in their society.

Hey.....He uses me. And if you knew my distant past, you'd find that amazing.

He uses imperfect people because that's all He can find. He can use you. In fact, He would prefer that.

Faith Profession: "I can be used in service to the Lord. He can work through me to His glory. The weaker the vessel, the more glory He gets."

Study Scriptures: James 2:5; I Corinthians 1:4-6

MORE ABOUT SALVATION

Scripture: I Peter 1:9

Salvation. It is, in fact, the "end" of your faith.....in the sense that is the object, or objective, of that faith.

Now, we know that salvation gives us eternal life with the Lord in Heaven. But too many of us have been led to believe that it ends there. I'm not trying to minimize the importance of eternal life.....please don't misunderstand. But I am trying to get across to you that it is so much more than that.

Did you know that your New Testament was written originally in Greek? Did you know that many Greek words have multiple meanings? Take, for example, the Greek word that is translated "salvation" in your Bible. It means salvation, of course.....but that's not all it can mean. Do you know what Greek word is translated "healing" in your Bible? It's the exact same Greek word that is translated "salvation" in other places. Do you know what Greek word is translated as "deliverance" in your Bible? Yep.....the same word.

So, why is it translated differently, and what does it all mean? Well, another possible translation of this Greek word (used for salvation, healing, deliverance) is "wholeness." That is, when you get saved, you are MADE WHOLE spiritually. Why is that true? Because at the moment of salvation, you become one with Jesus. You are imbued with the same power that He has, and you are given the right to use the authority of His Name .....as if it is your very own.

Salvation is more than just eternal life. It is deliverance. It is healing. It is wholeness. It is completeness. You have become one with the God of Creation, and are no less His child than Jesus Himself. That's why the church SHOULD be focusing on the gifts given by the Holy Spirit.....instead of treating them like some sort of nasty plague.

Faith Profession: "By definition of the word in the original language, my salvation has made me healed, delivered, and whole. It is much more than I had been led to believe. I have the authority to use the Name of Jesus!"

Study Scriptures: I John 4:17; John 14:12

BLUE FLASHING LIGHTS

Scripture: Philippians 2:9-11

The NAME.....the one that means something to the devil.....the one that will be exalted eternally.....the one through which heavenly power is unleashed.....is the Name JESUS.

You hear many church people talking about "Christ," or, more generally, "God." Now, some would say that they're all the same. But they are not, and our enemy knows that. He isn't bothered by you referring to "Christ," because that word is not Jesus' Name..... it is a title. It means "anointed one." Did you know that satan is a "christ".....or at least was one when he was Lucifer? Did you know that the devil isn't fazed by your referral to "God? Why not? Because the devil is a god, too (see study Scriptures).

Sometimes on the highway, you see cars slow down suddenly when they see the flashing blue lights up ahead. Why? Because those lights represent AUTHORITY. Although the policeman can't personally stop a car with his own power, the authority he holds does it for him.

As a child of God, you have been given the same authority that Jesus has. You have the right to use His Name, and that Name has AUTHORITY in the spiritual realm. When that Name is spoken, the devil and his foul helpers HAVE to bow to its authority.....and they know it.

So, they have made it their business to see to it that you DON'T know it. Too many Christians DON'T. Have you ever wondered why there is so much devil activity in our world? Perhaps it's because the devil sees no "flashing blue lights".....nobody speaking the NAME JESUS, and invoking its authority.

Faith Profession: "I have the right to speak the Name of Jesus into my life, and the world around me. I am determined to do just that. When I do, devils MUST get in line with that Name's authority!"

Study Scriptures: II Corinthians 4:4; Acts 4:7-18

DEVOTIONAL # 194
THE FOLLY OF REALISM

Scripture: Romans 4:17

I know something about being a realist. I openly claimed to be realistic in my view of the world for more than 40 years. Then I came to the place where I saw that the point of view of the realist is not much different than that of the pessimist. I always maintained that I was "calling it like it is," but you'd be surprised how negative that tends to be.

What changed my mind was coming to understand that God is not a realist.....at least not in the traditional worldly way. Today's Scripture is part of a larger body of information, and you'd understand it more fully by reading verses 1 to 22. Notice that promises were given to Abraham by the Lord, and Abraham believed them so strongly that he spoke today as if they had already come to pass.....even though these particular promises didn't manifest for about 25 years. Abraham is commended by the Lord for this. He is called a man of great faith. Why? Because he considered a promise from God to be a "done deal".....which, of course, it is.

That's why I say that God is not a realist, and He wants us to be like Him. That is, God always calls things the way He WANTS them to be, NOT the way they are. It is called planting faith seeds, and it is the Lord's most basic manner of operating.

He expects us to operate the same way. We are to "call those things which be not as though they were." Or, we might say it this way.....we are to place so much faith in God's promise that we call it so in advance of actually seeing it. We consider it done because it is God's Word.

In reality, that is the much more sane approach to this life. And, it is the only approach that God can bless consistently.

Faith Profession: "God's promise to Abraham defied logic and reason, yet Abraham placed total faith in it, and spoke that. I am to operate the same way. I will call the promises in God's Word so.....then wait to see them with my eyes."

Study Scriptures: I Corinthians 1:28; Hebrews 11:11,1

DEVOTIONAL # 195

HE WAS DEAD

Scripture: Romans 8:11

If you study the Word, and read information about the Word for as long as I have (37 years), you run into an amazing amount of crackpots who are writing about Bible events. One central target of these well-meaning, but misguided (and guess who misguides them?) writers is the crucifixion. Specifically called into question is whether or not Jesus actually died on the Cross.

One theory is that He only fainted on the Cross, coming out of it after He was taken down. This brainstorm is known in theological circles as "the swoon theory" (swoon being the old word for fainting). And, although there are other theories, you should know that all of them attempt to discredit the work of Redemption.

Today's verse would be enough by itself to refute these unbelieving ideas. It says that Jesus was raised up from the dead. If Christ is raised up from the dead, then He must have been dead!

Besides that, if He didn't actually die, then our salvation is not valid. No.....Jesus died on the Cross. There were more than a few witnesses to that, among which was a Roman Centurion.....a man well acquainted with death through his occupation, which involved hand-to-hand combat.

The devil is always at work trying to place doubt on the truth of Scripture. He is always counteracted by a verse or verses of Scripture. Jesus died on the Cross physically, and then willingly died spiritually.....to pay the whole debt against mankind. The devil.....and those deceived by him.....would have you believe otherwise. Let's be smarter than that. Let's believe the Scriptures.

Faith Profession: "Jesus died on Calvary's Cross, and paid the total debt for sin. I will believe the Word rather than some half-baked theory that is not supported by the Scriptures."

Study Scriptures: I Peter 3:18; I Corinthians 15:1-4

DEVOTIONAL # 196

BELIEF AND...

Scripture: I John 3:23

Everybody likes answered prayer, and everybody who prays is at least hopeful of a positive result. Those who know the Word a little better are aware that there will be no answered prayer without faith, or belief.

Today, I'd like to introduce you to something I'm going to call the "important connector," and it's found in our verse above. In actuality, there are four things that are needed to insure answered prayer: you must be born again; you must be free of unconfessed sin; you must be aware of the power of the Name of Jesus and how to use it; and.....today's subject.....loving one another.

We tend to downplay that last item; but, if you'll take some time with the "study Scriptures" listed below, you'll see that there is a connection between the verses on prayer and the verses on unforgiveness.

In loving one another, we know that this involves our relationship with our friends; our spouse; our children; our extended family; those in our workplace and church. But, have you considered that it also includes the Lord Himself? We are to love Him, too.....not just in the abstract sense, but in a real way.....in a daily way..... in a way that HE will be sure that you love Him.

It's so important to Him that He ties His ability to answer your prayers to it. Do you have a grudge against someone? Has somebody hurt you terribly, and you can't forgive them? Have you neglected your Lord and Savior? Why not take a few minutes right now and get that right. Forgive them. Tell Jesus about it (which means you'll be repairing that relationship, too). Then watch your prayers get answered. They WILL get answered if they're based on a Scripture verse, and you pray them free of these other bondages.

Faith Profession: "I love the Lord, and I'm going to show Him that I do. I forgive those wrongs done to me, and release those who committed them, in Jesus' Name."

Study Scripture: Mark 11:23-26 (notice the "And" that begins verse 25)

THE KEY TO MIRACLES

Scripture: John 2:5

This passage of Scripture is probably familiar to you. It is Jesus' first miracle in His earthly ministry.....changing water into wine. But maybe you've never noticed, as I hadn't, the importance of verse 5. It is not only the key verse in this account, but it is the key to you experiencing miracles on a regular basis in your life.

Notice that, in verse 4, Jesus expresses little interest in the wine problem after being informed of it by His earthly mother. Her response is to address the servants. She says, "Whatsoever He saith unto you, do it." She addresses servants on purpose because servants were used to doing what they were told.....unlike modern Christians.

Notice that they were told to do something odd.....seemingly unrelated to the problem, and somewhat difficult to do. The water in these containers would have weighed over a hundred pounds. After doing this work, the servants are commanded to draw some of this water out, and give it to the governor of the feast. This seems crazy! Surely the servants realize how angry the governor will be when he tastes water, not wine! So, it defies logic. It seems weird. It seems downright foolish. But.....when the governor drinks, he is impressed with the quality of this delicious wine, and says so.

And now we know the key factor in seeing a miracle. It is to DO whatsoever He says to do. Where do we find this instruction? In the Bible. In the verses that tell us to express faith.....to speak in line with Scripture.....to believe His Word no matter what. We are to speak the end result as described in the Scripture promise.....and to do all that while loving the brethren with a forgiving heart.

This is missing in the church today, and explains why so few miracles are seen by the average Christian. Hey.....Jesus didn't hide the information. It's right here.

Faith Profession: "I will serve the Lord obediently, and follow His Word even though it may not be scientific or logical. And, I will see miracles."

Study Scriptures: Mark 11: 23-26 (yes, I know we saw these yesterday.....it's okay to read them again); I John 5:4; II Timothy 2:15; John 8:32

DEVOTIONAL # 198

ADOPTION

Scripture: Romans 8:15

Adoption. You know how it works. A child (usually) is taken into a family he/she was not physically born into. That child, however, becomes part of the family through a legal process. Once that is done, the child is just as much a part of the family as a child naturally born into it.

Before you were born again.....whether you knew it or not.....you were not part of the family of God. In fact, John 8:44 indicates that you were part of the devil's family. In order to be brought into God's family, God has to WANT to make you His child, and then has to be willing to go through the legal process to MAKE you His child. Praise God, that's exactly what He's done through Jesus' death on the Cross.

The fact that He sent Jesus to die for you is proof that He WANTS to make you His child. The legal process was accomplished on the Cross and during the three days and nights immediately afterward. So, His part of the process is completed. All that's left is you.....your willingness to become God's child. You have a choice in this matter. It is NOT automatic. But.....all that needs to be done for you to become His child has already been done.

So, the question becomes this: "Will you choose to become His child?".....because He WILL NOT make that choice FOR you. If you're willing to become His child, then all you need to do is bow your head and tell Him that in prayer. When you do, you will IMMEDIATELY become part of the family of God. You will be legally adopted into His family, and will have every right and privilege that a natural-born child has.

You will be SURE of this because you have Scripture that tells you that it is so. Therefore, you have God's Word on it. Nothing could be more solid. So..... WILL you? If so, tell Him right now.....He's waiting to hear you.

Faith Profession: "I have chosen to become a child of God. I prayed for salvation; God heard me; and He said "yes" to my request. I am a child of God!"

Study Scriptures: Romans 10:9-10,13; John 1:12

Joint Heirs

Scripture: Romans 8:17

You know what an "heir" is, right? Perhaps you have been one at some time in your life. Someone dies, and they leave their possessions to others.....usually their closest family members.

I have been an heir on several occasions in my life. When my last remaining parent died, the estate was divided among the four surviving children. That's how it works in most cases. Technically, I was a "co-heir." That is, I was one of four children, and the estate was divided among all four of us, each child receiving one-fourth.

Now, if you are saved, you are a child of the Living God.....and make no mistake about it, He IS alive spiritually. On the other hand, Jesus DID DIE. That is why today's verse speaks of us as heirs.

Notice, though, that we are not called "co-heirs," but "JOINT-heirs." What's the difference? A "joint heir" doesn't have to share the inheritance.....,he/she inherits the WHOLE THING!! That is, each one of us, as children of God, receive ALL that He owns.....and He owns ALL OF IT!

So, many Christians say, "Wow, that's great! I'll have quite an inheritance when I die." But.....wait a minute. You don't receive an inheritance when YOU die. You receive it when the GIVER dies. Our giver is Jesus Christ, and He died some 2,000 years ago.

Do you know what that means? It means that the inheritance.....ALL of it.....ALL that Jesus is and has.....belongs to you and me.....RIGHT NOW! Are you enjoying yours? Or are you just letting it sit there, as if it wasn't yours until later? Here's a hint.....enjoy it now!!!

Faith Profession: "I have my inheritance now, and I live in it every day. I possess all that Jesus earned on the Cross, and all that the Godhead owns.....right now!"

Study Scripture: Galatians 4:1-7

Devotional # 200
A Marriage Proposal

Scripture: Romans 10:9-10

Even though you may not be married as you read today's lesson, it's safe to assume that you know a few basic things about the subject. A marriage proposal is basically a question: "Will you marry me?" I'd like you to think about that for a second. Let's say that you are the one asking that question. If you get a "yes" answer, or a "no" answer, you are at least sure of what you have to work with.

But, what if you ask, and the other person just says nothing at all? Do you take that as a "yes," or a "no"? Well, you take that as a "no," because you didn't get a "yes".....and I believe we all understand that.

Okay.....so the Lord died and rose from the dead for your sin. Then He asks you: "Will you receive my free gift of salvation?" Some people answer "yes." Some give it a flat "no." More often than not, though, people give no answer at all, and they believe they're "neutral" on the subject. They say, "Well, I don't deal with it either way.....I just don't think about it." That is, they're trying to stay "neutral".....not getting saved, but not rejecting God, either.

But, isn't the offer of salvation exactly like a marriage proposal? Yes, it is. When you give no response to God's invitation, does He see it as a "neutral" response? No.....of course not. And neither would you if you were the one asking.

The truth? You cannot be neutral on the issue of salvation. There IS no neutral. Unless you answer "yes," and do something about it, you have rejected His offer to save you. Silence is a "no" answer. Whatever you do, don't be silent about this. Your eternity depends upon it.

Faith Profession: "I realize that there is no such thing as a "neutral" position when the Lord offers to save my soul. I choose to give Him an answer.....He deserves at least that much from me."

Study Scriptures: James 1:8; Isaiah 7:15

NO MIRACLES

Scripture: Acts 1:1-9

Did you notice that Jesus performed no miracles on earth between the resurrection and His Ascension? Doesn't that strike you as odd? After all, there were lots of skeptics out there who doubted the validity of the resurrection.....a couple of miracles would have gone a long way toward convincing them. Plus, when Jesus returned from the dead, He was still God.....right? You may have been taught that He performed miracles because He was God.....or, more specifically, God's Son. And you may have been taught that you can't be involved in miracles because you AREN'T God; and that miracles happen only if and when God decides to do one.

Well.....He was God in the forty days before His ascension. What was the difference? The difference was that He was no longer in a purely human form. He now had a glorified body. Miracles are done by the ministry of the Holy Spirit working in co-operation with a human being. That's the way Jesus did them during His earthly ministry.....every time. That's why Jesus states that YOU can do anything He did while He was on earth (John 14:12). It's because you are still in a human body, and you have the Holy Spirit available to you.....the exact situation He had.

The teaching that Jesus did miracles because He was God is simply not true. The teaching that you play no part in miracles on this earth is likewise simply not true. I wonder who would want you to believe that you play no part in miracles? God? I don't think so.

We need to get our theology straightened out, my friends. Jesus said what He said in John 14:12 because miracles work through human beings working in tandem with the Holy Spirit. Miracles work through faith in the promises of God as found in the Scripture. When Jesus returned to earth after the resurrection, he was in a glorified body.....and it does make a difference. Don't receive the devil's lie that you play no part in miracles. The truth is just the opposite!

Faith Profession: "I see how the power of God is released. It is through a human speaking faith, which releases the power of God to change a situation for good."

Study Scriptures: John 14:12; I John 4:17

Romans 8:28 Clarified

Scripture: Romans 8:26-28

Those of you who are traditional in your theology are going to have some difficulty with today's teaching. I know that because I was saved in a traditional church, and went to a traditional seminary, and was ordained in a traditional denomination. But today's teaching is just pure Bible.....and you either believe the Bible, or you are not a Bible Believer (though you might be saved).

Lots of bad doctrine has come from teaching on Romans 8:28 by taking it out of context. I was taught that verse 28 means that anything that happens in life is from God (because He is sovereign), and, even though we don't know how, it will work out eventually for good.

Nice thought, but I've noticed that things DON'T always work for good. Did you notice the word "and" at the beginning of verse 28? It is a conjunction, and serves to CONNECT the verses before it with verse 28. What is being discussed in verses 26 and 27? Praying in tongues.....a vital ministry of the Holy Spirit in the New Testament church. Sorry.....tongues is NOT just Pentecostal belief.....it is Bible truth.

Verses 26—28 tell you that, IF you pray in tongues (a language unknown to you, but known to the Holy Spirit), the Holy Spirit directs the prayer like a laser into the heart of the issue.....in ways that you alone could never do. Once THAT is done, all things will work together for good to them that love God. Why? Because the prayer is being directed supernaturally, thus magnifying its effectiveness.

God does not operate alone. He uses you.....if you will speak His Word in faith. When that happens, things change. Miracles happen. Prayer gets answered. Power is released to change the devil's destructive purpose into a blessing. Things DO work together for GOOD. THAT is the Bible meaning of verse 28.

Faith Profession: "I accept the reality.....and Bible truth.....that I operate in partnership with the Lord in the faith realm. When I pray in my supernatural prayer language, the Holy Spirit directs the results, and all things work together for good."

Study Scriptures: John 14:16; John 16:13-14; I Corinthians 14:18,39

Devotional # 203
Saved to the Uttermost

Scripture: Hebrews 7:22-25

I have two points to make in today's lesson.....each of which should be a blessing to you.

First, notice with me the word "surety" in verse 22. This is an Old English word that isn't in common use these days.....but it will become plain to you if I tell you that it means "guarantee." Did you know that there is a guarantee that comes with your salvation? And that this guarantee comes in the form of the only sinless person ever to have walked the earth.....Jesus Christ? You and I are flawed creatures.....we sin. The devil knows that, and tries to accuse us to God when we do sin. But Jesus sits at God's right hand, calmly countering every accusation with His own sinlessness on our behalf. We are solid in salvation because our guarantee is Jesus!

In verse 25, it says that He is able to save us "to the uttermost." Hey, folks.....that is as good as it can possibly get! In the Greek language in which your New Testament was originally written, the word "save," and its companion word "salvation," have the meaning of "wholeness." So, verse 25 can be translated that we are made whole to the uttermost. Being "made whole" covers all aspects of our life. In other words, we are saved to the uttermost. We are also healed to the uttermost. We are blessed to the uttermost, too. We are protected to the uttermost (see study Scriptures), and prospered to the uttermost

God never does anything halfway. God's willingness to bless you, and love you, knows no limits. Receive this beautiful truth.....it will lead to abundant life!

Faith Profession: "The guarantee of my salvation is not my own actions, but Jesus Christ Himself. More than that, He has made me WHOLE.....in every respect.....to the UTTERMOST!"

Study Scriptures: Psalm 91; Matthew 8:17; Psalm 1:3

Devotional # 204
Your Body's Redemption

Scripture: Romans 8:18-23

You may have noticed, as I did, that your salvation did not appear to include your physical body. Nothing about it was changed when you asked Jesus to be your Savior from sin. It still tends toward a desire to sin, and this is something you have to fight from the moment you are saved until you go home to be with Him.

So.....why is that? Why not just complete the transaction all at once: spirit, soul, and body? Good question......and the answer is that you need to be in a physical body.....an unredeemed body that isn't yet in a glorified state.....to fight the fight of faith against the world, the flesh, and the devil.

You have probably been taught that Jesus does everything, and that you have no part to play in the spiritual battle of the ages. That is a false teaching, and causes Christians to be passive in the battle. In truth, Jesus left you on earth in an unredeemed body because you are His mouthpiece since His ascension. He is in a glorified body, and can't operate on earth.....technically. YOU are the key now. YOU are the one who speaks the Word in faith. YOU are the one who releases His power into a situation.

He did it while He was on earth, ministering as a human being in the power of the Holy Spirit. Now, He depends on YOU. That is why the devil works so hard to get you to be passive.....to wait for Jesus to do it all.....to pray for HIM to do whatever you need, and then wait for Him to do something. BUT.....that's not how it works. And the fact that He left your body unredeemed is proof of that. You are in a physical body, and so have legal right to exert authority on this earth. You do it by speaking God's Word in faith. Only you can do that now that Jesus is gone on to Heaven.

Are you doing what He intends for you to do? Or are you sitting around waiting for Him to do what He cannot do now??

Faith Profession: "My body was left unredeemed on purpose. In this state, I have the legal right to exercise authority on the earth. I intend to do just that by speaking God's Word, releasing His power into the spiritual realm."

Study Scriptures: I John 5:4; James 4:7; Matthew 16:19

YOUR PRAYER LANGUAGE

Scripture: Romans 8:26-27

Uh-oh.....we're going to be entering an area that will raise red flags for our traditional brethren. What I'm about to discuss is sometimes called Pentecostal or Charismatic doctrine. Actually, it's just Bible.....and anybody who is a true Bible believer will need to take a close look at it, because it's part of the Holy Spirit's ministry of power and blessing to the New Testament church.

What's being discussed in our verses today is praying in tongues. The word "infirmities" in verse 26 can better be translated "weaknesses." The point? We pray, but we often don't know much about the person or situation we're praying about. These verses say that the Holy Spirit DOES know EXACTLY what to pray, and, if we'll have faith enough to allow it, He will pray using our voice in a language unknown to the devil and his demons.

There are two advantages to this: First, the devil can't understand what is being prayed, so he can't take action against it. Second, the Holy Spirit can direct the prayer to the heart of the matter with supernatural accuracy.....accuracy you and I could never attain. Therefore, this type of prayer is much more effective than our regular praying.

Notice in verse 27 that the Spirit prays "according to the will of God." So, this prayer language will be in words that YOU won't understand either. But, if the Holy Spirit is doing the praying, what does it matter if you or I understand the words? Why do we feel the need to always be in control? Why would we do a better job than God's Holy Spirit?

So.....relax. The Holy Spirit is God.....He would never speak anything harmful through you. Yes, I know.....you've heard a story that someone interpreted tongues speaking as blasphemy against God. I've heard that, too. But I don't have a name, or any documentation of that story.....and neither do you. It isn't true, my friend. Read verse 27 again..... your prayer language is prayer in the will of God.....and it is more pure than any prayer you've prayed where you understood the words.

Faith Profession: "My prayer language is based on Scriptural evidence. It is prayer in God's will, and it is recommended for every believer in the New Testament church. It is violently opposed by the devil, who has invented damaging rumors about it to scare off Christians."

Study Scriptures: Jude 20; Ephesians 6:18

Three Powerful Things

Scripture: Ephesians 5:19-21

Sometimes the Bible packs loads of potent information in just a few verses, and today's Scriptures are one example of this.

First, verse 19 tells us that, when we are filled with the Holy Spirit (see verse 18), we will be moved to SPEAK, or sing, the Word of God. Speaking the Word is how we plant spiritual seed into the world around us. Singing worship music, hymns, and spiritual songs makes us happy, and is one great way to keep yourself filled with the Spirit.

Second, the giving of thanks should be part of every Christian's daily conversation with the Lord. Jesus loves it when we're thankful. It is one of the few things specifically mentioned as being the will of God (see study Scripture). Thankfulness keeps us focused on Him, and His loving kindness to us. He deserves our thanks, because He has done things for us that nobody else could or would do. He has made it possible for us to live in abundant life here on earth, and then enjoy eternal life with Him forever afterward. Saying "thank you" is the least we can do.

Third, an attitude of submission is vital to walking the "love walk" that Jesus wants us to live. I'm not talking about being a "doormat," but about giving the other person the benefit of the doubt.....focusing on giving rather than receiving.....focusing on others rather than on self. Submission to the Lord is a "no-brainer," but submission to those He's put into your life makes sense, too. You are the bigger person when you put the other person first. It won't hurt you, and it will give them a warm feeling. It's what love does, and the Lord will see to it that you are blessed for this kind of action.

These three things.....if practiced regularly.....would go far in making you the kind of child the Father could more easily love and bless. It's how Jesus Himself operated and, as His children, we'd do well to follow His example.

Faith Profession: "I will concentrate on speaking the Word in melody and in prayer. I will be a thankful child of the King. And I will operate toward others in an attitude of submission.....just as Jesus taught me to do."

Study Scriptures: I Thessalonians 5:18; Colossians 3:17

WHOSE SIDE IS GOD ON?

Scripture: Romans 8:31-33

Today's title may seem like an odd one, but it is a valid question to believers in these end times. You see, many Christians have been taught that their disease, or marital trouble, or accident, or money woes are sent by God (or at least that He "allows" them). The reasoning is that the Lord can teach you certain lessons through pain and suffering, so He permits such things for your greater good in the long run. Often, He doesn't let you know the reason for your suffering, and that, they say, is when you need to have faith that it is in your best interest.

All of this is predicated on the belief that you have nothing to do with what happens to you.....that God is "in control," and authors everything that happens to you. To this I say.....respectfully and with grace.....HOGWASH!!

Can you read today's Scripture? Can you answer the question posed by verse 31? Is God FOR you? Okay.....if He is, then how can He be against you at the same time? Some of you believe that you suffer because of sin in your life. Okay, then how does that reconcile with verse 33? Didn't Jesus pay your debt in full? How, then, do you have to pay for your sin again through sickness and suffering??

In verse 32, it says that He has freely given us all things. Yes.....that's what love does. So, how does this line up with the thinking that He gives you disease or trouble? Have you ever read James 1:13? That word "tempted" can also be translated "trials" or "troubles."

I think God is getting a bum rap. I think God's children are falsely accusing their Savior of things that are actually being done by the devil. I know that God's children have more authority over the devil than they think they have. I also know that God's children have a say in whether or not they suffer physical troubles or not. I know that the Holy Spirit was sent to assist us in this spiritual battle. I also know that the devil works hard to deceive God's children, and he has succeeded with you if you believe that God sends or allows sickness into your life. Maybe you need to step up to the plate and accept some responsibility for your own circumstances.....instead of laying it all on a Holy God.

Faith Profession: "God is FOR me, not against me. He has freely given me all things. I am pure and righteous, because He made that possible for me."

Study Scriptures: II Corinthians 5:21; James 1:13-15

NOTHING CAN SEPARATE US

Scripture: Romans 8:38-39

Let's look today at some information that will build you up, and put a smile on your face. That will be a wonderful way to start the day!

When Jesus died on the Cross.....and defeated death, Hell, the devil, sin, and the grave during the three days and nights immediately afterward, He COMPLETELY defeated all the enemies that you'll ever face. Then, at salvation, He freely gave those victories to YOU.

Notice the list of things that have been defeated totally. First is death: we have no fear of it after salvation because it no longer applies to us in the most important way.....spiritually. Angels have no power over us, either. Not that they would oppose us, but it is a reminder that we stand in a more important place than even angels.

Next are "principalities and powers." You have heard of them in Ephesians 6 where the armor of God is discussed. They are the satanic forces arrayed against us. Next in the list are things present and things to come. Why didn't He mention things past? Because they are gone.....we can't do anything about them, and the best thing is to leave them go and look ahead. With the Lord, we are encouraged to look FORWARD. So, we can't be defeated by anything present, or anything future. Now, THAT'S some good news!! Lastly, height, depth, or any other creature is mentioned. That just about covers everything.

We are in Christ. Nothing.....NOTHING.....nobody.....no circumstance.....nothing can separate us from Him. Why? Because we have become ONE with Him at salvation. We have become part of Him in a real, eternal way. When we pray, we bow our head because that's the best way to speak directly to Him. We are IN Jesus, and nothing can separate us from that. Nothing.

Faith Profession: "I am persuaded that, with Jesus as my Savior and Lord, nothing can prevail against me. I will do my part and speak His Word into my circumstances, and I will live an abundant life on this earth."

Study Scriptures: Isaiah 54:17; Ephesians 6:10-12; Proverbs 18:10

TRANSFORMERS

Scripture: Romans 12:1-2

Transformers. These days, they are famous as children's toys, and movie characters. Yet, the original "transformers" are born-again Christians who have been studying the Word of God. In fact, as a saved Christian, YOU should be able to call yourself a "transformer."

End-times Christianity, it's sad to say, is full of teaching that is based upon an interpretation of the Bible that focuses on the physical. We think that spirituality can be measured.....in the size of a congregation; how frequently we come to church; how zealous we are at "serving" at our church; etc.

The Bible, however, is not a book that focuses on the physical. Instead, its focus is on the spiritual. Because of that, attempts to understand the Bible by the accumulation of facts about it will result in failure. You can study the Bible for years without a real understanding of what it is about. Why? Because the focus needs to be on your spirit rather than your brain. The Words of God are to be received into your heart.....by faith.....believing them without your brain comprehending them totally. And that's OKAY. The Bible is supernatural, so parts of it won't make sense to your physical understanding. As you receive the Word into your heart, you will, over time, see that your mind comes into agreement with your spirit. But that is a process, and it is called in Romans 12 "transformation."

It's OKAY.....that's how it works.....that's how it was DESIGNED to work. So, you don't comprehend supernatural healing.....or tongues.....or authority over the devil. If you're honest, you don't fully comprehend salvation, either.....you just believe it because the Bible says it. Somewhere along the line, your mind came into agreement with it.....it was "transformed." It will work the same way with any other Bible truth. As you accept supernatural Bible truths, and your mind finally "gets it," you will be fulfilling the will of God.....as it says in verse 2.

Faith Profession: "I don't fully understand some Bible concepts, but I believe them because they are Bible truth. Later, my mind will catch up with my spiritual understanding.....it will be transformed."

Study Scriptures: Titus 3:5; Ephesians 4:22-24

Devotional # 210
The Measure of Faith

Scripture: Romans 12:3

Faith. Everybody needs some. Some believe that they have lost theirs. Others aren't sure they EVER had any. But, in reality, we ALL have faith, and we exercise it every day. For example, you probably don't stop to check out your chair before you sit down in it.....you just trust the manufacturer that it will hold you. That's faith. And you are exercising some form of it constantly.

Here in today's verse, we are told that every person is given what is called "the measure of faith." That is, according to God's Word, every person has faith given to them by the Lord. And, each person is given an equal measure of faith to begin with. The faith you are given happens to be HIS faith.....the same faith that He used to call things into existence in Genesis 1 from nothing. The same faith Jesus used to cast out devils, heal the sick, and, ultimately, to get victory over the devil and Hell.

So, you DO have faith, but the Bible describes several forms of it. There is strong faith..... weak faith.....little faith.....great faith. So, how do we account for these differences? Well, although every person is given the measure of faith, the amount of faith that you have at a given time can be measured.....at least by the Lord. How is it measured? By the amount of the Word of God that you have taken the time to put into yourself.

OH.....did you think it was automatic.....or that God took care of that entirely? No, like most Bible things, it is a matter of what YOU choose to do with it. YOU are responsible for the measure of your faith. The more time you spend in the Word, the greater your faith becomes (see study Scriptures). The greater your faith becomes, the easier you can handle the devil's attacks, and the more blessings you live in daily. It is not automatic..... or accidental. It is up to you. How strong is your faith today??

Faith Profession: "I have the measure of faith as a gift from the Lord. I intend to exercise it by the study of God's Word until it becomes great faith."

Study Scriptures: Romans 10:17; Luke 7:1-9; II Timothy 2:15

DEVOTIONAL # 211

THE POWERS THAT BE

Scripture: Romans 13:1-2

The powers that be.....now here is a phrase that is so universally misunderstood that it must be in the top ten. Generally, these verses are understood to mean that we are to be obedient to the laws of the land, and to those who are responsible to enforce them..... like policemen, the courts, judges, etc. Okay.....there's certainly nothing wrong with that.

Where we get snagged is in taking the rest of the verse to mean that every official in America has been placed there by the Lord. Using this false interpretation, some have thought it prudent to attack the Lord for His supposed choices, and be resentful of Him because of them.

Now, let's calm down and just look at the words. It says that the powers that be are OR-DAINED of God. So, if you look up the word "ordain" in the dictionary, you find that it means "to establish or order." That is, the Lord established structure in society.....a system of laws and enforcement to maintain order. He set up the SYSTEMS.....the general order of things, and that has proven to be effective over time.

What it does NOT say is that the Lord PLACES specific people in certain positions of authority. If that were true, then we'd have no reason to vote. I've noticed, though, that elections are held, and people do vote. THAT'S how specific people get into positions of authority. How convenient it would be to blame God for what WE have done.

God doesn't elect people.....WE do. Maybe we ought to take responsibility for our own actions for a change and stop pushing the blame onto the Lord who has no more to do with it after setting up the system. It helps to READ THE VERSES. If you don't understand a word, look it up! Don't just make stuff up, then get huffy with God about it. Maybe it's US.

Faith Profession: "I will be careful how I interpret Scripture, and will look up words that I may not really comprehend. Above all, I will expect the Lord to be fair, loving, and reasonable in all things."

Study Scriptures: Titus 3:1-4; Psalm 25:8

223

Devotional # 212
What's Required

Scripture: I Corinthians 4:2

I spent my early years in Christianity in a denominational church which was very conservative and traditional in its views of the Bible. Of course, they firmly believed that they were right, and everybody else was wrong.....so much so that they discouraged contact with others if they did not believe the same.

The outside world sees these kinds of things, and draws the conclusion that church people are no different than regular folk, except for the fact that church people profess to be holy.....and act like hypocrites. Coincidentally, that's what Jesus called the Pharisees of His day. It would seem that Pharisees in any generation are blind to their own shortcomings.

Our verse today is simple. What is required of God's people is simple. All He is looking for is FAITH. As a child of the King, you are required by your Father only to be faithful. He does not ask that your church contain a minimum number of members. He doesn't keep a total of how much you have given in the offering plate. He isn't interested in how many times your name appears in the Sunday bulletin. He isn't even focusing on how many souls you have led to Him.

He notices the times you are in faith. He rejoices over the times you follow His Word, even though it makes no sense to your brain. He loves it when you trust Him, and speak the solution to your problem.....as indicated in His promise.....before you see the outcome.

In short, He knows that you tend to fail in this conduct thing. He's not surprised at that. But having faith in Him and His Word.....just because you believe.....and even though you can't see the end yet.....is what touches His heart. If you are faithful to His Word, He is pleased with you, and that's about all there is to it!

Faith Profession: "I believe God's Word, even when it makes no earthly sense. My Lord is supernatural, and is the God of miracles. I believe that."

Study Scriptures: Hebrews 11:6; I John 5:4

Your Body

Scripture: I Corinthians 6:19-20

If you've been saved for very long, you've probably heard that you are part of the body of Christ. At the moment of salvation, many things happen.....many gifts are given to you..... many aspects of your spiritual situation are changed for the better.

You immediately possess eternal life.....you are given the righteousness of Jesus Himself.....you are adopted legally into the family of God.....you become a saint and priest..... and you are an heir to all that belongs to your Father. You are given His power, His authority, His wealth, His protection. Hitting the lotto seems puny by comparison.

All of this is GIVEN.....it is free. Yet, there are a few expectations (not requirements) that come with this package, and one of those is mentioned in today's verses. Your body has become the temple where Jesus resides. He paid a high price to redeem you, and He has some rights, too.

We live in a society that is convinced (because satan has been working hard to establish this belief) that their body and their actions are their own. That isn't true, whether you're saved or not. But, if you've trusted Jesus as your Savior from sin, then your body is, technically, not your own any longer. In fact, Jesus bought it with His own blood. Did you notice the verse immediately before today's verses? It gives the context of verses 19 and 20.....and the context is fornication.

The bottom line? You are not the legal owner of the body you inhabit after you are saved. And you don't have the right to do with it as YOU please, but you are to do with it as HE pleases. He is pleased when you glorify Him in it. That can't be done with a harlot..... an alcoholic drink.....curse words.....drugs.....premarital or extra-marital sexual activity..... pornography. Can you choose to subject your body to these anyway? Yes.....He won't interfere. But it still isn't right to abuse property that is no longer yours.

Faith Profession: "I realize that my physical body is not my own property after salvation. I will consult the owner before I do things with it from now on."

Study Scriptures: Romans 14:7-8; I Thessalonians 4:3-4

DIVORCE

Scripture: I Corinthians 7

Oh, go on and read the whole chapter for a change.....it might do you some real good. For one thing, you'll discover more information on divorce than anywhere else in the Bible.

I've studied this subject more than most. I've seen sincere Christians do substantial damage to younger believers through their misunderstanding of this subject. The bottom line? The Lord has not been taken by surprise by modern divorce rates.....they are a by-product of the enemy's attack on families.

Though you may disagree.....and you have the freedom in the Lord to do that.....my study has located three Biblical grounds for divorce. They are: death (of course—see verse 39); adultery, based on Matthew 19:9 and other Scriptures; and desertion, based upon I Corinthians 7:15, 27, 28. In verse 15, the departing spouse is called an "unbeliever" in the sense that he/she is not following the Word. Just as in Matthew 18:15-17, where the disobedient person is called a "heathen" (because that is what they're acting like), you are to treat them the same way you would treat an unsaved person.

In all three cases, remarriage is permitted, based on verses 27-28. Though a single life is recommended, "but and if thou marry, thou hast not sinned...," you are warned, however, that you will have "trouble in the flesh" (verse 28). What does that mean? It means that some traditional Christians, who think that divorced people are somehow "tarnished" more than they are, will cause trouble for you by making an issue out of your divorce..... and that can hurt.

Is the Lord in favor of divorce? Obviously not.....any difficulty in a marriage can be healed. But that effort requires TWO people who want to try. Often, one does not, and insists on divorce. It is a tragedy, and surely the work of the devil, but the Lord handles it with grace and understanding. He would never heap more hurt onto souls who are already deep in pain.

A difficult subject, to be sure.....emotions on this run high. I have presented a view shared by many. Some believe in only two grounds. We can agree to disagree on the number of grounds, but not on God's view of divorce. He can forgive it.

Faith Profession: "I will study this subject on my own, letting the Lord guide me into all truth. I believe the Word as my final authority."

Study Scriptures: Colossians 2:13-14; Romans 7:1-3

Devotional # 215
Escape From Trials

Scripture: I Corinthians 10:13

Early in my Christians life, this Scripture was introduced to me as a memory verse. I suspect that many of you had the same experience. I was taught that the verse meant this: that God might send trials (temptations) into our lives, but that He would never let those trials be too much for us to handle, and that He would give us a way of escape, even if it came only at the last minute. It makes for a nice, neat sermon. Unfortunately, it just isn't true.

The traditional interpretation of this verse has one large flaw.....it ASSUMES that it is God sending the trials (temptations). Please notice that this verse does NOT SAY THAT. It says that the trials and temptations that come upon you are the same ones that come upon most people. It doesn't say that God sends them. Obviously He would not do that. Trials and temptations are the work of the devil and his helpers.....EVERY TIME. God is the One who is faithful to limit the trials, and to give you a way to escape from them. THAT'S what this verse SAYS.

Why do we assume that God sends the trials? Because most Christians don't understand their standing with the Lord.....and don't understand who the Lord is.....enough to get this verse straight. Why else would you accuse a loving God of sending cancer, rape, starvation, poverty, leprosy, and a myriad of diseases on you? You mean to tell me that your God can't think of any other way to teach you some Bible than to put hideous diseases and pain onto you?? Wow.....have you got Him wrong!

Your Trinity IS LOVE. Love is defined for you in I Corinthians 13, where it says, in part, that "love is kind, and thinketh no evil." It says in James 1 (see study Scriptures) that the Lord NEVER sends trials to humans. Why, then, do His own children persist in making these outrageous accusations against Him? Let's just read this verse without putting in any assumptions. You'll find the correct interpretation and one consistent with the Lord's character.

Faith Profession: "I will be careful not to place assumptions into my reading of Scripture. I have a loving Savior, who seeks my good, and is always on my side."

Study Scriptures: James 1:13-15; Psalm 118:6

Devotional # 216

Jesus is Lord

Scripture: I Corinthians 12:3

Jesus is Lord. It's a simple phrase, but holds such power! That's true because of the fundamental truth of today's verse. By virtue of what He accomplished at Calvary, and during the three days and nights immediately afterward, Jesus completely defeated the devil, Hell, the grave, sin, and death. That makes Him Lord over all things; or, more simply put.....Jesus is Lord.

Notice that a person saying this phrase does so through the power of the Holy Spirit. That would make sense, because of John 16:13. Notice also that nobody calling Jesus accursed (using His Name as a curse, for example) is under the influence of the Spirit when doing so.

Now, you might think that this is just another phrase.....but you'd be wrong. This phrase has some of the same power as the great Name that God calls Himself.....the great "I AM." The sheer power of that name knocked people off their feet (see study Scriptures). This phrase.....Jesus is Lord.....has that same kind of power in the spiritual realm.

If you would take some time to study Philippians 2:9-11, you'd see that, at the mention of the Name Jesus, all spiritual beings are forced to bow their knee. I'm sure this infuriates the devil's crowd. That's why I like to say "Jesus is Lord" out loud every time I sense a strong demonic presence near me. Despite themselves, they MUST obey the Word, because they are defeated beings, and they know it. So, I repeat this phrase, over and over, picturing in my mind these scowling, slobbering slime-balls dropping to one knee every time I say it. I get the greatest delight out of that!!

Jesus IS Lord.....over your life.....your possessions.....your family.....your job.....your ministry.....your future.....your health.....your safety.....and your eternity. Saying it out loud will give you an infusion of spiritual power, as well as tormenting those demons who can hear you.

I'm so glad that Jesus is MY Lord. Aren't you?

Faith Profession: "Jesus is Lord. He is not only Lord, but He is MY Lord. Praise God!!"

Study Scriptures: John 18:1-6; Exodus 3:13-14

GIFTS

Scripture: I Corinthians 12:4-11

You know, it's kind of difficult to expound on New Testament verses in a study like this without bumping into things like tongues, healing, and prophecy. I guess I could wish that these things weren't so prominent in the Bible, but, in fact, they are. The average Christian might do well to ponder that fact, since teaching against these precious gifts is present in too many churches these days.

Please notice that these things are said to be GIFTS. The Giver goes out of His way to provide them because He expects the recipients to be excited, and joyful, with them. The Giver knows that they are vital to spiritual health in the end-times church. The Giver has gone to considerable trouble to provide them. And, the Giver must be quite shocked to see that His generosity is being rejected by so many of His own children.

These things are GIFTS. They are from YOUR LORD. They are part of the ministry of the Holy Spirit. The use of them imparts LIFE into church services, and into lives. They are powerful. Proof of their effectiveness is recorded for us all over the New Testament. Some churches, like this one at Corinth, went overboard on some of these gifts, and had to be brought back into balance. That certainly doesn't negate the gifts!

Did you notice verse 7? It says that these gifts are given to every person (every saved person) to profit "withal" (KJV).....which means to profit everybody. These gifts are given to every believer (see study Scriptures). But, as always, the Lord will not force ANY believer to receive them.

How sad, though, for the body of Christ to have been given potent tools to use against the enemy, and then not to use them.....or worse, to believe that they are actually HARM-FUL. What gift of the Holy Spirit have you ever heard of that was harmful?? This guy is trying to HELP you. But, because He is a gentleman, He will not force the issue. So, powerful gifts like these go to waste for many.....to the dismay of the Holy Spirit.....and to the delight of the devil.

Faith Profession: "I will not permit the devil to deceive me about the gifts of the Holy Spirit of God. I will look into them in a search for truth, asking the Lord to guide me into all truth about them."

Study Scriptures: Mark 16:17-18; I Corinthians 14:39

DEVOTIONAL # 218

ONE BODY

Scripture: I Corinthians 12:12-27

Today's verses introduce a wonderful concept for Christian believers, and that is the truth that, when we receive Jesus Christ as our Savior, we become part of what He calls "the body of Christ."

Every saved person is part of this body, but that is why today's verses spend so much time discussing its diversity. The body of Christ contains people of many different cultures, races, countries. Conformity and sameness is not encouraged in this body. In fact, its diversity is almost celebrated. As it says in the text, the foot isn't going to say that it isn't part of the body just because it isn't a hand. A body has both hands AND feet.....different parts, doing different functions, and shaped differently, but each necessary in its own way, and each valuable.

I've been in churches and schools that believed that, if someone had a slightly different belief than you, you should refuse to fellowship with them. These kinds of people are in for quite a shock when they get to Heaven and find out that there is no special section walled off for just them. Such folks have missed one of the primary points of the New Testament. Sameness is not valued that highly in this Testament. Differences are celebrated.....variety is looked upon with delight.....the Holy Spirit is likened to LIQUIDS (water, oil, streams, wells, rivers) because He has infinite choice of action. That's best, too, because He can adapt to any situation.....any personality.....any slimy trick thrown at us by the enemy

Did you notice that verse 25 says that there should be no "schism" in the body? That word means "division, discord, and disharmony." We are to be about out Father's business.....not bickering about length of hair; type of jewelry; facial hair; or whether or not to wear makeup.....to name a few pointless items of discord. (By the way, I've seen some people who could benefit from the application of a little makeup.....haven't you?) Let's resolve to focus on the TRUTH, and to get His message to a lost and dying world. We are not the same, but we ARE all saved.

Faith Profession: "I will focus on the things that are truly important.....prayer; the Word; and bringing glory to my Savior. I celebrate the variety in the body of Christ!"

Study Scriptures: I Corinthians 6:19-20; Ephesians 5:28-30

A WORD TO THE WISE

Scripture: I Corinthians 12:4

I thought I'd pause here near the beginning of this chapter of I Corinthians to discuss an important issue. We have already encountered mention of the gifts of the Holy Spirit, and they are going to appear often in the next couple of chapters of the Bible. Among them will be tongues.....healing.....authority over the spirits of darkness......prophecy.....and some less attacked gifts, like "helps" and teaching.

You need to understand that what we're dealing with here is not some doctrine of the devil. It is not some temporary phenomenon, either. These things are part of the ministry of the Holy Spirit, and each one has been given to you by God Himself.....not the devil. They are ministries of God's Holy Spirit, and you are told that over and over. By the way, they are not just Pentecostal or Charismatic doctrine.....they are BIBLE. If you look at the study Scriptures today, you'll see plainly that they are from the Holy Trinity, and that there is NO QUESTION ABOUT THAT.

So, if you are in fear of these gifts, you might want to ask yourself how that happened. You are avoiding powerful tools given to you by your Lord. Why would you do that? And who taught you to do that? Who would want you to avoid powerful ministries that chase away demons.....chase away the curse of sickness.....chase away fear.....and give you a prayer language that the devil can't understand, so he can't work against it?

So.....what are you doing avoiding these things?! Can't you see that it's the devil who wants you to stay away from them? He is afraid of the gifts of the Holy Spirit because he has no defense against them. They are ministries of the Holy Spirit, and, as such, are direct from the throne of God. They are the backbone of the New Testament church.....or, they should be. We're going to be seeing them a lot. Look at them through the eyes of faith!

Faith Profession: "I believe the Bible is the Word of God, and the final authority on all matters. I will not be deceived into believing that gifts from the Holy Spirit are harmful, or that they are to be avoided."

Study Scriptures: Acts 2:4,17; Acts 5:38-39

LOVE IN ONE CHAPTER

Scripture: I Corinthians 13

Whenever I need to refresh myself about just what love is.....and what it looks like.....I turn to this chapter. Love is defined in verses 4-8. True love will have these characteristics.

What is possibly even more important is the lofty position given to love. As you observe the world, you'd think money was the most important thing. Christians might guess faith, since you cannot please God without that (see study Scriptures).

But notice what is said about love ("charity" in a King James Bible). Verse one says that, if I don't have love, even speaking in tongues.....or speaking in the language of angels (whatever that is).....would be no better than the dull clang of a cymbal. Verse 2 tells us that we might have the gift of prophecy, and understand all mysteries (which I don't); and though we have all knowledge (which I don't.....and neither do you), even though we might have faith enough to move mountains .....if it isn't combined with love, these things are NOTHING. Further, it says in verse 3 that I could be the most compassionate person in the world, and give myself to be martyred for Christ.....but it would be worth nothing without love.

It is summed up in verse 13. Faith, hope, and love are gifts that last.....but it clearly says that the greatest of these is LOVE. Why? Because the Lord looks upon the heart. With Him, motive is everything. And, besides that, love is what God Himself is!

Do you want to be more like Jesus? Do you want His favor upon your life? OK.....then follow that which is written in verses 4-8. Easy? No. But worth the effort to try? Absolutely. Nothing pleases Jesus more than His children operating in love.

Faith Profession: "I will read I Corinthians 13 out loud each day for a month. Then I will seek to put these principles to play in my daily life. In doing so, I will be working on the most important thing to Jesus."

Study Scriptures: Hebrews 11:6; Matthew 22:36-39

ARE TONGUES FORBIDDEN?

Scripture: I Corinthians 14:1-5

Have you noticed how often the Bible speaks about tongues? There's a lot written about it for something that many Christians believe is "of the devil," or "not used since the last apostle died."

I Corinthians 14 is an excellent chapter, and it is devoted almost entirely to a discussion of tongues. With a whole chapter of information on it, you'd think God's people would be clear on the subject. Instead, confusion reigns due to fear and bad scholarship.

Look with me at today's verse, particularly verse 5. Paul is explaining to the Christians at Corinth that there needs to be more of a balance in their use of the gifts of the Holy Spirit. Like the more modern Charismatic movement of the 1970's and 1980's, the gift of tongues has received too much attention. Paul writes this chapter simply to get them back into balance. In verse 5, he points out that prophecy edifies (instructs) the church, and that tongues and their interpretation ALSO edify. They both accomplish the same purpose.....but one gift is not greater than the other, nor is one to be emphasized more.

Some believe that Paul forbade the use of tongues in this chapter. For those who think that way, please read verses 18 and 39. Neither did he recommend the use of prophecy instead of tongues. He didn't forbid the use of either. He was simply explaining that, if their congregation spoke in tongues most of the time, then those who didn't yet understand the gifts of the Spirit would be confused and untaught. That is, they wouldn't understand anything going on in the service. So, he suggests a more balanced approach.....a combination of both tongues AND prophecy.

Balance is the key. Balance is Paul's point. Nothing is being forbidden.....these Christians had just gotten over-enthused about one gift, and were going a little overboard with it. Read the whole chapter to get context, and you will see what I mean.

Faith Profession: "Balance is a key component of any Christian life. An over-emphasis on any one aspect of the Bible is never recommended by the Holy Spirit."

Study Scripture: I Corinthians 14

THE GOSPEL

Scripture: I Corinthians 15:1-4

The Gospel.....everyone knows what that is.....right? Some say it's the first four books of the New Testament. Some say it's the message of salvation. A few know that the word itself is defined as "good news." But what is the Gospel exactly? If you were to write it down in a few sentences, what would define it?

Well, the answer is right here in today's reading. Notice that Paul identifies it as "the Gospel" in verse 1. Notice, too, that it is the Gospel that saves you.....in the sense that you are saved when you believe it.

The Gospel is defined in verses 3 and 4. Notice that there are four parts to it. These parts are: 1) Jesus Christ died (verse 3). It was a voluntary death, since He had done no sin that would have caused Him to die. He died on purpose, and out of love for you and me. 2) He died for our sins (verse 3). He died for OUR sins (see study Scriptures), not for His own. His death was, therefore, a substitution and paid a debt that we ourselves could never have paid.

3) He was buried (verse 4). That He actually died was verified by Roman soldiers.....men who knew death intimately, since they were familiar with hand-to-hand combat. He was buried in a rich man's tomb (see study Scriptures), as predicted 800 years before in the Book of Isaiah. He died, having BECOME SIN for us (see study Scriptures), and went into Hell itself.

4) He rose again (verse 4). Resurrection.....the event that changed the world forever, and made it possible for us to become part of His body.....part of His family.....a recipient of the salvation that He earned. (He offers it as a free gift to anyone who will receive it.) The resurrection is proof positive that the devil was defeated, since no other man has ever risen from the dead.

Lastly, notice that all of these events have a qualifier..... "according to the Scriptures," it says in both verses. That is, the Gospel is only the gospel IF it is according to the Scriptures. No other source will do.

Faith Profession: "I now know exactly what the Gospel is according to God's own Word. I believe it, and I am saved because I have believed. More than that, I am not ashamed of the Gospel, and will tell others of its saving power."

Study Scriptures: Hebrews 4:15; Isaiah 53:9; II Corinthians 5:21

No Last Name

Scripture: Matthew 16:17

Have you noticed as you read the Bible that some of the people have last names? Here in our verse for today, Jesus refers to Peter by his full name.....Simon Barjona. We know him as Peter, but this more formal name is his also. What does "Barjona" mean? Well, Bible last names are often connected to the person's father. The word "bar" means "son of." "Jona" is the Greek language form of the name Jonah. Obviously, Peter's Dad's name is Jonah, and the name Simon Barjona simply means Simon, son of Jonah. We have similar names in our society today. Think of the last names: Williamson, Robertson, Jackson, Peterson.....for example.

Similarly, Judas has a last name.....Iscariot. In this case, the "is" part of the name is short for the Hebrew "ish," meaning "son of." "Cariot" can also be spelled "Kerioth," and is the town in which Judas was born and raised. Thus, Judas Iscariot means Judas, son of Kerioth (or, "from the town of" Kerioth).

Have you noticed, though, that Jesus has no last name? It is just Jesus. Actually, that's all there needs to be, because everyone recognizes that name. However, there is a good reason that Jesus has no last name.....He had no earthly father. He was supernaturally conceived by the Holy Spirit. Joseph was Mary's husband, but not the physical father of Jesus.....no man fathered Jesus. So, it is no mistake that He is never called by a last name.....He is not the "son of" any earthly man. If anything, He could accurately be called the Son of God.

That's why, in Philippians 2, it says, "That at the name of JESUS every knee should bow..." Just Jesus. That's more than enough!

Faith Profession: "Jesus was virgin-born because He was not conceived by an earthly man. He was conceived supernaturally by the Holy Spirit. Although He has no last name, it is enough to say that JESUS IS LORD!

Study Scriptures: Luke 1:30-35; Philippians 2:9-11

DEVOTIONAL # 224

EYEWITNESSES

Scripture: I Corinthians 15:5-8

In a modern courtroom trial, there are few things that are more convincing than eye-witnesses. People who have seen an event with their own eyes.....especially if there are several of them, and their testimony agrees.....make the basis for an excellent case that an event is fact.

So, how good would a case be if there were over 500 eyewitnesses, all of whom testi-fied to the same facts? It would be, as they say, "open and shut".....there would be NO DOUBT AT ALL that their testimony was true.

Today's Scripture reading gives that kind of testimony about the resurrection of Jesus Christ. As you know, Jesus died on the Cross, and His death was confirmed by several Roman soldiers (who knew a thing or two about death). He was wrapped in traditional grave clothing, and sealed in a tomb. Then, three days later, He appeared, and He was very much ALIVE! That is, He had resurrected from the dead.....the only "religious" figure in history to have done so. (That's what sets Him apart from all other "religious" leaders.....and how you know He is the "real deal.")

Knowing the tendency of human beings to doubt things, especially supernatural things, Jesus appeared to many people during the forty days that He walked the earth after His resurrection. Today's Scripture lists those who saw Him with their own eyes: Peter (Ce-phas); the twelve apostles (including the "new guy," Matthias); then over 500 people at one time; then James; then all the apostles again; and lastly Paul himself. That's a lot of eyewitnesses by anybody's count!

Why was this done? To prove to a skeptical world, and a wondering body of Christ, that Jesus DID resurrect, and that He IS ALIVE.....even now! It would be more than enough proof for any courtroom in the country!

Faith Profession: "Jesus showed Himself alive by what the Bible calls "many infallible proofs." The number of eyewitnesses is just one of those proofs, but it is probably the best. Jesus died, but He rose from the dead, proving that He is THE ONE!"

Study Scriptures: Acts 4:12; Acts 1:3

THE FIRST RESURRECTION

Scripture: I Corinthians 15:20-24

Hey.....what do you mean, the FIRST resurrection!? We know there's only one! Okay.....relax a little, and check our first study Scripture before you go too far. Why would it specify the "first" resurrection if there was only one?

In fact, there are two resurrections.....one for those who are saved, and part of the family of God by their own free will choice.....and one for all of those who fail to make that choice. The first resurrection can be a little confusing because it has three parts, each separated by a period of years. It's not that hard to understand, even though it may not be written at a first grade level.

The three parts to the first resurrection are listed for us in today's Scripture reading. Notice in verse 23 that Jesus Himself is the first of the three parts. Notice, too, that His part of the first resurrection is called by the name "first fruits." So, this resurrection is being compared to a typical harvest.....something familiar to the people of Jesus' day. (For those of us who aren't familiar with harvests.....they were divided into three parts: first fruits (self explanatory); the main harvest; and "gleanings" (where the "leftovers" were gathered)).

So, Jesus is called the "first fruits" of the first resurrection. The "harvest" part of it occurs at the Rapture of the church.....an event soon to happen. This will involve the largest number of people, just as it was the greatest part of a harvest. The third part..... compared to the "gleanings" part of a harvest.....will include any people saved during the seven-year Tribulation period that takes place immediately prior to Jesus' return to earth. So, all three parts are completed before His Second Coming.

The second resurrection takes place just prior to the Great White Throne judgment (see study Scriptures), and will include, for the most part, those who chose not to receive the free gift of salvation that Jesus offered to them.

Two resurrections.....the first of which has three parts. THAT is what the Bible describes, and that is what you can expect.

Faith Profession: "I have received the free gift of salvation paid for by Jesus, and offered to anyone who will receive it. Therefore, I will be part of the first resurrection..... the one Jesus is part of!"

Study Scriptures: Revelation 20:6; Revelation 20:11-15

DEVOTIONAL # 226
SHAPED BY COMPANIONSHIP

Scripture: I Corinthians 15:33

Today's verse is an easy one to miss. It looks innocent enough, and the wording, especially in a King James Bible, tends to fog up the real meaning of it. Put into plainer language, this verse says: "It's all in who you hang around with."

Notice that the verse begins with a warning about deception. We know where THAT comes from, and now we know that there is going to be specific deception with regard to whom you choose as friends.

Most people scoff at this warning, and believe that they can "handle" any temptation that comes at them. Most people will have a hard time believing that their friends would introduce anything that would do them harm.

So...think about it. Who is it that introduces you to smoking; drinking; drugs, etc? People aren't even aware of it, but they like to have company in their sin. Someone who is doing drugs will encourage those around him/her to join in because "it's fun".....or "a little bit won't hurt you." Or, they'll gently nudge you to "go along with the crowd." We all like to be part of the group. Nobody wants to be an "outsider." We tend to move away from anything that might make us lonely or different.

Make no mistake about it.....you will become like those you choose to hang around with..... and you will adopt their habits.....both good and bad. Today's verse is talking about bad habits, and it offers some wise advice. Be warned: bad behavior and destructive habits are deceptive. They sneak up on you, and before you know it, they have you ensnared..... much like they have ensnared those with whom you have chosen to spend time.

The solution? Choose your companions wisely. Good companions, who practice good habits, will influence you, too. The difference? You won't be sorry.

Faith Profession: "I will pray about my choice of friends and acquaintances, and choose them carefully, knowing that I will be influenced by them."

Study Scripture: Galatians 5:9

RAPTURE

Scripture: I Corinthians 15:51-57

The word "rapture," though not found in the Bible, is descriptive of the end-times event when the Lord will come back and take His followers off the earth bodily. That event is described in today's reading, and it is the next great event in Bible prophecy. It is eagerly anticipated by all who are saved and love their Savior.

It is said in verse 51 to be a mystery. That is, it was not understood for many centuries, but here in the last days before this event, the Holy Spirit has revealed much more about it. As you can see, it is a sudden event. Actually, it will happen without warning, as the Lord expects us to live in such a way that we are always ready for it. It begins with a trumpet blast, simultaneous with the voice of the Archangel Michael announcing it with a loud voice (see study Scriptures). At that instant, those who have died in Christ will be raised from the dead in a bodily resurrection. "We shall be changed," it says. Yes, decayed bodies will be supernaturally re-assembled, but will be made incorruptible. That word means "not subject to decay." Your mortal human body is corruptible, as you know. Your glorified body is not.

When this happens, your body will also be changed from mortal to immortal. The word "mortal" means "subject to death." Your new, glorified body cannot die. It is not subject to decay of any kind.....and cannot sin. This new body, instantaneously changed, will be pulled up to Heaven. Those who are alive.....and know Jesus as their Savior.....will also be taken up.....to be with the Lord Jesus forever!

It is the beginning of eternity, or at least the best part of it (since your eternal life began at salvation, technically). It is the most anticipated event on the Christian calendar. Listen! Look up! Be ready! Jesus is coming for us.....SOON!

Faith Profession: "I live in anticipation of the Lord's soon return. I can't wait to see Him, and to begin my eternal life in my glorified body!"

Study Scriptures: I Thessalonians 4:13-18

DEVOTIONAL # 228
THE LETTER KILLS

Scripture: II Corinthians 3:6

It's rare in the New Testament to find something as negative as this verse. The ministry of the Holy Spirit, which is the engine that powers the New Testament church, tends to focus on the positive.

So, this wording is worthy of our close attention. In speaking of the New Testament in general, it says that the "letter" kills, but the Spirit gives life. Okay.....so what does that mean?

The "letter" of the New Testament refers to the tendency to follow the Word so exactly that there is no room to breathe or relax. Operating this way will result in a series of rules.....do's and don'ts".....and requirements that are rigid, unbending, and restrictive. Many churches interpret the New Testament this way, and spend their time evaluating other Christians according to their strict guidelines. It leads to negativity and judgment, and too often it is harsh.

Instead, we are told to follow the "spirit" of the Word. That is, we are to look for its intended meaning.....not necessarily its strict wording. The Holy Spirit, who is always compared to liquids in the Bible, tends to flow as opposed to being confined to a man-made box. He operates in freedom, so that He can adapt to my personality and situation as well as yours.....and still be adhering to the Word.

Just because somebody doesn't act like you; dress like you; and believe everything exactly as you do, doesn't mean the Lord isn't using him/her. He has the freedom to operate in whatever way He sees fit, and that is better, because He can adjust to any situation and personality.

A strict view of Scripture "kills" in this way.....it confines the Holy Spirit to a narrow set of rules, therefore limiting His effectiveness. That reduces His power, and ultimately quenches Him (see study Scriptures). So.....loosen up! Let the Spirit flow as He is intended to do. So what if He isn't consistent.....that's what makes Him so powerful!!

Faith Profession: "I will give the Holy Spirit the freedom He desires in my life. I will not limit Him by expecting Him to operate the same way every time."

Study Scriptures: I Thessalonians 5:19; Ephesians 4:30

DEVOTIONAL # 229

BELIEVE AND SPEAK

Scripture: II Corinthians 4:13

It is so basic to the effectiveness of the Christian's walk with God that it is shocking to see how little it is practiced. With faith being the cornerstone of Christianity, and the Bible so full of examples, you'd think every Christian would know that speaking what you believe is vital to the faith process.

Today's verse says "it is written," and then quotes from the Book of Psalms (see study Scriptures). It then says that we have also believed, and therefore speak. It is the speaking of what you believe that plants the spiritual seed. It is the speaking of God's Word on this earth that is the primary duty of Christians, since Jesus is no longer physically present to do it Himself.

The believing of the Word is the foundation of the process. That involves taking in the Word over and over until it becomes part of you. You believe without even thinking about it, because you have worked to plant it in your spirit. Once you have done that, you are to speak it out into the spiritual world around you. THAT'S how it has effect on the invisible spiritual world in which we live. Every time you speak the Word of God, you plant spiritual seed for good.....you activate angels in the unseen realm (see study Scriptures).....and you put your spiritual enemies on the run.

If you haven't been TAUGHT to do that, then you probably don't do it. That's exactly what the enemy wants, because that gives him uninterrupted freedom to work his evil against you. Have you noticed that God spoke in Genesis 1 and things popped into existence? Did you notice that Bible prophets spoke the Word before it came to pass? Why? Because that's how it works.....that's how God's system operates. You believe and speak, and that releases His power into the situation. No speaking.....no power release. So..... believe.....then SPEAK the Word!

Faith Profession: "I see that I have a vital part to play in the faith process. It is important that I plant the Word in my heart, then speak it out loud. Otherwise, God's power cannot be released."

Study Scriptures: Psalm 116:10; Psalm 103:20

DEVOTIONAL # 230

LIGHT AFFLICTION

II Corinthians 4:17

Have you ever studied the life of the Apostle Paul? If you have, you know that he endured more hardship for the sake of the Gospel than most people can imagine.

In II Corinthians 11, he reveals some of this hardship. Beginning in verse 24, he mentions that he had been beaten with 39 stripes five times. The reason the beating was limited to 39 stripes was that 40 stripes killed many men. This beating was done with a whip that contained multiple strands of tough leather. At the end of each strand, pieces of glass, rock, or sharp metal were attached. This was done so that, when the whip was pulled back, it tore out chunks of flesh. It was a brutal punishment, and crippled many who bore it.

In verse 25, he mentions being beaten with rods three times. For this punishment, the victim was tied down with his feet sticking over the edge of the table. Then a metal rod was used to beat the soles of the feet. It crushed bones to the point where many victims never walked again. (Paul had this done three times, and walked all over the known world delivering the Gospel!)

You can read the rest of the account later. It is safe to say, though, that Paul had endured some of the most brutal beatings, punishments, and burdens that any human could have suffered.....all because he was preaching the Gospel.

So, here in today's reading, he refers to all of this suffering and outrageous violence as "light affliction"!! I wonder if you can possibly imagine how discouraging that verse must be to the devil! What an amazing thing to write.....and what an effective blow it struck in the spiritual battle we all face. Better yet, it has been sitting there in the Bible for 2000 years, jabbing at the devil every day. AMEN!! What a victory for our side!

I don't know about you, but I can't wait to meet someone who could have endured this unprecedented pain, and then casually call it "light affliction." What a man!!

Faith Profession: "Whatever I may face in the way of opposition from the enemy, please give me the grace and wisdom to refer to it as light affliction. I can't think of anything more discouraging to my enemy."

Study Scriptures: II Corinthians 4:8-9; II Corinthians 11:24-28

DEVOTIONAL # 231

WALKING BY FAITH

Scripture: II Corinthians 5:7

The last church that I pastored full time had a large sign hanging over the front of the room with this verse on it. What a great guideline for life on this earth! Did you know that the people of this world walk by sight? And that they think it is odd.....if not grounds to persecute.....anyone who walks any other way? Have you considered that, once you are saved by grace, you are a spiritual being.....changed forever from a person of the world? And have you considered that your primary motivator in this renewed life is FAITH?

Faith is the engine that runs the Lord's system in the Kingdom of God. He says that without faith it is impossible to please Him.....and that the victory that overcomes the world is our faith.....OUR faith, not His.

We walk by sight when we trust our own brain, and our own experience, to get us through the problems of life. We walk by sight when we believe the doctor's report more than the Word of God. We walk by sight when we convince ourselves that we can't afford to tithe, or that we can't prosper by giving away a tenth of our income. We walk by sight when we interpret the Bible in physical terms instead of spiritual truth. We walk by sight when we trust the facts rather than the truth.

Walking by faith is work.....you may as well know that up front. You'll need to spend time in the Word every day. You'll need to be in contact with Jesus at least as much as you talk on your cell phone. You'll need to know, and apply, the promises in the Word to your daily situations. You'll need to live in constant expectation of a miracle in whatever situation confronts you. And you'll need to have as much fellowship with believers.....others who walk by faith.....as possible.

Walking by faith gives you victory in life. It ushers in "abundant life." It brings you close to your Savior. And it opens the windows of Heaven for blessing.

Faith Profession: "Lord, open my eyes to the faith life. I want to live in victory daily, and to experience the blessings that come only through a walk of faith."

Study Scriptures: Hebrews 11:6; I John 5:4

DEVOTIONAL # 232

ABSENT FROM THE BODY

Scripture: II Corinthians 5:8

I can't remember a single funeral service I've conducted that I didn't refer to this verse..... providing, of course, that the deceased was a saved person.

There is abundant availability of Bibles in our land (they are everywhere), and anyone who wants one can get one. (It is not so everywhere.....I've been in Kenya, and have seen Bible school graduates who were going to pastor churches without a Bible! We corrected that problem by giving Bibles to them.....which they hugged and celebrated with tears of joy). So, it is somewhat surprising to find that many people don't know where they are going at death.....or even if they are going anywhere. You'd think this information was hidden away someplace.

The bottom-line truth of the matter is that your only assignment that matters while you are on this earth is to receive the free gift of salvation so generously offered to you by Jesus Christ. That being done, you are immediately moved into the Kingdom of God, and become part of His family.

Technically (spiritually), you are seated in Heaven from the moment you are saved (see study Scriptures). Physically.....bodily.....you are still on earth. But, when the time comes that you are to depart from this earth.....and from your body.....your saved spirit goes "home" where it belongs. That is, it goes to Heaven to be with the Lord, and today's verse is one guarantee of that. It is a guarantee because it is stated.....in print.....in your Bible. More than that, you are present with the Lord immediately.....and He will greet you with a big smile and a warm hug. Jesus will be the first thing you see in Heaven.

Think about it. When you get saved, you become part of His body. When you are loosed from earth, where else could you go? What a wonderful thought!!

Faith Profession: "I have received Jesus Christ as my Savior from sin. Therefore, I will be with Him immediately when I leave this earth."

Study Scriptures: Ephesians 2:6 and 5:30

CHRISTIAN INSANITY

Scripture: Matthew 15:6

"...Ye have made the commandment of God of none effect by your tradition." We might word it slightly differently.....You make the Word ineffective by your tradition.....but it has the same meaning.

My wife and I were discussing this concept today as we rode along in the car. I was thinking that Baptists tend to hang around other Baptists.....Catholics move in Catholic circles.....Pentecostals tend to be around others of like faith and belief. It is natural, I guess.....but is it the best thing?

One definition of insanity, the saying goes, is to do the same thing over and over and expect a different result. So, you notice that your church services are getting colder..... boring even.....and that attendance is dropping. Or, you notice that attendance is rising, but mention of the Word, and the teaching of it, are virtually absent.

How do you expect that to change if you keep doing the same things? You don't see many miracles? You don't get many "yes" answers to prayer? Your Christian life is just "the same old same old"? Why? How could that be if the Holy Ghost and His power reside in you? Why aren't miracles happening at least as much as they did in the early church?

Well, perhaps it's because you never progress in your Bible learning. Do you know why? Because you never look at anything different than you have been taught. Are you sure Pentecostals are wrong? Have you personally done the study of the Word to confirm that? Or are you just being lazy, and taking as truth what some other Christian said?

That's what tradition is.....just accepting the same old things as true, without ever doing your homework. Tradition.....in any form.....nullifies the effect of the Word. No fruit? No miracles? Very little answered prayer? Maybe you're stuck in tradition and don't even know it.

Faith Profession: "I resolve to believe only what I have personally studied in the Word. I will not let the laziness of tradition rob me of blessing and growth!"

Study Scripture: Acts 18:24-28

DEVOTIONAL # 234

CHRISTIAN JUDGMENT

Scripture: II Corinthians 5:10

If you want to see a group of Bible students thrown into terror by a verse of Scripture, then you should have seen my freshman class at Bible Institute. Oh no, we thought..... Jesus is going to publicly expose everything I've done since I've been saved?! Jesus is going to be angry with me in front of the angels and everybody in Heaven!!? (—Because we surely knew that we had failed Him.)

Then, of course, you grow up in the Lord. You get to know Jesus as a person: His character.....His love.....His tendencies. You begin to see that He is a God of love above all else. You begin to understand that no member of the Trinity would ever publically embarrass you. You begin to realize that the people teaching you to be afraid of this event were using it to keep you in line. They were shaping your conduct based upon a false interpretation of today's verse. Were they aware of what they were doing? I hope not.

But, as I've studied, I've come to realize that Jesus forgave our sins when He paid for them at Calvary. How many did He forgive? ALL. Every last one. Even those we committed AFTER salvation, you ask? Hey.....they were all future when He died.....right? ALL means ALL, and Jesus never asks you to pay for the same thing twice.

Are you responsible for what you do in this body since you were saved? Absolutely. Is it a good idea to live with that in mind? Sure. But Jesus isn't going to publicly air your dirty laundry in front of everyone.....He simply wouldn't do that. Anyway, your failures have been paid for. You will have a talk with Him, though, about what you did with His commission to take His Word to others.....to love others.....to seek out the lost. Give Him something to talk about with you. Now is the time, and it's running out.

Faith Profession: "I have responsibility to serve Jesus with my new life. He is interested in what I do with what He has given me. I will be a good steward of all that He has given, so that our discussion will be joyful."

Study Scriptures: I Corinthians 3:12-15; Colossians 2:13

DEVOTIONAL # 235

A NEW CREATURE

Scripture: II Corinthians 5:17

Obviously this Scripture is talking about a saved Christian.....one who has received the free gift of eternal salvation that Jesus paid for at Calvary. Once that is done, you are "in Christ." So, this verse is addressed only to you.

It says that, when you become born again, you become a "new creature." Some translations say a "new creation." Either way, you instantly become unique.....a creature who has not existed before. That's what a child of God is.....a one-of-a-kind creation.....who has had the image of God restored to him/her self.

It says that old things are passed away and all things are become new. But I noticed right away that I had the same face.....body.....personality.....car, etc. as before I accepted Jesus as my Savior. So, it can't be talking about physical things. However, spiritually.....all things have become new. Like what? Well, you are placed in Christ.....He is placed inside you..... your body therefore becomes the temple of God. You become part of His body.....you are given a clean slate as far as sin is concerned.....you are made completely righteous..... you are made a partner with Jesus in this spiritual struggle on earth. You become a child of God.....your Dad is a King.....actually, the King of Kings. You are royalty.....you have the ministry of a priest.....you are free from satan's kingdom and grasp.....you are released from bondage to sin. You have direct access to God's throne room.....you have authority over the spirits of darkness.....you are given supernatural gifts to use in the spiritual battle, as well as solid, proven armor.

That's not the whole list, but even if that was all of it, it would be almost too good to be true. That's who you become at salvation. Don't let the devil deceive you into believing that you are saved, but really not much different than before. That is a lie from Hell. You are a NEW CREATURE! Now.....go act like it!

Faith Profession: "My salvation changed everything for me.....both on earth and later in eternity. I refuse to let the devil talk me out of my rightful privileges."

Study Scriptures: I Peter 2:5,9; John 1:12; Mark 16:17-18

Devotional # 236

Ambassadors

Scripture: II Corinthians 5:18-20

Ambassador. You've probably heard the term on the news, or in the newspaper. Some rich, lucky person who gets appointed to a cushy job doing nothing, you might think.

The word is defined as follows: "a diplomatic agent of the highest rank sent to a foreign government as the official representative of his own government." An ambassador speaks on behalf of his/her country to the officials of a foreign land. An ambassador receives direction from the leader of his/her own country, but is, in fact, the primary representative of the country to the foreigners.

YOU have been appointed an ambassador for Jesus Christ. He has gone back to Heaven, and has left you here in this world to represent Him.....to speak for Him. He gives you His direction, and you take that to the leaders of the foreign land in which you dwell.

His direction is found in His Word. The foreign land to which you have been sent is the same world you came out of when you got saved. The leader of this foreign land, with whom you are to communicate, is the devil. As an ambassador, you are not a citizen of this foreign land; but you are the highest official representative of your Lord Jesus Christ to it. In plainer words, YOU speak for Jesus. YOU are His spokesperson on this earth. YOU are the one who speaks His Word into the darkness of this world, and if you don't do it, it doesn't get done.....because Jesus is not going to do it FOR you.

It is an honor to be His representative. It is important work, and requires knowledge of Him.....His will.....and His Word. That becomes yours to the extent that you spend time learning it.

Are you a good ambassador? Do you speak up boldly for your King? Do you know what He wants, and how He operates? It's all written down for you.....but it won't jump into your brain by itself. You are an AMBASSADOR for the greatest kingdom in the universe!!

Faith Profession: "I am humbled by the realization that I am given so noble and responsible a position by the Lord. I will seek to please Him as I represent Him, and I will speak for Him boldly and with assurance, because I believe His Word."

Study Scriptures: II Timothy 2:15; Ephesians 6:10; Ephesians 4:15

NOW IS THE TIME

Scripture: II Corinthians 6:2

Generally speaking, people don't like to be hurried. They are operating at their own pace, and chafe at anybody who tries to push them to move faster. Okay.....the Lord knows that; but, here in today's verse, it looks like He's being pushy. He's telling us that it must be done today.....that tomorrow may be too late. I don't like that.....I want to go at my own speed.....tomorrow is another day.

Is it? You had a tomorrow yesterday; but, are you sure about the next one? Maybe the Lord isn't being pushy at all. Maybe He is saying today's verse because He knows something you may have forgotten.....that salvation is so important that nothing else matters more. That today is the time.....NOW is the day.....because tomorrow is not guaranteed to you or anybody else.

People are surprised to find that they have no tomorrow every day. Maybe you know someone who left this life so suddenly that you were shocked. How many chances do you think you will get? Is it unlimited? I heard someone say once in a movie, "You are guilty of the worst extravagance, because you live as if there will always be another chance." You may not like that, but it's true. There are no guarantees of another day. Suddenness happens to people all the time, and it invariably surprises them.

But.....you have today. You are sure of that. I don't wish any harm on you, but the Lord has placed this verse in His Word for a reason. Now is the time. Today is the day. Receive Jesus as your Savior.....right now. Do it. Stop waiting. Make the decision. It will free you from the problem of another day, because you'll have an eternity of them to look forward to.....guaranteed by HIM.

Faith Profession: "I receive Jesus as my Savior from sin right here and right now. I believe that Jesus died for me; paid the penalty for my sin; and rose from the dead to prove He had the victory. Now it is mine. Thank you, Lord Jesus."

Study Scriptures: John 3:16; I John 5:12-13; Acts 4:12

Devotional # 238
Seeming Contradictions

Scripture: II Corinthians 6:8-10

There are some things written in the Bible that simply cannot be comprehended unless you know Jesus, and have the Holy Spirit to guide you into the spiritual truth of the words. Today's verses are one such example. Verses like these are what cause unsaved folks to complain that the Bible is difficult to understand.....or that it is full of blatant contradictions.

Of course, there are no contradictions in the Bible. It only seems that way to the untaught or to those who don't know Jesus personally. Everything Paul writes in today's Scriptures is true. Some of it is true physically.....some of it is true spiritually. For example, Paul says in verse 8, "by honour and dishonour." That is, what he's doing to minister the Word is honorable to the Lord, but dishonorable in the sight of men (a waste of time, they think). He says, "by evil report and good report".....so it depends upon who is giving the report. Both are true.

He says, "as deceivers, and yet true".....that is, those outside Christ believe that Paul is leading people astray. They think that is so because what he is teaching is not what they have learned. Pharisees always see things this way.

In verse 9, he says, "as unknown, and yet well known." Yes.....unknown in terms of worldly popularity.....but well known in Heaven. "As dying, and, behold, we live." Dying to the world.....dying to the flesh.....yet very much alive (spiritually) in Christ. "As chastened, and not killed".....see study Scriptures.

Verse 10 goes on..... "as sorrowful, yet always rejoicing." Why sorrowful? Because one's heart grows heavy seeing the rejection of eternal life by those who desperately need it, and because it is sad to see Christians stray from the Word. Rejoicing, though, because Jesus is pleased with faithfulness to Him. "As poor, yet making many rich." Again, Paul had very few earthly possessions, yet he had treasure in Heaven whose wealth could never be totaled. "As having nothing, yet possessing all things".....which is similar to the last explanation.

A Christian possesses all that His Father owns, and so possesses all things. All contradictions, yet all true. It is the Christian life in a nutshell.

Faith Profession: "I know where my real treasure lies, and it is not on this earth. "

Study Scriptures: II Corinthians 6:4-7 and 11:23-28

True Repentance

Scripture: II Corinthians 7:8-10

It seems like long ago now, but there was a time when my former spouse ran off with another man (unsaved!) and never came back. I have mentioned to my wife (the real one.....the one sent from the Lord) that my former spouse has never repented of her sin. My wife expressed doubt that I could know that, but today's Scriptures explain why I can know.....and so can you.

There is a difference between sorrow and repentance. Sorrow is a worldly thing that often involves regret (to some extent), maybe a tear or two, and a couple of days of an unsmiling face. You see lots of this in prisons, for example, but the reality is that the sorrow there is all too often sorrow for being caught, not sorrow for what was done, or, better yet, who you are. Notice in our verses today that the sorrow of the world works death. That is, it comes to no good end.....it accomplishes little.....it is more of a selfish thing.

There is another kind of sorrow that is real, deep, and heartfelt. In verse 10 it is called "godly sorrow," and it is said to work repentance. Repentance is quite different than mere sorrow, in that it compels the person involved to action. Repentance has been defined as "a change of mind that leads to a change of action." It is more than sorrow, or regret, or some other emotional response. Godly sorrow that works repentance will change a person.....move the person to do certain things to make the situation right.....to reimburse that which was taken, if possible.....or at least to try to make amends.

You might say, as my wife did, "How do you know that your former spouse isn't repentant?" Because, if she truly was, I'd be the first person she'd tell. Repentance compels one to try to make it right, or at least to convey some semblance of the sorrow for what they've done to you. Repentance moves you to go to the target of your hurtful deeds or words and tell them how much you regret what you've done. The absence of that is nothing more than the sorrow of the world.

Faith Profession: "If I ever do harm to anyone.....accidentally or on purpose.....I pray that I would be moved supernaturally to make it as right as possible through repentance."

Study Scriptures: II Samuel 12:13; Philemon 10-18

Devotional # 240
A Little Common Sense

Scripture: II Corinthians 12:9

Although I have covered the issue of "Paul's thorn in the flesh" elsewhere in this book (#147 and #256), I want to concentrate today on verse 9 (today's Scripture reading) because it is almost universally misunderstood.

The context of verse 9 is Paul discussing his "thorn in the flesh" (verse 7), and his confession that he asked the Lord three times to have it depart from him. The Lord's answer is verse 9. This answer has been interpreted by many Christian leaders as the following: God said that He would not remove this "thorn," but that Paul would just have to endure it; and for him to rely on God's wisdom that it would be best that he do so. Therefore, it is taught that Paul's prayer for healing was denied.

Well, dear reader, you won't find a better example of one's own beliefs changing what the Lord said. Because, if you just read the verse, you can see that God did NOT deny the request. He said, "My grace is sufficient for thee." Okay.....where have we seen that kind of thing before? Yes.....in Ephesians 2:8, where we're told that we are saved BY GRACE through faith. That is, we exercise faith in God's grace, and it is done.

Well.....WHAT is done? When we're saved, ALL of our sins are forgiven (see study Scriptures). That's what grace does! As applied to salvation, grace removes all of my sins. So, why do we interpret it differently in II Corinthians 12? Paul had a problem.....he prayed for its removal.....and God's answer was that His grace was sufficient. Sufficient for what? Well, in the case of salvation, it took all sins away. In this case then, it has to be that Paul's problem is taken away.....all of it! (See more on Paul's thorn in #256.)

That's true unless you are going to insist on making the Word say something that it doesn't really say. The Bible is consistent, and so is the Lord. If so, then when grace is involved, the problem issue is resolved completely. As always, a little common sense, and consistency, will work out the kinks in human thinking. Paul lived free of this "thorn" from II Corinthians 12:9 to the end of his life.

Faith Profession: "God's grace is always sufficient because it removes the entire issue facing me. Praise God for His grace and mercy!!"

Study Scriptures: Colossians 2:13; Ephesians 2:8-9; Romans 3:23-24

Our Warfare

Scripture: II Corinthians 10:3-5

You have been in a war since the moment you got saved. You knew that, right? You have no doubt been attacked by the devil and his slimy helpers.....over and over again.

If you're like most Christians, you have retreated under the attacks, pleading with the Lord to help you. What you may not have been taught is that YOU have weapons, and YOU can fight back. In fact, the Lord gave the weapons to YOU, and He expects YOU to use them.....not to come whining to Him to help you. He has already done more than He should have.....He left Heaven.....came to earth to live as a human.....died a horrible death in your place.....defeated the forces of darkness for you.....and then gave that victory and its authority to you. And now you want Him to do the little bit that He's asked YOU to do? I don't think so.

Do you see verse 4? Our weapons.....the ones given to us by a victorious Savior.....are MIGHTY. Why? Because they are from God, and have already succeeded in defeating the enemy. Our weapons are well able to pull down the devil's strongholds because they have already worked!

So, Jesus did all the hard work.....then gave you His victory for free. He does ask that you participate in the process by expressing faith in what He's done, and speaking that faith into the spiritual battle around you. You can do that, can't you? You can open your mouth and speak. That is all He's asking from you.....but it is not incidental.

Your willingness to speak His Word into your battle is what releases His power.....His victory.....into it, and that gives the final victory. We have weapons, and they are MIGHTY THROUGH GOD! No force of darkness can stand up to them.....but YOU need to put them to use!

Faith Profession: "I have powerful weapons at my command.....weapons that have already proven effective. I will use them against the enemy, and put him to flight.....every time!"

Study Scriptures: James 4:7; I Peter 5:8-9

False Apostles

Scripture: II Corinthians 11:13-15

With today's reading, we enter the heavyweight division of the Bible. In these verses is revealed the fact that devils have the capability of "transforming" themselves into other forms. When they are "transformed," they appear to be something that they are not. They will be false.....they will be telling lies.....they will be deceiving people.....and, sure enough, people will follow them (including some saved Christians, unfortunately).

Satan himself is a "changeling." In his original form, as Lucifer, he was the "light-bearer" of Heaven. He can change himself into what appears to be a being of the light (of truth).

Satan has ministers, just as Jesus does. There are people in this world sold out to satan, and who minister (serve) on his behalf. Some of these ministers transform themselves into "ministers of light." That is, they can effectively pretend to be God's people, when in fact they are not. They are, as today's verses indicate, "false apostles, deceitful workers." And their goal is to lead you away from the truth of the Word.

How do you recognize them? What is your defense? As always, it is the Word of God. Now, here's the part that modern Christians don't like to hear.....it is YOUR responsibility to fill yourself with enough of the Word that you will recognize they are ministers of deceit. How? By knowing the Word well enough that you recognize their teaching is false. They don't glow in the dark. In fact, they are usually the most smiling, pleasant, and friendly of folks. You will recognize them only by the fact that they speak contrary to the Word of God.

The world around you is not always what it seems. Good soldiers learn to recognize infiltrators. The Lord is counting on you to do your homework, and be one of those good soldiers.

Faith Profession: "The Word of God is my most valuable possession for many reasons. The transforming ability of the enemy is only one of those. I will study the Word to hone my recognition skills for Him."

Study Scriptures: Galatians 1:6-9 and 2:4

DEVOTIONAL # 243
SERIOUS PERSECUTION

Scripture: II Corinthians 11:24-28

Persecution, as we have seen before in this book, comes in different forms.....some physical.....some spiritual. With regard to physical persecution, you won't find a more impressive list than today's reading.

Most of the list explains itself, but I'd like to comment on just a few of the items mentioned. The beatings described in verse 24 are called "scourging" elsewhere in the Bible. It was commonly believed that 40 stripes would kill a man, so the Romans, in their deep compassion, limited the beating to 39 stripes. In fact, this type of flogging often DID kill the victim. Paul not only survived five such beatings, but operated just as if he was never beaten at all.

The process of beating a man with rods, as mentioned before, was as follows: the man was tied down flat with his feet sticking over the edge of the platform. Thick, solid rods were then used to smash the bottoms of both feet repeatedly. The normal result was for the bones in the victim's feet to be shattered, and that man would never walk again. Notice that Paul endured this atrocity three times, and then walked all over the known world at the time delivering the Gospel.

It's common belief that Paul was never healed from bad eyesight. That teaching is not correct, but there is certainly no more evidence of the miraculous healing wrought in Paul over and over again than this list. The Lord healed this man many times, and did so completely. None of these punishments.....meant to stop him from being able to preach..... ever even slowed him down! Yes.....the Lord heals. This list is proof positive of that.

Faith Profession: "If the Lord could.....and did.....heal Paul from these outrageous tortures, then He certainly will heal me."

Study Scriptures: II Corinthians 4:17; Galatians 2:4; Acts 20:18-21

PAUL VS. PETER

Scripture: Galatians 2:11-17

This interesting passage of Scripture gives us a glimpse into an incident that sparked temporary conflict between Paul and Peter.....both of whom were leaders in the early church at that time.

The Book of Acts is a time of transition for the church.....moving away from the Old Testament law and toward salvation by grace alone. The change was not always graceful..... as you might expect with humans.

Peter had defended Paul's right to preach to the Gentiles in front of the assembled church leaders at Jerusalem (see study Scriptures). Now, some time later, he comes to Antioch. And, when certain officials from Jerusalem come to visit, Peter withdraws from the Gentiles and separates himself unto the leaders.....causing others (who knew better) to join him. Before this time, Peter had freely associated with the Gentile believers.....but now, he separates himself. This action, called "dissimulation" in verse 13, created a division among the members of the church along the lines of Gentiles and Jews. Paul immediately recognizes this, and confronts it.

Notice that, in verse 14, Paul confronts Peter.....who had started it all.....openly in front of the whole group. Before you condemn Paul for being insensitive, remember that the division had been created openly and publically, and the Holy Spirit does not take offense at Paul's actions. Though it is not stated, it is safe to conclude that Paul's words were heeded, and the separating of the church into distinct groups came to an end.

Churches today could learn from this. "Cliques" (small groups who keep themselves separate from others) are rampant in the end-times church. Those left out feel hurt, and the body of Christ suffers.....as well as its Head, Jesus Christ. Let's take a lesson from Paul.....we are all one family, each member having the same value. Let's take care to operate that way.

Faith Profession: "The church is to be marked by its UNITY, not by fracturing into exclusive groups. I refuse to be part of any clique at my church."

Study Scriptures: Acts 15:1-12; Proverbs 6:16-19

DEVOTIONAL # 245
CRUCIFIED WITH CHRIST

Scripture: Galatians 2:20

This would be a wonderful Scripture to add to your list of those your say aloud daily. It is true of you if you have received Jesus Christ as your own personal Savior from sin..... just as it was true of Paul, who wrote it.

Because I'm saved, I AM crucified with Christ. It is exactly the same as if I'd have hung on the Cross the same way Jesus did. Though crucifixion meant death.....a most horrible death at that.....“nevertheless, I live.” So we are dealing with spiritual truth here. I have died spiritually, just the same as if I'd been crucified. I live, though, both physically and spiritually, because Jesus paid the price FOR me.

Yet.....the life I live now.....since salvation.....is not the same. I am a changed person. As an old pastor of mine from Tennessee used to say, my “want to” has been changed. In spiritual fact, I am NOT the same person (see study Scriptures), but a new creature.....or new creation.....in Christ. I have become that unique form of life called a “son of God;” and, as such, I am different than any other creature. I am special. I am unique. I am given supernatural abilities as I yield to the Holy Spirit to minister them through me.

The life I now live on earth.....in this flesh body.....is lived by faith rather than by my own abilities, experience, and brain power. I am no longer subject to random chance.....like those in the world without Jesus (or at least that's the way it SHOULD be. Many Christians have been taught otherwise, and have bought that lie).

My life is no longer the same, because it is no longer mine. It belongs to the One who paid a high price to purchase it. When it was mine, I messed it up anyway.....I'm so glad it's HIS now. As I yield to Him in faith, He will work supernaturally through me. THAT's what it means to be crucified with Christ!

Faith Profession: “I AM crucified with Christ, and I willingly place my faith in Him and His Holy Word.”

Study Scriptures: II Corinthians 5:17; Ephesians 2:10-22

DEVOTIONAL # 246

REDEEMED

Scripture: Galatians 3:13

If you spend some time meditating over today's verse, you would have to begin to wonder why so many people.....Christians included.....want to stay under the law. (By the way, meditating would be okay; meditation is not originally an Eastern religion idea, but a Bible concept. It means turning a thought over and over in your mind.) Obviously, the law brings you under a curse.....the curse of sin. (Have you noticed that the Old Testament ends with the word "curse"?)

Okay.....now that you're back from checking the Book of Malachi, what did I mean by that last remark? Just that, if you look at most denominational and/or traditional churches, they all operate under some form of the law. Oh, they're sure they're saved, and they know it's by grace through faith. Yet, these same folks will teach you that you need to DO certain things to be "spiritual".....things like visiting the sick; participating in church ministries; being faithful in attendance; tithing. They won't come right out and say you're not saved, but they sure are good at making you feel inferior if you're not performing to their standard of conduct.

It's one of the main things wrong with modern Christianity. It's nothing short of the same judgmental spirit that kept the Pharisees from believing in Jesus.

Today's verse, though, says that Jesus Christ was made a curse for us when He hung on the Cross. In doing that, He redeemed us from the curse of sin. That is, He "bought us back".....He paid a price FOR us that released us from sin's penalty. We can actually HAVE that payment IF we will receive it by faith.

That's why Christians are so devoted to Jesus. He did something we could never do, and then gave it back to us.....free for the asking. All we need to do is ask. Have you asked Jesus for the free gift of salvation? Right now would be a great time.

Faith Profession: "Jesus became a curse for me when He volunteered to die on the Cross in my place. Thank you, Lord, for loving me that deeply, and for caring more than anyone else ever could."

Study Scripture: Romans 10:9-10,13

Heirs of the Promises

Scripture: Galatians 3:26-29

Today's Scripture reading is one of the greatest promises in the Bible. When I got saved, I knew only people who attended a traditional church. So, I attended similar churches. Later, when I attended Bible school and seminary, I stayed with what I knew. Unfortunately, these good folks had incomplete revelation of the Scriptures, and never focused on today's verses. In failing to do so, they missed a vital truth.

Verse 26 states something we already know.....we became God's children when we received Jesus by faith. What I wasn't taught.....and what SHOULD be taught in every Bible school.....is the connection between verse 26 and verse 29. Notice, in verse 29, that it addresses those who are in Christ. That's you and me if we're saved. It says, "If ye be Christ's, then are ye Abraham's seed..."

Okay.....let's hold up there for a second. Being saved places me in the family line of Abraham (Abraham's seed being his offspring.....his children and ancestors). I was taught that Christians were NOT part of Abraham's descendants.....yet here it is in plain English.

Furthermore, it says that, since we are Abraham's seed, we are also "heirs according to the promise." What promise? The one given to Abraham. Essentially, that is the Old Testament covenant with the nation of Israel, detailed in Deuteronomy 28. Yes, I know that we're under the New Covenant, but the difference between the Old and the New is that the Old was based on personal conduct, but the New is based on Jesus Christ and HIS conduct!

But, the elements of the covenant, listed in Deuteronomy 28, never changed. What does that mean? It means that, since I received Jesus as my Savior, I have inherited the promises given to Abraham, including everything under the Old Covenant.....and that's quite a treasure!!! What a magnificent God we serve!!

Faith Profession: "As a New Testament believer, I have inherited the promises given under the Old Covenant. They are mine if I will receive them by faith!"

Study Scriptures: Deuteronomy 28; Deuteronomy 7:13-16

CASSIE'S GIFTS

Scripture: Matthew 7:11

Yesterday we celebrated Cassie's birthday.....she was six years old. Cassie is our grand-daughter, and is, of course, the cutest and smartest kid in town. Among the gifts given to her were three things from us, and I noticed that Cassie opened all three of those gifts.

What would you have thought if I'd told you that Cassie only opened one of the three gifts? What if I told you that we told her there were two more gifts, but she insisted there were not? What if I told you that she stubbornly refused to look at the other two gifts, and that they are still sitting there.....unopened.....and that all she'd have to do is open them to have them for her own?

Well, you'd tell me I was nuts. Who would fail to receive gifts from someone who loved them, and went out and bought them, and gave them freely? How silly would that be? Okay.....Cassie didn't hesitate to open all three gifts, and they have been hers since she did that.

Why do I tell you such a story? Who would refuse free gifts? Well.....quite possibly..... you. If you're like most people reading this book, you know Jesus as your Savior.....and you'd be dogmatic about that. He offered salvation as a free gift, and you received it..... probably immediately.

But did you know that Jesus brought more than one gift to you that day? Why did you open only one? Jesus went out of His way to purchase several other gifts for you. He brought them to you, all wrapped in colorful paper, and with your name on them. One is called healing.....one is called authority.....one is called protection.....one is called prosperity. You opened the salvation gift, but walked away, leaving the others unopened. Why? Isn't that just as inconceivable as a six- year-old refusing to open some of her gifts?

Check out the study Scriptures. They will confirm that you may have left a few gifts unopened that Jesus bought for you.....and the price was high.

Faith Profession: "It must have hurt Jesus when I refused to open the other gifts He brought for me. I'm resolved to make a correction. I'll look into these honestly, and determine from the Word that these things are mine,"

Study Scriptures: Psalm 1:3; Matthew 8:17; Psalm 91; Isaiah 54:17; James 4:7

DEVOTIONAL # 249

OUR "DADDY"

Scripture: Galatians 4:6

Because you have become a child of the Most High God, He has sent forth His Spirit.....
the Holy Spirit.....into your hearts to cry out "ABBA, Father." This phrase, "Abba, Father," is used only three times in the Bible.....each time in the New Testament (see study Scriptures). There is only one good way to describe what it means: it is a term of intimate affection that means, in essence, that God the Father became our Daddy when we got saved.

We're often given the impression that the Lord is someone removed from us, sitting on a big throne, judging us harshly. Who came up with THAT??! Talk about false teaching!

No.....quite the contrary.....the Lord has become your Daddy. His relationship with you is very much like the one you have with your own small children.....or your grandchildren. He loves you more than He can express. He can't wait to see you, and when you appear in the door of His throne room, He looks over and gets a huge grin on His face! He kneels down with arms outstretched and yells, "Hi! I'm so glad to see you!! Come over here and let me give you a hug!" Oh, yes He does!

Then, when you do come over, He puts you up on His lap and listens closely to every word you say. He wipes away tears.....He laughs with you.....He gives you encouragement that your problem will be okay. He is your Daddy, and nobody loves you more. Nobody delights in you more. He thinks about you, and misses you when you are away.

Daddies are like that. And Jesus Christ the Lord is YOUR DADDY!

Faith Profession: "I love the thought that Jesus is my Daddy. It gives our relationship a whole new feel, and I like it!"

Study Scriptures: Romans 8:15; Mark 14:36

DEVOTIONAL # 250
THE WORKS OF THE FLESH

Scripture: Galatians 5:19-21

The works of the flesh: they are listed here for all to see, and there is nothing pretty about any of them. Seventeen things appear, some of which are apparent, and some which are not. You know what adultery is, and fornication. (The difference? Adultery is fornication committed by a married person.)

Idolatry.....hatred.....wrath.....strife.....murder.....drunkenness.....we know what these are. Lasciviousness is defined as wild lust and lewdness.....sort of fornication on steroids. The witchcraft that's mentioned includes drug use, as the Greek word from which it's translated is the same word from which we get our word "pharmacy."

Variance is the annoying tendency to be against anything and everything. Emulations is a word for "keeping up with the Joneses".....and it is similar to the word "envy." Seditions are rebellions against established governments. Heresies are beliefs contrary to plain Bible teaching (and are rampant in the end times church). Revellings are loud, wild parties which often include many of the items mentioned elsewhere in the list.

The flesh, left to its own tendencies, will head in the direction of this list.....and you can count on that. That's why the Lord came down to earth to die for us. He knew that there was no hope for humans without a fundamental change in our inner nature. When changed supernaturally.....from within.....a person has some weapons at his/her disposal to use in the fight against these tendencies of the flesh. Without any inner change, destruction is just a matter of time and method.

Do you know Jesus as you own personal Savior? Have you asked Him for the free gift of salvation from sin's penalty that He wants to give to you? Why not? It's free.....it's easy.....a "yes" answer is guaranteed if you'll just ask. Go ahead..... right now.....and let Him give you something that can make a real difference for you.

Faith Profession: "I know the Bible is true because I can see the kind of things in this list going on all around me. Jesus is the only one who can make a difference."

Study Scriptures: Revelation 21:8; Galatians 5:17

GOOD FRUIT

Scripture: Galatians 5:22-23

The fruit of the Spirit of God would have to be good fruit, of course. And, it is listed right behind the works of the flesh.....to serve as a sharp contrast to the ways of the world. There are nine fruits mentioned, and it is no surprise that love is first on the list. The characteristic that most closely relates us to the Lord is love.

Joy is next. Joy is different than happiness, in that joy is a more permanent condition. Some have described it as "a calm delight," and it is based on the assurance of God's gifts that we have in our Bible. Peace is ours because we know we have the victory, in this life and the next.

Longsuffering means that we can be patient with oppression, knowing that it is defeated, and that help is always on the way. Gentleness is one of my favorites, not because I possess much of it, but because I appreciate it so much. My wife has this in abundance.....it is a soft approach to life that is not judgmental, and tends to see the good in things.

Goodness is tied to longsuffering, and is the tendency to find what's right about a person or situation rather than what's wrong. Faith is unconditional trust. The Lord values it highly because it is the key that unlocks His blessing to us, and because we believe without having seen. Meekness is sometimes mistaken for weakness, but it is an inner strength..... an iron resolve.....that never seeks to glorify itself, and tends toward the background.

Lastly, temperance can also be translated as "self-control." It is valued because the Lord has not yet completed the redemption of our bodies, but He appreciates it when we exercise control over them.....it keeps us out of trouble.

These nine things are not developed by your efforts, but are part of the "gift package" Jesus gives you at salvation. You need not strive for these things.....they simply describe who He made you to be when He saved you. Just be these things, and you will see them become part of your daily walk.

Faith Profession: "The fruit of the Spirit describes who I am in Christ, not what I'm trying to be. They are His gift to me, and to those around me."

Study Scriptures: II Corinthians 5:17; I John 4:8; Philippians 4:7

DEVOTIONAL # 252

LIVING LIKE HIM

Scripture: Galatians 6:1-2

One of the saddest things about saved Christianity is that there is some truth to the old saying that "the Christian church is the only organization in the world that kills its own wounded." I commented to the dean of a Bible school one time that it would be great to attend the school and be around all Christians. His response? "You haven't been around too many Christians, have you?"

Our Christian brothers and sisters get wounded in the battle. Sometimes it's because they do something really stupid. Sometimes they just can't bear another battle, and fold up for a time. Sometimes it's something from their past that they can't change, but for which they are held at bay by the Christian community. If you've ever experienced a divorce, you'll know what I mean when I say that the Christian community can be downright cruel.

But, I've noticed that Jesus spent time with prostitutes, traitors to their country, thieves, and loud-mouthed braggarts. He had compassion on the unfortunate, and even on those who had done something awful. Today's verses tell us to be like Him. If you are truly spiritual (many folks THINK they are, but they are just Pharisees), you will minister lovingly to those who have screwed up their life. The goal is to restore them.....to get them to see that they are forgiven.....to build their confidence back up.....to convince them that they're still useful and valued in God's work. Why? Because they could easily be YOU, and it says so at the end of verse 1.

Mary Magdalene was a hooker. Paul was a murderer and an ex-con. Matthew was a traitor and a thief. They were probably shunned by the Pharisees of their day, but the Lord had compassion on them, and considered them useful and valuable in His work. So.....ease up on people when they fail. Look for ways to help them get right. Encourage them to go on for Jesus. That will make you just like HIM.

Faith Profession: "People are human, and they mess things up sometimes. I will seek to help them.....to restore them.....to encourage them to move forward."

Study Scriptures: Acts 7:59-60; Luke 22:54-62 with John 21:15-17

SOWING AND REAPING

Scripture: Galatians 6:7

As you know, there are certain laws at work in the realm of physics in our natural world. For example, there is a law called gravity. If I drop something, it goes down (under normal circumstances). We have learned to live within the limits of laws like gravity.

Well, there are laws in the spiritual world, too. They are just as fixed.....just as certain.....as the law of gravity. One of those spiritual laws appears in today's reading. It is called the Law of sowing and reaping. Sometimes you hear it this way: "Whatsoever a man sows, that shall he also reap." It is a certainty, because it is a law written down in God's Book.

Plant rose seeds..... get roses. Plant corn.....get corn. You can't plant corn seeds and get carrots. We know that in the physical realm, but do we know it in the spiritual? It works the same way there. If you sow kindness.....you'll get kindness back. If you sow financial seed into God's Kingdom, you'll get back prosperity. But, you can't sow discord and expect to reap peace. It isn't going to happen.

Some folks want to spend all their money on themselves, and then expect God's blessings in their lives. They get all upset when it doesn't happen, and actually blame God for their lack! Hello.....can you read today's verse? It means what it says, and it is just as fixed a law as gravity.

So, what kind of seed are you sowing today? You realize that, once something goes out of your mouth, it can't be taken back.....right? Are you planting spiritual seed into your life by speaking and hearing the Word of God? Or are you wasting your time on junk that will give you no return? Do you listen to yourself speak? What do you hear.....negativity, doom and gloom, impending illnesses.....or expectations of blessing, positive comments, cheerfulness, and confidence in God's provision? It does make a difference. You reap what you sow. It is a law fixed by the Hand of God.

Faith Profession: "I intend to sow good things, profitable things, and positive things into my life. I will reap the same as time goes by. The Lord has promised it."

Study Scriptures: Philippians 4:8,13,19

DEVOTIONAL # 254

GOD'S WAY

Scripture: Galatians 6:7

Yes, I know we used this Scripture yesterday, but I have one other point to make about it. Have you noticed how often God's way is different than the world's way? In fact, it is often just the opposite of the world's way. Just as the earth revolves in the opposite direction of the way the sun travels across the sky, it is so consistent that you'd wonder how Christians could miss it.

Did you notice that, in today's verse, the sowing comes first? That is always God's way. In the world, we like to reap FIRST, then give AFTER we have accumulated what we consider to be enough. That is, we give IF we can afford to.

But in God's economic system, you give FIRST. You often give when it doesn't seem like you are able to do so. Hey.....if you give only after you have gotten.....where is the faith in that? You know that you can't please Him without faith, right? Well, faith does the sowing first.

I know of a church in Florida where the congregation begins to cheer when the announcement is made that the offering will be taken. They CHEER! You know why? Because they've understood today's lesson.....that their giving is the same as sowing. They sow financial seed in faith, and wait expectantly for the Lord to bless and multiply it (see study Scriptures). He does that, by the way.....every time.

Want to find out if you're "worldly" as a Christian? Check out your attitude toward giving. When the offering is announced at church, is it a time of rejoicing for you? If it isn't, then you've got the wrong financial system. Why not try the supernatural one.....the one that doesn't make sense to your mind, but works just because of faith? It does work..... some of us KNOW that. Why? Because of the order of the wording in today's verse. Sowing comes first.....then reaping.

Faith Profession: "I am so glad that I can participate in God's economic program. I do that by giving in faith.....then waiting patiently for the reaping that WILL surely come."

Study Scripture: Luke 6:38

DON'T LOSE HEART

Scripture: Galatians 6:9

Sometimes you hear people talking about promises in the Word of God, and you think, "What promises? I can't think of even one!" Well, if that's you, take another look at today's verse. It is a promise.....one of many hundreds in the Bible.

Another way to translate the phrase "Let us not be weary..." is "Let's not lose heart," meaning that we need to stay optimistic about our outcome. When a person loses heart, there are certain physical signs. Their shoulders sag.....their head goes down.....their smile fades. Listen.....I know the Christian life isn't always easy. Sometimes it seems like God is a million miles away, and you are slogging through knee-deep mud. In those times, try thinking about this verse.

The Lord PROMISES that you will reap if you won't give up. He promises.

David struggled with this same thing back in the Old Testament. He writes, in Psalm 27:13, "I had fainted" (KJV) (or, "I would have lost heart"), "unless I had believed to see the goodness of the Lord IN THE LAND OF THE LIVING."

That is, He says he would have given up, but he KNEW that he would see the goodness of God come through for him.

It's almost like he believed today's verse before it was written! Better yet, notice that David expected to see this goodness "in the land of the living." That is, here on earth.....in this life......not some day out there somewhere in Heaven!

Are there days when you feel like just quitting? Sure. But, consider this.....if you refuse to quit, the devil can NEVER defeat you. Don't lose heart, my friend. Jesus promises that your efforts for Him WILL BEAR FRUIT. We shall reap!!

Faith Profession: "In those times when I feel defeated and consider giving up, I will read today's verse out loud until it begins to change my outlook. The Lord's promises never fail.....I believe that, and will see the day that I reap!"

Study Scriptures: Psalm 27:13; II Thessalonians 3:13

Devotional # 256
Whose Bad Eyesight?

Scripture: Galatians 6:11

Here's a verse of Scripture that has been used to confirm some poor Bible teaching for many years, and I'd like to clarify it a little through the application of some simple common sense. Paul mentions that he has written a "large letter." This can be taken two ways. It can mean that the letter itself was long, or it can mean that the writer used large letters. We know that Galatians is only six chapters in length, so today's verse must mean that Paul wrote in large letters. Because of this, many have concluded that Paul had bad eyesight, and he couldn't see what he had written unless he used large lettering. It confirms, they say, the passage in II Corinthians 12 where Paul prays three times for relief from his "thorn in the flesh," which, they say, was bad eyesight.

Well, it all sounds nice, but it breaks down under scrutiny. First of all, Paul's "thorn in the flesh" is never said to be bad eyesight in the Bible.....that's an assumption made by scholars. In fact, the "thorn" is people harassing his ministry (see study Scriptures).

Secondly, Paul's eyesight was healed supernaturally following his salvation in Acts 9 when Ananias laid hands on him. I've never known the Lord to do halfway work. If the Lord healed Paul's eyesight, then that was one physical characteristic he NEVER had trouble with again. (See more on Paul's thorn in #240.)

Lastly, you need to think about this assumption. When I write in large print, it's because I know my READER has bad eyesight. People publish large print Bibles, right? Is it because they themselves can't see well, or because their readers need larger print? Come on, folks.....let's use some common sense here. This verse doesn't confirm Paul's bad eyesight because Paul went to Heaven with 20/20 vision.....and that's not what his "thorn" was according to the Word.

Faith Profession: "I will exercise care in my study of the Bible not to be led astray by the assumptions of even Bible scholars. I will compare Scripture with Scripture, as the Bible instructs us to do."

Study Scriptures: Joshua 23:13; Numbers 33:55

Devotional # 257

Amani Ku

Scripture: Psalm 119:165

Some years ago, I had the opportunity to spend two weeks in Kenya, teaching and preaching the Word. Kenya is what they call a "third world country".....most people walk to where they are going.....their buildings and systems are equivalent to those of about the 1940's or 50's in the USA. Yet, I have never been among a happier people. In the two weeks I was there, I never saw anybody angry.....never heard a criticism.....never heard negative talk.

In fact, one day when I was traveling to a church to preach, my friend James, who was driving the vehicle, stopped when he saw four young men sitting by the road. He talked with them a few moments, then they got into the vehicle. James looked at me and said..... smiling..... "These boys will go with us. They will get saved today." No doubt in his mind, even though I was doing the preaching. You know what? Three of them did get saved..... the other one already knew Jesus.

In Kenya, some people speak English (it was an English colony at one time), and others speak Swahili. In my short stay, I managed to learn a few Swahili words. Every time I tried to speak one or two in a service, the Kenyans would break out into large smiles and laughter. One of those phrases I learned was "amani ku," which means "great peace." I wrote that down for two reasons: one, it describes the Kenyans that I met. Despite poverty, lack, need, and backward conditions, they possessed what many Americans lack..... amani ku.

Second, this phrase describes what the Word gives to you if you will study it. Not just peace.....which is certainly good.....but GREAT peace.....the kind that is moved by nothing.

Today, I would wish you AMANI KU!

Faith Profession: "I have much to be thankful for. Jesus has given me both eternal life and abundant life, plus authority over the dark spirits that seek me harm. Thanks to Him, I have GREAT PEACE."

Study Scriptures: Philippians 4:7; Isaiah 54:13; I Peter 5:14

ALL SPIRITUAL BLESSINGS

Scripture: Ephesians 1:3

Did you know that the word "blessed" means "happy"? Today's verse says that it makes the Lord God.....our Father.....happy to bless us. Isn't that a wonderful thought? It's certainly contrary to the popular belief that God sends sickness and trials into our lives to teach us some lesson! No, what the Lord likes to do is BLESS us.

Notice, too, that He chooses to bless us with ALL spiritual blessings. I wonder what that word "all" means? I'm pretty sure it means exactly what it says.....A-L-L. That is, Our Lord God holds back nothing from us with regard to blessing. Nothing! So, what are these blessings?

Well, eternal life, to start with. Access to Him any time, 24/7. The privilege of being part of His family.....indeed, part of Jesus Himself! (We're part of His body). We have been made a temple. We have been given His righteousness. We have been given victory over death.....and Hell.....and sin. We have been given victory over fear (if we'll receive that). We have been blessed with prosperity (if we'll plant "seed"). We have supernatural protection in this world. We have been given authority over the spirits of darkness (again, if we'll receive that).

We have the blessing of being partners with Jesus in the battles of this present world, in that we are charged with the responsibility to speak His Word so that He can move it forward with His power. We have victory over sin and temptation (if we'll use it). We have been healed, because healing was part of the Redemption (if we'll receive that). We have access to His Royal Throne Room.....anytime. We have constant contact with God's Holy Spirit, who empowers us to do miraculous things in this earth.

We are a blessed people, and our future is even brighter than our abundant life on earth! What a Savior! What a Father! What incredible, wonderful blessings we have!

Faith Profession: "I am blessed beyond my wildest dreams by my oneness with Jesus Christ. On top of that, God Himself is blessed to bless me!"

Study Scriptures: II Corinthians 5:17,21; James 4:7; Colossians 2:15; II Peter 1:4

I'M ADOPTED

Scripture: Ephesians 1:5

I've noticed that, in this world, some people seem a little embarrassed to say that they're adopted. I don't mean to speak for them, but I would think that it's a great privilege to be an adopted kid. It means that someone chose you.....on purpose.....to be part of their family forever. That's quite a loving thing!

Today's verse says that we were predestinated to adoption. Of course, the verse is written to saved believers (see verse 1), but we need to be careful about this word "predestinated." Some folks have tried to make this word apply to salvation, teaching that the Lord picks out some folks to be saved, and others to be lost (by not being selected to be saved).

Of course, one can easily see from reading the verse that the predestination here applies to the word "adoption." That is, God decided in advance that anyone who would choose to receive the free gift of salvation would immediately, and permanently, be adopted into His family.

Once adopted, we have the same family rights as Jesus Himself (oh, yes we do.....check the study Scriptures for verification). We are placed under the Blood Covenant.....we become princes/princesses.....we become joint heirs.....we become priests, permitted to intercede in prayer for others on this earth. We are, in every sense of the word, part of God's great, unending, blessed family!!

Why did we need to be adopted? Because, as people born on this earth as descendants of Adam, we had inherited our earthly ancestor's fallen nature, which denied us access to Heaven. The act of receiving Jesus Christ as Savior from that nature gives us a new "image".....actually, a restored image.....that of our Savior, Jesus. Since we were not originally born into God's family, we have need of adoption when we get "born again" (spiritual birth). As we see in today's verse, the Lord had that adoption all planned out for you in advance. He thinks of everything!

Faith Profession: "I am adopted into the family of God immediately upon my choice to receive Jesus as my Savior from sin's penalty. The Lord planned this in advance because He loved me long before I turned to Him."

Study Scriptures: Romans 8:15-17; I Peter 2:5,9; Genesis 5:3

Devotional # 260
The Deal is Sealed

Scripture: Ephesians 1:13

Occasionally in the Bible you run across a verse that sums up a ton of teaching in a few words. Today's verse is one of those places. It gives us a capsule version of salvation..... the things that transpire in nanoseconds as you choose to believe the Gospel.

Notice first that you TRUST. What do you trust? You trust what you heard from the Word of God. This means you must have been reading the Bible, or listening to someone else speak about it. You heard, and you made a conscious decision to trust that what you heard was the TRUTH.

Secondly, that trust led you to take the next step.....BELIEF. That is, you made the choice to act on what you heard. What action did you take? You told the Lord.....in prayer.....that you believe what you heard from His Word. You believe that Jesus loved you enough to die a horrible death in your place.....that He shed His blood for you.....that He raised from the dead in victory over death, Hell, the grave, sin, and the devil. And, you asked Him for the precious free gift of salvation from sin that Jesus is willing to give you.

And thirdly, the instant that you prayed that prayer, you were SEALED.....with the Holy Spirit of promise. The Holy Spirit came to live inside you.....to permanently indwell you.....from the moment you received Jesus. He's called the Holy Spirit of promise because He was promised.....by Jesus.....in Acts 1. And, He showed up for the first time in Acts 2, and has been indwelling believers ever since! It says you were sealed, as in "locked in place".…..."a closure that must be broken to be opened" (and which no spiritual being can break). SEALED, as in permanence.

There are three steps described here. You experienced all three if you have received Jesus Christ as your Savior. All three, not just the first two. Jesus never goes back on His Word.....we can trust that, too.

Faith Profession: "I have a Savior I can trust absolutely. He is ALWAYS true to His Word, and He will always love me dearly."

Study Scriptures: Ephesians 5:30; Romans 10:9-10,13

YOUR GUARANTEE

Scripture: Ephesians 1:14

We like things that come with a guarantee, don't we? It gives us a feeling of confidence in the product or service, and we naturally feel that it must be a good product or service. So, we have a level of comfort with a guarantee.

Salvation, as you know, is a spiritual thing, and so is invisible. Since it is based upon faith.....another thing you can't see.....it doesn't come with the kind of guarantee that worldly things do. Or does it??

Today's verse is talking about the Holy Spirit, who seals you at the same time He comes to permanently indwell you (see verse 13). Notice that verse 14 says that this Holy Spirit is the "earnest" of our inheritance. Now, most of us don't recognize that word in that usage, but the word "earnest" here can also be translated "guarantee."

Jesus knows us.....better than we know ourselves. He knew that we'd need some sort of reassurance about something spiritual and invisible like salvation, so He provides a guarantee. That guarantee is the Holy Spirit Himself.

Are you having doubts about your salvation, or about your promised inheritance (which you receive at the moment of salvation, not at your death.....inheritances are issued when the GIVER dies, not the receiver. Jesus is the giver in this case, and He died over 2000 years ago)? Any time the devil begins to plant seeds of doubt in your mind about spiritual things, all you have to do is realize that you have the Holy Spirit within you. His presence is your GUARANTEE that you are His child.

Don't you just love the Lord!? Can you appreciate the tenderness and foresight required to plan for the possibility that you might doubt what He did for you? And what better guarantee than a Being who permanently resides in you! You have access to Him any time you want. No wonder the Book calls Him the Comforter.....it would be hard to beat this level of comfort.

Faith Profession: "I know that I have passed from death to life because I can see it in the Word. But my Lord has given me an extra guarantee.....just in case.....in the person of the Holy Spirit."

Study Scriptures: II Corinthians 1:22; Romans 8:23

DEVOTIONAL # 262

YOU ARE QUICKENED

Scripture: Ephesians 2:1

Isn't it comforting to know that you're "quickened"? Well, you say, it might be…..if I knew what "quickened" meant!

"Quickened" is one of those few archaic words that you find in an older version of the Bible. It means "to be made alive." If you meditate on that for a minute, you might find the word instructive. When I think of something being quickened, I picture it moving better and faster. I think of it being motivated by a renewed excitement. I imagine one's heartbeat rising with anticipation of something really good!

And that's exactly what is meant by "quickening." This "quickening" happens when you receive Jesus Christ as your Savior. In effect, your whole life is given an added excitement, and it is exhilarating!

Notice, too, that verse 1 says that you had been "dead in trespasses and sins." Of course, this is speaking spiritually. Your spirit had been dormant until it was acted upon supernaturally by the Word and your faith. So, being born again is exactly like a dead person come to life…..a raising from the dead…..which gives you something in common with Lazarus! As a result, you have a sense of "quickening"…..excitement…..energy…..life!

Have you been "quickened"? Do you know for sure? If you have any doubt about it, you probably have not. There is a simple fix…..just receive Jesus as your Savior. You can do that right now, right where you are. Just go to Him in prayer, and tell Him that you believe in His death, burial, and resurrection for you…..and you now receive His free gift of salvation. That's all there is to it! Do that, and you will understand the word "quickened"!

Faith Profession: "I love Jesus. He is my Lord and Savior because He has quickened me spiritually, and I am alive forevermore!"

Study Scriptures: Galatians 1:4; Colossians 2:13

Devotional # 263

Seated in Heaven

Scripture: Ephesians 2:6

One of the difficulties of the Christian life is the fact that, when we got saved, Jesus left us on earth in the same earthly body. Because this body is flesh, and has gotten used to operating by satisfying itself, and has done so by copying what it sees and hears in the world, it is difficult to comprehend verses such as today's.

It says that we (saved folk) are seated "together in heavenly places in Christ Jesus." Now, we can easily see that we are here…..on earth, so how does this make sense?

The answer is that not everything is physical, even though we have been conditioned to think so. The Bible is a spiritual book, about spiritual things. There is no real comprehension of it unless you start with that realization. And, spiritual things…..although real….. are invisible, and exist in tandem with the physical world.

So, physically, you are here on earth, and you can see that. But, spiritually, you are seated in Heaven in Christ Jesus. How do we know that? Because the Book says so. And where exactly is Jesus seated? Immediately to the right-hand side of God the Father…..on His throne (see study Scriptures). Do you understand what that means? It means that you are in an exalted place. Even angels are not seated in Jesus on God's throne. Therefore, you must be far more important than you ever thought possible! Somebody taught you that you were a lowly, unimportant worm in the scheme of things…..but that's just not true!

You are seated on God's throne…right now! In the spiritual world, you're something else!! If you can get a grasp of that, it will change your opinion of yourself, and it will tend to give you a quiet confidence in this life. You're special!!

Faith Profession: "I am physically present on the earth for now; but, spiritually, I am seated at God's right hand in Christ Jesus. What a privilege, and what an honor!!"

Study Scriptures: Mark 14:62; Ephesians 1:20

Devotional # 264

It's a Gift

Scripture: Ephesians 2:8-9

Here's an old standby verse that almost everyone knows. It contains simple information about your salvation, and most folks agree with it. How ironic, then, to find that many Christians don't actually live their lives by it. It says that you're saved through faith…..and faith alone. It adds that it is "not of yourselves," which says, in plainer words, that you have nothing to do with it except to exercise faith. Faith is indicated when you make the choice to receive. It then goes even further by saying that it is a GIFT.

Now, you know about gifts…..right? You've probably received some, and given some in your life. Gifts are free, and you don't pay someone back for them. You aren't obligated to them either…..you needn't cut their grass for a year, or pay them money later…..and you understand that.

The Lord goes to these lengths to get across these seemingly obvious facts because He knew that Christians would have trouble with this concept. Sure enough, you find well-meaning Christians telling you that you HAVE to go to church every service; or you HAVE to visit people; or you HAVE to read your Bible. Of course, it would be nice if you DID do these things. But…..and I want to make this as plain as possible…..you don't have to…..at least not to get saved or to stay saved. Not convinced? Maybe you should read today's verses a few more times.

A gift comes with NO OBLIGATION. "Doing things" for the Lord comes under the heading of fellowship with Him. It is a relationship thing, not a salvation thing. As the end-times church, we really need to work on getting this concept into our walk with the Lord. Perhaps more people would be attracted to church if they found less judgment there.

Faith Profession: "I am saved by grace, plus nothing. It is God's gift to me, received by faith alone. Thank you, Lord, for your generosity."

Study Scriptures: Romans 3:24; 6:23

HIS WORKMANSHIP

Scripture: Ephesians 2:10

This very important verse of Scripture is perhaps one of the most misunderstood and seldom believed in end times Christianity. Do you see that it says that we are HIS workmanship? Okay.....have you ever known the Lord to do shoddy work? When He created the heavens and the earth, didn't He comment almost every day that it was good? Yes..... the Lord makes things in perfection. When you received Jesus as your Savior, you became His workmanship.....and it was done right.

Of course, this is talking about the spiritual you.....not about your physical body or person. Perhaps that's where all the confusion comes from, but the average Christian certainly does not think of himself/herself in terms of perfection. No, in too many cases, you are told you're "only a sinner saved by grace".....that you aren't worthy to lift your eyes toward Him.....that you are a person of shame and guilt.

But, do you know that the Bible says things about you entirely different from that? Check out the study Scriptures today, and try believing what God says about you rather than what some well-meaning, but mislead Christian has said. Your shame and guilt were paid for. Your sins have been taken away. You are, in fact, an innocent man/woman because He bore your sins for you. You are a child of the King, and a person who has been lifted up out of the muck and slime of this world into new life.

Let's not live in the past. Let's be who the Lord says we have become. Let's take our opinion of ourselves from God's Word, not from men.

Faith Profession: "I am God's workmanship, and, as they say in some youth groups, God doesn't make junk!"

Study Scriptures: I Peter 2:5,9; John 14:12; John 1:12; Ephesians 1:1-6

Devotional # 266
Not Strangers Any More

Scripture: Ephesians 2:11-15

Back in Paul's day, there was the need to reassure Gentiles that they had, through Jesus Christ, become one with the nation of Israel. It was a revolutionary thought for its time. Today, we usually don't need that same reassurance, but we do need to know that we have become part of the same family with all believers, Jew and Gentile alike.

Because we have, through our salvation in Jesus, become part of a new family…..God's family…..we are no longer strangers…..to the Lord, or to His people. Notice, in verse 12, that we are also no longer strangers from the Covenant of promise. That is, the Blood Covenant promises to Israel; the promises to Abraham; the promises to David; any of the promises in the Old Testament…..belong to us.

That's one of the most startling revelations I can give to you! The Blood Covenant promises are staggering in their scope. The only difference for us is that we aren't required to "do" things to earn these blessings. Jesus paid the price FOR us, and we have these incredible promises for free…..just like salvation! This realization changed my whole life. It freed me from the bondages that had been placed on me by teachers of the Word who apparently didn't realize that these great gifts were ours.

I'd recommend that you look closely at today's study Scriptures…..in order…..and begin to realize what you have….right now, in this life on earth! It is some of the most precious and wonderful news that I could ever share with you!

Faith Profession: "I knew Jesus loved me, but these amazing promises give His love more depth than I had ever imagined! Oh, how I love Jesus!"

Study Scriptures: Galatians 3:26-29; Deuteronomy 28:1-13

DEVOTIONAL # 267

WE ARE HIM

Scripture: Ephesians 3:14-15

Yes, I know it looks like bad grammar…..hang in there a minute, and I'll explain. Today's verses reveal something that will come as a shock to many Christians, but that "something" is simply Bible truth, as stated in the Word. That "something" is this: that the Name of Jesus Christ is OUR name…..or, as stated in today's title…..."We are Him."

Let's look at the verses. The context is God the Father according to verse 14. Verse 15 says that the whole family in Heaven and earth is named for Him. So…..are you a child of God? Have you received Jesus as your Savior? Okay, then this is referring to you.

As you might know, your salvation places you into His body in both a spiritual and literal way. You enter in to His body…..called the body of Christ. And, He enters into your body in the presence of the Holy Spirit. You are in Him, and He is in you. In every way that's practical, you have become one.

So, when it says that the whole family is named for Him, then you have His Name as your own. What Name is this? It's the one mentioned in Philippians 2:9-10…..the one to whom every knee will bow. It's the Old Testament name for God, spelled in the Hebrew as "YHVH." Yes, WE are these names!! YOU are Him…..and He is you.

Maybe now you can see why the spirits of darkness are subject to your authority, and why they have no real power over you. You turn out to be far more important and potent in the spiritual realm than many in churches would have you to believe. WE ARE HIM!

Faith Profession: "I realize that I am in Jesus, and He is in me. We have become one person, much like an earthly marriage. And, just as in an earthly marriage, I have a right to His name…..which is now MY name, too!"

Study Scriptures: Ephesians 5:30; Philippians 2:8-11; Ephesians 1:10

DEVOTIONAL # 268

ONE

Scripture: Ephesians 4:1-6

It is often considered "narrow-minded" to limit the choices available to folks to one selection…..especially in the church realm. People are fond of saying that "there is one Heaven, but many paths to it." That is, they're telling you that they believe that God will honor any desire to get to Heaven (or its equivalent), regardless of what denomination it is, or what religion it is, or what belief system it is. These folks have designed a god who fits their way of looking at the world.

Their god is infinitely tolerant and would never insult someone by telling them that they're wrong (after all, the goal is no hurt feelings, right?) Sorry, but that's not right, and today's verses make that plain. According to the Lord and His written Word, there is only one faith…..only one Lord…..only one baptism…..only one hope.

There IS only one way to Heaven, but He has made it free, simple, and available to all. So, if someone believes differently, does that make them wrong!? (Heaven forbid!) Well, actually…..yes, it does. Jesus was plain about there being only one way to Heaven, and He made no apology for it. Since only one person ever rose from the dead, it would not be hard to figure out who you need to believe to get to Heaven.

Some say it isn't fair. Some can't believe that so many people who have chosen to believe otherwise could be wrong. Some get downright angry and confrontational in opposition to what I've presented today. But here's the thing…..it isn't my idea, it's the Word of God. You'll have to tell Him it's not fair. I warn you though….. I don't think He's going to agree.

Faith Profession: "Since Jesus is the only person who rose from the dead, it's reasonable…..and Biblical…..to believe that the only way to Heaven is by believing on Him."

Study Scriptures: Acts 4:12; John 14:6

DEVOTIONAL # 269

HE DESCENDED

Scripture: Ephesians 4:8-10

We all know that Jesus died on the cross and that He rose from the dead. But…..what happened during the three days and nights in between? Was He just asleep? Was it just total darkness?

Today's verses give a rather veiled reference into what actually happened. One thing is clear…..He descended…..and if He did, then He went DOWN. Okay…..down where, you ask? Exactly into where you have suspected…..into Hell itself. You see, His physical death on the Cross is the usual focus, but that is only one aspect of His work. Since all humans experience two deaths…..physical AND spiritual…..then He had to do the same.

On the Cross, Jesus was made to BE sin for us (see study Scriptures). That's why He was forsaken by God the Father…..and it explains why He labored so violently in prayer in Gethsemane. He knew He would become sin, and the thought of it was His most difficult challenge. If He became sin, then He had to go where sin must go…..into Hell. And that's exactly where He went. For you.

It was devastating, but He did what He expects you and I to do…..He began to pray. He prayed Scripture, in faith, while the forces of darkness danced around Him in what they thought was victory. But…..after 72 hours of intense prayer, Scripture promises exploded forth, freeing Him from the sin He bore; from death; from Hell; from the grave; and from the devil's control!!!

He rose up in Hell in victory. The devil and his companions were stunned! They realized they were defeated, and they have known that ever since. Jesus rose from the dead in the greatest victory of all time, and now seeks to give to you every aspect of that victory. He calls it abundant life…..He calls it your inheritance.

Have you received it yet? What a disaster it would be for you to get to Heaven and find that you neglected to take what He worked so hard to provide for you. Receive His gifts. You'll be glad you did.

Faith Profession: "I am amazed at what Jesus did for me. No one ever loved me more than He did…..and does."

Study Scriptures: II Corinthians 5:21; Colossians 2:15

DEVOTIONAL # 270
SOME OF HIS GIFTS TO YOU

Scripture: Ephesians 4:11-12

When the Lord shifted His people from the Old Testament to the New, He made a great many changes with regard to how His people worship; how they operate; how they are empowered; and even the day upon which they worship.

Today's Scriptures introduce us to five of these new concepts. They are gifts given to the body of Christ. (Remember, there was no body of Christ until Jesus paid for sins and rose from the dead.) And these are, by no means, all of the gifts given.

You are familiar with some of these gifts…..pastors and teachers…..from attending church. Evangelists are preachers who travel around, delivering special messages to various churches. The word "apostle" means "sent one," and we can equate them to our modern-day missionaries. Prophets are people who hear supernaturally from the Lord, and relate his message…..usually to a church congregation.

All of these gifts are given by a loving Father who wants you to have access to as much information about Him as possible, because that makes the relationship between you and Him so much better. Verse 12 tells us that these gifts are given to "perfect" you. The word "perfect" means "to mature" you. Secondly, they are to perform the work of the ministry, which calls for people who have the extraordinary capability to serve without fair reward, and to do this in obscurity in many cases.

Lastly, they are intended to "edify"…..a word meaning "to build up." You need this ministry because the enemy will work against you tirelessly, and without "building up," you will lose energy for the fight…..and it IS a fight. Does Jesus love you? The presence of these kinds of people is proof of it.

Faith Profession: "I realize that my Savior has provided special people in special ministries to help me in my Christian walk. I will honor those called to these invaluable positions."

Study Scriptures: Ephesians 2:20; Acts 13:1; 21:8

Devotional # 271

Cunning Craftiness

Scripture: Ephesians 4:14

Some Scriptures are especially applicable to end-times Christians, and today's reading is one of those. I think it's safe to say that there is general agreement that we are living in the last days before Jesus' return. That's why I'm so surprised to see so many Christians running headlong into the predicted apostasy, and into conformation with the church of Laodicea (see study Scriptures).

Having been warned in advance, you'd think we'd be smart enough to avoid the obvious. On the contrary, the three biggest churches in the area in which I live have moved away from the preaching of the "meat" of the Word and into the area of entertainment. Why? Because they have become "seeker" churches (their term, not mine…..and not the Lord's, either), meaning that their goal is to get people into the church instead of staying out of it.

Okay…..that's a start, but…..what then? If no teaching is provided…..no sound preaching…..no discipline…..what real good has been served? Unfortunately, churches like this enjoy telling you how many people attended last week. A number…..a marketing goal, not a spiritual one. Jesus, you might remember, had a small following numbers-wise….. He concentrated on teaching the few who followed Him, grounding them in the truth of the Word.

What is happening today? Folks are being carried away on winds of featherweight doctrine…..being seduced by entertainment and numbers…..being deceived by the enemy to pursue meaningless goals (at least meaningless to Him). It is the end times, my reader. See that you get yourself under the sound, uncompromising teaching and preaching of the Word. Happily there are many churches where the focus is on Jesus and the Word is preached. If you look, you can find one." It might not be flashy, but your Father will be pleased.

Faith Profession: "I realize that I live in dangerous times, filled with the devil's attempts to deceive God's people. I will study the Word, and find a church that preaches and teaches it without apology."

Study Scriptures: Revelation 3:14-22; II Timothy 3:1-7

Volunteer Bondage

Scripture: John 8:32

The other day at the golf course, a lady I know walked past me heading for the first tee. In friendly greeting, I said, "Have a good round." Her reply was stunning in its simple resignation to the effect of evil in our world. She replied, "I probably won't, with all of my aches and pains." My instant thought was …..."Too bad you don't know the truth….. it would set you free from that kind of thing."

I guess I've been in the Bible for so long that I just have that reaction when I hear something like that. In truth, though, the truth WOULD set her free…..from what she thinks are the unavoidable aches and pains of advancing age. You know, many, many people think that way. They see sickness, disease, aches, troubles, and problems as unavoidable facts of life that you just have to deal with. This fatalistic point of view has invaded the New Testament church, too, because many Christians see their life this same way. They think sickness is inevitable because it flies through the air in the form of germs and viruses, or that it's inherited from your ancestors. (They say, "My Dad had cancer, so it runs in the family, and I'll probably get it, too.")

Now, why would that be the thinking of Christians who have the Holy Spirit of God residing within them? Why would that be the thinking of Christians who have the Bible promises from Jesus Himself with which to counteract disease? Have we become so like the world that we have adopted their fatalistic views on life? Have we ignored clear promises in the Word on health and healing? Did Jesus pay for our sicknesses and infirmities in vain on the Cross?! (See study Scriptures).

Are you free? You should be. Free from disease, fear, worry, financial concern, care about the affairs of the world. If you aren't, it isn't because Jesus didn't provide that freedom for you…..He certainly did. What's missing, then? You receiving it as your own, by a free will choice.

Faith Profession: "Thank you, Lord, for providing me a life that's different from that of the world. I'm free, because You died to set me free from all aspects of this lost world. I receive that for myself right now."

Study Scriptures: Isaiah 53:4 with Matthew 8:17

The Devil Needs a Place

Scripture: Ephesians 4:27

One major difference between the Lord and the devil is that the Lord went out of His way to become part of the human race by physical birth. The devil has no physical body to call his own. Therefore, he can only operate in the physical realm…..where you and I live right now…..by getting someone with a physical body to do his dirty work FOR him. This is accomplished when he convinces some human…..through deception, of course….. that it would be in their best interest to cooperate with him.

Now, he doesn't announce himself as the devil. He shows up instead through self pity; pride; selfishness; feelings of being isolated; feelings of being treated poorly; feelings that you deserve better than what you have; feelings that you are being denied certain things in life. When you give in to these deceptions, you give the devil a place inside you….. spiritually…..from which he can work. In effect, you have given him permission to use YOU to carry out his plans to do harm (his intent is to do harm ALL THE TIME). Or, put another way, you "give place" to the devil.

Today's verse tells us NOT to do that. Though it is a command, it is given in love, and with the realization that you might do it, or you might not…..it is left up to you. The Lord does NOT script things in advance, nor does He MAKE certain things happen for or against you. He gave you free will, and He would never interfere with your right to use it (which is why sin is possible). It's not His will, but you get to choose.

You have the power, the right, and the ability to choose NOT to give the devil place in your life. That's what is recommended in today's verse. The devil WILL try to get place…..but YOU CAN PREVENT IT. If you do, you defeat the devil, and give glory and victory to the Lord. It's your choice.

Faith Profession: "This verse gives me choice in this matter of giving the devil place in my life. I choose to shut him out. He has no right to me, and I choose to honor my Lord with my decisions."

Study Scriptures: James 4:7; I Peter 5:9

IT HITS LIKE A HAMMER

Scripture: Jeremiah 23:29

The Word of God is compared to a number of different things in its own text…..apples, bread, milk, meat…..to name a few (see study Scriptures).

Today's reading compares it to something quite different…..a HAMMER. At first glance, this seems like a rather brutal thing for the Bible to compare itself to. In fact, many people see the Word in this light. They believe the Lord to be a harsh, unsmiling judge who looks down on us, searching for something we've done that He can punish us for.

Of course, that's not a true picture of our Heavenly Father, whose outstanding characteristic is LOVE, not judgment. No, when it says that the Word is like a hammer, it is referring to its effect on the things the devil has tried to build up in your life. These things are called bondages, because the devil is busy every day trying to get you all twisted up in the things of the world…..addictions; fears; things that waste your time; bickering; worry; anger…..anything that will be counter-productive to helpful, Bible things.

The devil builds up these bondages in such a way that people don't even realize it's happening. This is possible because, at the same time, he's been busy removing the Bible from your daily life. If, on the other hand, you insist on bringing the Bible back into your life each day, it serves to pound on these bondages…..like a hammer.

Each time you read your Bible (as you've done today with this devotional), those bondages receive a shock as they're struck a powerful blow. As you do this day after day, the bondages begin to crack, and eventually will break into pieces…..as stated in today's verse. Then, they'll be gone…..replaced by firm Bible convictions, and positive Bible blessings. The Word is like a hammer…..try it out, and you'll see!

Faith Profession: "My life will be characterized by a daily time in the Word of God. That way, bondages inside me will receive the hammering they need to be pulverized."

Study Scriptures: Proverbs 25:11; I Peter 2:2; Hebrews 5:12-14

Devotional # 275
Don't Be Sad, Holy Spirit

Scripture: Ephesians 4:30

I have to tell you.....this Scripture gives me a twinge of sadness. I don't like to think of the Holy Spirit of God being grieved. Grieving is what you do at the death of a loved one. Tears are often involved.....sadness.....hurt.

This member of the Trinity has agreed to come and live inside the bodies of God's children. He has come out of the glory and comfort of Heaven to exist in this foul, sinful world for OUR benefit. Among other things, He has come to SEAL us unto the day of redemption (of our physical bodies). To think that we would repay Him with grief is a difficult thought to bear.

Yet, human beings tend to have short memories, and their level of appreciation for a kindness is quick to fall off to nothing. So, the Holy Spirit can be grieved, and all too often finds Himself in this state of sadness. It happens when God's people neglect Him..... refuse to listen to His still, small voice.....refuse to believe that He communicates with them.....or just plain don't think about Him that much. Of course, He's grieved when we sin, and His grief is borne of His intense love for us. It hurts Him to see us do damage to ourselves.

We are asked here to "grieve Him not." Please notice that the context is communication.....what you say.....how you speak (see verse 29). Christians generally pay no attention to what they say. "God knows what I mean," they say.....as if that excuses it. No.....what you say is what the Lord has to work with in the spiritual realm (see study Scriptures). It <u>does</u> matter. Too often, what you say.....or fail to say.....causes big tears to roll down the Holy Spirit's cheeks. Let's not do that to Him.....okay? Let's appreciate what He does for us, and show it in what we do and what we say.

Faith Profession: "I am amazed at the Lord's care for me. He sent the Holy Spirit to be my constant companion, and Comforter. I will appreciate that by taking care not to grieve Him."

Study Scriptures: Hebrews 3:1; I Timothy 6:12; Philippians 4:8

DEVOTIONAL # 276
REDEEMING THE TIME

Scripture: Ephesians 5:15-16

Here and there throughout the New Testament, you will find "recommendations" given to you by the Lord. They are not exactly commands, but are still things you would be wise to heed. Such are the two verses that comprise today's reading.

First, you are advised to "walk circumspectly." Your "walk" is your manner of life.....the way you conduct yourself in general. The word "circumspectly" means "with care; with honor and honesty; to be morally right." So, it matters to the Lord what kind of testimony you present as His ambassador. Your manner of life is observed by those around you, and is a reflection of the Lord's place in your life.

What others observe reflects on Him.....positively or negatively. It's not a command, but He wants you to know that how you hold your temper.....how you react to crisis.....how you treat others.....does matter to Him.

Secondly, verse 16 tells us to "redeem the time." Why? Because there's not as much of it available as you might think. Someone who is redeeming the time would be spending some of it in the Word each day. That person would also be spending time with the Lord in prayer daily, too. These things are meant to prepare you for the events of your day, and the attacks the devil is sure to launch at you. It says that the days are evil.....as we knew they would be in the end times.

Let's focus on the Lord and His Word in our lives. It will reflect positively on Him, and keep us prepared for the daily battle we face with the world, the flesh, and the devil.

Faith Profession: "I will re-arrange my schedule to make time for prayer and the Word each day. I will heed the Lord's gentle recommendations for me."

Study Scriptures: Colossians 4:5; II Timothy 3:1-7

A LEAKY TEMPLE

Scripture: Ephesians 5:17-18

We have two verses today, with two important thoughts connected to them. You may be surprised to find that verse 17 says that you are "unwise" if you don't understand what the will of the Lord is. What??! Why, many Christians claim that you can't know God's will! So, how could He say such a thing?

The answer is that you certainly CAN know God's will. Why would He hide it from you? Where is it? It's in everything that Jesus did on earth (see study Scriptures). It's in every single promise in the Word of God…..and they're EVERYWHERE in the Bible. And, a few verses plainly tell you what His will is (see study Scriptures).

Next, you are told…..commanded, really, though He won't force you…..to be filled with the Spirit. In the Greek in which your New Testament was originally written, it reads, "keep being filled with the Spirit." So, it is an ongoing process. Why, you ask, is that so? Because your temple leaks, my friend. What you put into it spiritually today will trickle out by tomorrow or the next day.

The answer? Keep being filled! How? By spending time reading the Word…..or listening to it on some electronic device…..or by watching some decent Bible show on TV. OH…I know…..you don't think have time for that…..you're too busy. Well, you have time to feed food into your face, though, and you find time for that several times a day. Why would you think your spirit needed any less nourishment than your body? The truth of the matter is that the nourishment of your spirit is much more important than the feeding of your body…..though both are necessary. As end-times folks, we would profit by the filling of ourselves with the Spirit.

Faith Profession: "I CAN know His will…..and I purpose to fill my spirit with The Lord and His Word daily."

Study Scriptures: John 6:38; I Thessalonians 4:3; 5:18

DEVOTIONAL # 278

BALANCE IN THE HOME

Scripture: Ephesians 5:21-33

In my 37 years of ministry, I have seen and heard some pretty wild stuff, but perhaps none as nutty as the guy in a traditional church who had taken this passage of Scripture to new heights of misunderstanding. The fellow in question was showing a colleague how much he had his wife in submission by ordering her to do ten push-ups at his command. She promptly did them, and she was pregnant at the time!

This outrageous display of pride and lack of discernment.....on the part of both husband and wife.....is one indicator of how Scripture can be twisted into something other than what it is. A marriage is all about submission.....but <u>both</u> parties are to submit. When a marriage occurs, two people become one. There is no such thing as a superior person and a subordinate one.

This passage is showing men that they are held responsible by God for spiritual leadership in the home. The man is held responsible for the spiritual state of his home, and is to teach the Word both by speaking and by action. He is to LEAD his family in following the Lord. His wife is to follow that leadership as it honors the Word. The bottom line is that the man has the tougher end of the deal, as he is the one held responsible.

Too often these days, we see the wife taking the kids to church.....the wife praying.....the wife setting the example of spirituality. Some men these days think "that church stuff is for women and children." It sounds "macho," but it is ignorance and neglect of responsibility.....and it minimizes blessing toward that home.

Husbands are to love their wives AS CHRIST LOVES THE CHURCH: sacrificially; with love; with affection; with care; with tenderness; and in the Word. Wives, as partners, are to respond to that leadership, and follow it. Both parties are in submission.....that is true balance in the home.

Faith Profession: "I will follow the Word in my relationship with my spouse, trying my best to be submissive to that Word no matter what."

Study Scriptures: Colossians 3:19; Genesis 2:24; I Peter 3:7

HONOR TO PARENTS

Scripture: Ephesians 6:1-3

As I observe the world around me in these end times, I'm forced to conclude that many of today's generation will die young. There are several places where God's children are promised long life, but there are also places where that can be negated. I see children disobeying parents everywhere I go. I see babies pitching a fit because they're not getting their own way, and parents doing nothing at all about it.....just ignoring the loud wailing as if it isn't happening. Something about our society has changed, and it has led children to hold an attitude of contempt toward the parents who are raising them.

The Word of God holds the expectation that children will obey their parents. Why? Because, according to the Lord God Almighty, "This is right." Notice that it mentions the commandment from the Old Testament to honor your father and mother, and it says it is the first commandment "with promise." Do you know what the promise was? Long life and blessing if you obeyed, but death if you disobeyed.

Of course, we live in the Age of Grace.....but the expectation has not changed. One sign of the end times (see study Scriptures) is that children will be "disobedient to parents." The implication is that it will be rampant, not just an occasional thing. And these days, it is rampant!

The devil has been hard at work in our schools.....in our churches.....in our homes..... to change our thinking, and therefore our practices.....to open the door to this kind of thing. Once again, Christians have been asleep instead of diligently watching, and have given the enemy another victory. Only this time, we are losing our heritage.....our kids.

It's not too late. Homes centered on the Word WILL produce respectful children. Even in the end times, satan can be defeated. Let's pray for one another, and let's battle the trend of the world around us. Let's do it for the sake of our precious children.

Faith Profession: "I intend to pray fervently for saved children.....that they might be moved to obedience to the Word.....that they might make choices in line with the Word, and honor their parents, as the Word recommends."

Study Scriptures: II Timothy 3:1-7; Colossians 3:20

DEVOTIONAL # 280

NURTURE

Scripture: Ephesians 6:4

Yesterday, we discussed the responsibility of children to their parents, but that responsibility goes the other way, too. Today's Scripture addresses fathers with regard to raising children. Why not Mom? Because the Word gives primary responsibility to Dad, expecting both parents to be working together…..in balance…..in agreement…..with regard to the raising of kids.

Dad…..you are specifically warned not to provoke your child to wrath. You provoke your child by being unfair; by being selfish; by being unreasonable (insisting on your own way no matter what); by being sarcastic. You are to treat children as you are told to treat your wife…..as the Lord treats His own children. It is done with patience….. understanding…..consideration…..love…..care…..a listening ear…..and the willingness to make right decisions, even though your child may not agree. (Remember, YOU are the parent. There's a reason for that.)

Above all, you are to provide sound spiritual leadership…..leading by example. TAKE your child to church…..don't send them. Pray with them. Study the Word with them. SHOW them what a Christian is like, and be the parent first. As they grow up, it's NOT your first duty to be their friend. That will come later.

You are to be the parent…..to make the decisions that are best for your child…..and to do it according to the Word of God. You won't always win a popularity contest with them, but you will be operating inside the protective shield of God's Word…..which means that everything will be all right in the end. Trust Him. Follow His Word. You will make lifelong friends of your kids by doing so.

Faith Profession: "I will raise my children according to the guidelines in the Word. I will nurture them…..by being fair, firm, honest, and Biblical."

Study Scriptures: Proverbs 22:6; II Timothy 3:15

RHEMA

Scripture: Ephesians 6:20

The Apostle Paul was a man who had persecuted the church prior to his salvation in Acts 9. He had spent some time studying the Word, and then began his ministry to the world. Here in Ephesians 6…..toward the latter part of his life on earth…..we find Paul speaking boldly…..with certainty…..about the Word. Why is he able to do this? Well, you might say, he's the Apostle Paul…..the greatest Christian ever. HE could do that, but you can't expect ME to do it.

Okay…..this is where the buzzer goes off, because that's wrong. The reason Paul spoke the Word with such conviction is because his speech is characterized by the Greek word "rhema." "Rhema" is the Word spoken, but only after one has had a supernatural conviction about it. This conviction comes from the fact that you BELIEVE it with every fiber of your being. This is the result of EFFORT…..of meditating on a Scripture…..repeating it…..saying it…..until it becomes a part of you. Then, when you speak that verse, it has power because it is backed by this solid conviction of its truth, or….. "rhema."

Success in the faith realm is not about waiting until a problem comes along, and then just saying the words. It IS about speaking them with a deep conviction borne of the effort to plant the verse into your spirit. THEN it is spoken in "rhema," and goes forth from you with supernatural power…..and things happen!

No…..it's not easy. Yes…..it takes time and effort. Sorry, but it's not instant like our society. But…..it does work, and it works every time if spoken in "rhema"!

Faith Profession: "I have work to do, and I need to get started today. I will say Bible promises…..think about them…..repeat them…..until they become part of me. Then, when I speak them, the problem CANNOT STAND."

Study Scriptures: II Timothy 2:15; Matthew 21:22

SAINTS

Scripture: Philippians 1:1

When we hear the word "saint," our mind tends to bring us the picture of an old painting of a man with a halo, his hands folded piously. Tradition has led us to believe that certain individuals have lived such holy lives that they have "extra credits" built up in Heaven….. more than they themselves need to get there. The teaching is that these "extra credits" can be applied to you if you meet certain requirements.

Wow. That sounds almost reasonable! It certainly has a little logic behind it. And, you might take it seriously unless you knew that you don't get to Heaven by doing good deeds or by being holy. In fact, the Bible says that no human can possibly be holy enough to get to Heaven (see study Scriptures), let alone have "extra credit."

The bottom line is that only one man ever existed who lived a sinless life. He didn't put His "extra credits" in some heavenly bank, but died in your place…..when He had done no wrong to die for…..so that you could go to Heaven by simply receiving what He did as a free gift. This idea that God weighs your good deeds against your bad deeds on some sort of massive heavenly scale to determine if you deserve entry into Heaven is just a bunch of baloney…..there is no truth in it AT ALL.

So, what is a saint? According to the Bible, it is any person who has received the free gift of salvation from sin's penalty that Jesus died for and offers to everyone. Most of the New Testament Pauline epistles begin just like today's verse…..calling all saved people in that church SAINTS. So, I am a saint, and so is my wife. You are, too…..if you're saved.

Faith Profession: "I believe the Bible…..the Word of God…..rather than the traditions of men. Thank you, Lord, for making me a saint as part of my salvation."

Study Scriptures: Ecclesiastes 7:20; Romans 3:23

Devotional # 283
Ruth...Four Seasons...#1

Scripture: Ruth 1

The Book of Ruth contains four chapters, each of which describes a "season" in the life of Ruth. As is often the case with the Bible, these seasons have application to you and me as well.

Ruth 1 describes the first of these seasons.....Famine. Naomi and her small family move to the foreign land of Moab in response to a famine that has hit Israel. By the end of the chapter, all three men of the family are dead, proving that the decision to go to Moab was not the best of choices.

Our God, however, is in the business of taking what the devil meant for harm and turning it into something good, and this will eventually happen. However, in chapter 1, it is famine. For us, this famine represents loss, heartache, sorrow, and suffering. Some of us have been there, or are there right now. It is a bitter time, and it is easy to fall into the temptation to give up. Yet.....you need to know this about famines.....they are always temporary. They always end, and you can count on that.

I don't know what terrible situation you are facing today. Perhaps you have been diagnosed with an illness. Maybe you are having problems with your spouse or children. It could be that you have been betrayed.....or have lost someone you love. You are in a time of famine, and it hurts. And, though it might not seem like it right now, it WILL END.....famines always do.

Everything's going to be alright.....Jesus will see to it.

Faith Profession: "I'm going to place my faith in the One who loves me, and has never let me down. Jesus will make my situation right again."

Study Scripture: Isaiah 61:1-3

RUTH...FOUR SEASONS...#2

Scripture: Ruth 2

As we leave chapter 1 of Ruth, Naomi has lost her husband and both of her sons in Moab. One daughter-in-law has also chosen to remain in Moab (never to be mentioned in the Bible again). Only Ruth has accompanied her as she returns to Israel.....to Bethlehem.

When they arrive, and her old friends greet her, she identifies herself not as Naomi (which means "pleasant"), but as Mara (which means "bitter"). As she says in 1:21, she went out full, but has returned empty. Of course, this is her grief speaking. In fact, she has returned with Ruth at her side.....a woman from Moab who has chosen to follow her..... and her God.....because of what she saw in Naomi.

And, according to 1:22, they have returned at the time of the barley harvest, which, in Israel, is a time of plenty and rejoicing. This, then, is the second "season" in the Book of Ruth.....harvest! Naomi had left in a time of famine, but returns to a time of harvest. Though she has suffered loss, her life has moved out of that dark tunnel of seemingly endless sorrow, and into the light that is always present at the end of a tunnel. She has returned to a time of harvest.

Your time of sorrow.....loss.....pain.....bitterness.....crying.....will end, too. Though it might not be apparent to you immediately, you will have entered into a time of harvest that the Lord has prepared for you. Yes, life may have changed.....in some ways permanently. But did you know that every ending is also a beginning? And, when the Lord has a hand in your new beginning, it is a time of harvest.....renewal.....life.....possibilities. That light at the end of the tunnel? It's a HARVEST.....made especially for YOU.

Faith Profession: "I had just about given up when the Lord brought me into the sunlight at the end of the tunnel. I believe it is the beginning of the harvest time for me."

Study Scriptures: Isaiah 54:17; Psalm 1:3; Jeremiah 29:11

DEVOTIONAL # 285
RUTH...FOUR SEASONS...#3

Scripture: Ruth 3

Today's chapter introduces us to the third "season" in the Book of Ruth, which I will call Transition. By way of introductory comment, I'll need you to know that, in the Old Testament, widows were identified by the wearing of certain clothing that made their status apparent to others. (See Genesis 38:14.) As widows, both Naomi and Ruth would have worn such clothing.

But, here in chapter 3, Ruth has met Boaz.....having chosen his field to glean out of the hundreds of fields available (the Lord's hand appears again!). And, Boaz has shown favor to Ruth.

So, here in 3:3, Naomi instructs Ruth to put off her widow's garments in preparation for a second meeting with Boaz. The meeting itself is somewhat unusual, but would have been understandable based on the traditions of that time. The point, though, is that Ruth put off her widow's garments. That symbolizes the anticipation of change.....the expectation of a miracle that will involve LIFE.....rather than the death symbolized by the widow's garments. It is an exciting time of transition for Ruth!

So, too, in your life.....as your crisis or tragedy passes.....the time will come for you to "put off the widow's garments." You cannot change the past, but satan will surely try to keep you locked in it. It is tempting to remain there.....to wallow in your misfortune. Don't do it! It is the equivalent of a "dead man walking."

There comes a time when you need to move on with life. It isn't over just because it has changed. Take it from someone who knows.....change can be a wonderful and beautiful thing! Very often, it IS!

Expect a miracle of life.....embrace the changes.....look to the Lord to make lemonade out of those lemons! He WILL DO THAT!

Faith Profession: "I know that Jesus loves me deeply. He wants to bless me. I will 'put off my widow's garments' and look expectantly for MY miracle."

Study Scriptures: Jeremiah 29:11; Acts 10:38

Ruth...Four Seasons...#4

Scripture: Ruth 4

Chapter 4 of Ruth is a picture of what the future could be like for you. I call this chapter "Fulfillment."

Ruth has found favor with Boaz, and he is willing to perform the task required by Old Testament law known as "the Kinsman Redeemer." That is, the debts owed by Naomi and her family must be paid for Ruth to be free to marry. Boaz, as a rich man, is not only able to do this task.....he is quite willing!

Having done this, he and Ruth are married, and, some time later, have a child named Obed. Why is this significant? Well, for Ruth, it is the beginning of a wonderful new life with a loving husband and a child.....something she probably had thought was not possible. For Naomi, she holds a grandchild in her arms, and appreciates the miracle that this represents for a woman who had lost both of her sons.

Better yet.....Obed turns out to be the Father of Jesse.....who turns out to be the Father of David. Ruth's son.....the child of this miraculous rebirth of two lives seemingly lost in death.....is part of the lineage of the promised Messiah.....Jesus Christ! It is a miracle of miracles!!

So.....let's talk about you. It's never over if the Lord is involved.....no matter what the world or the devil tells you. IF.....you will "put off those widow's garments" and choose to believe in the impossible.....you just might find yourself living in a life more spectacular than you had ever imagined possible! Our God is a God of miracles, and the God of abundant life. There is no reason why He would not do a miracle of life for you. Believe, my friend, and you WILL SEE!

Faith Profession: "My God routinely does the impossible. He wants to turn my ashes into beauty. I believe.....I expect a miracle!"

Study Scriptures: Mark 10:27; Isaiah 61:1-3; John 10:10

DEVOTIONAL # 287

A PASTOR'S HEART

Scripture: Philippians 1:8

For those of you who have never been a pastor, today's verse might be easy to skip over. But, if the Lord has ever given you oversight of a flock, you can see Paul's heart for the people he loves in today's words.

He says that <u>God</u> is his record…..not people…..not facts. God knows the deep things of the heart, and would be the only one certain of Paul's love. Paul says that he longs for them in his bowels. This, I think, is where you have to have been there. When you are truly called of God to a pastorate…..not just taking the pastor's job because you need work…..He gives you a depth of love and care for your flock that defies explanation.

I have pastored three groups of people. Today, my wife found a letter in a Bible given to me by the members of my first church. The words were very nice, and it was signed by every member of that group. Reading it, you'd never suspect that they would later turn their back on the man they professed to love and appreciate so much at that time. So, I read the letter with mixed feelings, yet that old "shepherd's concern"…..that pastor's heart for his flock…..came flooding back to me. Almost thirty years later, my heart still "longs after them," despite their insincerity.

My point is this…..your pastor (if he is truly called of God)…..has been given a super-natural depth of care for you. Even he can't explain it completely, but he has you on his mind, and he desires the best for you. That has been given to him by the Lord…..if he is truly called. That "pastor's heart" keeps him from doing anything that would hurt you, and tries to get as much of the Word into you as possible.

Some pastors are just not called…..you can tell by their actions. Real pastors…..the ones supernaturally called…..are priceless, and should be treated with the respect and apprecia-tion that they deserve. They are one of God's gifts to you.

Faith Profession: "I will seek a pastor who is truly called by God. That man will serve me as a shepherd would tend to his beloved sheep."

Study Scriptures: Ephesians 4:11; Psalm 23

Devotional # 288
Seeing the Bright Side

Scripture: Philippians 1:12-18

One interesting by-product of much time spent in the Word is the tendency to see things in a positive light. In the world, there is much focus on the negative…..TV news and newspaper stories tend to emphasize fires, crimes, murders, death, and disaster.

In today's verses, Paul is attempting to ease the concern of those he loves who are saddened by the fact that Paul spends lots of his time in one prison or another. Paul is so well thought of in Christian circles that it's difficult to remember that he was an ex-con…..a jailbird…..a man who was in and out of prison all during his ministry. You wonder how well he would be accepted in today's end-times church.

Paul's point in today's Scripture verses is that some preach the Gospel because they are encouraged by his tenacity…..he even writes powerfully from prison, and his writings have become much of our New Testament. But he also points out that those who oppose him are busy telling others why he is a bad man…..why he has been put into prison….. why his teachings are worthy of his imprisonment (in their opinion). This negative talk is still information about the Gospel, and it is being passed from person to person despite themselves! Paul sees that, and rejoices over the irony of it.

For Paul, the goal was that Jesus Christ be preached to as many people as possible. The fact that Jesus was preached by those who were gossiping about Paul was not Paul's main concern. Paul's own reputation was secondary…..in his mind…..to the fact that the goal was being reached. The Name of Jesus was being spread around, and people were coming to know Him as a result. That is, for Paul, the fulfillment of the Great Commission was welcome in any form. THAT'S true love for the Lord!

Faith Profession: "Lord, please deepen my faith and love for you. I want to see the Name of Jesus lifted up, and my own personal gain is far secondary to that."

Study Scriptures: Philippians 4:8; Colossians 1:9-18

NO TERROR

Scripture: Philippians 1:28

You hear lots of information these days about terrorists…..their attacks on the USA and places around the world…..their threats…..suicide bombers…..etc. As always, such things are given priority by the news media, and the result is the maximization of fear in our society. The goal of terrorists, by the way, is to spread terror. They merchandise fear, and take it to an art form. Since they try to be undetectable, your fear of the unknown kicks in, and it is a very powerful force.

Paul, and other Bible writers…..inspired by the Holy Spirit…..repeatedly encourage us NOT TO FEAR. They know that fear is satan's biggest weapon, and that when people are in fear, they cannot be in faith. Failure to be in faith cancels any action the Lord can take to assist you, since the Lord operates only in an atmosphere of faith.

The phrase "fear not" occurs over 60 times in the Word. Did you know that God did not give you a spirit of fear? (See study Scriptures). Are you aware that fear is a spirit, not just an emotion? (See study Scriptures). Can you take heart from the message contained in today's Scripture, which is: your adversaries think that they're getting the victory over you through fear, but we know that they are taking this action because we are God's children.

Their attack against us is our proof that we belong to Him. In fact, the reason they promote terrorism is that THEY FEAR YOU. Yes, that is true. Something inside them recognizes the power that you have…..even potentially…..and they know it is superior to what they have. So they make lots of noise, and threats, and other bluster. The bottom line is that we already have the victory. Why worry about some puny threats?

Faith Profession: "I have been given power, love, and a sound mind…..but not fear. No weapon that is formed against me shall prosper."

Study Scriptures: II Timothy 1:7; Isaiah 54:17

DEVOTIONAL # 290
HOW TO GET ALONG

Scripture: Philippians 2:2-4

Paul, writing under the inspiration of the Holy Spirit, tells us some things in today's verses about getting along together. The Trinity is very pleased when God's children get along.....it is called unity in some other Bible places. Unity and harmony are part of the make-up of peace.....another highly-treasured spiritual value to the Lord.

How is it possible to "get along"? Well, verse 2 says to be "likeminded." That is, if you're spending time in the Word, and are yielded to it, your thinking will be similar to others doing the same. The purposes of any group need to be similar to avoid conflict. And love must be the glue that holds it all together.

Verse 3 says that nothing.....even if it represents gain.....is to be done through strife (conflict) or vainglory (that which exalts one person over another), because these are tools the devil uses for gain. Pride is also to take a back seat, because it is equally destructive. We are told to esteem others more than ourselves, or, in other words, be humble. This point cannot be overstressed. It is the emphasis on "self" that is ruining the end-times generation (see study Scriptures).

Verse 4 reinforces this thought.....if we are busy looking out for others, we won't have time to focus on ourselves. If all of us are focused on others, then our own needs will be met by the fact that others are focused on us. It is a brilliant and foolproof system.....as you might expect from the Lord.

The bottom line? Peace and harmony are only obtained by attention being paid to the needs of those around you. This will cause you to witness.....to give comfort.....to be of value to the rest of the group. It is also one definition of the word "love." Remember..... God loved you enough to GIVE His only begotten Son.....for your benefit, not His.

Faith Profession: "I will focus more on others, and less on myself. In this way, the Lord will be both pleased and obeyed."

Study Scriptures: II Timothy 3:1-7 (especially verse 2); John 3:16

NOT A WORM

Scripture: Philippians 2:10

It is popular in traditional Christian circles to think of oneself as a lowly worm…..only a sinner saved by grace…..a publican who can't even lift his eyes toward the Lord. All of this is done in the name of humility, and on the surface, it seems very pious. The problem is that it is contrary to Scripture. Put in plainer terms, it is directly against the revealed Word of God…..making it false humility at best.

The truth is that you USED to be a lowly worm…..but then you received Jesus as your Savior. That choice forever changed who you are, and the New Testament gives dozens of Scripture verses telling you so.

Today's verse is one of those. Now, you might say, "Wait a minute…..this verse is talking about Jesus Christ, not me." And I would agree with you…..it is exalting the Name of Jesus Christ our Lord, and is one of the most important verses in the Bible.

Yet, we are told to compare Scripture with Scripture if we are to study the Word properly. When we do that, we bump into Ephesians 3:14-15. Those verses clearly point out that Jesus' family is named after Him. So, the question becomes: "Are you part of His family?" If you can answer "yes" to that question, then you are confronted with this fact…..WE are this Name! YOU are this Name, if you are saved! Jesus has given YOU His name….. the Name to which every knee will bow! You have inherited this Name….. it is now legally yours…..and Jesus is glad about that!

That being said…..don't you DARE call yourself a lowly worm…..only a sinner…..a person not worthy to even lift your head toward Him. NO!! You are His child…..a prince or princess in the Kingdom of God! Your Dad is the King of Kings and Lord of Lords! You are special…..a new creation…..and you have an exalted position WITH HIM! That's who you are!!

Faith Profession: "I will be careful how I speak of myself from now on. I will not be arrogant about my status, but I will be confident about it, because it is a gift from my Savior, Jesus Christ."

Study Scriptures: Isaiah 45:23; Ephesians 3:14-15

Devotional # 292
It's No More Than Dung

Scripture: Philippians 3:4-8

There is such an emphasis in our world on the things of the flesh. Fame…..wealth…..looks…..status are the focus of even God's people. Diet plans are popular…..fitness centers are packed…..the amount of money spent on cosmetics in a month would feed most third world countries. We fuss about our hairstyle…..our car…..the image we project. As we age (inevitably), we get hair weaves, dye jobs, plastic surgery, tummy tucks. (Hey, don't get me wrong…..many of the people I meet could USE a little makeup, at least). Compare that activity and expense to the amount of time spent in the Bible…..going to church…..spending money on spiritual things…..and tell me that it isn't so far out of balance that it is downright embarrassing.

The Christians I know are victimized by TV news so badly that they speak the negativity they hear…..as if there were no Holy Spirit or Word of God. Most Christians live in fear every day. What is the problem? It is the flesh…..driving their every thought and word. It is the end-times church of Revelation 3 personified.

The Apostle Paul had "credentials" that rivaled any of his day. He lists them in today's reading, and they are impressive. He was, compared to the average person in his time, very educated, very important; very wealthy; and very well-known. His conclusion? It is no better than dung. Paul gave all of his worldly advantages up, and he couldn't have cared less. You know why? Because he had a firm understanding of what was TRULY IMPORTANT…..and it had nothing to do with how you dress…..how much money you have…..how popular you are…..etc.

Faith Profession: "I see the trends around me, and I want to be different. I want my priorities to be the things of God, not the things of the world. I will take steps to change my thinking and my actions…..starting today."

Study Scripture: Revelation 3:14-22

Yokefellows

Scripture: Philippians 4:1-3

Paul was a name-dropper. Unlike many in the world, he did not do it to display his pettiness.....nor to show others who he knew so as to be impressive (and develop false pride). Those who drop names probably aren't very well known by those they name anyway.

No.....Paul drops names like Euodias.....Syntyche.....Clement. You know them..... right?? You have at least heard of them.....right? Hmmmm.....they were important enough to Paul to mention in Scripture.....and they are strangers to you?? How much do you know about Timothy.....Titus.....Epaphroditus..... Luke.....Tertius? Tertius penned the book of Romans for Paul. Luke wrote two Bible books, and was a doctor. These other fellows traveled with Paul..... ministered with him.....risked their lives for and with him.....put it all on the line for the Lord.

Paul calls them "yokefellows".....a reference to the wooden device that was placed between two oxen to keep them together as they worked. Paul considered himself "yoked" with these people, and he was glad to mention their names as he wrote sacred Scripture.

All true laborers for the Lord have "yokefellows".....people who labor with them, and for them. They are the truest of friends. They don't just visit you in jail.....they are sitting there beside you in the cell. They are sold out to the Lord, and you can count on them. They are some of the most precious gifts the Lord could ever give.

Who are your yokefellows? This might be a good time to think about that, and spend some time in prayer for them.....and thank God for them. Two of my yokefellows live and minister in Kenya, East Africa. One lives right with me in my own house. Who are YOUR yokefellows? Better yet.....who would consider you THEIR yokefellow?

Faith Profession: "I thank God for giving me yokefellows, but it is my goal to BECOME a yokefellow for another person of God."

Study Scriptures: Romans 16:22; Acts 1:1 with Luke 1:3

DEVOTIONAL # 294
DON'T WORRY, BE HAPPY

Scripture: Philippians 4:6

Our title today is taken from a quirky little song that used to be popular, but you'd probably have to be my age to remember it. At any rate, it gets the point across.....today's verse is telling us not to worry.....that is what "be careful for nothing" means.

Worry is so common in our society that some people think it is inevitable. But, have you ever thought about worry? It is concern that the worst will happen.....or at least something bad will happen. In reality, it is an expression of faith in the work of the devil. And, it is based upon fear.....which is clearly of the devil. If you want to see how deeply our society is deceived, just listen to the number of people who express worry.....or feel that worry is some sort of duty for them.

Our verse gives an alternative. Give your concerns to a loving God, who is interested in giving you the best outcome in each case. He has promised you success. He has entered into a Blood Covenant relationship with you to guarantee you success.....on this earth..... in this life. He wants to help.....and He certainly CAN.

The time we spend worrying is time spent in subjection to the devil, and time spent out of faith in God's Word. It's truly amazing that God's people would give themselves so fully to such an unproductive endeavor. More than that, though, today's verse is NOT a suggestion. It is put in the form of a command.....not to bully you, but to emphasize its importance.

You are hurting yourself when you worry. You are not in faith, and so are out of the place where He can bless you. And, you are out of step with God's Word. Worry, my friend, would be a wonderful thing to eliminate from your life.

Faith Profession: "I will take my concerns about life to the throne of Grace, and give them to the Lord. Worrying has done no good anyway."

Study Scriptures: Matthew 6:25; I Thessalonians 5:17

DEVOTIONAL # 295

POSITIVE THOUGHTS

Scripture: Philippians 4:6-8

Although it is not the subject today, the Word recommends that you watch what you say…..very carefully…..because what you say creates a spiritual atmosphere around you which gives freedom of movement to either the forces of light or the forces of darkness. Similarly, it matters what you think, because who you are and what you do is shaped by what your mind dwells upon.

In today's reading, you are first told to eliminate worry from your life. Then, you are told that it would be best…..for you…..if your thoughts focused upon the kinds of things mentioned in verse 8. Everything in the list is positive. Everything in the list will tend to lift your spirit…..put a smile on your face…..give you a sense of contentment. As it says in verse 7, "the peace of God…..(a supernatural peace that transcends the events of the world)…..will be upon you."

The Lord wants what's best for you, because He loves you intensely. When He makes statements in His Word like verse 6 or verse 8, He is doing so for emphasis…..to impress the importance of these things to you. Why? So that YOU will benefit…..not Him…..so that YOUR life will be better (which, in the end, does make Him happy).

Some folks look at me funny when I tell them that I don't read the daily newspaper, or look at TV news. I avoid both because I don't need to be filling my mind up with all of that negativity and fear. It makes it easier for me to concentrate on positive things….. and there are lots of those! Some people will say I'm uninformed…..or living in a dream world. I believe I'm living as the Word has recommended, and it sure is a peaceful life!

Faith Profession: "Lord, I need to change my thought life and my speech patterns. Please convict me each time I say or think negative things, and guide me toward the more positive aspects of life."

Study Scriptures: Colossians 3:15; Deuteronomy 28:1-13

I CAN

Scripture: Philippians 4:13

Here and there in the Word of God you find Scripture promises, some of which are so good that they just beg to be committed to memory. Today's Scripture verse is one of those.

This particular promise is even put in the right form for you to say. By saying it.....and doing so over and over again.....you will be planting it inside your spirit. The more you repeat it, the more real it becomes to you on the inside. In effect, it becomes part of your being, and therefore part of your consciousness. In this way, your mind is transformed (see study Scriptures) until it accepts what had previously seemed impossible to it.....or at least impractical. One of the main deterrents to your faith is your mind, particularly if you are a "realist." If you are, you tend to take the world at face value, and pride yourself on being realistic.....looking at the facts of the world, and forming your viewpoint according to what you have seen.

Of course, we're dealing with the Word of God here, so it isn't realistic.....it's supernatural. Because of that, it supersedes and changes the facts of the world. It does so when you apply your faith to a verse.....like today's verse.....after you have firmly planted it in your heart.

Our verse eliminates the phrase "I can't" from your vocabulary. It is the world, the flesh, and the devil that has tried to convince you that you can't. This verse.....this PROMISE FROM GOD.....says that you CAN, and it doesn't matter what you are talking about..... you CAN. This, by the way, is going to force you to speak positively instead of negatively (the worldly way).....as the Lord always intended.

You CAN do ALL THINGS through Christ!

Faith Profession: "I can do all things through Christ which strengtheneth me."

Study Scriptures: Romans 12:2; John 15:5; Mark 10:27

The Reason For the Thanks

Scripture: Philippians 4:14-17

As we near the end of this Bible book, Paul communicates his appreciation to the Philippians for their thoughtfulness to him. In verse 15, he mentions something that had happened some time ago when he first left to travel from Macedonia. At that time, he was apparently short of money. He mentions that no church sent help except for the church at Philippi…..and he notes that they helped more than once. This financial help enabled Paul to continue on in his ministry, thus fulfilling the will of God.

So, they gave him some financial help, and he says thank you. Why is that worth mentioning? Because of what is said in verse 17. Paul says that his point wasn't that he received money, but that fruit might abound on their account. Thus is revealed the "background blessing" connected to generosity.

You know, so many people get bent out of shape about tithing. They make the accusation that churches just want their money. Of course, churches are just like banks…..stores…..homes…..people…..they require money to function in this world. The Lord set up a system in which tithing is central, but the real benefit comes to the GIVER, not the receiver. The idea is this: if you give willingly…..even cheerfully…..into spiritual things…..with no thought of personal benefit, then the Lord will bless your life.

I've provided study Scriptures which verify this, and you can read them for yourself. The key is MOTIVE. If you give in order to GET BACK, it won't work. If you give out of obedience, or just because you want to help, you will be blessed accordingly. That is, you shovel out of your "pile" to others…..just to be of help to them…..and the Lord will see to it that your "pile" is always full.

Faith Profession: "I give with a pure motive…..without looking over my shoulder to see if I benefit. When I operate that way, the Lord always provides me with more than enough."

Study Scriptures: Luke 6:38; Ephesians 4:28

DEVOTIONAL # 298

ALL YOUR NEED

Scripture: Philippians 4:19

Just before this book ends, the Holy Spirit deposits one more dynamite Scriptural promise into the text for us. Today's verse is one of those wildly general promises that seems too good to be true. In fact, many Christians treat it exactly that way…..they scoff at the idea that the Lord will provide money…..protection….. health…..supernatural safety…..a job…..a friend…..when you need them.

I feel sorry for those folks. They have an unconditional promise of provision…..from the Lord God Almighty…..and they can't find faith enough within themselves to believe it. And, because they won't believe, it doesn't happen for them…..which they take as proof that they're right!! Amazing circular reasoning!

The truth is this: you have a Heavenly Father who loves you, and isn't shy about showing it. He trusts you enough to provide for you, expecting that you will appreciate it…..and not take advantage of it or take it for granted. Now…..the verse says that he will supply ALL your need. So, what do you need?

My wife and I were traveling from Pennsylvania to Missouri a few years ago when we discovered that a tire on our car was going flat. It was about 8 AM, and we had a seven-hour drive ahead of us. We put some air in the tire, and prayed today's promise over the tire. We stopped every so often to check the tire, and it held air all day. We stopped at a tire repair place in Missouri (a place we'd never been). They took the tire off the rim, inspected it, and told us they could find nothing wrong. Then, they told us there was no charge, despite the fact that they had performed some service for us!

It's only one example of this verse working. There are thousands and thousands more. YOU could be someone telling this kind of story…..IF you can find it within yourself to believe today's verse…..without reservation…..without doubt…..trusting the Lord totally. It DOES work, but not without your faith. He will provide ALL your need.

Faith Profession: "I believe that I can put my complete trust in the King of Kings and Lord of Lords. He loves ME. I can put total faith in any promise He makes."

Study Scripture: II Corinthians 9:8-11

DEVOTIONAL # 299
YOU'RE NOT IN THE DARK

Scripture: Colossians 1:9

I've been ministering for almost 38 years now, and I've noticed some things as I have met Christians. Too many of them are "in the dark," so to speak, when it comes to knowing God's will. If you asked most Christians, they'd tell you that you can't know God's will. Some others would say that it doesn't matter anyway, because God is "in control," and will do whatever He wants to do, when He wants to do it.

How do you suppose we got to such a place as God's children? Certainly not by studying the Word, and today's Scripture reading is one proof of that. In it, Paul is praying for the members of the church at Colosse, and his prayer is that they might be filled with the knowledge of God's will. The word translated "knowledge" here means…..in the original Greek language from which it was translated….. "complete knowledge." You can reference the Scripture in John in the study Scriptures below for verification.

The Holy Spirit is given to you to give you COMPLETE KNOWLEDGE of HIS WILL. Therefore, you are NOT in the dark, because He has given you all the knowledge of His will that He can give. Well…..at least you SHOULDN'T be in the dark about it. We tend to accept almost anything thrown at us from a pulpit or a Christian classroom. But the Lord didn't ask you to do that. He asked you to study the Word of God, and conform to what IT says.

So…..if you are unaware of God's will, and He has provided it for you…..then what, do you think, is the solution? Yes…..a little more study on your part. The setting aside of what you've heard from men, and an openness to what the Word teaches. God's will is not some dark secret known only to a few. It is revealed in every Scripture promise…..in every work of Jesus on earth…..and in several verses which plainly tell you they are God's will. If you're in the dark, it's because you have chosen to be there by your own inaction. You can get into the light…..you know how.

Faith Profession: "I will take my beliefs from my study of the Word of God, not from the teachings of men. I will study the Word diligently."

Study Scriptures: John 14:26; II Timothy 2:15; John 6:38

Devotional # 300

Delivered

Scripture: Colossians 1:13-14

Did you know that you were changed into an entirely new creation when you accepted Jesus as your Savior? You did not merely have something added to your life. You didn't just "get religion." You were changed into a new creature, unique to the earth.

This new creation has certain features that aren't found in the old, earthly, physical-only model. This new creature has some supernatural elements, and they're REALLY NEAT!! One of those new features is mentioned in today's Scripture.....it's the fact that you're delivered from the power of darkness.

Now, traditional Christians will agree that Jesus got the victory over the devil through the events of Calvary and the resurrection. But they would NOT agree that THEY have power over these same forces of darkness. Why? Because they have been taught that they are powerless, insignificant beings.....that, at best, they are only sinners saved by grace, unworthy to even look skyward, and subject to whatever whim the Lord might take with their life today. (That is AWFUL teaching, and it comes straight from Hell.)

Do you believe the Bible? Okay.....do you believe verse 13 in today's reading? If you do, then YOU believe that YOU have been delivered from the power of darkness. It has NO POWER over you anymore. That's one of the benefits of being this new creature the Lord made you to be.

The problem? It's true, but it only WORKS for you IF YOU APPLY IT. Should you choose to stay in the old belief that satan has power over you.....or if you choose to wait for Jesus to chase the devil away.....you will be allowing the devil to keep power over you that he really doesn't have any more. But, he'll use it if you let him. IF YOU LET HIM. Why would you do that?? Hey.....believe the Word. Receive it for yourself. And apply the study Scriptures for today. Do it, and see the devil run from YOU.

Faith Profession: "My beliefs are based upon what is written in God's Word. I have been delivered from the power of darkness, and I will live in that reality."

Study Scriptures: James 4:7; I Peter 5:9; Ephesians 4:27

Devotional # 301
Held Together By God's Hand

Scripture: Colossians 1:16-17

Here and there in the Bible are placed statements of absolute truth that are absolutely stunning. Today's reading is one of those. In it, you are told flatly that ALL THINGS were created by Him.....things in Heaven, in earth, visible, invisible, even the beings that we know as darkness (principalities and powers). Notice that, originally, all these things were created FOR Him. Of course, as we know, some chose to turn away from Him and become His eternal enemies.

So, these two simple verses blow away evolution as you know it (see study Scriptures). And that's okay, because if you look at it closely, evolution is only a theory anyway, and it is the result of human reasoning applied to certain facts in a certain way. That is, give humans a chance, and they'll find a way to contradict God Almighty's eternal truth with some invention of their own mind.....which is puny in comparison to His.

In verse 17, we're told that our Lord is before all things. That should be apparent, since the Creator is always greater than the creation. More than that, though, notice the phrase "and by Him all things consist." So, I need to take you back to 4th grade science class, where you learned about atoms. Atoms are made up of protons and electrons, which have opposite charges magnetically. The nucleus of the atom contains one or more protons, which all have a positive charge. What happens when you try to put two positive poles of a magnet together? They repel. Yet the atoms of your body are made up of closely packed protons. The obvious question then is, "What holds them together?" The answer is in verse17. You see, they naturally want to repel each other. What happens when they do that? An atom bomb.

So, what keeps YOU from exploding? That's right.....your heavenly Father. "By Him all things consist." Treat Him right, my friend. You don't want Him to let go.

Faith Profession: "My Lord literally holds my life in the palm of His hand. I'm so glad that His outstanding attribute is love!"

Study Scriptures: Hebrews 11:3; Romans 8:38-39

Devotional # 302
It is Revealed

Scripture: Colossians 1:26-27

The fact that Christ comes to live inside us at salvation seems to be known to almost every believer….. "Christ in you, the hope of glory." We live in that realization, yet…..I wonder if we fully comprehend it.

I used to teach seven mysteries in the Word of God. In fact, there ARE seven things called "mysteries," yet it says right here in today's verses that they are no longer mysteries…..they have been revealed to us!

One of them is the indwelling of the living God in every believer. This was unknown to the Old Testament saint…..it did not become a reality until Acts 2. Therefore, we are a privileged people to be living in New Testament times. However, for too many Christians, the truth of an indwelling Lord is nothing but a statement on paper. For them, He is in there, but there is no change in their life because of it. My question is….."How can that be!?" You have the power of Almighty God inside you, and you don't notice anything different??!! That, folks, is what should not be.

The Lord, among His many wonderful attributes, is a gentleman. He never forces Himself, or anything, on the New Testament believer. All of His blessings are a matter of choice on your part…..all are manifest for you when you receive them by faith (just like you did for salvation). So, the greatest power in the universe resides inside you. It is called the riches of His glory because it is the Anointing. The Holy Spirit is not just indwelling, but providing power and glory…..IF you will choose to allow that. It is, however, revealed only to those who are searching for it…..and receiving it by faith (see study Scriptures).

Why do some believers have power? Why do miracles occur in some ministries and not others? Because some receive by faith, and others do not. It's that simple…..and that profound.

Faith Profession: "Oh, Lord, I don't want to be one of the unbelieving Christians who have the power of God residing inside of them, but never tap into it. What could be worse for a Christian?"

Study Scriptures: Ezra 7:10; Mark 11:12-24

BEWARE!

Scripture: Colossians 2:6-8

"Beware," Paul says to the Colossians. He is warning them for their own good, and so they will protect themselves from things that will move them away from Christ. "Beware".....or, we might say..... "Be AWARE."

Aware of what? Well, your enemy is subtle, so you're going to have to stay on your toes to "be aware." The devil will try to gently guide you just slightly off the path of truth. If he can do that, you will be on your way to being so far away from truth that you won't believe it. What does he do? He slips traditions of men into your life. They seem okay at first, because so many other Christians are sucked in by them. He'll also try to move you toward the "rudiments of the world".....that is, worldly practices and goals that will slowly replace your emphasis on the Word of God.

What does this look like in a practical way? Well, your church might begin to emphasize the number of people in attendance instead of the teaching of the Word. They might even slowly change the service toward an emphasis on entertainment-oriented services.....so that it will appeal to the people of the world. The preaching of the Word will become watered-down.....the goal will be to make people laugh rather than bring them into the truth.....and eventually the stated character of the church will be said to be "seeker-friendly."

You know what, my friend? Getting people in the door of the church is not an end in itself. The idea is to get lost people saved, and to get newly-saved people discipled, and to get discipled people serving the Lord. Therefore, much of the ministry of the church should be the teaching and preaching of the Word. When churches get pulled into this "worldly" approach, they have been "spoiled," as it says in verse 8. They then become churches exactly like that described in Revelation 3 (see study Scriptures). BEWARE!

Faith Profession: "I will stay focused on my most important assignment.....filling myself with the Word of God. THAT is always to be the emphasis for the child of God."

Study Scripture: Revelation 3:14-22

DEVOTIONAL # 304

WATER BAPTISM

Scripture: Colossians 2:12

When you receive Jesus Christ as your Savior from sin's penalty, you are declared righteous; you receive eternal life; you become part of the family of God; etc. You know that all of these things are spiritual, and therefore invisible…..right? Did you also know that you were baptized at the moment of salvation? Yes….. and that baptism is described in I Corinthians 12:13. Notice that it is a spiritual transaction, and therefore is invisible. That is, it is a spiritual thing rather than a physical thing.

What, then, is water baptism all about? Clearly it is a visible, physical thing. The answer is this: the Lord provided water baptism to be a visible picture of the real, spiritual baptism that occurred at salvation. Water baptism was originally done in the most public place possible, because it is for the unsaved…..it is something that they can SEE (because they best relate to things like that). It is an outward, visible picture of the real, internal, spiritual transaction of new life.

So, water baptism is recommended as a testimony to the unsaved people. Perhaps it will make them curious enough to find out about salvation. BUT…..some church groups have made water baptism an end in itself. They tell you that water baptism cleanses you from sin. NOT TRUE! If anything, water baptism gets you WET. It does NOT cleanse sin…..it COULD NOT. A physical thing cannot cleanse a spiritual thing.

You need to be careful in today's world. ANY emphasis on water baptism is a wrong emphasis. There's nothing wrong with it as a testimony to others, but it is not to be exalted…..especially at the expense of REAL baptism. It is a physical thing, and the end-times church likes physical things that it can see. But, it does NOTHING for you spiritually….. where it really counts.

Faith Profession: "I will be obedient to the Bible's recommendation to be water baptized AFTER my actual salvation, but I will be aware that it is NOT salvation, nor does it cleanse me from sin."

Study Scriptures: Romans 6:4; I Corinthians 12:13; Ephesians 1:19-20

NOURISHED IN THE WORD

Scripture: Colossians 2:19

For the Christian, there is nothing more important after salvation than the Word of God. You cannot hear it too much. You cannot get enough of it. You sometimes learn something completely new from a verse that you have looked at hundreds of times. It is truly a miracle Book, unlike any other.

Today's verse talks of nourishment, and lists three ways we are nourished by the Word. First, it "ministers" to us. That is, it serves us.....which is what "minister" means. The Word provides all you need for any situation in life. It comforts; corrects; encourages; convicts; teaches; loves; guides; counsels; and heals. It has been placed on earth by a loving God to give us guidance in this crazy world system.

Second, it "knits together." An understanding of the Word.....what it means.....how it all fits together.....how it reveals God to us intimately.....brings us into a true family relationship. We know our Dad. We love Him with abandon. We appreciate Him. And we love to be with others who feel the same way.

Third, it "increases" us. Our knowledge is increased. Better yet, our understanding is increased to the point of wisdom. As we know the Book, we know it's Author, which increases our peace, contentment, love, and joy. Belief in the Word gives us health, prosperity, love, safety, and authority over the dark spirits who oppose Him, and therefore us. In all ways, the Word of God increases us.

What, then, could be more important than spending time in the Word? Do we have certain obligations? Of course. But.....is there still time that COULD be set aside to be in the Word.....every day? The correct answer is yes.

Faith Profession: "The Word of God, which is equated with Jesus Christ, is my most important possession. Neglect of it is done at my own loss. I seek to be nourished by it.....by spending time in it."

Study Scriptures: Hebrews 4:12-13; II Timothy 3:16

DEVOTIONAL # 306
THE RIGHT PERSPECTIVE

Scripture: Colossians 3:1-3

As I look closely at the Book of Colossians, I'm startled at the number of verses that gently prod us toward more attention to the Lord, His Word, and spiritual things in general.

Today's verses admonish us to set our affections on things above.....on Heaven.....on the Lord.....on eternity.....on our commission to go and tell the world the good news. In verse 3, Paul tries reasoning.....why would you set your affection on earthly, visible, physical things when you have heavenly, spiritual things which are of infinitely more value? Why would you who are now dead to the world (for all practical purposes) focus your attention on it? Why?

In an attempt to lure the people of the world into their services, some churches have themselves become like the world.....they are giving their attention to earthly, visible, physical things. What does this look like? Entertainment.....flashy videos.....an unusual emphasis on water baptism rather than spiritual (real) baptism. They place an emphasis on physical things like numbers of attendees; the amount of money in the offering; the need to go to two services, or build a bigger building; and a corresponding decrease in emphasis on the teaching of the Word of God.

Jesus tells us that, "If ye then be risen with Christ, seek those things which are above...," that is, heavenly things.....invisible things.....spiritual things.....the kinds of things that are important to HIM. After all, HE is the focal point.....right? Not us.....or our ministry..... the size of our church.....or how nice our building looks. His Word would also be a focal point. His Word would be emphasized, loved, studied, taught, used, and believed. Hey, it's what Jesus recommends for you.....not just what I recommend. That ought to make a difference to you.

Faith Profession: "Lord, forgive me for any over-emphasis I've placed on the things of the world. I resolve to set my sights on the things that are important to YOU."

Study Scriptures: II Timothy 2:15; II Corinthians 6:14-17

Devotional # 307
Satan Can Only Hinder

Scripture: I Thessalonians 2:18

The devil has been waging a propaganda campaign against the church for as long as we can remember. It has increased as technology has made that possible. Today, he can feed us garbage through the TV, newspaper, magazines, movies, books, and, of course, the internet, among other possibilities. The advent of increased communications, then, is both a blessing and a curse.

Because of advances in technology, satan can spread his lies much more rapidly, and in more volume. Thus, modern Christianity is filled with saved believers who think that satan is more powerful than they are, and that they're powerless to resist him…..that all they can do is appeal to the Lord, and wait to see if He will help.

Notice in today's verse that satan is attacking Paul himself. Paul mentions that his intention to visit the Thessalonians had been hindered several times. Now, don't jump to a negative conclusion on this. You say, "Well, if the devil was successful against Paul, then who am I to stand up to him?"

Wait a minute. Let's calm down and just look at this. The word "hinder" means "impede" or "detain"…..NOT STOP. In fact, the devil CAN NOT stop a Christian…..neither Paul nor you…..unless you LET him by being passive and believing his lie. No…..the Scripture tells us that "no weapon formed against us will prosper…" (see study Scriptures). The Word also says that we triumph in Christ EVERY TIME (see study Scriptures).

The key? Our faith. In Paul's case, it was his faith. Once he realized what satan was doing, Paul simply commanded him to stop…..and he HAD TO. It works the same for you, because Jesus gave that same victory over the devil to you. Use it, and you'll see him flee…..from YOU. He can hinder, but that is all. In other words, he's nothing but a nuisance.

Faith Profession: "Once again, I will take my authority from the Word of God. Though satan can try to hinder me, he cannot stop anything I do."

Study Scriptures: Isaiah 54:17; II Corinthians 2:14; James 4:7

Devotional # 308
Jesus is Coming Back

Scripture: I Thessalonians 4:13-18

Though the word "rapture" does not appear in your Bible, the word has become associated with the event described in today's verses because it means "a joyous reunion...a joyous meeting." It describes so well our next meeting with our Savior, which is explained in today's reading.

You need to know that the word "sleep" in today's verses refers to death. That being said, notice that Jesus is coming back for the church. This is NOT the Second Coming at Armageddon.....that takes place a little later. The Rapture will involve saved believers only. Notice that, in verse 17, Jesus does not touch down on earth in this event.....as He surely will at the Second Coming.

Instead, He comes into the earth's atmosphere to meet us. The event is signaled by a shout from Heaven, and with a trumpet blast. It says that those who have died in Christ prior to this event will raise from their graves with a glorified body. Those of us who are alive when this happens will be taken off the earth supernaturally, and our bodies will be instantly changed as we go. We will be "caught up," it says, to meet the Lord in the air. From that point on into eternity, "so shall we ever be with the Lord."

Well.....A...M...E...N!!! How's THAT for good news?! It's just the BEST!! The details of what happens next are recorded for you in the Book of Revelation, plus a few other places in the Word. A good study of the end times will give you all the rest of the information on this. Today, I simply wanted to introduce you to this fabulous concept. Some of us will not see physical death, but will be taken alive into Heaven. It is the very next event on the prophetic calendar. So, keep one ear open, and an eye on the sky. Jesus is coming back to take us home!!

Faith Profession: "I love the Lord. He is coming back for me, to take me to Heaven..... where I belong.....forever!"

Study Scriptures: I Corinthians 15:51-57; Luke 24:36-43

Let It Go

Scripture: I Timothy 1:12-16

I don't know what your past was like, but chances are that it wasn't as bad as the Apostle Paul's. In today's verses, Paul does a brief review of his past. He says that he had been a blasphemer.....a persecutor.....and injurious. In fact, before his salvation in Acts 9, Paul was among the most zealous of the persecutors of the church. When Stephen was stoned to death, the man holding the coats of those who killed him was Paul (see study Scriptures).

Paul then thought he was serving God by harming Christians. He imprisoned many..... broke up families.....had people put to death.....ruined lives. Death and destruction in the name of the Lord.....you'd think religious folk would know better. Now, as a saved man, Paul recognizes an important fact.....Jesus has forgiven him for all the harm he did. In verse 14, he says, "The grace of our Lord was exceeding abundant with faith and love...."

So.....what about you? You have a past. We all do. In mine (before I was saved), I mocked God and Christians.....cursed like a trooper.....lived like the devil.....and defied the Lord. When He saved me, I was reasonably certain that He could not use a person like me. But.....I found the same things that Paul mentions in verse 14.

The reason it's called "the past" is because it's all over. It can't be changed. There are no "do-overs." There are only two things left.....for the past to be forgiven, and then for it to be forgotten. The first thing is given to you as a free gift by Jesus. The second thing has to be given to yourself.....by you. It's over. The Lord has forgiven you. Now, forgive yourself, and let it go. Don't let the devil beat you up with memories. Forgive yourself, just as Jesus has forgiven you.

Faith Profession: "One weapon the devil uses against me is the replay of memories of past sin. I reject these memories. I am forgiven, and I will leave my past in the past."

Study Scriptures: Acts 7:58; Colossians 2:13

Devotional # 310
Pray for Leaders

Scripture: I Timothy 2:1-4

Today's devotional mentions praying for leaders, but verse 1 also tells us that we should make intercession for them, and give thanks for them. This is a tall order when the leadership in question is not of your liking. In fact, though, it's the less competent leaders who need prayer more than others. If God can work miracles through donkeys and whales, He can surely do so through humans…..however incompetent they may be.

So, we are to pray for our President…..our Senators and Representatives…..our Governors…..our local political leaders…..our policemen…..our military…..our firemen…..our emergency responders…..our parents…..our teachers…..our pastors…..our boss at work…..even the crossing guard at the corner. It says that "this is good and acceptable in the sight of God our Savior."

So you say, "Well, I don't like some of my leaders." Okay…..then apply verse 4 to them. It's placed in the same context as the recommendation to pray for these people. If they choose to receive Jesus as their Savior, you just might like them a whole lot more.

One more thing. Much of what we know about others is based on hearsay, or something we read in the newspaper or heard on TV. If possible, try to get to know those leaders personally. You might be surprised to find that they're decent folks who are really trying to do what's right. You might also be surprised to discover that their job isn't so easy…..that they have frustrating obstacles placed in their path…..that they get opposition when they try to do right. Things aren't always what they seem to be.

No matter what, pray for them. How can that hurt? The injection of some spiritual power into their life HAS to be of help…..to them, and to you.

Faith Profession: "I am exhorted by the Holy Spirit to pray for the leaders around me. They have a tough job, and I resolve to help them in this way."

Study Scriptures: Ephesians 6:18; II Peter 3:9

Devotional # 311
What is Jesus Doing Now?

Scripture: I Timothy 2:5

Jesus completed the most difficult work ever done on earth.....the redemption of mankind.....then resurrected from the dead as proof that He is the only way to Heaven. He re-appeared for forty days, then went back to Heaven. So, what is He doing up there? Has He been resting for 2000 years?

Quite the contrary. He has been as busy as a one-armed paperhanger, being a mediator for you, me, and every other saved child of God. What is a mediator? It is somebody who represents another. Think of a courtroom scene. The devil, who is called "the accuser of the brethren," is busy blaming stuff on you. The judge would be the Father..... you would be the accused. Jesus acts as your defense lawyer.....countering each charge against you with the fact that your sins have been washed in the blood of the sinless Lamb of God. Every charge is nullified in this manner.

In addition, Jesus is said to be your Advocate. An advocate is someone who is FOR you, not against you. He is on your side. He is your defense; your comforter; your helper; your redeemer. No matter what happens, Jesus is there to bail you out, and to counteract the accusations of the enemy. Let's face it, if you could choose only one person to be "on your side," who else would you choose but Jesus Christ?

Resting? No, I don't think so. I think He's been as busy as ever keeping the devil's accusations off of His children. How good is He at this? Not a single accusation has stuck in all the time He's been our Mediator and Advocate. He paid for all sins, including those you committed after salvation. They were ALL future when He died for them.

Faith Profession: "Jesus is my Advocate and Mediator. As such, He is on my side, and is defending me every day. For my part, I will strive to make His job easier."

Study Scriptures: I John 2:1; Psalm 118:6

DEVOTIONAL # 312
WHO CAN BE SAVED?

Scripture: I Timothy 2:4

As you travel through life as a saved Christian, you encounter a wide variety of viewpoints on the various truths of the Word of God. It's surprising to discover how many of them are NOT based on the Word, but on chunks of Scripture taken out of context, or pre-conceived notions which are "proved" by applying <u>parts</u> of verses.

Some people believe that everybody is saved because Jesus died for all. Some believe that few are saved, and even less "endure to the end".....that is, they get "unsaved" along the way (of course, not THEM). Some believe salvation is a process. Some think it isn't real at all.

The Bible, though, is very clear on this subject, and today's verse makes it abundantly plain.....He would have ALL...to be saved. Yet, other Scriptures tell us that, in fact, MOST people remain unsaved.....despite the fact that they COULD be saved.

Certain things are clear from the Word. Jesus made it possible for every person who ever lived to be saved and have eternal life. It is His will that every person receive this free gift of salvation. Yet, most people die without it (see study Scriptures). Why? Because it is a GIFT, and, as such, has to be RECEIVED. That is, there is a choice involved.....a decision. Just as you do on your birthday, or at Christmas, you need to RECEIVE the gift in order for it to be yours.

Who can be saved? Anyone. Everyone. Jesus made no distinction in the giving of His miraculous gift. The question is....."Have YOU received it?" I can't answer that for you. But, if you haven't chosen to receive salvation, I'd recommend that you do it NOW!

Faith Profession: "Based only on the Word of God, it is clear that salvation is available to every person. It is Jesus' will that ALL be saved."

Study Scriptures: II Peter 3:9; Matthew 7:13-14

DEVOTIONAL # 313
CLOTHING AND COMMON SENSE

Scripture: I Timothy 2:9

Oh, boy…..what a mess Christians have made of verses like today's. I was raised in a very strict, traditional denominational church setting which took verses on modest clothing to a ridiculous extreme. Earrings; makeup; anything tighter than a potato sack; anything shorter than your ankles; anything shiny…..were absolutely forbidden. If you had the audacity to wear any of these things, you'd be frozen in your tracks by the icy stares of the "righteous enforcers."

For men, no shorts…..you could go without a necktie in an extreme situation…..and no facial hair. I even know of a man who was "spoken to" because he wore a nice, expensive leather sport coat to church (it was leather, which apparently was a "no-no"). When challenged on the facial hair issue (because he had a moustache), a friend of mine pointed out that the accuser had eyebrows…..so the facial hair rule was somewhat selective.

Is this what the Word intends? Nit-picking among God's people…..the development of a judgmental attitude about others based on their physical appearance? I'm guessing the Lord Himself would not be welcomed into many churches today. He wore a beard. He wore sandals. His feet were dirty. He slept in His clothes. He had no access to underarm deodorant.

Modesty? Sure. There are reasonable limits to fashion. The idea is to dress in a manner respectful of the Lord. Will that be different for you than for me? Yes. But…..love dictates that we make no issue out of this kind of thing. Common sense tells us the same thing. Don't judge others, folks. Some people just don't have the money for clothing that others do. We aren't to be seeing the outward appearance anyway. We need to look at people as Jesus would…..seeing the need of their soul, not what they are wearing.

Faith Profession: "I will live my life in common sense, and with a minimum of judgment of others. I will show the love of Christ to all."

Study Scriptures: Romans 14:1-10

Mute Women

Scripture: I Timothy 2:11-15

Well, this chapter of I Timothy is turning out to be a gold mine of controversy! Today we have some of the Scripture that folks used to teach that women should not ever be permitted to speak in church. I used to attend church business meetings in which, if a woman had a question or comment, she had to whisper it to her husband so that he could say it out loud! Such are the extents to which some people go to be "correct." The Pharisees would be so proud!

Yes, I know that the man is to be the spiritual head of the home. Yes, I know that the woman was created second. I also know that woman was created from man's rib…..from his side…..not from a part lower than him, and not from a part above him. I know that the woman in a marriage is to be the man's "helpmeet," meaning "partner." Though he has final spiritual responsibility, the decisions are shared…..because two heads are better than one (no matter how big you think yours is).

The word "usurp" in verse 12 means "to rebel or overthrow." A woman in such a state needs to be silent, and these verses say so. Apparently this was an issue that Timothy had to deal with in his church. But, are we to take it to such an extreme that we have women whispering rather than talking out loud? Doesn't that seem ridiculous to you?

Would you be surprised to find out that these same women…..in these same churches….. are permitted to teach Sunday School classes? How is THAT talking different that what is done in a business meeting? Folks…..have you read about the woman at the well? Or Priscilla? Or Lois and Eunice teaching Timothy? No, these verses can't mean total silence. But they could mean silence in the event of rebellion or usurping the authority of the man in the home. Let's stick to being reasonable, shall we? That's what the Word does.

Faith Profession: "I will search the Scriptures to get the whole story on every issue. It will, of course, be consistent with common sense in all cases."

Study Scriptures: Acts 2:17; John 4:4-30; Acts 18:24-26

Devotional # 315
Qualifications

Scripture: I Timothy 3:1-7

Today's reading gives the qualifications for the office of "bishop"…..we would say "pastor," or "minister," or "reverend." The person who is called to be the leader of a local church is expected to meet certain minimum requirements…..the position is that important to the Lord.

You can see that there are quite a few qualifications. Each one is, if you look closely, a matter of simple common sense. The person called to lead a church group is to set an example for the group…..in word and deed. Notice that this person is to be, among other things, "apt to teach." That is, there will be an "anointing" on that person from the Lord that will cause his/her teaching to be easily understood, and that will pull truth from the Bible's verses.

This "bishop" is not to be in the position to make money ("not greedy of filthy lucre"). So, it is NOT a job, but a calling. Of course, a reasonable salary is to be paid, but it is to be in balance with the congregation…..not too extravagant…..not too miserly.

This person called of the Lord is not to be a novice. That is, he/she is to have some experience in the application of spiritual things to life situations; the handling of crises; the patience required to counsel others; and the diligence to spend time in prayer and the study of the Word. A novice will, in all likelihood, become prideful…...and will begin to see the work as his/her own…..will begin to focus on numbers (attendance/offerings)…..and will have, as his/her basic motive, the building of a work that will be noticed and praised by the world. A whole verse is devoted to this warning.

In short, a person called to lead a local church congregation must be skilled at the application and teaching of the Word of God…..must be a veteran of spiritual warfare…..and a person who conducts himself/herself as any leader would. He or she would recognize that he/she is to be an example to others in all aspects of life. Be careful who you place at the head of your church. These qualifications are given so you won't suffer at the hands of the wrong one.

Faith Profession: "I see that the office of pastor (elder, bishop, minister) is vitally important, since the spiritual well-being of an entire congregation rests in his/her hands."

Study Scriptures: I Peter 5:1-3; Titus 1:6-9

DEVOTIONAL # 316
THE MYSTERY OF GODLINESS

Scripture: I Timothy 3:16

In today's verse, we are once again confronted with one of the "mysteries" that are occasionally mentioned in the New Testament. In this case, it is the mystery of godliness. Since it is defined in the next few words of the verse, it is plainly not a mystery any longer. It had been, though, for many years…..mainly to Old Testament saints, who lived under an entirely different set of circumstances spiritually than we do.

The mystery of godliness is this: God was manifest in the flesh. Think of that. God Almighty…..Creator and Sustainer of the universe…..the Great "I AM"…..El Shaddai (all-sufficient One)…..King of Kings and Lord of Lords…..arranged to become a flesh and blood human. He accomplished this through a master stroke of genius that we call the Virgin Birth. Had He become flesh as God, He would not have been just like us. Had He become flesh just as a human, He would not have had the necessary connection to Heaven.

So, He arranged to have a young girl become pregnant supernaturally (without the help of a man). In doing this, He became human, because the girl was human. But, He avoided the passing on of the sin nature of humans by making the conception a supernatural thing. So, He appeared in the flesh…..making Himself part of the human race (so that His payment for sin would be valid for mankind).

Think about this…..God was a tiny baby. Someone had to change His diaper. Someone had to feed Him. He was essentially helpless, at least for a time. How much love do you have to have to be willing to do that!!?? And how do our simple minds ever comprehend that situation?

I don't think we ever will. But, it was a stroke of genius that caught the devil totally by surprise, and led to his final defeat without violating any point of the law. Masterful. Amazing. That's our God!!

Faith Profession: "The mystery of godliness is, indeed, a wonderful thing to think about. Our Lord is so incredible…..so wonderful! Thank you, Lord."

Study Scriptures: John 1:14; Matthew 1:18-25; Luke 1:26-38

Devotional # 317

Refusing Nothing

Scripture: I Timothy 4:4-5

It has been established since Noah departed from the Ark.….a diet can include meat, and no form of it is excluded in the New Testament. It is true that certain foods were prohibited for Old Testament Jews, but the idea was to prevent disease. Most of the prohibited animals and birds were scavengers, and the world back then was not conducive to disease prevention.

At any rate, Acts 10 makes it clear that the Old Testament laws concerning unclean animals are no longer in effect. In our day, when we are promised healing as part of our Blood Covenant relationship with our Father, we have supernatural protection from these and other things (as long as we place our faith in it). These days, you find people trying to impose restrictions on God's people. Certain foods have been forbidden on certain days, for example. Some folks refuse to eat meat at all.

Now, while your choices are yours, and my choices are mine, we should be aware that all things are permissible to the Lord. He will not fuss if you don't choose to eat meat, but you need to be aware that my choice of eating it is not wrong in His eyes. According to today's Scripture, every creature of God is good, and nothing is to be refused. Nothing.

Therefore, we can all live in harmony if we just make our own choices, and not try to impose them on others.….realizing that ANY choices of what to eat are acceptable to the Lord. That's the bottom line.….what HE thinks. If the Word is really your final authority, you'll make your own choices, and give others the freedom to make theirs. That's what Jesus does.

Faith Profession: "I have the liberty in Christ to make my own choices about diet. My choices are no more right than anybody else's. We all have the freedom to choose for ourselves, and nothing is refused as far as He is concerned."

Study Scripture: Acts 10:9-16

Meditation

Scripture: I Timothy 4:15

Today's lesson is centered on the first word in today's verse. Meditation has received some bad press in recent years…..it has become connected in the minds of Christians with Eastern religions, so much so that Christians tend to dismiss the concept as soon as they hear it.

Perhaps, though, we ought to hold on a minute. We know that the devil is our enemy. One of his main weapons against us is the fact that he counterfeits sound Bible concepts. The idea is to steer us away from them through confusion. Meditation is just such a concept. Would you be surprised to find that meditation is a Bible idea? That it was part of Scripture long before other religions "borrowed" it? I guess it isn't talked about too often these days, but it should be.

Meditation is simply the considering of a thing…..a verse, or a concept from the Word. It means to think about it…..to mull it over in your mind…..to look at it mentally from different angles…..to think about it carefully…..to get to know it intimately. Did you know that this process is one of the best ways to increase your faith in a Scripture promise? No wonder the devil wants to steer you away from it!

Scripture promises contain power, but they are activated by faith…..your faith. That faith is strengthened by how deeply you believe the promise in question. Your belief in it grows as you think about it…..speak it…..read it. What are you doing? You are planting it into your own spirit until it becomes real to you. Then, when you need to rely on that promise in a crisis, your faith in it will be already established, and it WILL WORK FOR YOU.

It all starts with meditation on the promise. It is a Bible concept, and it is important in increasing your faith. The Lord wants that for you…..the devil does not. Let's defeat him by meditating in the Word.

Faith Profession: "I now understand that meditation is a Bible concept, and that it is important for the increase of my faith."

Study Scriptures: Joshua 1:8; Psalm 19:14; Psalm 119:48

Devotional # 319
What You Value

Scripture: I Timothy 6:6-11

Although the Bible recognizes the things of the world, it places little priority on them. Today's Scriptures tell us to be careful with our attitude about money, because it can easily gain prominence in our lives. In fact, it is said in verse 20 to be the root of ALL EVIL. It is not a misprint.

Notice that <u>money</u> itself is not the problem. These days, it is virtually impossible to function without money, and the Lord knows that. The problem becomes our <u>attitude</u> toward it. Some think these verses are an indictment against rich people. But, poor people are often the ones with the negative attitude about money…..they are often resentful and jealous about not having enough.

The Lord recommends a completely different focus. He plainly says in verse 7 that you can't take money with you when you die, so why place an emphasis on it? Maybe it would be wise to focus on the eternal things, like righteousness; godliness; faith; love; patience; and meekness. All of these are free…..you need no money at all to have these. Yet they cannot be bought with money…..no matter how much money you have.

The inerrant Word of God says that the <u>love</u> of money draws a person away from faith, and leads to many sorrows. Evidence of this is all around us in the news media. Yet, those who seek after the qualities of verse 11 tend toward contentment…..that is, a life of peace; rest; quietness of mind; satisfaction.

I'll tell you what. You get into the money rat race if you want. As for me, I know that the Lord provides generously for His children, and does so without all the stress and strife of the world system. It seems odd to me that anyone would NOT choose His way. It's your choice. One way is frenzy and frustration…..the other is godliness and contentment. Your choice.

Faith Profession: "I know my Lord is the Great Provider. He provides well for birds and animals who know nothing of money. I know where contentment lies, and I will seek that as my life's goal."

Study Scriptures: II Timothy 3:2; Matthew 13:22

FIGHT THE GOOD FIGHT

Scripture: I Timothy 6:12

Fighting…..it's probably not the way you'd prefer to start your day. You'd rather slide into it on a more mellow note. Yet, if your day has begun, you need to know that the fight has, too. You don't have to be in the mood to fight; the devil brings the fight to you every minute of every day.

Some believe that their only recourse against the devil is to appeal to God for relief. When He doesn't respond, they rationalize that He wanted them to get sick, or hurt, to teach some obscure lesson. But, if I read today's verse correctly, it is addressed to the reader, and it says to FIGHT. It does NOT say that God will do your fighting FOR you. He's already provided the victory…..He gave His life…..He paid the price. And now you want MORE from Him!?

No, you have a choice in this, just like in all matters of faith. The Lord provides the power for you to win the fight, but you make the choice to participate. If your faith is strong, and you apply Scripture as it was intended, then you will kick the devil back into the hole he crawled out of…..every time. That is, fighting isn't so bad when you know you'll win. There's a sweet satisfaction in beating back the devil…..chasing him away…..putting a defeat on him.

When you got saved, you may have noticed that you weren't taken to Heaven right away. No, the Lord left you here…..in enemy territory…..because someone has to battle the devil in this war for the souls of men. He has left us here to fight…..for lost souls, and against the enemy of mankind. He gave you armor…..HIS armor…..for your protection. He gave you mighty promises that work every time if applied in faith. He's trusting you to do your part. It is a privilege to be given this assignment. Let's not fail Him.

Faith Profession: "I don't feel like a mighty warrior, Lord, but with Your power and my faith, we can beat back any enemy."

Study Scriptures: II Timothy 4:7; II Timothy 2:3-4; Ephesians 6:10-18

DEVOTIONAL # 321
GETTING GOD'S APPROVAL

Scripture: II Timothy 2:15

I think it would be safe to say that we would all prefer to have God's approval. It is certainly better than the alternative. To watch Christians, you'd think that getting God's approval is a matter of conduct.....do this.....don't do that.....dress this way.....say the right thing.....never curse, drink, swear, or chase loose women.....and don't hang around with those who do. No.....that would be wrong.

Funny how far from the truth Christians have gotten. Today's verse tells us how to win God's approval, and it is all about the study of His Holy Word. You see, the Lord knows that His Word is powerful.....life-changing, actually.....and He knows that your conduct will be altered simply by the study of the Bible. It will be more than enough. Modern Christians have it backward, it would seem.

Notice that it says "study," not just read. Notice, too, that the person studying is said to be a "workman." So, studying the Word is going to be WORK. It will take up some of your time. It will have to be a matter of priority for you. Some other things are going to have to be put aside.

Furthermore, you are to be a workman who needs not to be ashamed. That is, you'll have to give this some effort. You'll need to study and work in a way that you'll not be ashamed as you stand before HIM. A minimal effort simply will not do.....you won't get away with it.

Lastly, the study of the Bible involves the "rightly dividing" of it. So, there are divisions, and you need to recognize them. You will become confused if you mix up the Old Testament with the New, for example. Many, many people do that, and have a distorted view of the Lord and faith as a result.

Ahhhh.....but if you DO study.....if you DO work at it.....if you DO rightly divide..... you will enter into a place of blessing and intimate fellowship with Him such as you've never imagined! It is well worth the effort.

Faith Profession: "I'm going to have to re-arrange my priorities, and make the study of the Word of God a daily event. I want the approval of my Lord and Savior."

Study Scriptures: Proverbs 1:1-6; Proverbs 4:4-9

DEVOTIONAL # 322

IN THE LAST DAYS

Scripture: II Timothy 3:1-7

There are few more sobering passages of Scripture than this one, especially because, here in these last days, we can see these verses happening all around us. They are a description of the character of people in the days before the Rapture. Did you notice what is first on the list? Selfishness.....people thinking that what they want, and who they are, is all that matters. It is chillingly apparent in the world in which I live.

Disobedience to parents has rapidly escalated, now that parents have been deceived into believing that they need to "reason" with their children. Sometimes I wonder, as I watch a small child dominate an adult.....,"Is anybody in charge here?" The great national tragedy of abortion, along with the rampant abandonment of newborns, brings home the truth of the phrase "without natural affection." For me personally, I have experienced a lack of natural affection with my mother; my brother and sisters; and some of my children. Trust me, it is a plague from Hell, and causes hurt too deep to put into words.

True practicing Christians have experienced the truth of verse 3. If you love the Lord, and aren't afraid to show it, you will be on the outside socially. (It's not so bad.....the folks inside the social camp often don't even like each other, and usually can't remember whether or not they had a good time.)

Verse 5 says many will have a form of godliness.....that is, they'll look okay to the un-trained eye. In fact, they are lost folk who are just faking it. And, lastly, you'll find people.....Christians mostly.....who attend Sunday School; listen to sermons; and read books; but never come to a knowledge of the truth.

The unsaved world doesn't recognize the Bible as Truth, so they miss it completely. Saved folk tend to re-learn what they already know, and never look at anything different. Too many don't have any idea what a relationship with the Holy Spirit is like. It is the last days, my friend.....for sure.

Faith Profession: "I love Jesus, and will live like I do."

Study Scriptures: Matthew 24:3-34; I Timothy 4:1-3

Inspiration

Scripture: II Timothy 3:16

The Bible is a book which has over 40 different authors, most of whom didn't know each other.....was written over a period of about 1600 years.....yet has a basic message, and prophetic content, that is consistent throughout. Things predicted in the Bible come true at a rate of 100%.....and some of them are written 1000 years before the predicted event takes place.

Today's verse tells us that all of Scripture is inspired of God. That is, though it is written by many human authors, all have this in common.....they wrote what they were supernaturally inspired to write. This is the difference between the Bible and any other book. No other book on earth has been inspired by God Himself. More than that, the Bible writings are said to have been supernaturally preserved over the years (see study Scriptures).

This is important, since the Old Testament was originally written in the Hebrew language, and the New Testament was originally written in Greek (with a little bit of Aramaic). Copies of the text were most commonly written on papyrus, which is much like newsprint, and is perishable. Because of this, Bibles had to be re-copied constantly, just as they are today. Since the printing press wasn't invented until the 1400's, these copies were made by hand. This makes the doctrine of preservation very important. Bibles were accurately copied because they were supernaturally preserved by the Hand of God. What you have today can be counted on to be accurate to the original text, especially if its source is the Received Text (Greek).

All Scripture is not only inspired, but preserved. It is effective for doctrine (the basic truths of the Bible); reproof (conviction); instruction (on any subject in life); and correction (because all of us need this at times). It is the Book of books, and is spoken of in human terms as if it is alive (which it is spiritually.....see study Scriptures). It is God's Word, and it is available for you.

Faith Profession: "I believe what the Bible says about its own inspiration and preservation. As I read it, it speaks to my spirit. No other book does that."

Study Scriptures: Psalm 12:6-7; Hebrews 4:12-13

DEVOTIONAL # 324

END-TIMES ADVICE

Scripture: II Timothy 4:1-5

II Timothy 4 is the last chapter in the Bible written by the Apostle Paul before he died. In it, he includes some good advice for Timothy, but that advice also applies to you and me today. Notice that he says that the time will come when "they" will not endure sound doctrine...will gravitate toward teachers who will tell them what they WANT to hear rather than what they NEED to hear...and that they will turn away from the TRUTH. Is he talking about the people of the world? Yes, but he is also talking about saved, blood-bought Christians.

As the end nears, they will begin to focus on things like: the size of the church (attendance); the need to build new buildings; how to increase offerings. To attract more people, they will begin to focus on methods that will appeal to the world rather than the Lord. Preaching will be "watered down".....it will contain little truth, and even less sound teaching. The teaching of the Word in any depth will be neglected.

Services will become more geared toward entertainment, and less toward the Bible. I've recently seen a 5-minute stand-up comedy routine substituted for prayer as the introduction to the taking of the offering. In short, there will be a turning away from the Word; the truth; sound preaching; and the ministry of the Holy Spirit. It is happening as I write to some of the churches in my hometown.....and probably in yours, too.

Paul advises that we: preach the Word; be "instant" (prepared) at all times; deliver sound doctrine; rebuke (where necessary); and spread the truth of the Word wherever and whenever possible. Time is rapidly running out. The time for serious focus on the Word is NOW. It's as simple as this.....when He returns, what will He find you doing? I'm hoping He catches me praying, or preaching the Word.

Faith Profession: "I see that the need to focus on the Word becomes more critical as the time for Jesus' return grows near. I resolve to remain true to Him, despite the apostasy around me."

Study Scriptures: I Timothy 1:4-7; Titus 2:15; I Timothy 4:7-13

DEMAS

Scripture: II Timothy 4:10

Paul is writing from prison (nothing new there), and is winding up the last chapter he will ever write on earth. When you come to the end of a thing, you tend to mention those things that stand out to you. In today's verse, Paul mentions a man named Demas…..and in doing so reveals the pain in his heart because of this man.

Though not mentioned often in Scripture, Demas had been one of the men who had followed Paul, ministering the Word throughout Asia Minor and Greece. His name is mentioned two other times in the New Testament, and both times he seems to be a faithful companion of Paul. Sadly, here in II Timothy 4, Paul is remembering Demas as a man who had forsaken him…..and the Lord….. "having loved this present world." Whatever led to Demas' departure, he had obviously abandoned the faith for love of worldly things. What a way to be mentioned in Scripture!

Have you ever had a "Demas" in your ministerial life? They are all too prevalent in the body of Christ. They're faithful for a little while…..even effective. Then, their enthusiasm drops off. They begin to miss the things they knew in the world. One day, you look up, and they're gone.

I may be wrong in this, but I think that's the worst of all testimonies. I am dumbfounded that someone could know what Jesus has done for them, and how He loves them…..and then just walk away from Him because he/she misses drinking; parties; immorality; and the rest of the pointless nonsense.

You'd walk away from Jesus Christ for the temporary pleasures of the world?! Are you kidding? I think Demas is one of the most tragic figures in the Bible. I just wish there weren't so many like him in ministry today.

Faith Profession: Serving Jesus is one thing; sustaining the effort is another. I pray that my testimony will be….. "he/she didn't quit."

Study Scriptures: Colossians 4:14; Philemon 24

Devotional # 326
The Opposite of Demas

Scripture: II Timothy 4:11

As Paul gets ready to end his letter to Timothy, he is mentioning a number of people. Here in verse 11, he specifically mentions Mark…..saying that "he is profitable to me for the ministry."

To appreciate this statement, we'll need to go back in time to Paul's first missionary journey, which he took with Barnabas primarily (see study Scriptures). According to the Book of Acts, Mark (whose full name is John Mark) was with them on that journey. However, early on in that trip, John Mark departed and went home (see study Scriptures).

This abandonment made an impression on Paul (and not a good one). Paul obviously had little regard for quitters, and those with no stomach for the rigors of the ministry. (By the way, those of you who think the ministry is some "cake" job have lots to learn. True ministry results in scars….. "marks," the Bible calls them. They come from battle….. hand-to-hand combat on the front lines. It is not for the faint of heart.)

Paul's feelings on this matter are so strong that, when he and Barnabas decide to go back into the field and visit the churches they had established (we call this Paul's second missionary journey), there is an argument between Paul and Barnabas. Barnabas wants to take John Mark with them again. Paul, remembering Mark's desertion from the first journey, refuses to have him come along. Their disagreement is so sharp that they end up NOT traveling together. On the second journey, Paul travels with Silas. You can read up on all of this in the study Scriptures.

Yet, here in II Timothy 4, Paul is requesting John Mark's presence, commenting that he is profitable for the ministry. Something had changed. Mark had matured. And Paul, mature Christian that he was, recognized that. Mark didn't give up…..and wins Paul's respect because of it.

Faith Profession: "Lord, I want to be a "Mark" rather than a "Demas." I resolve to refuse to quit in my service to you."

Study Scriptures: Acts 13:1-13; Acts 15:36-41

Devotional # 327
Come Before Winter

Scripture: II Timothy 4:21

I don't know if Timothy made it to Paul before winter set in…..or before Paul went home to be with the Lord. I do know that II Timothy is the last book written by Paul, and this phrase, "come before winter," got me thinking.

We live in a busy society. I heard someone say yesterday that there just aren't enough hours in the day to go around. We get so busy that we tend to forget to live. We also tend to put off some things that we shouldn't.

Do you have a parent somewhere who would just love to spend some time with you? Couldn't you at least call, or send an e-mail? Is there some friend that you have been wanting to contact, but you've put off doing it until you were less busy? You know you're not going to be less busy…..so MAKE time to call.

Has the Lord has placed a desire to witness to someone on your heart, but you've been waiting until a more opportune occasion. How would you feel to hear that the person in question had died suddenly? Maybe waiting isn't your best choice. Have you been thinking about finding a new church? Or maybe setting some time aside each day to pray and spend time with your best friend…..Jesus?

Tick…tock…tick…tock. The seconds are moving by quickly. Soon they'll be minutes; then hours; days; months; years. It might be best to do some things now. Winter isn't all that far away…..it will be here before you know it. Act now…..before it's too late.

Faith Profession: "I purpose to reduce the amount of procrastination in my life, and do the important things right away. I especially promise to spend more time with Jesus….. starting today."

Study Scriptures: II Corinthians 6:2; James 4:13-14

The Glory of Jesus

Scripture: Hebrews 1:1-3

There are many reasons to exalt and glorify the Lord Jesus Christ. Today's reading gives us several of these, and I believe it would be a good exercise to look at them.

First, Jesus is said to be "heir of all things." Since that's true, then we can rejoice further because, at salvation, He placed Himself in us, and us in Himself.....WE are His body. Therefore, we also are heirs of all things!

Second, it says that the worlds were made by Him. So, He was present at the Creation as part of the Trinity.

Third, Jesus is "the express image of His person." That is, if you want to know what God the Father is like, just study Jesus. If someone or something is the express...or exact... image of another, then they are identical.

Fourth, Jesus "upholds all things by the word of His power." See Colossians 1:17 for further clarification, but this literally means that the very atoms that make up your being are held together by Jesus. You exist at all because of Him.....and that goes for every atheist and agnostic on the planet!

Fifth, He "by Himself purged our sins." Jesus did that alone, and He did it for you. In fact, nobody else could have done that.....only Jesus was virgin-born, and lived a sinless existence. His death, therefore, could not have been for Himself.....it had to be for YOU.

Last, He "sat down on the right hand of the majesty on high." The right-hand side is the "power" side, and Jesus took His rightful place there because the work of Redemption was FINISHED. You can have that finished work given to you as a free gift. All you have to do is believe, and ask Him for it.....He guarantees in advance that He will say "yes" to your request (see study Scriptures).

Faith Profession: "The Lord Jesus Christ IS WORTHY to receive all glory! He has paid the price for redemption of the entire human race, and sits at the right hand of the Father even as I read this."

Study Scriptures: Revelation 5:11-14; Romans 10:9-10,13

Devotional # 329

ANGELS

Scripture: Hebrews 1:7,13-14

Today's reading takes us into the realm of the unseen spiritual world around us. Though invisible, it is nevertheless quite real, and it contains very powerful beings called angels.

Angels are created beings, and are said to be "innumerable" in Hebrews 12:22. That is, there are too many of them to count. Angels are mighty (see study Scriptures), but not Almighty. For example, one angel wiped out 185,000 troops for Hezekiah in one night. Angels are said to be glorious (Luke 9:26), and are "ministering spirits" to the "heirs of salvation." That's every saved person on earth…..we are ministered to by angels every day.

When necessary, they are the executioners of God's wrath (II Thessalonians 1:7-8). They will also gather the "elect of Israel" from all the earth in the latter times (Matthew 24:31).

There is one archangel mentioned in the Bible, and that is Michael (see study Scriptures). (Yes, I know that some teach that there are many, and, some time ago, four cartoon turtles were named after them. I'm just telling you what the Bible says.)

Angels do NOT have wings, and they are always male. When they appear to humans, they are always mistaken to be regular human men….. (you'd notice a six- foot wingspan). Here are some reference Scriptures you can look at: Genesis 19:1,5; Judges 13:2-3,6,10-11; Revelation 21:17; Daniel 8:15-16.

Please note…..angels are NOT seraphim (Isaiah 6) or cherubim (Ezekiel 1:10; Revelation 4). Angels are unique beings who interact with people on the earth on occasion. They interact most often when they are activated by someone speaking God's Word (see Psalm 103:20). That is why it's so important to speak Scripture out loud. Angels move when you do!

Faith Profession: "I see that there is an unseen spiritual world around me. It interacts with me, and I can activate angels on my behalf by speaking God's Word."

Study Scriptures: II Thessalonians 1:7; Jude 9

A PARALYZED DEVIL

Scripture: Hebrews 2:14

Too many Christians think of the devil as a powerful enemy, and that we, as mere humans, would be unable to successfully oppose him. So, when we are attacked, we tend to wait for the Lord to "fix it".....while we meekly sit and wait, cowering in fear.

Today's verse contains two truths. First, it tells us that Jesus became a "partaker of flesh and blood" in order to legally be able to represent the human race in this matter of Redemption. When Jesus died, He did so as a human.....so His subsequent victories could be given to His fellow humans without argument.

Secondly, notice that, through death, Jesus was able to destroy the devil.....who, up to that time, had the power of death. So, Jesus dies.....as a human.....but defeats the devil in Hell, and then resurrects from the dead to prove the victory.

Now.....did you notice that it says that He did not just defeat the devil, but He DESTROYED him? That is a very significant thing. The word used for "destroy" in the original Greek can also be translated "paralyze; render completely useless; totally destroy." Can you see that it was far more of a victory than we have been led to believe?

When you got saved, Jesus gave that victory to YOU as part of your inheritance (see study Scriptures). I know.....you were taught that you get that victory in Heaven. But.....you get your inheritance when the GIVER dies.....NOT when YOU die. Jesus died 2000 yrs ago. You have this inheritance NOW!

Receive it! Live it! The devil's power has been PARALYZED. It has no effect on you UNLESS YOU LET IT. You WILL let it if you insist on living in ignorance of the truth of God's Word. Don't do that.....please!!

Faith Profession: "My enemy has been totally defeated, and I have been given authority over him just as if I had defeated him myself.....because I am in Jesus Christ, and I share all that is His."

Study Scriptures: Romans 8:16-17; James 4:7

Devotional # 331
Delivered From Bondage

Scripture: Hebrews 2:15

Every person lives in bondage through fear of death…..right up to the time they are freed by the salvation that Jesus earned, and gives as a gift to those who will receive it. For those who never choose to receive the free gift of salvation, fear of death grips them right to the end. Many of these poor souls try to rationalize away their fear, but it is there…..and they know it.

Fear of death is one part of a larger problem known in the Bible as "the law of sin and death" (see study Scriptures). All unsaved people are subject to the law of sin and death. Their lives are run by it…..they make decisions based upon it…..the constant fear that lives deep within them is fueled by it. It is one of the most ruthless bondages the devil has ever come up with, and he uses it to his every advantage. The fact that people in this condition find safety in numbers (as more people live by the law of sin and death than do not) does not validate it at all.

The moment a person chooses to receive Jesus as his/her Savior from sin, the law of sin and death is replaced by what the Bible calls "the law of the spirit of life in Christ Jesus." There is no fear connected to this law…..its driving force is love, and it wipes out the bondages the devil has tried to impose. Again, living under this new, better law is a choice…..just as living free of fear is a choice (see study Scriptures). But you should know that this choice does exist, and some of us live in this new law daily.

Free…..from fear…..from confusion about death…..from bondages…..IF we choose to live in the Scriptural promises that give these privileges. Check out the study Scriptures, and receive them. You'll be glad you did.

Faith Profession: "I choose to live in the freedom of the law of the spirit of life in Christ Jesus. Fear of death has no more hold on me."

Study Scriptures: Romans 8:1-2; II Timothy 1:7

Devotional # 332

Too Late

Scripture: Mark 16:15

A friend of mine died this week…..he was 82 years old, and I hadn't seen him face-to-face in over three years. I had known him for 28 years, and he was affectionately known to me and one other person not related to him as "Dad." "Dad" was my friend, and you don't get too many of those in life. I'm going to miss the fact that I can't call him anymore….. even though he had gotten crotchety in his old age.

My problem is regret. You see, I have no indication that "Dad" had received Jesus as his Savior. He was fiercely devoted to a large denominational church group which, unfortunately, does not emphasize Bible salvation. "Dad" knew I was a minister, and respected that…..but he never asked about my beliefs, and made it clear in conversation that he liked what he believed.

I'm bothered, though, by the fact that perhaps I could have tried harder to witness to him. Maybe I was being too polite…..maybe I didn't see any real openings to have a conversation about eternity…..maybe I didn't look hard enough…..or maybe I could have just broached the subject and let the chips fall wherever they might have.

I knew this man, and I liked him. But I never gave him a clear presentation of the Gospel, and I wish now that I had. Would he have listened? Probably not. But…..you can never tell. "Dad" had been my friend. I wonder now if I had truly been his.

Yes, I'm not the only one who might have witnessed to him. No, it is not my responsibility alone. Yet…..my counsel to you today would be this: go ahead and say something to that person who might not know the truth. One day, you'll be glad you at least tried. It doesn't bring them back, but you'll not be living with that "what if" in the back of your mind, either. It's about eternity, after all. Trust me…..say something now. You might be surprised at their reaction.

Faith Profession: "Lord, you have left me here on earth to be your witness to the lost. I want to be just that, and to be bold about it every time I get opportunity."

Study Scriptures: Acts 1:8; 8:4

DEVOTIONAL # 333
SAYING THE SAME THING

Scripture: Hebrews 3:1

Most Christians whom I know have no idea that what they say, and how they say it, makes a difference in the spiritual realm. In fact, the spoken word is vitally important in the faith process, and always has been. You might recall that God created the heavens and the earth with words. Perhaps you are aware that prophets were placed throughout the Bible. Their job? To speak things into the world around them so that the Lord could use those words, coupled with faith, to bring the thing to pass. We call the end result Bible Prophecy.

It works the same way today. Saved people were left on the earth to continue the work Jesus started. One aspect of that work is to serve as God's voice…..to speak His Word so that He can bring it into the physical realm where we can see it.

Today's Scripture tells us that Jesus is the High Priest of OUR PROFESSION. That word "profession" literally means "to say the same thing." That's one of our most important jobs while we're on the earth…..to speak Scripture, and Scriptural principles, so that the power of God can be released to cause those Scriptures to become a reality. We do the speaking…..we supply the faith…..and He makes it happen.

It's very much like using a car. The car carries you where you want to go. It has an engine, and tires, etc. that are well able to do that. However, none of it works unless YOU turn the key…..the car simply doesn't do that itself.

When you speak a Scripture promise, you are, in effect, planting spiritual seed. The promise is true in the spiritual realm. Your act of speaking it, in faith, is what moves it from the spiritual realm to the visible, physical realm. We call it an answered prayer, or a miracle. It is just Jesus performing His Word, and honoring your profession.

Faith Profession: "I will speak the promises of the Bible into my life, and will do so with faith and conviction. I will see them come to pass."

Study Scriptures: Hebrews 4:16; 10:36; Proverbs 18:21

DEVOTIONAL # 334

THE WORD IS ALIVE

Scripture: Hebrews 4: 12-13

Today's verses are some of the most powerful Scriptures in the Bible about the Word of God. The word "quick" in verse 12 means "alive" (as in "to quicken"). Your Bible is said to be "sharper than any two-edged sword." In the time this was written, the Romans had invented a small sword that was light, and had both edges sharpened. Prior to this time, swords were large and heavy, and were sharp on one side only. If you hit something with it, it did lots of damage. But, if you missed, you were vulnerable to counter-attack. This new lighter sword revolutionized warfare, and gave the Romans a distinct advantage, resulting in many victories.

Notice that the Bible is given human qualities…..it "divides soul and spirit;" it is a "discerner." These are traits not usually associated with a book. However, those of us who are familiar with the Bible know that these words about it are true. In verse 13, although the subject is still the Bible…..a book…..it is now being referred to as "his" and "him" instead of "it." Again, human qualities are being applied to an inanimate object.

Normally, this would be an obvious mistake. But…..the Bible is NOT an ordinary book. It is, as it says, "quick"…..ALIVE. It has human traits given to it because of its close association with Jesus Christ Himself. In many ways, Jesus and the Bible are one and the same…..and today's verses recognize this unusual fact.

Hard to believe? Fair enough…..then I'd invite you to see for yourself. Read it carefully, and then…..being entirely honest…..tell me that it doesn't see into your soul, and the deepest parts of your heart. The Word of God, my friend, is alive. Read it, and you'll see.

Faith Profession: "The Bible is unlike any other book on the planet. It is so far ahead of any other book that comparison is downright silly. The Bible is God's Word…..and it sees deep within a person's heart."

Study Scriptures: I Timothy 3:16; I Peter 1:23-25

He Understands

Scripture: Hebrews 4:15

We tend to think of Jesus as the supernatural Son of God who, despite being on earth in a physical body, was somehow immune to the devil's attacks. Today's verse refutes that thinking. In fact, Jesus set aside His supernatural characteristics while on earth (see study Scriptures), and operated as just a human being…..exactly like you or me.

There are numerous examples to support this…..He got tired and needed to sleep; He wept, so He was feeling sadness; He prayed; He got hungry; He even lost His temper once or twice.

Sometimes, when I'm feeling hurt, or sad, or angry, I get frustrated and vent on Him. It's unfair of me, and I always regret it. But, when I take time to think it through, I realize that He understands…..really understands. I guess that's why He's able to show such remarkable patience with us…..He's "been there and done that."

Today's verse tells us that Jesus has experienced everything that you have or ever will experience. It says that he is "touched" by this understanding…..meaning that it affects Him in His heart…..it brings back memories to Him of how that felt…..and it causes Him to reach out to us in compassion.

Jesus is not sitting in Heaven analyzing your every move, looking to condemn you. On the contrary…..He spends lots of time defending you from the accusations of the devil. He can do this with real conviction because He knows, from first-hand experience, the pain of betrayal; abandonment; rejection; hatred; and deception. He knows. And someone who knows is always better to talk to. He "gets it" when you come to Him with your current problem…..and He knows how to help you like nobody else.

Faith Profession: "My Lord is not only willing to help me, but He can do so as one who truly understands how I feel. He is my best resource for help."

Study Scriptures: Philippians 2:7; John 11:35

Devotional # 336
He's Glad to See You

Scripture: Hebrews 4:16

Much attention is given to the word "boldly" in today's verse.....that we have the right and privilege to enter directly into God's throne room to speak to Him. To be sure, it is a rare and precious privilege.

I think, though, that there are still some of God's own children who approach Him cautiously. They are not yet sure of Him.....somewhat fearful of His power.....and unsure enough about His character that they just aren't comfortable around Him. These folks have been taught to fear God.....that God spends much of His time barely controlling His anger.

We need to remember that we're in the New Testament.....that we're in the Age of Grace.....that, these days, our Lord's primary motivation is love, not anger. As such, we find a much different picture of His throne room when we enter it.

First, though, you will need to know that the Lord is not just your Heavenly Father, but He has become your Dad.....more specifically, your loving Daddy. So, picture this: as you enter the throne room, He sees you. His reaction? A huge smile crosses His face..... He is DELIGHTED to see you. I picture Him bending down with His arms open wide, encouraging you to run into His arms for a big hug! Then He sits you on His lap and wants to hear every word you have to say.....His full attention is on YOU. THAT'S the more accurate picture of the God we serve and love. He's not mad at you.....if anything, He misses you.

The Lord Jesus is very much like (maybe EXACTLY like) a loving, tender, caring grandparent.....doting on you; loving to spend time with you.....eager to help you.....missing you when you're gone.....thinking about you.....keeping your picture on His refrigerator.....and loving you like nobody else ever could. Think THAT way when you go to Him in prayer.

Faith Profession: "Jesus loves me, this I know.....for the Bible tells me so. He is delighted to see me enter His throne room.....every time!"

Study Scriptures: Romans 8:15; Galatians 4:6-7

Rightly Dividing

Scripture: Hebrews 6:4-6

Okay.....you read today's verses, and you instantly conclude that a person can lose his/her salvation.....if they "fall away." You take these verses and make assessment on the conduct of other Christians, deciding that, if they are doing or not doing certain things, then they're no longer saved. And, you hold firm to the belief that one is saved ONLY IF he/she does NOT "fall away."

This, of course, runs counter to scores of other Scriptures. You are told that, when you receive salvation, you become part of the Lord's flesh and bones (see study Scriptures). You are told that salvation is a free gift, and that you are part of a Blood Covenant that is unconditional. You are told (correctly) that your salvation paid for ALL your sins..... past, present, and future (see study Scriptures), and that your salvation is not dependent upon you, but upon Jesus and what he did.

How then, can we make sense of what we read in today's verses? Well, you can be sure that there are no contradictions in God's Word. With that in mind, we need to take a step back and look at the location of this passage. The name of the book is "Hebrews"..... because it is written to Hebrews. As you read Hebrews, you find numerous references to Old Testament practices.....the Law.....the Levitical priesthood. Why?

If you know anything about the end times, you know that, in the seven-year Tribulation, the Old Testament and its practices return to use. The Jewish Temple is even rebuilt, and is in use during that time, because the Lord is revisiting His chosen people to give them one last chance to see the truth. The Book of Hebrews has application to that time period, and in the Old Testament, you COULD lose your salvation, because personal conduct determined your status with Him. Rightly dividing the Word is essential.....otherwise, you'll begin to wrongly apply Scriptures, and get an incorrect picture of God's Kingdom.

Faith Profession: "I will 'study to show myself approved unto God' by rightly dividing Scripture.....thus avoiding errors in interpretation."

Study Scriptures: Ephesians 5:30-32; Colossians 2:13; II Timothy 2:15

DEVOTIONAL # 338

FOLLOWING THE RESULTS

Scripture: Hebrews 6: 12

Today's verse rather plainly says that you are slothful (the polite way to say "lazy") if you fail to follow those who "inherit the promises." Another way to say the same thing is to say that you are simply lazy if you refuse to follow those who get spiritual results.

An amazingly high percentage of Christians do NOT get results…..at least not too often. They get a prayer answered here and there. They see someone rise up from an illness now and then. Oh, they DO pray…..and they believe that the Lord <u>can</u> answer prayer. But, since He doesn't answer them most of the time, they invent excuses for their lousy results. "We don't know why God wants me to go through this, but He must have some higher purpose in mind," they say. Yes…..it sounds so pious and spiritual. And it would be, if it weren't dead wrong.

Some folk DO get results…..regularly. They see prayer answered on a regular basis. They see sicknesses healed all the time. They live prosperous lives that are immune to economic recession; poor job markets; and a fluctuating stock market. They enjoy victory over the devil's attacks on a regular basis, beating him back into his dark hole by utilizing the authority given to them by Jesus.

The problem? These people who get results are the ones who pray in tongues…..believe in the power of God, and use it…..and trust in His Word as a daily routine. "Ohhhh….. that stuff is of the devil," you say. Really? I wonder why it gets such wonderful spiritual results then? Is the devil giving us healing? And prosperity? And supernatural protection? OR…..could it be that you have been taught poorly (by well-meaning folks, of course)? The Lord says that, if people are getting results, and you're not following what they do…..you're LAZY (His words, not mine).

Faith Profession: "I will look into the gifts of the Holy Spirit to search for the truth about them. If they are truth, I will change my thinking about them."

Study Scriptures: Acts 2:4; Mark 16:17-18; John 17:17

Devotional # 339
Your Witness That Jesus Lives

Scripture: Hebrews 7:8

Hebrews 7 is a chapter that speaks about a person named Melchisedec…..who is simply an Old Testament appearance of Jesus Christ. It mentions that Abraham gave tithes to this person…..another indication that He is part of the Trinity. The subject of tithing always gets people fired up, because, I'm sure, it involves money. More specifically, THEIR money (or so they believe)…..so it is what used to be called a "hot button."

Recently…..without provocation…..my barber (who is a Christian) began to give me a dissertation on tithing. "Tithing," he postulated, "occurs only once in the Bible, and it involved Israel giving a tenth of their money to an enemy who had defeated them" (or something like that). I sort of zoned out after hearing him say it appeared only <u>once</u> in the Bible. He was, of course, making his case for NOT tithing. Many Christians who value a dollar too much have a reason why they don't tithe…..and it's always a Bible reason.

As you may know, tithing appears in many places in the Bible. It was in practice before the Law…..during the Law…..and after the Law. It is not an Old Testament relic, but a sound Bible financial principle. You tithe in order to give seed money to the Lord. If you want a harvest, you plant seed…..right? Okay…..your tithe is your financial seed, which gives the Lord something to work with FOR YOU. On top of that, your tithe is your testimony that Jesus is alive…..it says so in today's verse.

So, tithing does at least two good things…..it testifies that your Lord lives and gives Him seed to use for your financial harvest. And, it's a Bible principle….. not some fancy way to pry a dollar out of that wallet that you like to keep welded shut where the Lord is concerned.

Faith Profession: "Every time I tithe, I have given testimony that I believe that Jesus is alive. I do believe that…..He rose from the dead!"

Study Scripture: Luke 24:6; Malachi 3:10-11

DEVOTIONAL # 340

TO THE UTTERMOST

Scripture: Hebrews 7:25

Hebrews chapter 7 establishes the fact that Jesus has become our High Priest. However, unlike the earthly priesthood of the Old Testament, which had an earthly lineage, Jesus is High Priest of the Melchisedec Priesthood, which differs in that it is spiritual and eternal. Jesus earned this lofty place when He volunteered to die in my place and yours to pay the penalty for sin. He did that, and then turned around and offered it back to you and me as a free gift.

There's never been a gift like this one. Not only are your sins forgiven….. completely and unconditionally…..but it is done, it says in today's verse, to the UTTERMOST. That would be exactly what we would expect from Jesus. He never does anything halfway.

The word "save" in today's verse can also be translated "made whole"…..or "made complete." So, salvation is also wholeness, and it is wholeness to the uttermost. Comparing Scripture with Scripture, this "wholeness" means that we not only have eternal life when we receive this gift of salvation, but, since it involves "wholeness," it applies to our health; our financial well-being; our safety; and our inclusion totally in all that He accomplished.

What did He accomplish? Among other things, He defeated the devil completely. When you received His gift of salvation, you became part of Him, and He became part of you. Therefore, His accomplishments are now yours…..meaning that, as part of your "wholeness," you have the same authority over the devil that He has. (Yes, that's true! If you've become Him, and He's become you…..then it is true!! Don't believe me…..look at the study Scriptures).

You are saved to the uttermost…..healed to the uttermost…..blessed to the uttermost….. protected to the uttermost…..and have spiritual authority to the uttermost! Amen!

Faith Profession: "I love the Lord. He does things right. He has saved me…..made me WHOLE…..to the UTTERMOST."

Study Scriptures: John 14:12; I John 4:17

DEVOTIONAL # 341

HE BECAME US

Scripture: Hebrews 7:26

For a long time, I didn't understand today's Scripture. I was looking for some deep, profound meaning to the phrase "became us." Finally, the Holy Spirit prompted me to remember that the Lord tends to make things simple…..He speaks plainly, and to the point. When I looked again at this verse, it was clear…..Jesus BECAME US.

Despite all the rhetoric about salvation, most Christians still see themselves as separate from, and inferior to, the Lord Jesus. "He is the Son of God," they say….. "I am just a human being and a sinner at that."

Yes, you are a human being. You USED to be in sin, but Jesus forgave all your sins at salvation. And Jesus IS the Son of God. But what you apparently don't realize is that His work at Calvary covers far more ground than you have been led to believe. First of all, while you are still a human, you are NOT the same as you were before salvation. The Bible says that you have become a new creature, or new creation…..unique, because of what today's Scripture tells you.

Jesus BECAME YOU. As part of your salvation…..and part of the Blood Covenant that is a part of that…..you have exchanged names with Him. He takes your name, and you take His. You become ONE with Him, and He with you. In effect, the "new creation" that you have become is a mixture of the old you and Jesus Christ.

He became you…..and you became Him. That's why you have the right to use His Name against the devil and his slimy helpers. Can you see that? It is stunningly simple, yet totally life-changing. You and Jesus became ONE when you received Him as your Savior. It is much more than receiving only eternal life…..way…..way…..more!!

Faith Profession: "Because I am saved, I am one with Jesus. I am a new, unique creation upon the earth, and I have the right to use His Name, because it has become mine."

Study Scriptures: I Corinthians 12:27; Ephesians 5:30

Devotional # 342
A New Covenant

Scripture: Hebrews 8:6-13

Old Testament Israel operated under a Blood Covenant relationship with God. That Covenant was binding on both parties, and was conditional…..that is, it worked in a positive way IF…..you obeyed the Lord's commands. This Covenant had many priceless benefits…..they're listed in Deuteronomy 28:1-13; Deuteronomy 7; and other places. The Lord promised not to alter or break this covenant (see study Scriptures). However, Israel continually failed to obey God's commands, and therefore missed the blessings all too often.

Since the Lord is no dummy, He knew people would fail, and had a plan in place to take care of that. He promised not to alter HIS part of the Covenant, therefore His solution is on OUR side of the Covenant. He made it UNCONDITIONAL for us (those who have received His gift of salvation). That is, He removed the difficult part…..the part that tripped up folks all through the Old Testament…..the part about obedience to His commands.

Now, when a person gets saved, he/she is immediately included in this marvelous Blood Covenant. That person is NOT required to DO things in obedience to His word, but simply to believe. So, for us, the DOING part has been replaced by BELIEVING. All we have to do is receive what the Bible tells us, and it is ours…..just exactly as we did to receive salvation. When we believe it, the Covenant begins to operate in our life…..and it is magnificent! It is so good that Jesus calls it "the abundant life" (see study Scriptures).

If you're saved, the benefits of this Covenant are yours. Look them up in Deuteronomy 28. Then, believe it…..and live in those benefits. Your life will never be the same. Our God is a GOOD God!!

Faith Profession: "I know Jesus as my Savior, therefore I am part of the Blood Covenant with Him. I have what He says I have…..I believe, and I receive!"

Study Scriptures: Jeremiah 31:31-34; Psalm 89:34; John 10:10

DEVOTIONAL # 343

ONCE

Scripture: Hebrews 9:12

If you wanted to locate the one verse that pinpoints the exact event that finalized your eternal redemption, today's verse would be it. It is common knowledge that Jesus died on the Cross…..that's the physical side of it, and the part that's usually emphasized by a world that focuses on the physical. Of course, that's not all there was to it.

Jesus had to die spiritually, too, because all humans experience two deaths…..one physical, and one spiritual. By definition, spiritual death is separation from God, so Jesus volunteered to do that. He <u>became</u> sin (see study Scriptures) and went into Hell for three days and nights. He defeated Hell and the devil by speaking the promises of the Word in faith, and rose from the dead in total victory.

But, one of His goals was to fulfill the Old Testament Law, so He had to complete the vital act of placing His own sinless blood on the mercy seat in Heaven. In the Old Testament, this was done on the day of Atonement…..once a year…..and <u>covered</u> the sins of the nation of Israel for that year. To completely <u>wipe sin away</u>…..and to complete the fulfillment of the Law…..Jesus needed to move up to the Temple in Heaven and place His holy blood on that mercy seat…..the real one…..for the redemption of the human race to be complete.

Today's verse describes that eternally significant act. It closed out the Old Testament; completed redemption; and began a new chapter in God's relationship with humans. We call the this the New Testament, or the Age of Grace. Jesus paid it all, and completed every last detail of His mission perfectly. Now, you can be a beneficiary of all that He did…..just by believing. Though the price He paid was high, He offers the finished work to you for free. It is yours if you will simply receive it. Will you?

Faith Profession: "When Jesus presented His sinless blood onto the mercy seat in Heaven's Temple, redemption was complete. It was the final piece of a puzzle that the devil never saw coming. Jesus is Lord!"

Study Scriptures: II Corinthians 5:21; Hebrews 10:12-14

Devotional # 344
Iron Sharpens Iron

Scripture: Hebrews 10:25

I heard a Bible teacher say one time that all of his children were in ministry in some way or another. I remember thinking how wonderful that was, and having the same goal for my own kids. Then I volunteered for the pastorate and, 21 years later, my children were so turned off by what they had seen Christians do that they couldn't bear to attend church any more. In truth, Christians can be…..and have been…..some of the nastiest folk you've ever met. (I could tell you stories…..and my kids certainly could).

Yet, here in today's verse, the Holy Spirit is recommending the togetherness of Christians. Why? Because the Bible says that "iron sharpens iron" (see study Scriptures). It is simply better to be under the sound of the Word of God than to be away from it. Many Christians are truly lovely people who are really trying to serve Jesus, and do no harm to others. But, in any house, there are vessels of honor, and vessels of dishonor. The goal would be to find the real Christians…..the ones who are genuinely plugged in to the Word…..the ones who show love in a real way. The most likely place to find these folks is in a church, because that's where Christians assemble.

I've noticed that the people who avoid fellowship with other Christians, and who avoid church attendance, tend to be in a slow drift away from the Lord. They are praying less than they used to…..they have stopped tithing…..and they have questioned the Bible rather than believe it, and so have lost interest in that, too.

Listen, friend, the world is a lousy substitute…..even for the worst of churches. Will you find the perfect church? No. Are there bozos and ding-dongs in churches? Yes….. but that's true of your workplace; your bank; and your grocery store…..and you haven't stopped going to them. Jesus says it's better to be under the sound teaching of the Word than not, and to not forsake the assembling of yourselves together.

Faith Profession: "I will obey the Word of God in this matter."

Study Scriptures: Proverbs 27:17; Acts 2:42

WHAT PROMISE?

Scripture: Hebrews 10:35-36

One of the most difficult things about faith is the waiting. Most of us would prefer to pray, and immediately have the Lord perform some miracle, and…..Wham!…..our answer would arrive. You may have noticed that it rarely happens that way.

Instead, we are instructed to find a promise in Scripture…..speak it in faith…..and stay in faith about it until we see it come to pass. It tends to be a process…..a seed planting process…..and, like all seed-related things, takes some time to grow. The time between the belief in the promise and the end result is what we call "patience."

Today's reading plainly says that we will need patience, especially after you have done the will of God (finding and believing a Scripture promise). It says that, if you'll do that, and have patience while the answer finds you, you WILL receive the promise. Why? Because faith works, and the Lord always honors it…..as long as we don't give up on the patience part.

So…..what promise is being spoken of here? Is it Jesus' promise that we would receive the Holy Spirit as a permanent resident in our hearts after salvation? Yes…..it is that. But, it is also that promise that YOU are believing for. Now, I have no idea what that would be. I do know that today's verses tell us not to lose confidence in the Lord, His Word, or in the fact that He will bring the promise to pass, and you will see the answer to your prayer.

In layman's terms, He is telling you to "hang in there." Stay in faith. Don't waver. And you'll see YOUR promise change YOUR circumstance!

Faith Profession: "I believe the Lord when He says He'll honor my faith in His Word. I will pray a promise, then stay in faith (having patience) until that promise becomes a reality."

Study Scriptures: Hebrews 6:12; Isaiah 55:10-11

FAITH IS NOW

Scripture: Hebrews 11:1

Faith…..it is the most important element of the saved Christian's life. It is the victory that overcomes the world (see study Scriptures). Without it, the Lord is not pleased, and cannot operate. This last statement is very important, because many of God's children, who have some incorrect ideas about how the Lord works, believe that He does whatever He wants, whenever He wants, IF He wants. But, the Word is plain in telling us that God's power is released ONLY when we, as His children, exercise faith. It is this faith that acts as the trigger…..or key…..that releases His power into a situation.

In today's verse, let's notice a few things. First, faith is a "NOW" thing…..not a "later" thing, or a "maybe" thing. Second, notice that faith has substance. Like many, you have always been taught that faith is a concept…..something invisible…..a "mind" thing. No, Scripture says it has substance, and that substance would be whatever you're believing for. It might be healing from a disease. It might be money. It might be deliverance from an addiction. It might be something as simple as peace and tranquility. Whatever it is, your faith in God's Word produces tangible results that you can see, feel, hear, and touch.

More than that, faith is the "evidence of things not seen." When you're sick, you need healing. You might have cancer…..or a heart problem. Faith in God's promises will produce a report of NO cancer, and tests and x-rays that back up that miracle. You might have a financial need. Again, faith in the working of God's economy will produce a statement that says "paid in full." Whatever it may be, faith in the promises of God will produce a result…..evidence of something you thought was invisible.

The bottom line? Faith is not quite what you thought it was. It turns out to be something that "is," not "will be." Faith is "now," not at some unknown time out there somewhere. And faith produces evidence that you can hold in your hand, and show to someone. Faith…..use it, and see for yourself!

Faith Profession: "My faith is the key which releases the power of God's Holy Word into my situation. It WILL produce tangible results!"

Study Scriptures: Hebrews 11:6; I John 5:4

DEVOTIONAL # 347

GOODBYE, CHARLEY

Scripture: Hebrews 11:3

In today's Scripture, we come upon one of those Bible verses that simply opposes modern thought absolutely. It is becoming increasingly common to think of our earth as being part of a process of evolution that has lasted millions of years. Of course, those who profess belief in this idea have no idea how it all started. Their best guess is a large explosion called the "big bang"…..which carries with it zero documentation. They are not put off by the fact that their belief is properly known as the THEORY of evolution…..a theory being, by definition, a GUESS. The whole mess started with Charles Darwin and some thoughts he had just after visiting the Galapagos Islands.

At any rate, you need far too much faith to believe in such an unsubstantiated guess as that…..at least for me. I like what it says in God's Word. Here, in today's verse, it says that the "worlds were framed by the Word of God." That is, the Lord spoke them into existence, just as it tells us in Genesis 1. That's not as far-fetched as you might think. In fact, it is entirely consistent with the way faith triggers the power of God throughout the Bible. Things that previously did not exist were brought into being (in the physical realm…..they DID exist previously in the spiritual realm) by God speaking them into existence with words.

You have confirmation of this idea in Colossians (see study Scriptures), where you're told that "all things were created by him…" The nice thing about creationism is that it's not a guess, and doesn't profess to be. Plus, it's consistent with the way the Word works throughout the Bible and in life.

It's a free country, and you can believe a theory that guesses at time frames, often nonchalantly "supposing" that something happened a million years ago…..or five million….. or whatever. I think it's time we told Charley "goodbye" in favor of the truth of God's Word.

Faith Profession: "The Word says that God created the heavens and the earth with the power of words. It is not a "theory," or a guess, but is presented as fact. That is His Word on the subject."

Study Scriptures: Colossians 1:16; Genesis 1

DEVOTIONAL # 348
A CITY BUILT BY GOD

Scripture: Hebrews 11:10

Our Scripture reading for today has reference to Abraham, a man called by God to take his family and all his possessions to a place that was unknown to him when he left. I wonder how many of us would take such a large leap of faith. I wonder how many of us believe God enough to follow Him blindly with all we have.

Abraham did that, fully trusting that God would care for Him, and that He had Abraham's best interests at heart.....which He did. As you read about Abraham, you begin to see that his focus was not on earthly things, even though the Lord blessed him with material wealth. Throughout his life, Abraham was focused on something other than the things of earth.....his mind and heart were on Heaven.

In today's verse, it says that Abraham looked for a city built by God. So, it wasn't a physical structure, because Abe was not focused on physical things. Rather, his attention was on the unseen.....the spiritual.....the future, which was as bright for him as it is for us.

This same kind of statement is made about US as Christians, you know (see study Scriptures). It says that here.....on this earth, in the physical.....we have no continuing city. That is, this is not our home. Our attachment to the things of the world were severed when we received Jesus as our Savior. Ever since then, we live with a realization deep within ourselves that everything here is temporary..... that our real home awaits us up there.

Our real home's foundations are a product of the wisest Master Builder in the universe. He's preparing a place for YOU.....right now.....and it will be yours sooner than you think. Faith people always have their ears open to hear that trumpet blast, and that voice that says, "Come up!"

Faith Profession: "Something within me tells me not to get too comfortable in this world. My "city" is built by a loving God, and I will be there soon."

Study Scriptures: Hebrews 13:14; I Thessalonians 4:13-18

CHASTENING

Scripture: Hebrews 12:5-11

If today's subject isn't the most misunderstood concept in the New Testament, it certainly is in the top ten. Our dear traditional brethren teach that the sickness, financial trouble, divorce, betrayal, disappointment, and heartache you endure in this earthly life are all examples of the Lord chastening you. The idea? You sin in some way or another, and the Lord sends problems to you as punishment. That, they say, is how He chastens His children.

Well, I don't know if these folks have been the recipients of bad parenting, or they just don't know their Lord as well as they could, but that kind of teaching is simply not accurate.....and must bring a tear to the Lord's eye. Why, I wonder, do we insist on interpreting the Bible in physical terms when we know it is a spiritual book?

Folks.....your Savior (who is love, and who is good all the time) is not going to beat you physically to punish you.....or to teach you lessons. It's just not the way He works in the New Testament. But, you say, it says that this chastening is grievous.....doesn't that mean it's going to hurt? Yes.....but you can't think of any way for the Lord to teach you, and guide you into the light, without inflicting physical discomfort??

The bottom line is that the Lord DOES chasten.....obviously.....but He does it with <u>His Word</u>. If your relationship with Him is as close as it should be, that's all it will take to stop your sin, or straighten out your problem. When you are chastened from the Word, it IS a rebuke. If you ignore it and continue on anyway, you're out of His will, and have entered the area where satan can have access to you. THAT'S where the physical suffering comes in. If there is pain from chastening, it is the hurt you feel at letting Him down. If your relationship with Him is right, that's all it will take.

Faith Profession: "I really don't want to disappoint my Lord Jesus. When I do, He uses His Word to rebuke me, and it works.....quite well, thank you."

Study Scriptures: John 16:8-11; II Timothy 3:16

Devotional # 350
Entertaining Angels

Scripture: Hebrews 13:2

Did you know that you have entertained angels in your lifetime? Not in the sense of a catered party in your back yard, but in the sense that you have interacted with them without realizing it.

Today's verse reminds us to be careful to treat strangers with respect and love, and to do good to them. As we do that, we have unknowingly done it to angels. "Wait a minute," you say, "don't you think I would have noticed that big pair of white wings?" Yes…..you probably would have…..if angels actually had wings. You will search the Bible in vain for one example of an angel having wings (as previously noted).

And angels DO appear to humans on occasion, as, for example, the angel appearing to Samson's Mom…..the angel appearing to Daniel…..the angel appearing to Mary in the Christmas story. "But," you protest, "it says they fly!" Right again…..but what makes you think you need wings to do that? Jesus flew in Acts 1:9; Enoch and Elijah both flew….. but none of them had wings. For that matter, I'VE flown, and I can guarantee you I don't have wings. I had some help from an airplane, but I HAVE flown.

Jesus, Enoch, and Elijah didn't have wings or an airplane…..they just flew. Just because an angel flies doesn't necessarily mean he has wings. Maybe you've been looking at too many paintings down at the art museum…..they paint wings on heavenly beings, but who said they were right? And, just to be precise, you should know that cherubim and seraphim have wings in the Bible…..but they are not angels.

When angels appear in physical form, they are mistaken for regular human men…..because that's what they look like. They're around you more than you think. I'd say that you've probably had interaction with one or more angels already. Be kind to strangers (and friends, too)…..you never know who they might actually be.

Faith Profession: "Things are not always what they appear to be. Angels walk among us sometimes, and I purpose to treat everyone with kindness and respect. It's what Jesus would do, and will make a good impression on any angels I might meet."

Study Scriptures: Revelation 21:17; Daniel 8:15-16

DEVOTIONAL # 351
THE EVERLASTING COVENANT

Scripture: Hebrews 13:20

As the writer of the book of Hebrews draws his letter to a close, he mentions something that seems to have been lost in the shuffle in end times Christianity…..the magnificent Blood Covenant that the Lord has made with His children.

When Jesus died on the Cross and shed His sinless blood, it not only paid the price for the sin of all humanity, but it was also the seal of the Blood Covenant. This Covenant had been in effect throughout the Old Testament but, back then, it was dependent upon the obedience of the people. Well, you can imagine how that worked out.

So, the Lord made some changes. Having made the Covenant, and having promised never to break His word about it (see study Scriptures), He changed the only part He could…..He eliminated the requirement of obedience from the humans under the Covenant. Put His way, He "…put [His] law in their inward parts, and wrote it in their hearts" (Jeremiah 31:33).

In a stroke of genius that once again confounded the devil, the Lord preserved the Covenant and made it foolproof (or devil-proof…..hmmm…..maybe both). Our part of this great Blood Covenant is now supernaturally written on our hearts. That is, it has become a spiritual transaction that is covered under the Blood when you receive Jesus as your Savior. The terms of the Covenant remain the same (see study Scriptures). But, as you read Deuteronomy 28, you can eliminate any references to obedience for you as a New Testament believer. And, it applies to both Jews and Gentiles because of Galatians 3:26-29. [I am not encouraging disobedience. See tomorrow's lesson (#352).]

It is unbelievably clever. It is now unconditional. It applies to every believer, and all that believer need do is receive it in faith…..just like salvation. It is yours…..claim it, and live in its magnificence!

Faith Profession: "My Lord is so incredibly generous! I have great gifts given to me freely by a God who loves me without bounds."

Study Scriptures: Psalm 89:34; Deuteronomy 28:1-13

Double-Minded

Scripture: James 1:8

Today's Scripture describes what is obviously a problem in the lives of many of God's children. We look at the verse, and that seems apparent. What we may not realize is that double-mindedness is a far more vicious and devastating problem than it might initially appear.

Perhaps the most famous Bible person who struggled with this issue was Pontius Pilate. Here was a man who knew Jesus was innocent. He publicly declared that at least three times…..yet had Him put to death anyway. The problem? Pilate was convinced of Jesus' innocence, but was also trying desperately to please the crowd (who wanted Jesus dead). Pilate found out…..too late…..what all double-minded folks find out…..you end up making a choice, and double-minded people almost always make the wrong one.

Actually, there's lots of this going around in our world. .People know what is right, but are torn by peer pressure to do otherwise. Most of them go along with the crowd, and do the dope; have premarital sex; steal; lie; commit a crime. You see, the problem for double-minded folks is that there's no easy way out. It takes guts to do the right thing, because that's going to make you stand out from the crowd. Most are afraid to be different…..afraid of what people might say…..afraid of losing friends…..or just plain afraid. So, they ride the fence for as long as possible, and then they choose. When they choose to go along with the crowd, they find out too late that the crowd doesn't care about them even a little bit. Eventually, they're alone…..having made the wrong choice, and seeing it fail to accomplish what they had hoped for.

Doing right is often hard, and usually unpopular, but, in the end, you still have your integrity…..you can still look yourself in the face…..and you know inside of you that you have built character. You have also pleased the Lord, which may be the biggest benefit of all. Do right…..every time.

Faith Profession: "Lord, I pray for strength to make right decisions, and to avoid the devil's trap of double-mindedness."

Study Scriptures: James 1:12; Ephesians 6:11-13

GOD DOESN'T DO IT

Scripture: James 1:13-15

Well, dear reader, we've come to one of those Scriptures that's going to separate the true Bible believers from those who only profess to be that. If you're like most Christians, you've been taught that the sickness, problems, discouragements, pain, loss, and heartbreak that has found you in this life can be traced back to the Lord…..because "He is sovereign," or "He is in control."

In today's passages, you need to know this fact: the word "tempt or tempted" in a King James Bible can also be translated…..more accurately…..as "trials; tests; or problems." Now, let's read the verses using those words. Let no man say when he is tested, or has problems, "I have these problems because God sent them." God cannot be tempted, or tested with evil, NEITHER DOES HE TEMPT, OR TEST, OR SEND PROBLEMS….. to ANY man.

Does that make it clear to you? Somebody has been trying to blame God for what the devil has been doing. You've been hoodwinked!! (So was I for many years.) It's one of the devil's best deceptions on the end-times church. Shame on us for being so willing to believe that our God would act like that.

Verses 14 and 15 tell us that it's our own choices that get us into trouble. That sounds more like the truth to me. And, in fact, it IS the truth. Sin is a choice. We are drawn away because of our own lusts. But, in our world, it isn't popular to take responsibility for things, or to be accountable for our own actions and choices (more of the devil's deception).

Let's be different, shall we? Let's not try to pass the blame off onto God (who loves us anyway). Let's own up…..let's be responsible for ourselves. And let's not try to "pass the buck" onto someone who isn't to blame.

Faith Profession: "The devil has been passing the blame off on others since Genesis 3, and tries to get us to do the same thing, just as he did with Adam and Eve. I will be accountable for my own actions."

Study Scriptures: Genesis 3:1-13

BE CAREFUL WITH THAT TONGUE

Scripture: James 3:3-11

Most Christians have been deceived…..yes, I wrote deceived…..into believing that it doesn't matter what they say. If you ask them about it, they'll typically say, "The Lord knows what I mean." Yes, the Lord DOES know what you mean, but the question that should be considered is this: "Which actually counts in the spiritual realm…..what you mean, or what you say?" The answer? It is what you SAY.

There are dozens of Scriptures that tell us about the importance of the words we choose to speak. Since spiritual seed is planted by speaking words (see Genesis 1; Mark 11:23), we ought to be paying much more attention to what we say and how we say it.

Did you know that your negative speaking opens the door for the forces of darkness to become active in your life? Some of you will defend yourselves by saying that you're just being realistic. Yeah…..I used to say that, too, until I realized that realism and pessimism are pretty close to the same thing.

If you don't think the Lord is serious about what you say, then perhaps you should re-read verse 6. Today's whole passage is a warning to us about being careful in what we say. Of course, the best thing you can do is speak Scripture. Otherwise, speak in line with Scriptural principles…..and try to let only positive comments come out of your mouth. If you have something negative to say, just SHUT UP…..hold your hands over your own mouth if necessary. But please don't give the devil ammunition to use against you.

Instead, give the Holy Spirit something to work with. You'll be shocked at the difference it will make…..and it WILL make a difference!

Faith Profession: "What I say, and how I say it, DOES make a difference in the spiritual world around me. I will watch my mouth, and work to speak only that which can be used for my spiritual good."

Study Scriptures: Proverbs 18:21; Proverbs 21:23

Answered Prayer

Scripture: James 4:2-3

Answered prayer is an interesting subject among Christians. If you ask about it, most Christians can come up with one or two examples of answered prayer in their life…..but they might have to think about it for a minute.

Why do you think that is? Every saved Christian is indwelt by the Holy Spirit at the moment of salvation. God has sprinkled promises all over the Bible. We're told that the receipt of the Holy Spirit is also the receipt of power (see study Scriptures). We all know of examples of large numbers of people getting saved…..people miraculously healed….. miracles happening exactly as they did in the book of Acts. .Why doesn't it happen in our church, or in our life??

I think it's because we've been taught to accept little or nothing in the way of answered prayer. And, I think today's Scriptures tell us why…..either we don't ask, or we ask "amiss," which is the King James way of saying "wrongly." If you don't ask, you're just lazy, and, frankly, you don't deserve an answer. If you believe that God "might" answer…..or that His answer is sometimes "no" or "maybe"…..then you've ruined the prayer process right from the beginning. Those beliefs are DOUBT. Doubt is the opposite of faith, and you can't get prayer answered without faith.

Most Christians have few prayers answered because the results fall into the category of random chance…..which is exactly how the world has things happen. Come on, folks, you know it can be better than that.

Try this: find a promise in the Bible that applies to your issue. Place your faith in that promise, and call it done. Pray to Jesus, telling Him you believe that promise. Then, thank Him each day for bringing that promise to pass in your life. Keep doing that until you see it happen. Then you'll see answered prayer all the time!!

Faith Profession: "I will pray as indicated above, and I WILL SEE RESULTS."

Study Scriptures: Acts 1:8; I John 5:14-15

Devotional # 356
Power Given to Us

Scripture: James 4:7

It is simple, really…..and quite obvious in Scripture once you realize that it's there. You have been given power over the devil and his helpers. It's the same power Jesus used to cast out devils…..and the same power God used to raise Jesus from the dead (see study Scriptures). It's the power and authority Jesus earned when He defeated the devil during the three days and nights after Calvary. And now, it has been given to YOU.

Yes, I know…..this isn't what you've been taught at church. That's too bad, because your power and authority over the devil is a Bible truth. And, it makes sense when you think about it. At salvation, you were made one with Jesus Christ. His Holy Spirit permanently indwelt you, and you became His body. Your body became His temple, and He lives there. In a real way, you and Jesus have become one person. Factual teaching on the Blood Covenant would verify this: all that you have and are, have become His…..and all that He has and is, have become yours.

You therefore have His power and authority. That's why today's verse makes sense. Do you see it? Resist the devil, and he will flee from YOU. Why? Because he knows that the authority you have is powerful, and based upon the truth of the Bible.

The key, though, is your willingness to receive this truth. It is there…..it is Scripturally true…..but it won't work if you don't receive it, or you don't use it. Like most things in the New Testament, it is activated by your faith. But…..if you dare to believe, and use this potent tool…..you'll experience the exhilaration of having the devil flee from you in defeat. I'll include some extra study Scriptures today to verify this teaching.

Faith Profession: "I am one with Jesus…..therefore I have His power and authority. I use it to put the devil on the run, and it works!"

Study Scriptures: I Peter 5:8-9; Ephesians 4:27; Colossians 1:16; Colossians 2:15; Romans 8:38; Luke 10:17-19

DEVOTIONAL # 357

EFFECTIVE PRAYER

Scripture: James 5:14-16

Today's subject is prayer. You are familiar with prayer because of all the time you have spent doing it, and hopefully you have been doing it correctly. Prayer, you know, is designed to be a dialogue, meaning that both parties communicate. Too many Christians are taught that they can't and shouldn't hear from God (except through His Word). Where is the documentation for that? Why wouldn't He communicate back to you? No, it's not audible…..it's something that comes into your spirit…..it's a spiritual thing because God is a spirit. How else would He communicate?

Notice in today's verses that it says the "effectual" (we'd say "effective"), "fervent" (we'd say "intense") prayer of a righteous man avails much. So, you have an issue, and right away you begin to think that you need to take your request to someone "spiritual"….. someone you think is a person in touch with the Lord on a level that you haven't reached yet.

But, when verse 16 mentions a righteous man (person), it's referring to YOU. You don't need to find someone else…..YOU will do. That's true because you were given the righteousness of Jesus Christ when you received Him as your Savior (see study Scriptures). YOU are that righteous person. And, your prayer will be effective if you pray correctly.

What does that look like? Well…..find a promise in the Word that applies to your issue, and pray that promise (in effect, get into agreement with it). The promise is your answer. Since it is a promise, it WILL came to pass…..as long as you maintain faith in it. So, stay in belief until you see it come to pass. It's that simple. That's what effective prayer looks like. It works every time.

Faith Profession: "I am the righteous man referred to in James 4:16. My prayers are effective, because they're based upon Bible promises, and activated by my continuing faith."

Study Scripture: II Corinthians 5:21

Do You Have a Reservation?

Scripture: I Peter 1:3-4

I'm pretty sure that most readers will understand what a reservation is, and how it works. For example, if you want to fly on a plane to some destination, you arrange the flight in advance, reserving a seat for yourself. When you get to the airport, you know you have a seat, because you have a reservation.

Now, assuming the plane is full, you wouldn't be surprised if you tried to board the plane without a reservation, and were told you couldn't get on.....would you? You could tell the agent that you thought you had a reservation.....or that you didn't know you needed one.....or that you just assumed that everyone who wanted to board could just do so..... but that wouldn't change the fact that you wouldn't be able to get on board. No reservation.....no getting on that plane. We get that, and we live by it.

Okay. Let's talk about Heaven. Most people want to go there when they die. Most people EXPECT to go there. But, here is the question: "Do you have a reservation?"

Some of you will say.....''I had no idea I needed a reservation''....."Nobody told me"..... "I just thought everyone would go there automatically." No.....you are expected to make a reservation.....just like you would with an airline, or an expensive restaurant.

So.....do you have yours? You can get one for free.....just by receiving Jesus Christ as your Savior from the penalty for sin. You do that by bowing your head and asking Him for that free gift. The Bible says that, if you do that in belief, He will give that gift to you. And, when you have that gift.....called salvation.....you have your reservation. God bless you as you receive that great gift right now!

Faith Profession: "As a saved child of God, I have a place reserved for me personally in Heaven. Thank you, Jesus, for giving me that!"

Study Scriptures: Romans 10:9-10,13; Matthew 6:20

DEVOTIONAL # 359

A RANDOM BLESSING

Scripture: Malachi 3:10

As I was sitting here writing just now, the phone rang. As I picked it up, I recognized that the call was coming from someplace identified only as an "800 number." Such calls have been made several times recently…..the record is on our phone's listing of calls missed. So, as I picked up the receiver, I was expecting to be met by some telemarketer trying to sell me some useless item.

To my surprise, it was a representative from Kenneth Copeland Ministries, thanking me for our prayer and financial support to that ministry. The woman who called then asked me if there was anything she could pray for in my life. Since I had been asked to preach the Wednesday evening service at our church next week, I asked her for prayer about that. I again expected that she would write that down and put it on some list for later. Instead, she immediately began to pray a wonderful prayer for me; the organization of my thoughts for the message; and for the preparation of the listeners…..all so that Jesus might be glorified.

I was deeply touched by the whole event, and found tears welling up in my eyes. I was prepared to tell the caller to stop calling here…..we didn't want to deal with telemarketers. Instead, I found someone trying to bless my life…..and she surely did that.

I think there's a lesson in that for both you and me. When is the last time you called someone and asked them if you could pray for them? Some stranger, whose name I don't know, just did that for me, and I was truly blessed. Maybe you could call your Mom, or Dad, or a friend, and ask them the same thing. Maybe they'd be touched by the gesture as much as I was. You'd be doing what Jesus would do, and you'd be bringing blessing into someone's life. Why don't you give it a try…..right now?

Faith Profession: "I purpose to call someone I know once a week just to ask them if there is anything I can pray about for them. It will be my way of being a blessing to others."

Study Scriptures: Proverbs 10:6; Ephesians 1:3

Devotional # 360
Guaranteed Success

Scripture: II Peter 1:5-10

It's a common saying in the world that there are no guarantees. Others will tell you that the only things you can be sure of are death and taxes. The Bible, on the other hand, never avoids guarantees, since it is a supernatural book.

Today's reading gives us one such guarantee. In verse 10, it says that you will never fall..... provided that you build into your life the eight things mentioned in the verses immediately preceding verse 10. You are to do this building with diligence, it says in verse 5.....so it will take some work.

You start with faith, which is the basic building block in any Christian life. Without faith you cannot please God (see study Scriptures), nor can He take action for you. Virtue is next, and involves taking the moral high ground in any situation. Upon that, you build knowledge. In my Christian life, I originally thought that knowledge was first. It is important, but not first, as you see.

Once you have knowledge, you add temperance, which is self-control. That is, you put your body and its fleshly desires in the proper place, which is in subjection. Patience is next. This is not just waiting endlessly, but is the maintaining of consistency as you wait for your promise to manifest. Patience puts pressure on the devil.....which is always a good thing.

The next layer is godliness.....because you are becoming more and more like your Master. To this you add brotherly kindness.....doing good to others.....treating them as family members. Lastly, you top it off with a generous portion of charity (love). True love is last because it consists of all the previous elements, but it is the end result because God is love (see study Scriptures). These are the characteristics we strive for.....in order.....to become Christ-like. When we do this, we'll never fall.

Faith Profession: "I see what I am to work at, and I see the order these attributes are to be in. I will begin today to develop these vital traits."

Study Scriptures: Hebrews 11:6; I John 4:8

Devotional # 361
You WERE Healed

Scripture: I Peter 2:24

It is interesting to me that so many of God's own children seem to be unaware of some of the best and most priceless of the gifts He gave to them at the moment of salvation. Many of these are revealed through the promises He has sprinkled throughout the Bible, and one of them is found in today's verse.

It is an undeniable fact that healing was part of the Redemption that Jesus achieved at the Cross and through the Resurrection. Think about it.....was there any sickness or disease in the Garden of Eden? When did sickness first appear? That's right.....after the Fall in Genesis 3. Sickness is part of the curse of sin that entered the world at the Fall. When Jesus paid the price for sin, He didn't just remove your personal sins.....He paid it ALL. And, ALL includes anything associated with sin, or any of sin's by-products.

So, you're talking to a Christian, and you mention that God heals the sick. Most Christians believe that He CAN.....but they're not so sure that He WILL in their case, or that of the person they're praying for. Why? Because (and I'm not trying to be hurtful here) they've bought into satan's lies about healing and health. In doing so, they negate their own healing, and put themselves into the same boat as the unsaved world.....they are subject to random chance with healing.

Sometimes they get healed.....sometimes they don't. They reason that God wants them sick for some reason that they usually don't know. (Nice view of our Father.) Today's verse tells us that Jesus not only CAN heal, and that he WILL heal, but that He HAS healed. Look at the wording: "By whose stripes ye WERE healed" (emphasis added). Your healing was taken care of at the Cross. Why don't you have healing? Because you don't believe that, and you won't take God at His Word on it. Believe it, and you WILL SEE HEALING. Your faith is what makes it real in your life.

Faith Profession: "My healing was accomplished at Calvary. It has already happened. I can access it through faith in God's promises."

Study Scriptures: Matthew 8:17; Proverbs 4:20-22

DEVOTIONAL # 362

GOOD DAYS

Scripture: I Peter 3:10

The longer I am a Christian, the more the people of the world seem strange to me. I am appreciating what the Bible says about being a stranger and pilgrim in this world.

You can't help but listen to folks having conversation all around you. I've noticed that many people like to talk about their various ailments; their trips to the doctor; recent operations; their medications…..their physical problems in general. If weather is the subject, they can tell you that it's likely to rain, or snow…..that it will be hot and humid…..that a storm is coming. In winter, it's too cold…..in summer, it's too hot.

And then there's the daily news, whether it comes by newspaper or TV. Though a piece of good news occasionally finds its way in, the vast majority of what's presented involves fires; people being arrested; car crashes; deaths; injuries; falling stock markets (or markets that are sure to fall soon); failing businesses; housing crises; and conflict the world over. Personally, I've stopped taking a newspaper, or watching TV news…..I don't want all that negativity coming into my spirit.

Since people talk about what they've seen and heard, plenty of this negative junk tends to come out in their conversations. They don't realize it, but it is deadly. Today's Scripture reading cautions us about speaking evil or negative words. Such talk sets up an "atmosphere" around you that makes it easier for spirits of darkness to operate. It also warns about speaking "guile" (deceit…..lies…..deception). Again, this kind of stuff comes back to bite you.

Avoiding this kind of thing results in "good days"…..and lots of them. It is a promise from a God who simply cannot lie.

Faith Profession: "I will be more aware of what comes out of my mouth. It is not enough that the Lord knows what I mean. I will refrain my tongue from evil, negativity, and deceit."

Study Scriptures: Hebrews 3:1; Romans 12:9-17; Philippians 4:8

Devotional # 363
Proper Suffering

Scripture: I Peter 4:12-16

Make no mistake about it, if you live in this world, you will experience suffering. I don't mention that as a depressant, but to prepare you for it. It would be much worse to be surprised by suffering.

Many believe that their suffering is given by, or at least permitted by, God Himself. Personally, I believe it comes from a devil who is angry and irritated that saved children of God live in his domain; prosper there; and do the Lord's work there.....quite effectively at times.

Remember.....the people of the world are "of their father the devil" (see study Scriptures), and, even if they don't quite understand why, are often antagonistic toward saved Christians. Their father the devil most certainly is, and does all he can to deceive you; distort the truth; twist things; lie; and just plain attack you. Really now, would you expect him to do any less? So, he tries to get you to speak in such a way that his work is made easier. He works to convince you that the Bible is not relevant.....that church is useless.....that you can't make a difference.....or that he's more powerful than you, so you might just as well give up.

Today's reading is trying to encourage you, saying that, as a Christian, you will suffer things like mocking; betrayal; gossip; lies told about you (and people believing them). You won't be easily accepted into the worldly crowd because you don't join in on their habits, addictions, and ungodly ways. They see that as a reproach to themselves.....even if you don't say a word. So, they feel justified in attacking you, and they have no idea that they're being manipulated by the devil. It's okay. Jesus understands, and stands with you. You are a child of God who is temporarily in enemy territory.....but you'll be home soon!

Faith Profession: "It would be naïve of me to believe that I could exist in this evil world as a child of God without suffering opposition. I will glorify my Lord in my battles, giving Him glory for every victory."

Study Scriptures: II Timothy 2:3-4; I Timothy 1:18

A Word to Ministers

Scripture: I Peter 5:1-3

As I write this page, we as Christians are surely in the last days before the return of Jesus Christ. One way we know this is by looking at the state of our churches, and noticing, with great dismay, that they are frightfully close to the description of the end-times church in Revelation 3 (see study Scriptures).

We live in a country that has great numbers of churches, but a stunning lack of the truth. Some churches today are nothing more than social clubs. They are "fun" places, but so is the corner bar or the amusement park. Some churches are so uptight and formal that it almost chokes you. They pass judgment on what you wear; what you look like; and what you do. Others spend their time and money trying to entertain you with flashy video clips; stand-up comedy routines from the pulpit; games; and amusements. Some have compromised enough to state that their goal is merely to get people in the door. ("It's better that they're in church than out of it.")

Really? What about the teaching of the Word? What about discipleship? What about training? What about prayer? Today's verses clearly tell us that the primary responsibility of church leadership is to "feed the flock of God…" This can be done by the pastor, or any other spiritual elder sent to assist that pastor…..but it MUST be done.

Furthermore, a church is not to be a place where someone gets personal glory for being "the big cheese." It is not to be just a "job," either. When you step behind the pulpit, you are standing on sacred ground before God Almighty. You'd better be sure that He's not offended at what you're doing with His calling. And, you need to be led by His Holy Spirit (whom some church leaders haven't heard from in a long time). When Jesus returns, will He find faith? It is the responsibility of church leadership to be able to say "yes." Thankfully, there are some responsible, faith teaching leaders who will be able to. We need more.

Faith Profession: "It is my responsibility to place myself under the sound teaching of the Word. I will find a church which honors today's Scripture reading's principles, and be led into fellowship with my Lord."

Study Scriptures: Revelation 3:14-22; II Timothy 4:2

Devotional # 365

Hot Air

Scripture: I Peter 5:8-9

For nearly 20 years after my salvation, I worshipped and studied with traditional Christians who, although they were very sincere, tended to learn the same things over and over. For instance, they focused on verse 8 in today's reading, but never mentioned verse 9. That is, they emphasized that the devil was BIG.....like a lion. They taught he was powerful, strong, fast, and nasty.....and you were absolutely no match for him. The implication was that you should do your best to avoid the devil, or to stay hidden.

But.....look at the verses. It doesn't say the devil IS a lion, it says that he walks about AS a lion. There's a big difference. AS a lion, the devil would like you to THINK he's mean and powerful. He makes lots of noise.....he roars at you.....he certainly SMELLS like a lion.....and he has really bad breath like a lion. So, he rushes at you, making all this noise, and you get scared and run.

But.....what if you DIDN'T run? What if you just stood firm, as you're told to do in Ephesians 6 where it describes the whole armor of God? What if the devil's roaring and carrying on were just hot air? You're told in verse 9 to resist him steadfast in the faith. Resist him. Forget the fear.....refuse to budge when he starts all that posturing and loud noise and fuss. He is AS a lion, but he is NOT a lion.....or anything like one. It's all show. He's a defeated enemy, and he knows it.

He was destroyed by Jesus Christ, and he will spend his eternity in a lake of fire. So, resist him. Oppose him, in the Name of Jesus Christ. Show faith instead of fear. And you'll see him crawl back into that hole he came out of. With the devil, it's all just hot air.

Faith Profession: "I have not been given the spirit of fear, and I will not accept it. I stand firm in my spiritual battle. I resist the devil, and he flees from me."

Study Scriptures: James 4:7; Ephesians 6:10-18; Colossians 2:15

DEVOTIONAL # 366

YOU SURE ARE PECULIAR

Scripture: I Peter 2:5,9

As Peter writes his first epistle, he is acutely aware of the lofty and unique status granted to believers on this side of the Resurrection. Saved Christians in these days are said to be a "new creation," or "new creature" (see study Scriptures). As such, we have a number of characteristics that were not available to, nor present in, Old Testament saints. Some of those new features are mentioned in today's reading.

First, notice that you, as a saved child of God, are said to have become a "priesthood." Priests have always been those who serve as a "go-between," or "link," between God and people. This is important to Him, because His whole existence is about people…..His most basic characteristic is LOVE. As a priest, you are to offer up "spiritual sacrifices" (verse 5)…..that is, you are to intercede for others through prayer.

Second, you are "royal" (verse 9). This is true because your new Father is King of Kings (see study Scriptures). That makes you a prince or princess in the most magnificent kingdom in the universe! Maybe you thought you just got saved…..but you have become royalty, and have priestly duties now. You are NOT who you used to be…..by a long shot.

Because of these and other changes, you have also become "a peculiar people." Although that word can mean "weird," or "odd," it can also mean "distinctive; special; different from the usual." These last terms are the meaning in today's verses. Though, in truth, I've met some Christians who ARE weird, it is more to the point that we have become, at salvation, persons who are different…..and special.

We have special status with our Father…..we have special giftings (see study Scriptures)….. and there is just "something" about a true child of God that you can sense. It is a confidence, maybe…..a feeling that they know they're important to Jesus. They are. YOU are. We are distinctive from others in this world. Praise the Lord!

Faith Profession: "I now see that I have become a new creation in Christ Jesus. I am special, and important, to HIM."

Study Scriptures: II Corinthians 5:17; Revelation 19:16; Mark 16:17-18

The Word of God Made Plain

is available at:

olivepresspublisher.com

amazon.com

barnesandnoble.com

and other websites.

The E-book is available at:

amazon.com

Book stores and book distributors
may obtain this book through:

Ingram Book Company
or by e-mailing

olivepressbooks@gmail.com

Pastor Jim Kirkland and his wife Lyn have been writing, teaching, and doing ministry for many years. To schedule them to speak or lead a seminar contact:

Starfish Ministries
of Pennsylvania

www.starfishofpa.com

info@starfishofpa.com

(717) 201-1514

The name "Starfish" comes from the story of a boy saving starfish one at a time on a seashore. When told that he was not making a difference among the thousands of stranded starfish on the beach, he quickly responded, "It made a difference to that one."

The goal of Starfish Ministries is to "give hope and comfort to hurting souls in the Body of Christ."

www.ingramcontent.com/pod-product-compliance
Lightning Source LLC
Chambersburg PA
CBHW080454110426
42742CB00017B/2886